D0948435

DEATH IN THE SHAPE OF A YOUNG GIRL

## GENDER AND POLITICAL VIOLENCE SERIES

GENERAL EDITOR: LAURA SJOBERG

Muscular Nationalism: Gender, War, and Empire in
India and Ireland, 1914–2004
SIKATA BANERJEE

Female Soldiers in Sierra Leone: Sex, Security, and
Post-Conflict Development
MEGAN H. MACKENZIE

Death in the Shape of a Young Girl: Women's Political
Violence in the Red Army Faction
PATRICIA MELZER

PATRICIA MELZER

# DEATH IN THE SHAPE OF A YOUNG GIRL

Women's Political Violence in the Red Army Faction

NEW YORK UNIVERSITY PRESS  *New York and London*

NEW YORK UNIVERSITY PRESS
New York and London
www.nyupress.org

Book designed and typeset by Charles B. Hames

References to Internet websites (URLs) were accurate at the time of writing. Neither the author nor New York University Press is responsible for URLs that may have expired or changed since the manuscript was prepared.

ISBN: 978-1-4798-6407-2

For Library of Congress Cataloging-in-Publication data, please contact the Library of Congress.

New York University Press books are printed on acid-free paper, and their binding materials are chosen for strength and durability. We strive to use environmentally responsible suppliers and materials to the greatest extent possible in publishing our books.

Manufactured in the United States of America

10 9 8 7 6 5 4 3 2 1

Also available as an ebook

*For Karl, with love*

# Contents

# Acknowledgments

This book has been close to ten years in the making and as with all academic projects, could not have been completed without the support of various groups of people. I want to thank my family for supporting me through the process, including housing and feeding me during extended stays at the archives, beginning with my parents, Annemie and Klaus-Jürgen Melzer, who unfailingly have been there for me, all my life. I also want to thank my oldest sister, Kathrin, whose input into parts of this book has been invaluable. I cannot imagine myself having done this work without the encouragement of her and my two sisters Nanette and Temesgen and my sisters-in-spirit, Marina Walter and Natali Schirm. A special thank you to Michelle Matisons, whose friendship has been central in making me begin this journey; her radical dedication to social justice and creative thinking continues to be influential on my work.

Thanks to research grants from the College of Liberal Arts at Temple as well as a summer research grant and a sabbatical research year from Temple University, I was able to visit archives in Germany and the Netherlands and travel to conferences. My mentors and friends at Temple have been my intellectual and emotional "backbone" during this project. I enjoyed Kristi Brian's friendship and grounding presence in times of transition; since her move, they are sorely missed. Rickie Sanders has been a good mentor and friend for the past ten years. Beth Bailey's smart advice and consistent support of my endeavors are much appreciated. James Salazar has been a wonderful friend with a bagful of tricks who greatly facilitated the publication of the book. Laura Levitt has been unfailing with her backing of me and of my work, and I am grateful for her extending her support and friendship to my family. I greatly enjoyed smart conversations with Margaux Cowden about feminist theories of violence and appreciated her thoughtful input into my writing. I also want to thank my department chair, Louis Mangione, whose advice and support in the past two years have been central to the completion of this book. Outside of Temple, I am also extremely grateful for the support and encouragement I have received from my mentors of many years, Cynthia Enloe and Sabine von Dirke. Their patience and generosity with their time and energy have been crucial in moving this project forward. Thea Renda Abu El-Haj's feedback and our conversations in the local coffee shop are greatly appreciated. Thank you also to Robbie von der Osten, whose intellectual and personal interest in me and in my family has been a constant source of inspiration and encouragement to me.

I have had the opportunity to work with several amazing intellectual communities during the development of this project. As a research associate with the Five College Women's Studies Research Center at Mt. Holyoke College in fall 2005, I was able to conceptualize this project, and I fondly recall inspiring conversations with Mary Strunk and Coralynn Davis on women and violence. A few years later, a Faculty Fellowship at the Center for the Humanities at Temple (CHAT) in 2010–11 connected me with my amazing junior colleagues Naomi Schiller, Ashley West, and Judith Levine; I am grateful for their encouragement and feedback that year. In 2012–13, I had the privilege of spending my sabbatical year as a research fellow at the Newhouse Center for the Humanities at Wellesley College. It would be difficult to imagine a more spirited, intellectually challenging, and personally rewarding group of research fellows, whose input into my work has been invaluable. Special thanks go out to Carol Dougherty and Jane Jackson. I am particularly grateful to Genie Brinkema, whose brilliance and generosity directly impacted the theoretical underpinnings of this book. I also want to thank the best postdoc writing group one can ask for, Yasmine Ramadan, Alex Orquiza, Elizabeth Falconi, and Nikki Greene. I am particularly grateful for the friendship, support, and encouragement I received from Nikki during that year, and for her companionship during odd working hours when no one else was around. Thank you also to Quinn Slobodian, whose input into chapter 1 helped make it happen. Finally, during this past year, 2013–14, I have had the good fortune of working with an amazing and intellectually engaging group of research fellows as a Mellon Regional Faculty Fellow at the Penn Humanities Forum at the University of Pennsylvania. I have enjoyed the interdisciplinary discussions about violence, and the input of the other fellows has enabled me to think beyond this book about my next research project. A special thank you goes to Karen Beckman.

During the past years, I have been grateful for the less formal but crucial intellectual community of the *Wanderzirkus*, a wonderful group of people I have been meeting at conferences and with whom I have been presenting on numerous panels on women and political violence. Their work and our conversations have been central to this book, including those of Irene Bandhauer-Schöffmann and Vojin Saša Vukadinović. A very special thank you goes to Dominique Grisard, whose encouragement and feedback has influenced my thinking on women and violence in important ways. Her friendship and consistent belief in what I have to say mean a lot to me. Thank you also to Clare Bielby, whose friendship and thoughtful engagement with my work has helped me move this book forward. I feel lucky to have such brilliant and generous colleagues as friends.

Anyone working with archival material appreciates the assistance and logistical support of people who run archives. I am especially grateful to the late Herrn Stolle, who during his time at the Cilip-Archiv in Berlin actively assisted me in my early research on women in the RAF and Movement 2nd June. Thank you also to Herrn Schwarz and his colleagues at the Hambuger Institut für Sozialforschung, and to Herrn Lönnendonker at the APO-Archiv in Berlin. I also appreciate the work of the staff at the International Institute for Social History in Amsterdam Archive, who enabled my research in their archives. The work of (often volunteer) staff in the archives of the community-run centers Papiertiger in Berlin, Rote Flora and the feminist Denkträume in Hamburg, and the Infoladen in Frankfurt cannot be valued enough. Their activist work and dedication to preserving alternative political histories is amazing and inspiring.

I am grateful to the three women who agreed to be interviewed about their experiences as members of the RAF and/or Movement 2nd June in the 1970s and '80s. Their willingness to engage in the debate about their actions and the impact those have had on German culture and history has enabled me to integrate important insights into my study. I greatly appreciate them giving their time and sharing their thoughts with me.

I have greatly enjoyed the intellectual work with my students in my Women and Political Violence course in Fall 2013. As always, students keep my research grounded. This group in particular, with their enthusiasm for the material, their passion for social justice, and their feminist fervor, made me newly appreciate the relevance of my work to others. They have greatly inspired me in that final, important phase of finishing the book.

I could not be more pleased with the "home" I found for my book as part of the NYU Press series Gender and Political Violence. I am grateful to the editors and the advisory board of New York University Press and to series editor Laura Sjoberg for their enthusiasm for the project. The feedback from two anonymous readers for the series Gender and Political Violence as well as two outside reviewers has been very helpful in finalizing the book manuscript. Thank you also to the copyeditor, Emily Wright, for taking on those dangling modifiers so diligently. I could not have asked for better editors: Ilene Kalish's belief in my book and her support and practical advice have been invaluable. And Caelyn Cobb's unfailing technical advice and great patience have made this process bearable! Thank you both for all the work to make this book happen.

My work is only possible because of the community around me, and the network of support it provides. An especially warm thank you to my friends Agnieszka Christman, Jennifer Crowe, and Ilka Cassidy and their families. Their friendships in recent years, which included feeding me and my family, making sure I got to yoga, and taking care of our children when things got tight formed the backdrop to the writing of this book. Thank you to Lucy Brannon and Kasea Rowland Myers for always finding words of love and encouragement and for the important work they do that allows me to feel I can do mine. Jen Hemenway's presence during the final three months of completing this book has been a gift, and I am grateful for her being there for us. Thank you also to Damian and Anais, whose joy and love keep me grounded.

Finally, I want to thank Karl. For everything and always. More sushi dinners to come!

# Introduction: "An Excess of Women's Emancipation"

## Gender, Political Violence, and Feminist Politics

Must "every citizen" reckon that one of these days "he'll be confronted with violent death in the shape of a young girl?"

    ⋆ *Die Welt*, 1977

Violence can be defined *a minima* as the application of a force
that remains foreign to the dynamic or energetic system into
which it intervenes. [. . .] It denatures, wrecks, and massacres
that which it assaults. Violence does not transform what it assaults; rather, it takes away its form and meaning. It makes it
nothing other than a sign of its own rage. [. . .] From elsewhere
or beyond, violence brandishes another form, if not another
meaning.

    ⋆ Jean-Luc Nancy, 2005

## Introduction

On May 14, 1970, Andreas Baader, incarcerated in Berlin, Tegel, for
arson, was granted permission to meet with the well-known journalist
Ulrike Meinhof. The meeting was to take place in the research facilities
of the German Central Institute for Social Issues.[1] The reason given for
the unusual request was to discuss their collaborative project, a book
on youth at risk. Instead, Meinhof's visit with Baader was part of a plan
devised by several women (and one man), including Baader's lover,
Gudrun Ensslin, to break him out of prison. The freeing of Baader and
Meinhof's subsequent flight underground is generally thought of as the
"founding moment" of the left-wing terrorist group Red Army Faction
(Rote Armee Fraktion, or RAF). Within a day, Berlin's police initiated
the largest manhunt since 1945, with Ulrike Meinhof's picture plastered
throughout the city on wanted posters.[2] The fact that Baader's escape
involved five women and one man (who, as was learned later, was hired

from outside the group's political circles to lend some gendered authority to the armed action) stunned the West German public and would haunt its imagination concerning left-wing terrorism for years to come.

Seven years later, on July 30, 1977, the CEO of one of West Germany's largest banks, Jürgen Ponto, was shot in his home in Oberursel during an attempted kidnapping by the RAF. The murder was to be the prelude to the "German Autumn" of that year—an escalation of the conflict between the RAF and the German state. Public outrage over the event focused in particular on the role a young woman played in gaining access to the house: as a friend of the family, she brought flowers when ringing the doorbell. Responses to the violent political act framed it as a gendered deceit. In media coverage of the event, Susanne Albrecht—and by extension all the RAF's "terrorist girls" (*Der Spiegel*)[3]—embodied "violent death in the shape of a young girl" (*Welt*).[4] Secret Service Chief Günther Nollau observed that women's participation in left-wing terrorism felt "somehow irrational" and summed up the official response with the conclusion that female terrorists must be the result of an "excess of women's liberation." What is striking about these narratives is the central role that gender plays in defining the magnitude of the RAF terrorists' breach of the social contract through their violent political actions.

Public shock at women's participation in such violence is based on the equation of purposeful and systematic violence with masculinity. Women's participation in militant political groups in the 1970s and 1980s was not in accord with prevalent perceptions of women as peaceful and nurturing. Indeed, these women understood their actions as a means of liberation from restrictive gender norms. They present a cultural paradox—violent death in the shape of a young girl—raising critical questions about the gendered dimensions of political violence: How do masculinity and femininity operate as cultural parameters for political action? How does gender as an analytical variable contribute to our understanding of terrorism? *Death in the Shape of a Young Girl: Women's Political Violence in the Red Army Faction* engages with these questions by examining, through the specific case of left-wing West German female terrorists, how gender shapes our perception of women's political choices and of political violence more generally. The discursive convergences and divergences of mainstream gender ideologies, feminist theories of political violence, and the political decisions of women in the

RAF and other terrorist groups, while specific to the RAF and German history, in fact imply a necessity to rethink assumptions about women's and feminist politics.

In addition to the RAF, other armed underground groups sought confrontations with the state, such as the Movement 2nd June (Bewegung 2. Juni).[5] These groups included a striking number of female members: at times more than 50 percent of West German terrorists were women, many of whom took leadership roles and made strategic decisions. Seven years into the RAF's declared war against the West German state, public and official responses to the Ponto murder convey a pattern of gendered assumptions regarding women participating in militant actions: mainstream media as well as the state and its investigative units—law enforcement—oscillated between trivializing the "terrorist girls" and demonizing them as "wild furies." Said to have generated the directive within law enforcement of "shoot the women first,"[6] women in the RAF and Movement 2nd June were constructed by officials and media reports alike as particularly violent and dangerous. As the years of conflict between the RAF and the state progressed, so did speculations about the reasons for the increased participation of women in armed groups. The two most popular were, first, that terrorism was motivated by sexual devotion to fellow revolutionaries (this also included deviant sexual preferences such as homosexuality) and, second, that it was a result of women's emancipation, furthered by the growing women's liberation movement. Clearly, female terrorists, so the reasoning went, were acting against their natural disposition, *ergo*, feminism, which agitates against traditional gender roles, produces female terrorists.

Feminist activists were quick to pick up on the sexist framing of female terrorists' actions and voiced their opposition in feminist journals and other movement publications. They found themselves caught in the dilemma of condemning violent politics, which they viewed as being inspired by patriarchal and overtly masculinized revolutionary politics, yet feeling obligated to voice solidarity with the female terrorists imprisoned or wanted by the police in what they saw as a sexualized hunt against "excessively emancipated" women. The autonomous women's movement unambiguously condemned the conceptual link between women's liberation and violent politics, pointing to the newly formulated nonviolent feminist politics that dominated the women's movement in the 1970s.[7]

RAF and Movement 2nd June women arrested and/or on trial rarely commented on the *Feminismusverdacht* (charge/accusation of feminism)[8] the state harbored against them and continued to focus instead on speaking about their political actions outside of a gendered framework. Their understanding of their own involvement did not correspond with prevalent perceptions (both mainstream and feminist) of women's political participation. Some of them perceived themselves as feminists and saw their participation in the armed struggle as a logical extension of their liberation as women, while many others thought of revolutionary movements as superseding feminist aspirations of equality. This troubling position of leftist female terrorists rarely finds representation in Western scholars' accounts of women's activism—let alone of activism that is defined as *feminist*. So what are we to do with these conflicting understandings of women as political agents? And what is the place of terrorist women in a cultural memory of feminist activism? And finally, these women raise the question, "Can political violence be feminist?"[9]

The RAF symbolized a time of acute crisis for the young, post–World War II Federal Republic as traumatic events profoundly shaped the political climate in the 1970s. The Ponto shooting in 1977 was part of a series of events that led to the escalation of the conflict between the RAF and the West German state that began in 1970 and would continue into the 1990s. This conflict resulted in the state instituting increased security measures and laws restricting political formations, such as the 1976 passing of §129 in the criminal code, which went beyond targeting terrorist activities to criminalize any associations with potentially terrorist activists and dramatically expanded the police's reach into activist circles.[10] Media outlets created a forum for confrontations between a militant leftist activist culture and a mainstream German public discourse on political violence, with the inflammatory tabloid *Bild*, put out by the conservative Springer publication house, representing the most reactionary voice in the debate. The nation's self-interrogation into the meaning and processes of their post–World War II democracy was in part forced by the terrorism that became synonymous with the name of the RAF.[11]

The RAF, with its radical Marxist framework and critique of the FRG as a "fascist" state, has continued to spark political controversies up to the present day. Like other left-radical groups in West Germany, such as the Movement 2nd June, the RAF was formed in the beginning period of a growing political mobilization of the radical Left after the waning of the SDS.[12] The RAF bombed U.S. military facilities, kidnapped and assassinated influential businessmen and state representatives, robbed banks, and worked with Palestinian terrorists. When the Movement 2nd June dissolved in 1980, the remaining members joined the RAF. Politicizing their cause further with prison hunger strikes, the RAF maintained a consistent political presence in West German public debates until the group renounced its "armed struggle" in 1992 and officially disbanded in 1998.

The violence committed by the group and its mobilization of a small number of young people's political rage throughout the twenty-eight years of the RAF's existence still haunts policy makers and activists alike. Since their entrance onto the public scene, the historical and cultural meaning of the RAF has remained a subject of public debate, as the role of the state in the events is being reexamined, victims' families speak out, and former RAF members go public with narratives of their experiences. Art exhibits, feature and documentary films, literary works, academic conferences and scholarship, as well as mainstream publications continue to redefine the impact of the RAF on German society and political culture today.

Gender clearly shaped early public debate about the RAF, a focus that until recently has been absent in the scholarship on West German terrorism. In recent years, an increased attention to gendered aspects of the debate is reflected in selected scholarship on the RAF.[13] This study contributes to the emerging feminist discourse on the West German terrorism debate by providing a gendered analysis of the RAF and the Movement 2nd June that makes concrete some of their actions' implications for feminist political thought as well as for mainstream gender ideology. This approach in turn enables a more complete understanding of German political and social history, and of the construction of terrorism as an act whose gendered meaning is mediated to the public through mass media.

## Reading and Writing Women's Political Violence

This book adds to the current debate on West German terrorism in a significant way by utilizing original sources and by introducing original theoretical considerations. Tracing the concept of violence as it circulated through and connected the New Left (and its armed groups), the autonomous women's movement, and the Third World revolutionary movement is one example of such an original consideration,[14] as is my gendered analysis of the RAF hunger strikes and the significance of a gendered focus on the body for a political reading.[15] The sources and methods of analysis I utilize in the book are diverse; the book's methodology is informed by cultural studies (textual analysis and contextual framing of a phenomenon) as well as history (archival research on a specific period). The trajectory of the book is to investigate discursive convergences and divergences of important debates and the implications they contain, not to (re)create some definite historical or theoretical truth about the RAF and Movement 2nd June. The original sources I bring to the debate confirm this trajectory, such as the integration of a series of conversations with former members of the RAF and Movement 2nd June.[16] The interviews do not constitute a representative sample— methodologically, the information provided by the three women with whom I spoke functions in my study similarly to expert knowledge and is not understood to represent a generalized female RAF and Movement 2nd June member's point of view.[17] Instead, similar to the autobiographies I interpret, their narratives form distinct texts within a process of memorializing and historicizing the RAF and Movement 2nd June. While they constitute a very particular (and clearly limited) historical text in that they speak of personalized memories retrospectively, they provide a context for understanding the printed material that discusses their experiences and actions. They also form an important interjection informing an often heated public discourse on gender and political violence. These personal accounts are one of a variety of primary sources that create overlapping and contradicting strands of discourses on gender and violence in (West) Germany.[18]

Primary print sources consist of archival material that includes both mainstream media coverage of major national publications, such as *Der Spiegel*, and so-called grey literature: movement publications, event flyers/calls for action, prisoners' trial statements, etc. In particular, the response of feminist groups and the debates that took place in the feminist political subcultures at the time, which were ignored by mainstream media and largely by researchers to date, add a new dimension to the historical understanding of the autonomous women's movement in West Germany, and its relationship to political violence. Maybe more importantly, these varied debates that become visible in small feminist publications complicate the notion of a universal feminist subjectivity by making visible the historical specificity of women's activism.[19]

In addition, original sources such as private documents and letters, when placed in relation to the published autobiographies of former female terrorists, make visible the complicated relationship women in the RAF and Movement 2nd June had to feminist politics. Current scholarship usually posits that women in left-radical groups distanced themselves politically from the autonomous women's movement and thus from the question of feminist politics. To dismiss the connection between left-radical women and feminist activists/politics because their ties were not formally organized means to discount gender as an organizing force *beyond consciously politicizing it.* Instead, my analysis of memoirs and unpublished letters shows that armed women at times engaged intensely with feminist issues and politics and suggests that there existed a mutual influence between the different political groups of women that demands a reconsideration of what constitutes feminist politics.

I approach the RAF and Movement 2nd June as case studies primarily through textual analysis of historical documents. I read the material against mainstream gender ideologies and against feminist theories on gender and violence in order to make visible the process of "gendering" the meaning of terrorism and of women's political choices. One theoretical framework that critically informs my analysis includes the emergence of the women's movement campaign against violence against women, a paradigm that would dominate feminist theories on women's political activism. Other theoretical frameworks include liberal feminist political theory, Marxist and socialist feminist theory, and poststructuralist concepts of feminist subjectivity and gender performativity. My reading of this variety of sources makes evident forces within the history of political violence in Germany and the cultural discourses that generate a previously unexamined understanding of this history. With this reading, I expose implications for feminist theorizing about political violence, furthering the debate on political violence as it is taking place in gender studies more broadly.

What I am finding in my analysis of the RAF and the implications their actions have for feminist politics and theories is a dilemma posed by a feminist claim to nonviolence that, in its theorizing of women's relationship to political violence, ultimately upholds a dominant gender ideology. The claim to nonviolence as inherent to women's politics is clearly contradicted by RAF women's commitment to armed struggle. I argue that their actions need to be reviewed from within a conceptual framework that recognizes the gendered dimensions of their decisions without denying the contradictions these decisions pose for feminist politics.

In a post-9/11 world, in the West, the term "terrorism" connotes first and foremost activities of Islamic fundamentalists against Western targets or their ideological and economic extensions. In 1970, the term was also used in a much more localized way within the domestic landscape, in addition to its use to refer to international acts of terrorism. By the late 1970s, a series of airplane hijackings and actions like the kidnapping and murder of Israeli athletes during the 1972 Olympics in Munich by members of the PLO drew attention to conflicts in the Middle East. These incidents linked the term "terrorism" as it was used in West Germany specifically to secular armed Palestinian and other Middle Eastern groups. In several other European countries, terrorism was linked to ethno-national or religious conflicts that troubled the nation states, such as in the UK and Northern Ireland and by extension in Ireland (the Irish Republican Army) as well as in Spain (the Euskadi Ta Askatasuna), or to domestic left-radical terrorist groups, such as the Brigate Rosse in Italy. In West Germany terrorism referred primarily to activists who were working in so-called revolutionary circles, radical leftist movements that identified with a larger global struggle. Until the mid-1970s, media and state officials primarily referred to the RAF and other militants as "gangs" (*Banden*) (such as in the term "Baader-Meinhof Bande," which was used early on to refer to the RAF) and/or as "anarchists" in the tradition of politically violent Russian anarchists within radical Marxist movements. Only later did they advance to be considered the more dangerous category of terrorists, which is reflected in the 1976 addition to the criminal code of §129, which explicitly equates radical activism with terrorism.

Perception is everything in defining the nature of political violence. Phrases like "one person's terrorist is another person's freedom fighter" and bumper stickers like "Terrorist: What the big army calls the little army" reveal a reluctance to accept the criminalization of violence from the perspective of the state/majority alone. The criminalization of political violence is thereby always historically specific and culturally distinct. Clarification of the terms "political violence" and especially "terrorism" as they are being used in this study is thus important. The term "political violence" as I use it here indicates the politically motivated strategic employment of violence by a group against objects and structures (and, in certain cases, humans) that in the worldview of the group represent either state or systemic power. The aim of political violence, therefore, is to destabilize the existing government through strategic attacks, as well as to direct public attention to issues of perceived injustice. More specifically, political violence in the 1970s and early 1980s was viewed by Left militants in industrialized nations as "revolutionary violence" and "armed struggle"; they saw themselves as "guerrillas" and part of a worldwide fight against U.S. imperialism spearheaded by anticolonial movements in the Third World.[20] The state, in turn, classified these actions as "terrorism." The topic of political violence is necessarily an ideologically charged discourse reflected in controversies regarding terminology used to describe actions and groups.[21] To emphasize the ambiguous meaning of acts of political violence that always is historical, I use terms like "terrorism" and "armed struggle" contextually.[22]

Finally, the term "feminist" is central in formulating my main argument. As I apply it to publications, groups, debates, and political positions alike, the term is meant to connote a commitment to gender equality and/or the right of women to self-determination that is not homogenous. The shared belief in gender relations as an oppressive regime that is in need of correction does not necessarily extend to a shared analysis of its roots and/or its relation to other systems of oppression. Consequently, the term "feminist" here functions as an umbrella term for a diverse and at times contradictory or even hostile range of political and theoretical positions. To signal the fracturing within the feminist label in Western discourse, I add modifiers (such as "anti-imperialist," "anar-chist," "radical," "cultural," "socialist," and "mainstream") when discuss-ing feminist publications; when discussing feminist theories I specify their analysis of gender and violence. Overall, my interest is in feminist political *practices*, not in defining "the" feminist political subject, and my goal is to contribute to a careful reevaluation of a universalizing use of the term "feminist." Instead of trying to generalize about "feminist" politics, here the emphasis is on a contextualized use of the term.

## Feminist Practices versus Feminist Subjects: The Subversive Power of Gendered Violence

Any attempts to understand the ways in which the debate on the RAF was gendered, and in particular the implications its violent political actions have for feminist politics, necessitate a philosophical excursion into the question of what actually constitutes violence. If we understand the concept to include injuries other than physical ones, and injuries to be inflicted by both direct and indirect agents, the damage violence does goes further than blows directly aimed at bodies and objects. The RAF's terrorism constitutes what Slavoj Žižek refers to as "subjective violence," violence executed by an "identifiable agent."[23] Žižek argues that subjective violence, however, is only the most visible of three forms of violence that also include two kinds of "objective violence," namely, "symbolic" violence, which is embedded in language and its forms, and "systemic violence," "the often catastrophic consequences of the smooth functioning of our economic and political systems."[24] Objective violence is the violence material and ideological regimes impose, and it generates, according to Žižek, outbursts of subjective violence. Because objective violence remains invisible (the damage inflicted by objective violence is viewed as the "'normal' state of things"),[25] it is subjective violence that triggers outrage. Judith Butler addresses how the privilege of reacting to one's loss brought about by (subjective) violence silences the victim of (objective) violence, to which one's own complicity contributes; grief and the aggression that often follows are justified for some, and denied to others: "[T]he differential allocation of grievability that decides what kind of subject is and must be grieved, and which kind of subject must not, operates to produce and maintain certain exclusionary conceptions of who is normatively human: what counts as a livable life and a grievable death?"[26] Terrorist violence becomes measurable to the public because of both its identifiable agent and its unsuspecting victims (those not experiencing objective violence).

The flip side of systemic violence is the way that violence actually interferes with and *destroys* systems of meaning. In his essay "Image and Violence," phenomenologist Jean-Luc Nancy defines violence as "the application of a force that remains foreign to the dynamic or energetic system into which it intervenes."[27] Violence "denatures, wrecks, and massacres that which it assaults" and "it takes away its form and meaning," reducing it to "a sign of its own rage."[28] Violence does not replace order with new order, meaning with new meaning; instead, it "splits open and destroys the play of forces and the network of relations."[29] Finally, as Eugenie Brinkema points out, "violence is monstrous, but also monstrative: Violence demonstrates"[30] and, in Nancy's words, "exposes itself as figure without figure"[31]—it threatens to collapse meaning in its demonstration.

Violence relates to "truth"[32] in two directions: it does "not serve truth: it wants instead to be itself the truth."[33] As Brinkema writes in her discussion of Nancy, "likewise, the history of philosophy suggests truth's own violence";[34] its need to impose itself, to exist above all else, violates. So "the truth of violence" is "nothing other than the truth of the fist and the weapon," which contrasts with the "violence of truth," which is "a violence that withdraws even as it irrupts and [. . .] that opens and frees a space for the manifest presentation of the true." [35] Nancy points to the seductive danger of this ambiguity on which any direct or indirect approval of violence feeds. It is the "reason why one could speak of good and necessary violence, and of loving violence, interpretative violence, *revolutionary violence*, divine violence."[36]

The violence of RAF women is present in both of the ways in which Nancy sees violence relating to truth: the "blows"[37] of their "true violence," the damage their terrorism inflicts on human bodies and physical structures, on the one hand, and their "violent truth," their existence as violent women, on the other. Their 'true violence'—which assaults the German social and state system—is what they are primarily associated with; but rarely recognized to be at play here is their 'violent truth'—which assaults the gender regime, the system of meaning that explains and organizes gender norms.This truth regime is attacked by their gender transgression, effecting a violence that "denatures, wrecks, and massacres" any existing naturalized "truth" about femininity and masculinity and "takes away its form and meaning." Their "violent truth" can thus be understood as a very particular form of "counterviolence," as the gender regime's disciplinary technologies already inflict violence on lives.[38] The response of the state and the public to this "violence of truth" RAF women bring in turn is the "gendering" of the discourse on terrorism through the cementing of gender norms—the freezing and containing of the image of the female terrorist.

The image of the female terrorist stands in troubled relationship to violence and truth. As Nancy conceptualizes the image in general, it is separate from the symbolic of language; it is "*the distinct.*"[39] It is distinct from the thing: "The image is a thing that is not the thing: it distinguishes itself from it essentially."[40] As Brinkema puts it, "[T]he image is not an imitation (for mimeticism reinscribes the appearance/original binary) but the resemblance from which the thing is detached."[41] The thing it resembles is invisible (the woman, the terrorist), unlike the image itself (female terrorist).[42] Images of the RAF women as they circulated in media coverage, state documents, and the public's imagination more broadly are more than mere (distorted) representations of "real" women—that would suppose there are authentic "women" to represent. Instead, their image converses with the "truth" (of the gender regime) it violates, and thus becomes an *image of violence* (terrorist)[43] at the same time as it is a *violent image* that assaults us (death in the shape of a young girl).

However, the discursive reduction of the RAF's violence to its "violent truth" (read: its gender transgression)[44] in order to contain the violence it does to the gender regime backfires—the image of the RAF women actually makes visible, and thereby challenges, the truth(effect) of the gender regime itself. Now the question becomes whether or not their very image—as separate from the thing, terrorism, and the moral indefensibility of it—constitutes a feminist subversion in its violent performing of gender, regardless of their self-identification as feminist.

This investigation of terrorist women as potentially engaging in what I think of as feminist practices rests on a poststructuralist "letting go" of the definition of feminist politics as actions of a feminist subject.

The notion of a feminist subject is linked to the important theoretical presumption that feminism is the development of a subject towards an understanding of the personal as political; liberation hinges on an individual's consciousness of oppression in everyday life. Furthermore, this consciousness has been defined as oppositional to oppression—and violence is one of the most important markers of women's experience of oppression. Women participating in political violence thus run counter to a core principle of many of Western feminist theories and political movements, especially as they were formulated during the 1970s and 1980s: that a feminist subject rejects violence as a patriarchal mechanism of oppression. The historical representation of this debate quickly can become polarized into positions trying to claim certain strategies as "feminist" while dismissing others as "antifeminist."[45]

Letting go of the definition of feminist politics as actions of a feminist subject is not to say that an action has no agent, i.e., that there is no accountability and evaluation of sustainable politics. It however assumes that there are discursive political effects being produced outside of conscious subjectivity, including feminist ones. The concept of "practice" here allows for feminist countertruth-effects to develop through actions, bodies, and images ("true violence" and "violent truths") independent of the individual's subjectivity *as* feminist. I suggest that it is more appropriate to focus on feminist practices, which I understand to be actions whose gender constellations trouble, challenge, and potentially redirect existing oppressive gender regimes. While not necessarily "consciously" feminist in their orientation, these practices have discursive effects and shape power in ways that undermine essentialist notions on femininity and masculinity, and thus a heterosexist economy of desire. "Feminist" then is less a marker of progressive identity than of practices that affect gender relations in ways that challenge conservative and static traditions, and these practices might be controversial in their moral and ethical implications.

Thus, the analytical approach of this book should not be understood to be in search of the feminist subject in the RAF context. Instead, I am interested in reading their actions and existence as potential feminist practices that trouble existing gender norms. So while the RAF did not formulate explicit feminist positions in their texts and/or actions, it is important to ask how the existence of RAF women challenges not only mainstream ideas about gender but also feminist efforts to *abgrenzen* (demarcate, separate) the women's movement—and its efforts to change patriarchal structures—from these women's violent transgressions of gender expectations. The feminist practice is then constituted in the "violent truth" of terrorist women, which relies on the "true violence" of the groups' politics. In other words, does the *Feminismusverdacht* (charge/accusation of feminism) constructed by the West German state and public debate voiced from misogynist and sexist anxieties about loss of male privilege during times of social change not also somehow address the reality that gender norms were seriously confronted by women in revolutionary groups? Instead of declaring the "nonfeminism" of the RAF and Movement 2nd June and thus treating it as a phenomenon outside of feminist politics, I consider the impact their actions have both on mainstream gender ideology and on a feminist reliance on a preconceived feminist subject in assessing the meaning of political violence for feminist discourse. The repeated assertion by former members of the groups—echoed in many scholars' analyses—that the RAF and Movement 2nd June were not interested in "feminist" politics does not change the fact that their actions need to be examined in terms of their impact on discourse. The proposition that RAF women's violence can constitute feminist practices is only sustainable when we understand the term "feminist" not as a marker for moral, progressive politics but as a marker for—often troubling and violent—challenges to existing gender norms—"feminist" as signifying the "violent truth" of gender transgression. A feminist practice, if decoupled from a liberated subjectivity accountable to *all* women's freedom, can be evaluated for its sustainability in particular historical contexts as furthering (or hindering) gender justice, while the claim of acting out of a feminist subjectivity raises questions of who actually defines what a liberated consciousness is and who is in the position to "rescue" other women.[46] The concept of feminist practices allows for divergences in feminist reasoning and fosters feminist theory's core structure as counterdiscourse—a feminist action then cannot be assumed (because it is executed by a feminist subject) but needs to be examined and explained (in relation and contrast to other feminist practices).

The RAF women's "true violence" is destructive and morally indefensible to many, and their political effectiveness needs to be seriously doubted. Nevertheless, the question remains to what extent their existence and actions upset the existing gender regime, how they constitute a "violent truth." Some indications of this are the state's response to the RAF as gendered threat to the nation, and public discursive obsession with the gender of terrorists. Women in the RAF and Movement 2nd June might not have been feminist subjects (i.e., few identified as feminist activists who were targeting gender oppression as a primary system of oppression), but they were engaging in feminist practices whose impact on discourse was measurable and concrete. This approach to the RAF's relationship to feminist politics facilitates a historical understanding of women's political measures that is complex and accounts for dominant gender ideologies that shape the debate on women's choices of political resistance. The question "Can political violence be feminist?" then is recast as, "How do women arrive at their feminist politics?" and "How and why do feminist practices differ from each other?"

## Gender and Political Violence: The Terrors of a Violent Woman

This book approaches women participating in political violence with the understanding that this phenomenon intersects with a variety of what Foucault has termed "discursive technologies"—spaces and moments where cultural and political meanings relating to gender and violence are produced and disseminated through particular knowledge production. These sites of knowledge production range from media coverage, investigative reports, and hunger strike statements to prison letters, movement publications, and statements following violent political actions, as well as scholarly research and artistic expressions. Operating from the perspective that power is discursive[47] and gender is performative,[48] the book offers a multilayered analysis of how the RAF and the Movement 2nd June and their politics produced (and still produce) gendered discourses, how, as Dominique Grisard puts it, in fact "gender is constitutional for the phenomenon of left-wing terrorism on a personal level, as well as on an institutional and symbolic level."[49] The book accounts for the mechanisms and institutions of these discourses as well as counterdiscourses that result in RAF women's terrorism constituting what can be understood as feminist practices. It does so by engaging with three different (inter)disciplinary areas of debate. First, by placing the analysis of radical politics in relation to feminist theories of violence, this study engages in conversation with and contributes to feminist scholarship on politics in general and terrorism in particular. Second, it provides new insight into the historical discussions of the formation and political trajectories of revolutionary groups in the 1970s and how the public perceived them, with particular attention to how women's participation is explained in terms of their gender and sexuality. Finally, I reframe general conversations on political violence that treat the very notion of the female terrorist as a fundamental paradox, especially as they appear in media representations and in the dealings of the state with gender and terrorism, by offering a new perspective on the intersections of gender and politics: my study examines not how women have been figured as offering an alternative to violence but rather how the political violence exercised by women is rooted in, or emerges in relation to, the violence of gender itself.

## Feminist Debates on Political Violence

Our understanding of political violence is structured by gendered behavioral norms that, while always more ambiguous and overlapping in actual interactions, are powerful concepts that shape discourses: simply put, violence is associated with an aggressive, powerful, and strong masculinity, which opposes a passive, gentle, and vulnerable femininity. Normative gender thereby determines bodies, which, as Sarah Colvin points out in *Ulrike Meinhof and West German Terrorism*, "renders violence inseparable from biology": "Cultural belief says women give life—they do not take it."[50] Bodies are thus positioned in particular relationships to violence: men commit it, women do not; instead, they *experience* it. Appropriate social gendered behavior that originates in bodies includes heterosexual desire: reproduction is the center of sexual relations, and the identity as (potential) mother becomes that which defines a woman's relationship to violence. Violence in a woman becomes not only a criminal deed but an unnatural act. Historically, this association of ideal femininity with nonviolence in Germany is racialized as well as classed (the ideal is projected onto *bürgerliche*—bourgeois—Gentile women), such that nonconformist gender behavior is claimed to evince an aberration rooted in nonwhite, nonbourgeois background, such as in the case of poor and Jewish working-class women.

The association of feminism (women resisting social roles and claiming self-determination, including in terms of sexuality and reproduction) with terrorism (women committing political violence) as it appeared in West German discourse in the 1970s, is contradictory in many ways. It is contradictory specifically in terms of a feminist construction of violence as inherently male/masculine (which manifests in sexual, domestic, and social violence of men against women), which sides with mainstream ideology's definition of women as inherently nonviolent. The general association of violence with masculinity that underlies social interactions and political gestures, as well as state institutions (such as the military, which in most countries in the 1970s excluded women), was politicized by second wave feminists in an unprecedented campaign against violence against women that shook up public discourse on violence in the 1970s and 1980s: women were presented as living in a "daily war" waged against them by men and a male-run state.[51] Motherhood was reclaimed and politicized by feminists as the basis of women's peacefulness and (moral) superiority. In its demands for women's rights, the women's movement countered the depoliticization of women through mainstream ideologies with a declaration of women's experiences of violence as political and their nonviolence as the trait with the potential to create sustainable politics.

This paradigm shift that pointed to women's daily suffering of violence at the hands of men as central to defining the women's liberation movement's main political focus resulted in two major discursive phenomena. First was the alignment of mainstream gender ideology's view on women's nonviolent nature (which declares the female terrorist deviant or insane) with a feminist insistence that women experience, not execute, violence within a patriarchal system. The second discursive formation—which contradicts the first—conveys conflicts within the women's movement around the paradigm of violence against women as the main structural violence exhibited by the society and supported by the state: many feminists viewed patriarchy as only one of several major systems of oppression and thus resisted the binary characterization of violent men versus resisting women. They also urged women to disinvest from the notion that women are peaceful and instead viewed (counter)violence as a legitimate feminist means of resistance.

The violence-against-women paradigm, which positioned women as victims/survivors of male violence and which declared violence as the major structuring force in society, demanded radical (social and political) changes in gender relations for any social justice to become attainable.[52] This position throughout the 1980s was further developed to include commercial and sexual (including visual) violence against women in antipornography campaigns, as well as an analysis of the militarization of women's lives through institutions, the state, and nationalism. It also resonated in the developing feminist discourse on the ethics of care in the 1990s that emerged from discussions of maternal ethics and politics. Mostly, then, feminist debates on politics have highlighted women's nonviolent organizing against a global militarization in which underlying assumptions of gendered violence are carried over.[53] The result of this has been a naturalization of women's nonviolent activism as the norm in the historicization of women's resistance. In this history, the use of violence by women in "Third World" countries—in an anticolonial context—is at times acknowledged but mainly understood as alienated political work, furthered by feminist conclusions around the failure of revolutionary and nationalist movements internationally to commit to women's rights and concerns.[54] Actually, it is within the context of "Third World" women's struggle that the contrast between feminist subjectivity and feminist practice as it structures the mode of inquiry of this study becomes urgently visible: the movements women globally organize around, while recognizing gender as a crucial force, rarely foreground it as the primary system of oppression, and the political issues driving at times forceful social change do not center on the notion of "liberated women" as premise for success, as Western feminism traditionally does.

But why, as a feminist scholar, turn to women in the RAF and Movement 2nd June to examine these questions of gender and political violence and feminist politics? They clearly represent a radical political minority that—in the grand scheme of things—might be nothing but an anomaly in the tradition of women's political activism and whose impact on women's lives has been negligible at best, and damaging at worst. The political debate surrounding the RAF is actually of particular interest because it takes place within a geographical and discursive space of what in the 1970s was referred to as a "First World country" and today usually is identified as part of the Global North, i.e., industrialized, Western nations in which feminist formulations of nonviolence as women's prevalent form of activism are dominant. In other locations in the world, different experiences of, and relations to, violence (often state and structural violence) do not preclude women's participation in or support of what is seen as armed resistance; this was especially true in a world of the 1960s shaken by anticolonial and revolutionary struggles. A disruption of (universal) feminist claims to nonviolence as they were increasingly formulated by Western feminists in the 1970s happening "at home" thus becomes an important site to revisit assumed relationships of gender, power, and forms of resistance.

Until recently, feminist research on understanding the political work done by women in the 1970s and 1980s has created a cultural memory of women's activism that defines feminist political work as nonviolent. Women in the RAF and Movement 2nd June trouble these memories. They introduce questions of violence as a woman's or feminist's tool into the discourse on women and violence within the context of Western democracies that lack the context of anticolonial/anti-occupation struggles reserved as the area where women's activism is understandably compromised by necessarily violent resistance. As a *Western* armed group that cannot be understood in the context of ethno-national or religious conflicts, it raises unsettling questions about the use of violence as a political means within a democratic civil society neither at war nor destabilized by ethno-national disputes. Finally, the group's actions provide a historical precedent for the militant feminist groups in the 1980s and 1990s that did not operate underground.

*Death in the Shape of a Young Girl* examines how feminist disagreements on political violence have been flattened out in favor of a definition of feminist politics as nonviolent—not least because of the state's strategic conflation of women's liberation with female violence. Consequently, in much of the literature on women's political activism, the historicization of the feminist debate on political violence focuses on the premise of the violence-against-women political rallying point: a nonviolent feminist position often is presented as the normative one that rejects the aberrant female terrorist whose acts are undermining the "true" women's movement's agenda. Countering this presentation, my research shows that women's movement publications of the 1970s and 1980s actually reflect intense debates about the contradictions of feminist claims to nonviolence and show instances of overlap between feminist aims and uses of violence. Prison letters and autobiographies depict activists debating revolutionary violence and feminist rejections of violence. Within the discourses, ideologies of motherhood underlie much of the debate on feminist politics, and some RAF and Movement 2nd June women's rejection of their children emerges as a major theme of contestation. Ultimately, understanding how the women's movement—and its definition of violence as masculine, which corresponds with mainstream gender ideologies—engaged with women in armed struggle (and vice versa) enhances our understanding of the limitations of feminist theories of political violence. The critical question at stake then is not the necessarily limited "Can violence be feminist?" but rather "What constitutes women's political choices and feminist practices?" Asking this question allows for a critical evaluation of those practices.

## Women in Revolutionary Groups and Their Challenge to Gendered Ideologies

The second area of thought that underlies the analytical approach of this study concerns the perception of female terrorists in public discourse and how that diverged from (and/or corresponded with) their actual experiences. I reframe the historical approach to the RAF by considering gender ideologies as they circulated in mainstream life and in public policy (e.g., women as mothers and men as providers) and as they were challenged and/or reproduced in the political groups in question. Cultural narratives on gender here co-construct other important discourses on national identity, citizenship, and the role of West Germany in global politics.[55] Masculinity and femininity become parameters of political actions that are embodied by men and women, respectively, and transgressions of these alignments produce a moment of cultural crisis. Central to this political embodiment is social space: notions of the public sphere—heavily contested by 1960s counterculture and the Extraparliamentary Opposition (APO)[56]—traditionally privilege the masculine; politics were men's business. The private, the domestic space was delegated to women's influence; women's work was motherhood and housekeeping. Similarly to the autonomous women's movement's challenge to established gender roles in West Germany more broadly, women in revolutionary groups present a moment of such crisis. They destabilize cultural assumptions and political norms primarily on two accounts. First, their experiences and the way they relate to them counter existing ideologies on women's "nature," partly because they undermine spatial assignments. The revolutionary space they claim is political *and* violent. Second, their political beliefs and their very existences disrupt and shape discourses on terrorism in ways that make visible contradictions of gendered discourses.

Discourses on West German leftist terrorist formations barely consider women's gendered motivations for revolutionary violence, or their participation in terrorism as a gendered experience.[57] If gender is part of the debate, women are highly sexualized and/or infantilized; their political agency is reduced to their being victims of male seduction, or else their deviant sexuality (as lesbians or seductresses) is depicted as perverting and as inciting violence. However, my research reveals the ways that revolutionary spaces provided women (and men) liberation from confining gender expectations, such as in experiences underground. Overall, the 1960s and 1970s introduced new social spaces that challenged normative arrangements of nuclear family homes and monogamous relationships, and redefined politics as not simply happening in Parliament. For example, the infamous Kommune 1, a radical leftist living commune in West Berlin that later became a starting point for members of the Movement 2nd June, was synonymous with a sexually permissive, politicized living environment and grew to be the target of many a proper citizen's disdain.[58] Similarly, as a terrain "outside of" the social order (including that of gender), the underground symbolizes a counternational social space, society's "other" place characterized by its ultimate break with everything "normal." The underground loomed large in the German imagination, both in the Left's discourse on political legitimacy (with the RAF's claim of underground as the only *true* revolutionary space)[59] and in mainstream society's anxiety about "passing" terrorists among them[60] and their denouncing of neighbors as potentially harboring terrorists.[61]

Clearly, being underground demanded skillful organization, such as renting apartments illegally, "passing" as normal tenants when meeting neighbors, avoiding contact with family and acquaintances, and planning actions within restricted circumstances, from car theft and document forgery to bombings, bank robberies, kidnappings, and assassinations.[62] This life seemed to have generated gender constellations that differed from traditional gender roles regarding sexual relations, reproductive issues (particularly with regard to logistics around access to health care, such as abortions and contraception), and the division of labor in securing funds and planning actions. Fundamentally, being underground seems to have been experienced by many women as a more egalitarian space than other social arenas, such as the workplace and electoral politics. The media demonized this "outside" space of living without a legal existence by dismissing the activists as anarchist and their social relations as misogynist and hypersexual. Inadvertently, the media thus correctly marked it as a threat to the "proper" German order: sexual liberation was definitely a part of revolutionary groups' internal logic, lesbian relationships were accepted (or viewed as politically irrelevant and thus permitted), and while both men and women had to participate in "bourgeois drag" to pass within their neighborhoods, their understanding of gender relations seemed to run counter to those of "proper" German citizens.[63] While we need to be cautious of sensationalized representations of life underground and recognize it as a surface for projected anxiety concerning national security and stability, testimonies of women and men attest to the experience of living underground as being distinct from the experience of living in any other social space, in its limitations and social isolation, its radical, liberating separation from confining norms, and its political meaning.

Another area of women's experiences examined by the book are prisons as mostly sex-segregated spaces and as sites for political hunger strikes. Many RAF prisoners continued to politicize their incarceration throughout their prison terms, and the RAF was able to maintain a political presence in West German discourse for years through their hunger strikes. The core significance of the hunger strike for the continued politicization of the RAF demands an examination of it as a gendered political practice. Both printed and unpublished sources reveal women's accounts of their hunger strikes as a source of both political subjectivity and social isolation. Furthermore, the way the practice relates to sexual difference is rooted not simply in the bodies of the actual prisoners but in political customs organized by gender. The question arises as to how a feminist focus on the body redirects assumptions of a liberal, political subjectivity towards a more radical, collective identity produced in the collective hunger strike that uses bodies to insist on a political presence. The challenges that both underground and prison pose to the spatial division of democratic political traditions—the irrelevance they impose on concepts of "public" and "private"—invites a gendered analysis of how the violent actions of the RAF, which forced them out of public sight (first the strategic retreat underground, then the state's attempt to make them invisible/irrelevant by locking them away), undermine a political gender regime and thus constitute feminist practice.

## Gendered Terrorism

The third area of thought that structures this analysis concerns the ways in which women's participation in political violence discursively genders the meaning of terrorism (i.e., how it constitutes a "violent truth"). As recent feminist scholarship on terrorism shows, studies of women who participate in political violence enhance our understanding of terrorism itself and how it is shaped by the discourse of mass media and the class, race, and gender presumptions behind it.[64] Conversations about terrorism are often inadvertently informed by gender ideologies, and gender as an analytical variable provides important new insights. If women's experiences in armed groups counter prevalent assumptions, how does their very existence change the course of debates on political violence? How does gender structure the understanding of political violence for the public, for activists, and for the state through media outlets and scientific claims?

Terrorism as a political and social phenomenon is not simply produced by the violent actions of a group of activists. Instead, it is discursively constructed through the terrorizing act, representation and dissemination of knowledge about the act and its perpetrators, expert opinions, the public response, and the political framing of it—all contribute to the phenomenon of "left-wing terrorism" in West Germany.[65] The media as a forum for public debate, as a mediator of information, and as an agent of meaning making is central to an analysis of how terrorism is gendered.[66] The RAF's and other militant activists' relationship to the media was shaped by the broader counterculture's criticism of established forms of news media and their attempts at creating "counter public spheres." Despite its severe critique (and targeting) of corporate media, the RAF used and relied on media representations to relay their actions and to construct the group as a threat to national security. A new understanding of gendered ideologies and the RAF calls for a reevaluation of the particularly gendered way in which the mainstream media has historicized the RAF.[67] This reevaluation includes the responses by movement activists to media representations, as well as consideration of the increased pressure on intellectuals, civil servants, and average citizens to disassociate publicly from the radical Left so as not to become targeted by the state's investigations, especially after the legislative introduction of §129.[68] It especially includes a critical illumination of the ways in which the media *relied* on gendered ideologies dominated by the cultural paradox posed by RAF women to make the threat of the RAF intelligible.[69] These representations shaped and echoed people's general perception of terrorism. An examination of how masculinity and femininity function as central parameters of media coverage of terrorist acts thus counters a "mediated" cultural memory and historicization of the group that has dominated RAF discourses.

Media representations reached a large audience and contributed to a general public debate on women and violence. "Expert" knowledge on women, violence, and violent women, usually reserved for specialized journals and conferences, was disseminated widely into the mainstream debate primarily through the media's consultation of "terrorism experts"—criminologists, psychologists, law enforcement personnel, sociologists—whose theories as to why terrorist women committed their actions were paraded in news stories on the RAF and in government reports on the group.[70] Understanding how women's political violence was contained within a sexist framework of linking their crimes with the supposed physicality of female bodies and with essentialized feminine emotionality and irrationality clarifies the at times over-the-top, hysterical discursive construction of the RAF as threat to *the nation* (not just to its police officers or powerful representatives). Generally, the violent acts of the RAF and other groups seemed exacerbated by women participating in them; in the perceived pathological inversion of their gendered nature, they were more masculine than men: "If what we expect of women is [. . .] gentleness and passivity, then any level of violent activity looks relatively more extreme than in a man."[71] It is therefore important to consider the role that "experts"—and the truth-effects on gender and violence they generated—play in Germany's reading of terrorism.

Pseudoscientific claims that locate female criminal activity in a perverted or thwarted corporeality and hormonal/emotional determinism that needs to be stabilized through firm social roles find their way into law enforcement analyses of the group, most notoriously in the *Baader-Meinhof-Report*, a book-length document on the RAF issued by West Germany's Federal Criminal Bureau in 1972. The document reproduces some of the coarsest gender theories in criminology, including the association of female political crimes with sexuality (lesbianism, promiscuity, and physical and psychological effects of "the pill")[72] and gender inversion (RAF women as "more masculine and dominant" than their male counterparts, Andreas Baader as feminine, as an object of desire for homosexuals, and as "sadly underendowed by nature").[73] Recognizing how various elements of the state (politicians, law enforcement, the judicial system, and the prison medical and administrative system) gendered terrorism in an essentialized and sexist fashion speaks to the reliance of the social and political system on a gender regime these women were undermining. A gender analysis also illuminates the differential responses of the state to terrorism (e.g., counterterrorist measures, judicial sentencing), as well as strategies employed by political prisoners (e.g., hunger strikes). The significance the *Feminismusverdacht* (charge/accusation of feminism) had in terms of investigative measures taken for tracking, arresting, and trying members of the RAF points to the double violence the women were perpetrating: violence against actual people ("true violence") and violence against the gender regime ("violent truth"). As Colvin points out, "Like feminists, women terrorists were under attack as unholy aberrations from an ideal of womanhood."[74] The *Feminismusverdacht* speaks to the fact that the RAF posed a *gendered* threat to the state and society at large—mainstream ideology permeated a discourse that couched the RAF as posing a feminized threat (that is, the dark side of femininity: irrational, destructive, deceitful, and hysterical), whose violence originated not in masculine honor or heroism but in fantasies of self-empowerment to a masculine state/society (characterized by rationality, predictability, and just reasoning and as employing justified, because honorable, violence in order to protect its citizens).

Finally, the social and state perception of the RAF as a gendered threat raises the question of the political subjectivity of a "revolutionary." How are revolutionary theories that influenced the radical Left in West Germany gendered? How did terrorist women relate to the autonomous women's movement's and feminist theories on violence? Autobiographies and prison letters give some insight into how some women in armed groups, while not necessarily identifying as feminist "subjects," were impacted by feminist formulations of resistance and claimed armed struggle to be intimately related to women's liberation. They also give insight into how others only turned to feminist analyses and theories once they denounced the armed struggle, as if a revolutionary consciousness disallows a feminist consciousness. In all cases, gender (or the disavowal of its relevance for politics) informed how these women came to and experienced armed struggle and encountered it as a gendered phenomenon. Understanding the complex ways in which terrorism is gendered is a necessary step towards analyzing the subversive effect of the RAF women's violent actions: while they generated a reactionary and conservative backlash in media and much of the public, they also disclosed the continuous inherent sexism permeating German culture and facilitated a push-back—a counterdiscourse that critically challenged the gender regime.

## Debates on Political Violence in the New Left and the Women's Movement

The discourse on female political violence as it took place in West Germany was created in a particular historical moment in which leftist activists were debating and utilizing strategies of political violence. The question of violence in West Germany's Left, Ingrid Gilcher-Holtey emphasizes, needs to be localized "within the context of the strategies of action and transformation of the New Left"[75] (also referred to as "the 1968 movement") that linked it to the movement's "alternative scheme of order" and to its "method to alter society by subversion."[76] The idea that violence can constitute an important element in politics thus cannot be reduced to the bombs and bullets of the RAF. Instead, as a concept that circulated within various activist scenes in West Germany in the late 1960s and early 1970s, the question of violence proved to be a central component in defining both the *need* to resist (against state violence, against patriarchal violence, against the threat of military violence and war) and the *political means* of responding to that need (which were manifold and convey the complexity of the term). This study places debates about political violence that were taking place among leftist activists—in particular extremist positions as they solidified in the formation of the RAF and other militant groups— into conversation with feminist discussions on violence as they were emerging in the West German autonomous women's movement. While the formation of underground armed groups took place parallel to the emerging feminist movement, the separate strands of discourses on violence are rarely analyzed in relation to each other—they are assumed to be fundamentally oppositional.[77] Instead, I argue, more than simply coinciding in terms of temporal occurrence, they signify important divergences from originally shared leftist positions—many of the actors had at one point been politically connected with those who eventually represented opposing views on violence and others found themselves caught in the deepening schism between the Left and the autonomous women's movement. Understanding these strands of discourse illuminates their contribution to the phenomenon of "female terrorists" (and of "terrorist women") as it was constructed in West Germany in the 1970s and 1980s.

The differing theorization of violence within political resistance that took place in armed struggle and the women's movement was definitional for the relationship between the two political formations (and responsible for much of the schism between the two): there existed a tension between the concept of violence as revolutionary (counter)force as it was conceptualized by many in the Left's increasingly radicalized circles, and the gendered theory of violence as male/masculine and patriarchal, put forth by the developing autonomous women's movement, which imagined a countering of this oppressive violence with a female/feminine nonviolent alternative culture. While for both movements the *need* to resist was produced by existing violence, the origin of that violence and the *political means* of how to resist it differed. The RAF viewed violence as produced by an oppressive state and market system and—by extension—a social value system that necessitated a violent self-defense and/or defense of others. Emerging segments of the women's movement presented violence as originating in masculinity—and thus by extension in actual men and their socially sanctioned behavior as well as a state represented by men. This understanding of violence positioned it as a gendered form of political resistance that was rejected by a feminist sensibility that suspected violent responses to political oppression were simply reproducing masculine destruction. These seemingly irreconcilable theoretical positions were crossed by the lived experiences of armed women as well as challenged openly by feminist militants within the Left. Women in the RAF and Movement 2nd June undermined demarcations between assumed political movements and positions. They make visible important implications for a feminist theory that relies on a binary gender system to conceptualize violence.

## The *Gewaltdebatte* (Debate on Violence) in the West German Left

Somewhere between the terrorism of the RAF and the pacifism of radical feminists lies the complicated relationship of the West German Left to violence as political resistance.[78] Focusing on armed groups like the RAF generally, this study treats political violence as indicating the politically motivated strategic employment of violence by a group against objects and structures (and in certain cases, humans) that in the worldview of the group represent either state or systemic power. The aim of political violence therefore is to destabilize the existing government through strategic attacks and/or moments of resistance, and to direct public attention to issues of perceived injustice. The *Gewaltdebatte* (debate on violence) within the West German Left, however, as well as a consideration of the political strategies employed by it, reveals the concept of political violence to be less stable and actually quite ambiguous outside the context of armed struggle.[79] Its multidimensional meaning runs through three decades of political activism: it emerges in actions and strategies of the New Left aimed at violating social norms and rules of the 1960s, in the terrorism of the RAF and other armed groups and the increasingly brutal street battles between police and leftist activists, as well as the state repression and surveillance of the 1970s, and in the confrontational militancy of the radical leftists, referred to as Autonomen, as much as their anti-establishment lifestyle, in the 1980s.

The *Gewaltdebatte* became a major point of political discussions early on and would remain central. Its significance for the Left originated partly in the spirit of provocation and of challenging conventions that was inherent to the 1960s movements. Violating social and political norms meant resisting a systemic violence, often construed as a legacy of the Nazi past. The German "*Gewalt*" includes connotations of the English terms for both "violence" and "power," e.g., the power of the state is called "*Staatsgewalt*," and the monopoly of violence that it holds is referred to as "*Gewaltmonopol des Staates*." So the term signifies both legalized power to maintain order as well as violent acts against its rightful citizens. The perceived misuse of the state's power through violence was at the center of the debate about legitimized political violence. As Gilcher-Holey puts it, "This dual characteristic, which the German-language term brings to light, helped to make 'violence' a combat term in 1968, used on both sides to scandalize and delegitimize the actions of the respective opponent."[80] Borrowing concepts such as the "construction of situations" from International Situationists[81] and civil disobedience from the American civil rights movement,[82] the New Left adopted and transformed the relation of direct action and violence.[83] Contrary to political participation as it had been traditionally measured in its democratic representational forms in industrialized countries after World War II, the 1960s and 1970s introduced forms of political participation that were quickly construed as violence by the mainstream public. Protests, building occupations, boycotts, theatrical staging (and comical ridiculing) of conflict with the authorities, the use of flour and paint bombs, housing squats, petitions, and street barricades gave face to a new generation of activists who differed not only in political content from the "Old Left" but also and especially in their activist strategies that addressed the refusal of the political establishment to consider reforms.[84] Yet even in its most peaceful manifestations, such as sit-ins and strikes, direct action is often perceived as violent by mainstream society because of its violation of political convention.[85] As acts of civil disobedience, direct action activism actually often breaks the law. Its less peaceful forms, such as property destruction, violence against people, sabotage, and blockades, are quickly associated with terrorism. As Gilcher-Holey points out,

> The unconventional direct action in the border zone between legality and illegality broke with everyday life, with the normality of things. It violated norms, rules, laws, expectations. It caught the attention of the public and called for a reaction, for taking a position. [. . .] In many instances police, prosecutors and courts reacted sharply and took to stern repression and legal sanctions, which, as a kind of chain reaction, enhanced the movement's readiness to apply violence.[86]

This interactional element also becomes visible in the increased debates on violence following instances of police brutality, such as after the 1967 death of Benno Ohnesorg, who was shot by police at a protest, or after violent acts associated with right-wing ideology propagated by mass media, such as in 1968 when popular student movement leader Rudi Dutschke was shot and severely injured by a man who felt inspired by the spiteful hatred against leftist activists published in the tabloid *Bild*. Police brutality thus both generated feelings of radicalization and spurred actions of self-defense and/or counterviolence in the moment of confrontation.[87]

While police brutality against protesters created situations where activists felt directly threatened, political strategy sessions demanded clarification of the ways in which "violence against objects, which is a primarily symbolic gesture, related to violence against people."[88] Others thought this to be nothing but a technical distinction. By the 1970s, violence formed an important—albeit contentious—aspect of the radical leftist landscape: "'Violence,' without question, was one element of a variety of strategies leftist activists during the 1970s considered [. . .]: whether for self-defense against police or nonstate brutality, [or] as part of a 'theatrical' expression of one's opinion."[89] For some people, the line was drawn when it came to major destruction of private/state property (such as bombing of buildings) and/or the injuring of people. However, direct-action strategies established countless instances of "grey" zones of political violence that precariously navigated the conceptual lines between provocation and destruction, between generating shock and generating fear, between hurting those in power and terrorizing those who thought differently, between assault and self-defense. These concepts structured the movement's focus on the ethical distinctions between violence against objects and violence against persons. As Gilcher-Holtey points out, the strategy of direct action, "which later was adopted by the diverse movements that succeeded the 1968 movement (the alternative, peace, women's and environmental movements), gradually found its place in the 1970s and 1980s in the political culture of the Federal Republic,"[90] including a changed public perception of what constituted political violence towards more tolerance of direct action. However, those movements also inherited the New Left's precarious negotiations of what the limits of acceptable violence constituted.   .

Overall, the majority of leftist activists confined themselves to *discussing* political violence. At the same time, state violence left its mark on activists' experiences, impacting more than simply the "extremist" sections of the Left. For example, the intense battles between police and protesters, in particular in the *Häuserkämpfe* (housing battles) in the urban centers of Berlin, Frankfurt, and Hamburg that lasted into the late 1980s, deeply scarred many activists' relationship to the state. Police brutality against protesters increased during the 1970s,[91] in part as the state's reaction to the RAF. This began the cycle of leftist terrorist actions against a state they defined as inherently violent, which in turn provoked more national security measures, including increased surveillance and persistent persecution that defined the "leaden times"(*bleirne Zeit*)[92] of the mid-1970s. After the passing of the Emergency Laws[93] in 1968 that allowed for the limitation of democratic rights during times of crisis, measures by the state that increased pressure on leftist activists included additions to the criminal code that criminalized leftist activism, especially direct-action strategies and confrontations with the police. These legislative actions (§88, 129, and 130s) effectively limited freedom of speech as well as established the Decree against Radicals (Radikalenerlass, 1972) in order to protect the government from unconstitutional elements that resulted in the expulsion/exclusion of leftist thinkers from public service, including professors.[94] While formulated against unconstitutional elements, in fact the decree targeted leftists while not affecting large numbers of members of right-wing groups employed in the public sector.[95] By the mid-1970s, state and media discourse had succeeded in constructing all leftist activists as violent and as "sympathizers"[96] who all were potential RAF members, making political organizing dangerous and more difficult.[97] In this conflict among state, media, and leftist activists, the image of the female terrorist became central in defining the dangers that left-wing terrorism (and implicitly, feminism) posed to German society.

*Death in the Shape of a Young Girl* consists of five chapters; each addresses the three interdisciplinary areas that organize my reading of the material: the relationship of feminist theories to political violence, women's experiences in revolutionary groups, and the way gender structures responses—public and state—to terrorism. The historical and cultural background provided in each chapter does not serve merely to supplement but to *frame* the gendered analysis. Only when the specific context of the RAF and Movement 2nd June and the context of gendered ideologies in West Germany are established can we appreciate the work feminist theorizing on gender and violence does. The chapters are loosely organized around the chronology of events, beginning with an overview and discussion of political movements and groups and their theories in chapter 1. The seemingly oppositional politics of the RAF and feminism introduced very different models of thinking about resistance and violence; RAF women seem to represent a crossover between those models. The chapter introduces feminist theories (and claims) of nonviolence that—together with mainstream ideologies of gender—throughout the book are troubled by RAF and Movement 2nd June women's commitment to armed struggle as well as by gendered responses to their actions. Chapters 2 and 3 highlight German terrorist discourse during the "leaden times". Chapter 2 focuses on the ideology of motherhood as a major contested theme in this study. The cultural background for this is the feminine ideal constituted in a woman's realm of "Children, Kitchen, Church"[98] that centers around her duties of motherhood. The decision of RAF founders Gudrun Ensslin and Ulrike Meinhof to leave their children to go underground is revisited in this chapter in the context of feminist theories on "maternal ethics." As it turns out, both mainstream expectations of motherhood and the concept of feminist maternal politics are unable to account for the gendered experiences of Ensslin and Meinhof. The extent to which media structured public debate is the starting point of chapter 3. The emergence of violence against women as a major theme in feminist activism in the mid-1970s thereby forms the backdrop for this chapter, which analyzes movement publications as a discursive space in which mainstream ideologies of gender are countered with a set of diverse feminist positions on political violence. The chapter investigates an emerging dialogue among feminists, mainstream culture, and radical activists, in which these groups debated how terrorist acts constituted a disruption of both social contract and gender prescriptions. Chapter 4 discusses the years of the RAF hunger strikes, which span fifteen years of RAF activism, with a particular focus on the 1980s. I present an analysis of the RAF hunger strikes in terms of feminist theories on how embodiment relates to political subjectivity. The focus in this chapter is twofold: one is on hunger strikes as signifying a female (or, rather, feminized) political subject position in general inhabited by both women and men (the practice as a feminized trope), the other on women participating in hunger strikes in particular (female political subjectivity in the context of hunger strikes). Ultimately, the gendered dynamics within this political strategy reveal the limitations of the concepts of public/private, autonomy and state control, as they emerged in the state's conflict with RAF prisoners. In chapter 5 I read autobiographies of former female terrorists, as well as a set of unpublished prison letters by a former member of the Movement 2nd June. Their writings about their experiences and beliefs are narrative constructions of political subjectivities in the context of revolutionary violence. The departure point of each text is crucial: some memoirs and letters were written during the actual experiences (which, especially given long prison sentences, could span decades). Others were written in retrospect and/or are related through interviews, i.e., are coauthored. Thus the women's personal understandings of their political careers are mediated by time, context, and other voices. The time span in which these texts were written ranges from the late 1970s to the 2000s. All texts engage directly with the question of feminist politics and the women's movement; all create diverging narratives of how their revolutionary subjectivity intersected with or was separate from a feminist consciousness.

Prominent in all chapters is a tension among three discursive agents: voices of the autonomous women's movement (including feminist theories on political violence), the state and public opinion as representative of those threatened by the RAF and Movement 2nd June, and the women active in armed groups. This tension creates productive nodes of discursive connection that potentially transform the way gender functions as a structuring force. The main goal of this book is to revisit the question of whether political violence can be feminist by redefining what constitutes feminist politics. Instead of searching for the feminist *subject* executing the true violence of women in the RAF and Movement 2nd June, I explore the effects of their actions—their violent truth—on gender discourse as potential feminist *practices*. This can only be done in any sustainable way when we recognize that actions take place in certain contexts, and are not universal. Thus they need to be examined situationally (actions as constituting feminist practices) and not from a position of theoretical absolutes (actions are executed by feminist subjects). My hope is that this case study of women in the RAF and Movement 2nd June and the implications for feminist theories it raises will impact the discussion on political violence as it is taking place in gender studies to include less polarized, more complicated understandings of women's relationships to and use of violence as a part of their political choices.

# The Other Half of the Sky

## Revolutionary Violence, the RAF, and the Autonomous Women's Movement

Protest is when I say I don't like this. Resistance is when I put an end to what I don't like. Protest is when I say I refuse to go along with this anymore. Resistance is when I make sure everybody else stops going along, too.

　★ Ulrike Meinhof quoting a Black Panther activist, 1968

Women carry half of the sky on their shoulders and they must conquer it.

　★ Mao Zedong

Male violence has settled within my body, has broken my voice, constrained my movements, has blinded my imagination: the female body as microphysics of patriarchal violence, faceless identity, formless history, invisible labor, called love.

　★ Anna Dorothea Brockmann, 1981

### Introduction

During the early 1970s, a flyer with the image of a woman with her fist raised to the sky was passed around in radical political circles in West Germany. The upper part of the image displays a quotation from Mao Zedong: "Women carry half of the sky on their shoulders and they must conquer it" (see figure 1.1).[1] With the woman's Afro and raised fist, the image connotes anticolonial movements, evoking associations with movement icon Angela Davis of the Black Panthers. This flyer and its distribution in activist circles speaks to one of the central issues of this book: the role of women in revolutionary movements in West Germany (including their employment of political violence) and what that implies for feminist politics. Visually, the image makes two points: first, it offers revolutionary violence (symbolized by the raised fist) as a means to a

Figure 1.1. Circulated in activist circles in the early 1970s, this flyer placed women into the context of revolutionary violence. (APO-Archiv, Ordner: Frauenbewegung)

better world; second, it suggests that women have a central role to play in this process. The actual gender politics of the Left were much less integrated than Mao's statement suggests; however, the flyer does visualize a convergence of feminist goals and revolutionary violence that is mirrored in the RAF women's presence in the political scene. This convergence troubles the historical separation of feminist politics and violence and instead demands a realignment of categories of women's political activism.

Understanding the multidimensional approaches to violence that existed in the West German leftist activist scene is important to theorizing its gendered implications. The following reflections on the political and theoretical contexts that produced the RAF and the women's movement in West Germany are thus necessarily narratives about violence, focused on the role it (imaginatively and actually) played in various activist settings, the seduction and temptation it posed for some and the horror and repulsion it evoked in others. The seemingly dualistic approach to the complicated matter of movement activists arguing for diverse political positions does not imply that all leftist activists were violent or that all feminists opposed political violence. However, it acknowledges the center stage that the question of violence took in the political organizing of that time.

Before turning to feminist discussions on political violence, it is necessary to establish the context of this particular historical moment in West Germany of the 1960s to the 1980s. This context, in which the use of violence was intensely debated by activists in Western nations, sets the stage for the analyses of gendered terrorism in the rest of the book. During this time, domestic political issues were interpreted in the larger context of the Vietnam War, the Cold War détente, and anticolonial and/or liberationist struggles in Africa and anti-imperialism in South America, which cast U.S. imperialism as the contemporary manifestation of fascism. The context analysis in this chapter does not represent a history of social movements in West Germany, but offers instead a narrative of how the discursive force of violence (conceptually and actually) shaped political formations. This narrative is formulated around two main parts at the center of the debate on political violence in West German activist circles. One frames violence as the oppressive foundation of political resistance, thus creating a *need* to organize. Leftist activists (and later the RAF) understood this violence to be based in imperialism and its racist wars, fascism and its political workings, as well as capitalism's global and domestic exploitations. Feminist activists, on the other hand, understood violence to be based in patriarchy (an analysis that initially included what was viewed as patriarchy's destructive offspring/extensions, imperialism and capitalism) and to manifest in (sexual) violence against women.

Both leftist and feminist political positions harbored a particular suspicion of "democratic" procedures as simply disguising existing power structures (such as the West German parliamentary politics making invisible surviving fascist/authoritarian ideologies, interests, and practitioners, or promoting inherently patriarchal values and barring women from social and political power), and thus both groups took radical, antistate political positions. However, their takes on how to counter violence differed markedly on the basis of their opposing philosophical views. This second part of the debate, which focused on the *political means* to counter violence, conveys the diverging conceptual emphases around which activists would rally. Radical sections of the Left, and especially armed groups, viewed actual (not symbolic) violence as a necessary and singularly effective way of meeting systemic violence, while many feminists thought violent resistance would simply reproduce existing destructive patterns.

Maybe most importantly, in leftist discourse, power and oppression were externalized forces to be fought against. While a leftist analysis of capitalism and imperialism necessarily seems to include an examination of one's own class privilege, often a simple rejection of a "bourgeois" lifestyle and declared solidarity with Third World peoples seemed to establish shared grounds with those in need of defending themselves against state violence, and fascism was constructed as the parent generation's social disease. This is not to claim that all leftist activists were privileged or uncritical of themselves; the social background of many of them included the experience of poverty, an abusive foster care and/ or educational system, and social stigmatization. Rather, the point here is that the theoretical reasoning that solidarity can be the grounds for revolution (as it was initially formulated by the SDS and taken to its logical consequence by armed groups like the RAF) does not resonate with a feminist sensibility that locates liberation/revolution in the resistance against personal, everyday sexual oppression. Instead, feminist criticisms of the everyday privileging of men posited every individual man to be a representative of oppressive power relations (this criticism meanwhile problematically released women from accountability for *their* power, based on factors such as their class, nationality, and/ or race). The feminist claim that the "enemy" of patriarchal domination infested even activist circles challenged the construction of West German activist men as having successfully rejected their inheritance of social and political power, a narrative central to the legitimization of armed resistance.

## Revolutionary Violence

Placing revolutionary violence and feminist nonviolence into conversation means recognizing their shared historical and political context of the New Left and the new social movements in West Germany. The early 1970s saw both the consolidation of feminist organizing efforts in the emerging autonomous women's movement and the radicalization of activists resulting in the formation and political actions of the RAF, the Movement 2nd June, and other militant groups who viewed revolutionary armed struggle as the only effective way to achieve social change. For these activists in armed groups, violence signified not only a political strategy but also a philosophy that viewed actual, physical conflict as a necessary prerequisite for change. According to the statement on the formation of the Movement 2nd June in 1972, "The militaristic stance of the Movement 2nd June cannot be separated from its political stance and is not secondary. We view both stances as inseparably connected. They are two sides of the same revolutionary cause."[2] This group side-stepped the ethical dilemma activists of the New Left struggled with: whether violence—against property and/or people—is legitimate. Revolution, they reasoned, cannot be *talked* into existence. Instead, only *actions* can facilitate social change—in this case, actions of violent resistance. Instead of *writing* and *talking* about revolution, they demanded, people must *act* as revolutionaries. This call to action is addressed in the RAF position paper "*Das Kouzept Stadtguerilla*" ("The Concept of the Urban Guerilla") in 1971: "The Red Army Faction speaks of the primacy of practice. The question, whether it is right to organize armed resistance at the current moment depends on whether it is possible; whether it is possible can only be determined through practice."[3] This credo of the "primacy of practice" that would be the RAF's main argument against criticisms from within the movement reduced the New Left's principle that "solidarity [with the armed struggle of peoples in the Third World] must become practical"[4] to the one option of going underground and attacking the state.

These activists did not step out of nowhere into the underground: they formed their extremist political positions in the context of West Germany's leftist subcultural milieu. While some scholars suggest that the student movement propagated the use of violence much more than discourse had previously depicted,[5] others have convincingly argued that large numbers (probably the majority) of people organizing around leftist political issues sought alternative strategies from those presented by polarized positions.[6] Maybe more importantly, the way violence as a concept circulated in leftist circles was much more complicated than planting bombs and carrying guns. However, within the smaller radicalized circles whose members' direct-action strategies and street violence with police were already located in the "grey" zone of political activism, violent rhetoric (and action) was part of the political repertoire. So instead of constituting an isolated phenomenon, the prioritizing of violence against the state and its representatives over other forms of political strategies by groups like the RAF and Movement 2nd June can be understood as the development of an extreme section of a much broader discourse on violence that was taking place in the countermovements of the 1960s.[7] The terrorism of the RAF and Movement 2nd June thus needs to be contextualized in the wider narrative of revolutionary violence that in the 1960s shaped much of international and domestic organizing throughout the world, including in West Germany. Certain radical approaches to political issues dominated parts of the APO (Außerparlamentarische Opposition, or Extraparliamentary Opposition),[8] the New Left's most concrete formation in the 1960s, and the radical political scene throughout the 1970s and into the 1980s. During the 1960s, many members of the APO conceptualized their radical, countercultural lifestyle and their direct-action approach to politics as counterviolence to a brutal state and corporate system. Actions included the campaigns and protests against the publishing giant Axel Springer and its reactionary tabloid *Bild* as well as the massive and violent protests against the Iranian shah. During the 1970s, the reframing of medical discourse on mental illness as politically oppressive by groups such as the Socialist Patients' Collective (SPK),[9] militant actions against nuclear facilities (both weapon positioning and waste storage), and the increasing number of squatting projects in the urban centers all involved rhetoric and actions of violence. Finally, during the 1980s, the emergence of the Autonomen[10] and their militant street politics as the most visible element of radical leftist organizing form an important historical backdrop for armed groups like the RAF (1970–1998) and the Movement 2nd June (1972–1980). While the aim here is not to paint radical leftist German political activists as generally violent (the majority maintained a consistently ambivalent relationship to political violence), the goal is to avoid a defensive denial of the fact that violence has constituted an important part of leftist politics—in particular as a response to state and other violence.

This being said, it is important to understand the West German debate on political violence to have taken place in conjunction with international radical social movements (including armed revolts) against former colonial regimes, a brutally fought war on the Indochinese Peninsula, and an aggressive nuclear arms race between two superpowers.[11] Those in the West German Left who viewed violence as one necessary element of revolutionary change conceptualized their radical politics in close relation to happenings globally and to the theories on revolutionary violence that were circulating internationally.

## Snapshots of the 1968 Movement and the APO

If you were a young activist with radical leftist politics in 1968 in Paris, Berlin, Rome, Berkeley, Prague, or Montevideo, revolutionary violence as a means to disrupt the oppressive state was debated rigorously and passionately in your political circles. In West Germany two developments galvanized the protest movements leading up to the year of international revolts in 1968: one involved the impending Emergency Laws that would allow for the curtailing of democratic rights during times of crisis,[12] and the second was the formation of the "Great Coalition" in 1966 between the two major political parties—the Social Democratic Party (SPD) and the sister parties Christian Democratic Union (CDU) and Bavarian Christian Social Union (CSU)[13]—that effectively eliminated any opposition in Parliament. The "Great Coalition" spurred on the formation of the Extraparliamentary Opposition (APO) that had begun to emerge in the early 1960s. The APO saw itself as the only true oppositional force against the government; it stood separate from party politics and worked outside the electoral process. APO activists organized projects that challenged institutional and cultural authority. While the APO consisted of a variety of political groups, the student movement took a leading role; in particular, its formal body, the SDS,[14] and its leaders became the "faces" of the New Left, especially Rudi Dutschke. In their early years, the APO organized against rearmament, the basing of nuclear weapons in West Germany, and the proposed Emergency Laws. Later, their activities included campaigns against the conservative publishing house Axel Springer and its notorious tabloid *Bild*, the public exposure and confrontation of former Nazi officials and professors, protests against the Vietnam War and the Iranian shah's regime, and other organizational collaborations with international students and activists.[15]

The students' criticism of German politics and what was viewed as a static, conservative society in general was driven by a conviction that the country had never found productive closure with its recent fascist past and National Socialism. They condemned their parents' generation both for their complicity with the Nazi regime and for their selective silence throughout the official dealings with the issue that took place in the form of reparation discussions, the trials of Adolf Eichmann in 1961, and the "Auschwitz Trials" of 1963–65.[16] However, the New Left's dealings with the Nazi past was rife with ambiguities. In their introduction to *Coping with the Nazi Past: West German Debates on Nazism and Generational Conflict, 1955–75*, Philip Gassert and Alan Steinweis point out that while New Left activism "radicalized the discourse about the Nazi past,"[17] its targeting of what they declared a "fascist continuity"[18] in communal and federal administrations at times emphasized "a generic 'fascism' [that] also tended to universalize and dehistoricize that past."[19] Despite these ambiguities, activists were quite concrete in their charge that a fascist continuity was present, represented by former agents of the Nazi regime who now were major decision makers in the construction of the newly democratic West Germany. These included university professors and teachers, civil servants, influential businessmen and industrialists, as well as judges and politicians.[20] The young activists' confrontations with Germany's fascist past also shaped their social criticism more broadly: in accordance with the Frankfurt School and the psychologist Wilhelm Reich, they understood fascism to be "a cognitive structure and a cultural condition, manifest in subjects who were at once extraordinarily pliant and dictatorial, submissive and aggressive" and "the behavior of the adult generation—from the defense of order to disdain for nonconformity—as signs of the persistence of the 'authoritarian personality' integral to fascism."[21] Anti-authoritarian activism—including the *Kinderladen* movement[22]—thus was not simply a gesture against bourgeois values but part of an antifascist agenda.[23]

The New Left's approach to Third World issues was reflected in a shift in the way the concept of fascism was understood. Initially referring to an ideology underlying National Socialism, dominated by a theory of totalitarianism, the concept was subsequently broadened to include the cultural, social, and psychological conditions that produce a fascist mindset that can undermine the democratic process. Fascism was seen as underlying many of imperialism's impulses, and solidarity with the struggles of peoples in the Third World was central in West Germany in the three decades of activism after the launching of the New Left. In the early 1960s, transnational collaboration in particular between international students from African and Asian countries who were dissidents in their home countries encouraged West German leftist activists to analyze politics through the lens of international relations and human rights. These early, concrete collaborations presented activists with insights into Third World socialism that offered an alternative to authoritarian forms of Marxist traditions.[24]

After 1966, transnational activism in West Germany increasingly focused on Iran as well as the Vietnam War.[25] The Vietnam Congress in 1968 drew not only activists from the United States to Berlin (as is often noted) but many more from the Iranian student organization alone, in addition to other internationals.[26] However, the shooting and killing in West Berlin of the student Benno Ohnesorg at a protest against the Iranian shah organized mostly by Iranian students redirected the attention from Third World subjects to West Germans as victims of repressive state violence:[27] Benno Ohnesorg's death would be a catalyst for the radicalization of leftist activists, some of whom would later form or join revolutionary groups and move underground.[28]

The international influence on the West German New Left's ideological positions manifested concretely in German activists' support of the U.S. Black Panthers. The militant black activists represented the strategic and ideological move from the civil rights movement (and its iconic nonviolent resistance) to Black Power (and its no less iconic armed members). They signaled an impatience with liberal ideas of blacks' integration into white America and introduced Black Nationalism's radical demand for community self-determination and self-governance. To West German activists, the militant Black Panthers represented Frantz Fanon's anticolonial subjects who resort to violence as the necessary means to respond to and end colonial violence. As a racial minority who defined their oppression as an "internal" colonialism, they allowed West German activists, who had declared West Germany an "external" colony of the Unites States' imperialist Cold War politics (and an enabling ally to the atrocities of the Vietnam War), to forge an ideological connection to the Black Power movement by casting the United States as a fascist regime that was ready to exterminate (or enslave) whole peoples.[29] Despite the complete lack of shared racialized experiences or history, most West Germans leftists viewed their solidarity with the Panthers as real and founded in actual political realities.[30] The theoretical underpinning of leftist activists' solidarity with the Black Power movement in the United States was thus established through the notion of the two groups as anti-imperialist allies, and through the rationalization that while West Germany had no ethnic minority that would speak of its oppression in the terms of "internal colony," students were seeking conflict with the state to an extent that would eventually lead to the "emergence of a counter-milieu, which could then serve as a basis for radical social change."[31]

These countermilieus included ideas of alternative public spheres, as the New Left's criticism of fascist *Gedankengut* (ideas) that they saw as pervading West German consumer culture was extended to the media and the public sphere. They believed the latter to be poisoned by the influence of the conservative publishing house Axel Springer, in particular its flagship, the tabloid *Bild Zeitung*. The "Enteignet [Disown] Springer!" campaign that began in 1967 addressed the publishing giant's domination of the media market as well as the conservative, or even right-wing, content of its newspapers, in particular *Bild*. Perceiving *Bild's* right-wing coverage of the student movement—flanked by Springer's other newspaper publications—the APO faulted Springer for the shooting of the popular spokesperson of the student movement, Rudi Dutschke. In 1968 a right-wing fanatic apparently was inspired by *Bild's* coverage to shoot Dutschke, a link that the APO expressed in its accusation, "Springer shot too!"[32] The publishing house subsequently extended its inflammatory coverage from the New Left to the RAF and other armed groups.[33]

### "From Protest to Resistance": Armed Struggle and the Concept of the Urban Guerilla in the RAF and Movement 2nd June: 1970–72

Opening her *konkret* column titled "From Protest to Resistance"[34] with a quotation of a Black Panther activist she had heard speak at the 1968 Vietnam Kongress in Berlin, the well-known journalist Ulrike Meinhof introduced a piece of rhetoric to the German leftist scene that, according to Karin Bauer, had been circulating in the United States for quite some time:[35] "Protest is when I say I don't like this. Resistance is when I put an end to what I don't like. Protest is when I say I refuse to go along with this anymore. Resistance is when I make sure everybody else stops going along, too."[36] The shift from a mentality of protesting a state's policies and a society's value system to one of actively resisting an oppressive regime—with violent self-defense if needed—marked the theoretical justification for the formation of underground armed groups that would at times openly determine, at other times subtly haunt, the relationship of the West German state with its politicized radical leftist opponents. Nobody could predict that two years later Meinhof would put this shift into action by cofounding the RAF and that her actions would greatly influence public debates on gender and violence.

By the end of 1968, the West German SDS had pretty much dissolved. However, the number of students who were politically organizing actually grew after 1968, with many founding so-called *K-Gruppen*, small communist parties.[37] By the early 1970s, a street-militant scene emerged in local protests involving the Spontis,[38] such as against gentrification and nuclear armament. The times were also marked by the formation of militant groups, including the Tupamaros West Berlin and the Tupamaros Munich (Tupamaros München)[39] (1969) that committed organized violent acts, such as arson and bombing, the RAF (1970), Movement 2nd June (1972), and later the Revolutionäre Zellen with its feminist subformation Rote Zora (RZ, Revolutionary Cells [1973], and Red Zora [1977]).[40] The West Berlin left-radical *Agit 833* began publication in April 1969, serving as a discussion platform for the leftist scene and its armed groups.[41] In Heidelberg, the Socialist Patients' Collective (SPK) formed in 1970; its "antipsychiatry" framework operated under the premise that capitalist society produces all mental illnesses, which can only be eradicated by the abolishment of the capitalist class society. Later, members of the SPK would join the ranks of the RAF. These radicalized formations of the early to mid-1970s signaled the shift from "protest to resistance" that activists deemed necessary to establish conditions for a revolution.

The RAF was founded in May 1970, when a group of activists broke Andreas Baader out of prison. Baader, together with his lover, Gudrun

Ensslin, and two other men, had been sentenced to prison for setting off a fire bomb in a Frankfurt department store two years prior, an act that was framed in political terms as an anti–Vietnam War protest by the four defendants.[42] Upon his escape, Baader proceeded to cofound the RAF with the women who had organized his prison break, including Gudrun Ensslin and the well-known journalist Ulrike Meinhof, as well as the attorney Horst Mahler. The high ratio of women in the RAF (and other armed groups), which troubled traditional gender roles, would later dominate state and public discourses on national security. The RAF's founding manifesto/statement on June 5, 1970, "Die Rote Armee aufbauen" (Building the Red Army),[43] was published in *Agit 883*. In this text, written by Meinhof, the group explains its Marxist politics in relation to both domestic issues and international concerns. The RAF's fundamental ideological and political belief was that change can only happen through escalating conflict with the state, aimed at an overthrow of the existing system, and that that conflict can most effectively be achieved through armed struggle executed by underground, illegal cells: "To carry these conflicts [with the state and its institutions and representatives] to extremes means: that they cannot do what they want any longer, but have to do what we want."[44] Violence by the urban guerilla—the true revolutionary subject—forces the state to show its "true" repressive face and garners public support and politicizes the masses.

Even more so than for the RAF, the roots of the Movement 2nd June[45] began in a countercultural movement that viewed the use of drugs, certain musical influences, and liberal sexual habits to be as much the basis of radical politics as world politics and wars. Increasingly militant and politicized groups such as the Blues, "half subculture, half political underground,"[46] and the Tupamaros West Berlin and Tupamaros Munich preceded the formation of the Movement 2nd June. They attracted militant activists and participated in acts of bombing and targeting of individuals who were viewed as representatives of the system. After Georg von Rauch, a member of the Blues, died in a shoot-out with the police, a number of activists, including Ina Siepmann, Ralf Reinders, Gabriele Kröcher-Tiedemann, and Norbert Kröcher, founded the Movement 2nd June.[47] West Berlin remained both the logistical and political focus for the Movement 2nd June, more so than for the RAF, who early on shifted much of its attention and organizational emphasis to the FRG.[48] The

Movement 2nd June declared its strategic goals in its founding manifesto, circulated in June 1972: "Our goal is not the creation of a 'dictatorship of the proletariat' but the destruction of the domination of pigs over humans, [. . .] the destruction of the domination of capital, of the parties, of the state. The goal is the establishment of a democracy of councils."[49] While the manifesto was gender nonspecific, women made up at times more than half of the Movement 2nd June's members, which triggered much public anxiety about women using political violence and contributed to the gendering of the discourse on terrorism.

Both groups were socialist at the core, but the RAF relied on a more hierarchical, Leninist belief in armed groups serving an avant-garde function, while the Movement 2nd June, while also believing an avant-garde to be central in *sparking* revolutionary change, nevertheless was organized around "anti-authoritarian" principles, believing in the anarchist creed of "propaganda of the deed."[50] As with the New Left in West Germany more generally, the two groups were inspired, and felt called upon, by anticolonial and anti-imperialist movements, in particular the Black Panthers, who in the early 1970s found material and political support in the Black Panther Solidarity Committee. While the two groups identified and acted as distinct, their goals and methods overlapped, and upon the dissolution of the Movement 2nd June, most of its members joined the RAF, some of them while in prison.

As in other countries, the debate on political violence was propelled by the revolutionary writings of authors such as Frantz Fanon, Che Guevara, and, especially in West Germany, Herbert Marcuse.[51] International anticolonial groups such as the Black Panthers[52] and dissidents of the Iranian regime constituted concrete influences, whose activism provided the theoretical backdrop for West German activists' violent resistance.[53] Central to this was the theorizing of violent political resistance as the only viable response to a systemic state violence, both domestic and international. Guevara, Fanon, and other revolutionary writers addressed issues of international significance that spoke to young activists worldwide who related the left-wing, anti-imperialist critique of these texts to their respective Cold War contexts. The brutalities of the Vietnam War, the Black Power Movement's decrying of global black oppression, preceded by the Algerian War of Independence and other African and South American freedom movements, and of course the

Israel-Palestinian conflict, all represented crises produced by the perceived imperialist aspirations of the United States and its Western Allies. All of these revolutionary theorists rewrote traditional Cold War politics to pose the United States, Israel, and NATO as pushing an imperialist agenda in the Middle East, Africa, and South America and view violence as a necessary self-defense in the conflict between the First World/the North and the Third World/the South. Accordingly, violent resistance as a necessity for ending colonial oppression is the basis for Fanon's theoretical position that only violence can bring about true social change.[54] Thus, for the young West German activists, the Cuban Revolution and the Chinese Cultural Revolution became symbols of a socialist resistance to the global reach of capitalism.[55]

Forming in the urban centers of West Germany—more specifically, in West Berlin—the RAF and Movement 2nd June adapted the revolutionary *foco* theory of guerilla warfare, formulated by French writer Régis Debray, to their geographic and political specificities. Inspired by Guevara's theory on rural guerilla warfare as an effective way of toppling a sitting regime with popular support, *foco* theory relies on small, fast-operating paramilitary cadres to destabilize a larger military system while gaining the support for a general insurrection.[56] Transplanting Guevara's rural war strategy to the metropolis, Brazilian revolutionary Carlos Marighella's *Mini-Manual of the Urban Guerrilla* (1969) inspired activists in large urban areas around the world to further the overthrow of imperial states from within their urban centers. The *Mini-Manual* was widely circulated in West German activist circles. These influences on how to strategize, but especially also on how to *identify* as a revolutionary, become apparent in the early position papers of the RAF, such as "Das Konzept Stadtguerrilla" (April 1971),[57] in which they state that armed resistance has become a necessary addition to "legal" forms of resistance. Furthermore, they locate revolutionary identity in the sharp separation from the social contract, which in turn results in persecution by the state: "Red Army Faction and urban guerilla constitute those factions and practices that, by clearly drawing a demarcation line between themselves and the enemy, are being most severely fought. That requires political identity; that requires that a learning curve has taken place."[58] Finally, in the writings by critical theorist Herbert Marcuse, the militants found commentary on the limits of conventional political participation in democratic societies. Marcuse argues that these societies' repressive tolerance, which in itself is violent, controls and limits opposition and dissent. Tolerating resistance within the bounds of "democratic means" allows the state to create the illusion that dissent has a place in state formation, when in fact it limits the effect of any push for change. Violence employed by dissenters becomes a legitimate means to disrupt oppressive power relations that the democratic state enforces through its monopoly of violence. Political violence, it then can be argued, is warranted not only in places of extreme oppression but also in societies whose facades of democratic participation in actuality leave political control in the hands of those in power.[59]

The number of active members in the RAF and Movement 2nd June remained small (in sharp contrast to the thousands of supporters the emerging new social movements gathered in the early 1970s); they operated in individual cells responsible for separate political actions. The RAF raised funds for its underground operations through bank robberies; they worked with the militant wing of the Palestinian PLO (Palestine Liberation Organization) and other Middle Eastern terrorists. Over time, the state would categorize RAF members as belonging to three separate "generations" that marked the state's counterterrorism responses to the changes in members and strategies the RAF underwent. The Movement 2nd June, after a devastating series of arrests, dissolved in 1980, and all but a few of the remaining members joined the RAF. In the first two years, the RAF primarily built an infrastructure underground with bank robberies, document forgeries, and car thefts. During their May Offensive in 1972, the RAF bombed U.S. military facilities and German institutions, such as the central office of the conservative publishing house Axel Springer. The Movement 2nd June limited its actions to the geographical radius of West Berlin, until the group moved much of its attention to international locations. In the first year of its founding, the group robbed banks and bombed UK military facilities. The politics of the RAF and Movement 2nd June—despite the important differences that existed in the ideologies and strategies between the two groups—would dominate the West German Left's debates on resistance through violence until the "German Autumn" of 1977 that escalated the confrontation between the RAF and the state.

## Anti-Imperialism, Revolution, and the "German Autumn": 1972–77

The transition from the initial euphoria of 1968 to the dissolution of the SDS and the original student movement in 1970, and later the formation of armed underground groups coincided with the emergence of new social movements around women's and gay rights, environmentalism, and, eventually, the peace movement. A growing number of leftist activists were seeking more centralized political forums in the *K-Gruppen*, small communist parties.[60] Both the new social movements and the solidification of the Left in *K-Gruppen* signified a turn away from the New Left's decentralized, anti-authoritarian, utopian vision for a new society. Many former 1968 activists set out to bring about their transformational vision not through social and cultural revolution but through the "long march through the institutions,"[61] and, in a climate often hostile to leftist activism, reverted to what Belinda Davis calls "politics of the kitchen table."[62] More radical sections of the Left later formed the Sponti scene of squatters and antinuclear protests in urban areas such as West Berlin and Frankfurt. This street-militant scene, involving primarily local political campaigns, was to precede the later formation in the 1980s of the Autonomen, as well as the shift of some Spontis towards electoral politics that took place with the Greens[63] and that forced established parties to reckon with a left-leaning, environmentally concerned national political platform that would change West German parliamentary politics.

The transition from the 1960s to the 1970s also came with the rapid formation of an anti-imperialist focus on the "catalytic role of Third World struggles,"[64] as opposed to a focus on human rights violations against individuals. Anti-imperialism provided a framework for a more universal criticism of U.S. politics that did not rely on the problematic communism of the USSR. With its targeting of the United States and its NATO allies (including Israel) as the declared global driver of exploitation and wars, anti-imperialism would remain crucial for the theoretical underpinnings of the RAF.

A problematic, often contradictory, and apparently anti-Semitic position solidified within the anti-imperialist rhetoric of the New Left, with its criticism of the "new fascism" of imperialism. This position was mainly based on the New Left's definition of Israel as part of imperialist forces—the political solidarity and subjective empathy of West German activists were with the Palestinian people, the "underdog" of the conflict.[65] A troubling anti-Israel (and very pro-Palestinian) rhetoric, amplified by the collaboration of the RAF and other leftist terrorists with the Palestinian PLO and other Middle Eastern groups, made many of the New Left appear anti-Semitic. The anti-Israel position taken by many leftists stood in startling contradiction to the antifascist discourse the New Left had introduced, and the radical anti–National Socialism position taken by the RAF. Conceptually and rhetorically there existed a disjuncture between the consistent evocation of National Socialism's past and crimes, and the anti-Zionist casting of Israel and its Jewish population as fascist, genocidal, and imperialist. It would be too simplistic to reduce the New Left's global politics to beliefs that were rooted in anti-Semitism—without doubt the concrete National Socialist past of the country and a feared continuity of Nazism in its ruling body (political and economical) fueled the New Left's transformational goals.[66] The revival of a Leninist anti-Zionism (in particular within the K-Gruppen) that completely ignored the historical reality of the existence of Israel as well as the fact that it was populated by large numbers of Holocaust survivors was a rash und naïve radical position. The results were complicated and seemingly contradictory analogies that transferred specificities of Nazi crimes (in particular references to the Holocaust and specific concentration camps) onto historically unrelated instances, from German police brutality to the "fascist" genocidal war of the United States in Vietnam, conveying the limitations and dangers of an ahistorical use of (German) fascism and of universalizing analogies of suffering that are rooted in historic specificities.[67] However, it is also important to consider that these at times hyperbolic projections of Nazi-specific Holocaust crimes onto U.S. and Israeli politics were taking place in a climate in which National Socialism was declared a historical phenomenon that was dead, and in which the war horrors inflicted by the United States in Vietnam were being presented as a necessary measure against a rising global communism. Further, the virulent anticommunism rampant in the FRG was part of the official political program for the West German government, amplified in the face of the GDR (German Democratic Republic) across the border. It should thus not be surprising that this anticommunism was conflated with fascist sentiment since it evoked the historical parallel with the face-off between a fascist national socialist movement and antifascist Kommunistische Partei Deutschlands (KPD; Communist Party of Germany) activists during the Weimar Republic with the well-known, catastrophic outcome.

Hasty and manipulative analogies within the New Left's criticism of Israel (and the U.S. war in Vietnam) that ignored historical realities (such as declaring Israel a fascist state) created dubious arguments and were not helpful in resolving complicated political conflicts. However, it would be as dubious to declare the New Left's criticism of either Germany's unresolved Nazi past, the U.S. war in Vietnam, or Israel's uncompromising treatment of Palestinians as paranoid and unfounded, or as merely the product of a latent and violent anti-Semitism as the "true" survivor of the National Socialist legacy.[68]

After the arrest of the RAF's founding members in 1972, they were at times kept in solitary confinement and subsequently organized several hunger strikes to protest their prison conditions.[69] In 1975, Ulrike Meinhof, Gudrun Ensslin, Andreas Baader, and Jan-Carl Raspe were sent to a maximum security prison with a cell block specifically built for their incarceration during the trial, at Stammheim prison. The trial against the original RAF members lasted from May 21, 1975, until April 28, 1977. Ulrike Meinhof was found hanged in her prison cell on May 8, 1976; reportedly she committed suicide. The RAF's actions outside of prison meanwhile increasingly targeted individual representatives of the state and industry, such as with the murders of Chief Federal Prosecutor Siegfried Buback and the chief executive of the Dresdner Bank, Jürgen Ponto, in 1977. The release of RAF prisoners became a major focus of the group's actions after 1972, exemplified by the violent occupation of the West German Embassy in Stockholm in 1975, and the kidnapping and murder of industrialist Hanns-Martin Schleyer in 1977. Schleyer's kidnapping and the state's refusal to negotiate his return with the RAF resulted in the so-called German Autumn of 1977, which haunts Germany to this day: on October 13, members of the Palestinian PLO hijacked the Lufthansa plane *Landshut* and, among other demands, sought the release of eleven RAF prisoners in exchange for the passengers and crew. The successful storming of the *Landshut* by the West German antiterrorist unit GSG-9 at the Mogadishu airport shortly after midnight on October 18 kicked off a series of traumatic and violent events. Learning of the failure by the PLO to negotiate their release, and of the GSG-9's capturing of the airplane, the core RAF members Gudrun Ensslin, Andreas Baader, and Jan-Carl Raspe committed suicide in prison that same night (Irmgard Möller survived her suicide attempt), after which the RAF shot Schleyer, whose body was found on October 19.

Using collective hunger strikes to politicize their cause from prison (which resulted in the deaths of two RAF members, Holger Meins in 1974 and Sigurd Debus in 1981), the RAF maintained a consistent political presence in West German public debates. They continued to target representatives of what they believed to be an oppressive and exploitative system, including the fatal bombing of the chairman of the Deutsche Bank, Alfred Herrhausen, in 1989, and the assassination of Detlev Rohwedder, the manager of the Treuhandanstalt, in 1991, until the group declared a truce in 1992 and completely disbanded in 1998.

In 1974, the Movement 2nd June fatally shot Günter von Drenkmann, the president of West Germany's Superior Court of Justice, during a failed kidnapping attempt. The following year, the group kidnapped West Berlin politician Peter Lorenz and successfully negotiated the release of five prisoners in exchange for him, including Gabriele Kröcher-Tiedemann (the first and only terrorist action resulting in the release of political prisoners by the state). The Lorenz kidnapping is believed to have motivated the RAF to attempt to force the state into releasing political prisoners, such as with the siege of the West German Embassy in Stockholm and with the Schleyer kidnapping. In 1977, the Movement 2nd June successfully kidnapped the Austrian industrialist Walter Palmer in order to fund its actions. The Movement 2nd June also is known for several prison breaks (in 1976 and 1978). The underground group officially disbanded in 1980, with the remaining members joining the RAF.

## Street Militancy and Armed Struggle: Late 1970s and 1980s

In the late 1970s, a shift occurred in the landscape of social movements as the *K-Gruppen's* party communism increasingly lost influence to a protest culture of "politics of the first person" ("politics of the self")[70] that, as Sabine von Dirke points out, "signifies a new perception of political commitment and activism that is oriented toward the immediate and personal concerns of its practitioners."[71] Protests against the neoliberalism emerging from Reaganism and Thatcherism on both sides of the Atlantic were voiced by activists in the new social movements in terms of individuals sharing political and cultural concerns, and appeals to "the people" as a rallying cry for the masses as good as disappeared. The anticapitalist impulse of a number of the new social movements lacked the socialist orientation of the New Left but was significantly more successful in mobilizing "the people."[72] New social movements in West Germany included the peace movement, the autonomous women's movement, the antinuclear movement (against weapons as well as energy policy), the movement for gay and lesbian rights, and the environmentalist movement. The latter was later spearheaded by the Greens, who were elected into Federal Parliament in 1983 after having gained votes in communal and state elections since the mid-1970s.[73] After the mid-1970s, local campaigns created collaborations between diverse protesters, ranging from conservative environmentalists to concerned local citizens to militant Autonomen. One notable example of a collaborative campaign is the expansion of the Frankfurt airport with the Startbahn West, which was furiously protested against from 1980 until its completion in 1984.[74]

Entering the activist scene full force in December 1979 after the announcement of NATO's Dual Track policy[75] was the peace movement, which would prove to become West Germany's largest new social movement. Its massive protests and organizing against nuclear armament was mirrored in similar movements throughout Western Europe and in parts of the Eastern bloc. Its focus on peace politics attracted large numbers of women activists, many of whom organized a women's peace movement within the larger peace movement. However, the antiimperialist section of the peace movement charged organizers of the broader movement with acting out of self-interest (avoiding nuclear war in Europe) while ignoring military escalations in the Middle East and elsewhere, branding the slogan, "We don't want your peace!"[76] While the New Left's global and internationally socialist vision was modified to reflect the new social movement's focus on both the identity and the concerns of local politics, global relations maintained a central role in defining radical leftist politics—in terms of peace politics (arms race and long-range nuclear missiles in West Germany) and economics (protests against WTO and IMF in the 1980s), as well as regarding environmentalism and human rights issues.

With the rise of the new social movements, violence as a means of political struggle during these times manifested in particular with the Spontis, in the emerging Autonomen scene, and with underground armed groups, such as the RAF, who disbanded only in the late 1990s. The issue of political violence also divided activists in the emerging autonomous women's movement, for whom this became a point of contention in the formulation of feminist politics. Armed struggle thus had a role in this reconfiguration of leftist politics—a highly controversial and contested role that brought into relief the changing ideological positions within the leftist scene—but one that nevertheless left its mark on the confrontations of leftist activists with the West German state.

Public response to the RAF and Movement 2nd June was complicated and shifted in relation to the groups' actions and political development. In the early 1970s, there was wide logistical and political support in the leftist scene, with "sympathy" being expressed by large numbers of leftist intellectuals not for their violent means but for their political motivation. This tacit support resulted in an intense surveillance and regulation apparatus the state put in place to control popular support for the RAF.[77] Conservative media dominated by the Springer publishing house waged a now-personalized war against the RAF, and the liberal, "bourgeois" media clearly condemned the group, while at times questioning the state's violent response (which included not only legislative changes to regulate political formations but changes in trial law and the building of maximum security prisons especially for RAF prisoners). In the German Autumn of 1977 that resulted in escalations between the state and the RAF, the Left experienced a profound alienation from the group's violence as well as increased fear of the state. Broad public support (and sympathy) for the RAF dwindled in the following years, with a large segment of the radical leftists continuing their support especially for the political prisoners and their hunger strikes. Violence was a central motif in the diverse makeup of the Left's turbulent organizing since the beginning of the New Left and shaped discourse within the political radical scene and outside of it. The emerging new women's movement—which would self-identify as the "autonomous women's movement"[78]—was no exception to this, and violence would prove to be a crucial structuring concept for women as they were organizing in the 1970s and early 1980s.

## Patriarchal Violence

On September 13, 1968, in her speech at the SDS conference in Frankfurt, Helke Sander, a representative of the then still very obscure Women's Action Council[79] challenged the delegates of the SDS to seriously consider and integrate questions of women's liberation into their platform. Not only did the SDS not thematize women's issues in their political work, she charged, but the organization in fact reflected the sexist structures of larger society in its privileging of male organizers and their opinions, while women's work was reduced to supporting the men of the organization.[80] Despite a spirited response from the audience (some enthusiastic, others outraged),[81] the men of the SDS voted to ignore Sander's interjection into the conference's agenda and proceeded with the program. Sigrid Rüger, a well-known and respected female SDS member, hurled tomatoes at the next speaker, SDS chairman Hans Jürgen Krahl, calling out "counter-revolutionary . . . agent of the class enemy!" and hitting him on the shin with one of the tomatoes.[82] The incident became known far beyond the SDS and was debated in many corners of the 1968 movement, and in retrospect has been seen as the beginning of the women's movement by many.[83] The issues raised in Sander's speech, and significantly the immediate decision of the male delegates to ignore them, pointed to a fundamental contradiction the SDS embodied: on the one hand the organization's theoretical and political call for radical change of authoritarian hierarchies invited a critique of their own structure of power, and on the other hand the SDS's organizational success relied on the gendered division of labor of male leadership and female support.

September 13, 1968, would become the symbol for the eruption of the female discontent in the New Left that had been brewing for a while. During much of the debating and organizing of revolutionary politics that happened in the 1960s, the political roles of women were often reduced to those of muse and event organizer. Driven by critiques of leftist men's self-importance and of a broader structural patriarchy—such as capitalism's sexual division of labor—West German feminists in the early 1970s began organizing separately from the Left, launching one of the major new social movements of the 1970s. Thereby, the concept of "autonomy" that gave the new women's movement its name in West Germany (autonomous women's movement)[84] was "the most important characteristic of the new women's movement."[85] "Autonomy" derived its meaning from two levels. First, it signaled the organizing of women separate from "the male-dominated Left and men as such."[86] Second, the term "autonomous" also connoted a rejection of the state and its institutions as patriarchal. The feminist battle cry "the personal is political"[87] demanded a politicization of all circumstances of life and all social structures. The call for "autonomy" also defined the new movement as separate from (and more radical than) the established women's organizations that were aiming for gender equality within the existing social system.[88] In contrast to the established women's movement that advocated for the representation of women's interests in politics, the church, and the sciences, the autonomous women's movement rejected the notion that a male-dominated system could be liberating for women.[89] Instead, women in autonomous feminist groups viewed patriarchy to be the primary system of oppression, concentrated on the creation of a female subculture (one that increasingly also integrated motherhood and [homo]sexuality as important components of female identity),[90] defined violence as a product of patriarchy and as part of the systematic oppression of women, and moreover originally refused to work together with the state. However, already after the mid- to late 1970s, more and more women's groups began to rely on state funds for the implementation of feminist projects (such as battered women's shelters and cultural centers), which precludes the political concept of autonomy. The conflict around the acceptance of state funds also dominated discussions within the autonomous women's movement of the 1980s.[91]

In the course of the formation of autonomous women's groups (first within, and increasingly separate from, the New Left), more and more feminists increasingly distanced themselves from what they perceived to be male-defined revolutionary violence, as women's activism began focusing on women's issues such as reproductive rights and what activists saw as male structural and state violence against women. While many activists in the autonomous women's movement maintained an ambivalent relationship to the gendered approach to violence (one that viewed violence as a symptom of male aggression and power), by the mid-1970s any discussion of the potential for women to be violent was reduced to a focus on violence against personalized attacks by men. Self-defense was valued in the daily conflict and against perceived dangers; in contrast, revolutionary political violence was rejected as furthering a masculine, militarized culture. This increased rejection of militant activism on the side of feminists followed what was probably the most significant development—in terms of a lasting theoretical premise—in the autonomous women's movement: *the reframing of the political debate on violence into one of violence against women.* Originating in radical feminist grassroots anti–domestic violence and anti-rape politics of the early 1970s, this framework declares a patriarchal culture that condones and rewards the physical and sexual domination of women to be at the heart of any social conflict. Social justice in all areas can thus only be achieved if this violent male/masculine culture is exposed and rejected. While this idea took hold in almost all sections of the autonomous women's movement by the second half of the 1970s, its prevailing interpretation of women consequently as inherently nonviolent did not extend to some factions of feminist groups, who viewed women's effective resistance to male violence to *be* violence. These factions included primarily self-defense groups, but also groups whose analysis extended to the state as a form of male violence.

While the autonomous women's movement's campaign against violence against women set up the paradigm of violence as inherently patriarchal and women as the victims of violence, the peace movement after the late 1970s also independently generated a gendered analysis of state militarism as patriarchal and the arms race as male. However, many feminists took issue with this analysis because of its concealment of a historical violence against women by men in their lives, and therefore its failure to consistently gender violence in its manifestations beyond militarized threats. Violence as a tool for activists (such as political militancy and the use of force against the state and other political opponents) was hotly debated by women activists, especially by those who were coming from or were still active in the post-1968 Left, where the *Gewaltdebatte* (debate on violence) still formed an important part of political discussions. Only in the mid-1970s did the majority of feminists mobilize around violence against women. This, and the fact that influential feminists whose political work did not start out in the 1968 movement (such as *Emma* founder Alice Schwarzer) framed feminist issues primarily around reproductive rights and violence against women, in retrospect, created a homogenous depiction of the autonomous women's movements as ubiquitously nonviolent. This incomplete narrative does not account for the political and organizational overlap between feminists and leftist activists who were deeply influenced by the questions of the *Gewaltdebatte*.

## *Aktionsrat zur Befreiung der Frau* and the Feminist Analysis of the Left: 1968–69

By the late 1960s there existed no coherent feminist movement in West Germany (aside from the established women's movement that was represented in the political parties), only individual voices and actions. Thus when the West Berlin Women's Action Council was formed in 1967–68, it constituted one of the first efforts to organize more broadly around women's issues. At the core of the council's work stood efforts to address the sexual division of labor that stood in the way of women's full participation in politics and other arenas of society, and to formulate the aim of anti-authoritarian education for children.[92] By the time Helke Sander held her speech, the council had established five *Kinderläden* (childcare cooperatives) that were to relieve leftist women from their double burden and contribute to an anti-authoritarian (and hence less susceptible to fascist and other authoritarian regimes) raising of a generation. The council was still wedded to an overall socialist theoretical framework but challenged the view that women's oppression is a "minor contradiction"[93] within capitalism's "major contradiction," class struggle.[94] The *Kinderläden* took practical aim at women's oppression by creating alternatives to women's role as primary (and isolated) caretaker within the nuclear family.[95] However, when the council conceded control of the *Kinderläden* to the SDS in the summer of 1968, the initiative's emphasis shifted increasingly to a discourse of anti-authoritarian childrearing and away from one of women's liberation.[96]

Both shaken and inspired by the events of the SDS conference in Frankfurt in September 1968, delegates returned to their cities and founded so-called *Weiberräte* (women's councils) that became regional feminist voices of the New Left. Already by the next SDS conference

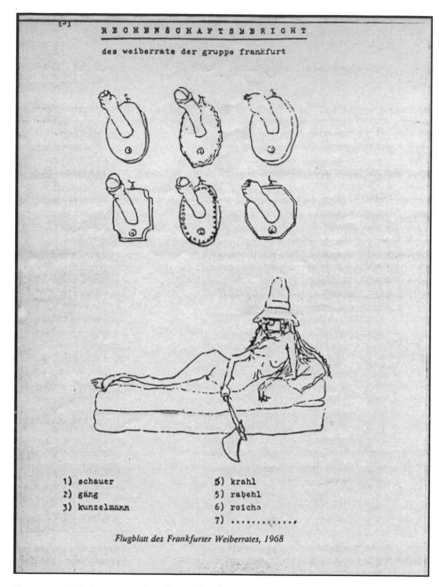

Figure 1.2. This flyer was distributed by the Frankfurter Weiberrat at the SDS conference in November 1968 and utilized sexualized symbolic violence that was typical of the New Left to voice criticism of male activists' sexism. (APO-Archiv, Ordner Frauenbewegung)

in November of that year, the women's councils formed an organized and self-confident voice. They were represented most famously by the Frankfurt women's council, which distributed a flyer with a critique of men's condescending and patronizing treatment of women in the SDS, ending in the provocative demand to "liberate the socialist eminences from their bourgeois cocks!"[97] with a cartoon of a woman with an ax lying underneath the mounted penises of male SDS leaders (see figure 1.2). The flyer's symbolic violence is quite typical of many of the Left's visual representations of its radical positions, and its language reflects the women's attempt to invite self-irony through the use of oversexualized jargon. However, leftist men were not amused and overall refused to engage with their feminist comrades.[98] The early feminist rumblings within the Left soon were joined by women *outside* the organized Left who would form groups separate (autonomous) from the socialist Left.

### The Emergence of the Autonomous Women's Movement: 1970–74

The disbanding of the SDS spoke to an overall reorientation within the New Left, including many feminists who began organizing separately from leftist groups, and the autonomous women's movement emerged. Never constituting a homogenous movement, autonomous women's groups included activists coming from diverse political places, such as from within the student socialist groups, the unions, and/or humanitarian groups. In the course of the next five years, women from all walks of life—including those who had never before organized politically—began forming a social movement that was causing a recognizable stir within mainstream society with its demand for legislative and cultural changes.

In 1970, the Frauenaktion 70 (Women's Action 70) launched a series of political actions against the infamous §218,[99] the restrictive abortion law in West Germany. This was the first visible political action of an autonomous women's group (i.e., they were independent from either socialist student groups or from labor unions).[100] The fight against §218 would become the main focus of the growing women's movement nationally, providing a shared political rallying point amid increased discussions of and political organizing around questions of motherhood, women's economic status and labor rights, women's education in schools and universities, as well as the situation of women internationally. Networks of women's groups began forming throughout the country, with the first national conference of women, in 1972, solidifying a national networking and strategy discussion.[101] The fight for reproductive self-determination through the right to abortion spoke to the larger issues of women's health, overall economic position, and rejection of male dominance. This particular struggle for abortion rights and the larger issues it spoke to had its roots in the first women's movement and the socialist labor movement,[102] and thus it also represented a tradition of feminist resistance against a patriarchal state. The campaign reached mainstream attention in particular through the 1971 manifesto, published in the weekly news magazine *Stern*, that consisted of self-disclosures by women of having had abortions and the demand to abolish the criminalizing anti-abortion law. A total of 374 women—both famous public figures and "regular" women—signed the manifesto: "I had an abortion"[103] the appeal read, underlined by the pictures of dozens of women on the cover of *Stern*. The action was initiated by the journalist Alice Schwarzer with the support of local groups such as Frauenaktion 70 and the—initially reluctant—backing of socialist feminist groups such as the Munich Red Women (Rote Frauen) and the Berlin Sozialistischer Frauenbund.[104] Within weeks, the original manifesto resulted in declarations of solidarity by both women and men that gathered more than eighty-six thousand signatures and the formation of the national umbrella organization, Aktion 218, which loosely connected the hundreds of local feminist groups protesting the abortion law.[105] The repressions of feminist activists by the police increased as the protests grew nationally. "My body belongs to me!"[106] was the battle cry of women organizing around abortion rights and became one of the representative slogans of the entire autonomous women's movement.

Meanwhile, new women's groups began emerging that focused on issues beyond reproductive rights. However, the struggle to overturn the punitive §218 connected diverse sets of activists; in 1972, women formed an autonomous women's group within the gay rights movement in Berlin, the Homosexuellen Aktion Berlin (Homosexual Action Berlin, HAW), making visible the political concerns of lesbians and declaring solidarity with the fight against §218. They, together with the socialist collective Brot und Rosen (Bread and Roses), established the Women's Center in 1973, the first of a myriad of feminist cultural and political centers that were founded during the 1970s throughout the Federal Republic. Creating women-only spaces—including bookstores, music festivals, bars, cafés, and other "safe spaces"—the centers became important social locations in which feminist projects could be conceived and implemented. From the women's (self)health care movement to artistic collectives and consciousness-raising groups, women throughout West Germany were creating cultural spaces separate from what they perceived to be destructive patriarchal social environments. The confrontation with patriarchal society and feminist challenges to it took various forms, reflecting the diversity of women active in the movement, from the militant feminist squatters in Frankfurt in 1973, whose women's collective was brutally and selectively evacuated by riot police with water cannons to the women who experienced the violent police evacuation of a building occupied for a future women's center in Heidelberg in 1974. Both incidents pointed to the targeting of feminist projects within the squatter scene. Working women organized factory women's strikes in various cities and protested wage increases for jobs exclusively done by men (often these women were migrant workers who faced wage discrimination), thus making visible the economic disparity within the working class. A women and film seminar highlighted women's contributions to and marginalization within the film industry, and women's courses at universities thematized women's position in the artistic professions as well as in academia. These all represented points of intervention by the autonomous women's movement into a patriarchal culture.[107]

Such feminist projects presented a wide range of theoretical understandings of women's oppression; once the activism against §218 had ceased, the core issue women would rally behind had been removed. By 1975 these different positions on women's oppression had solidified into three main currents of feminist thought that broadly can be categorized as socialist, cultural, and radical feminism. Socialist feminism continued to locate women's oppression in relation to a larger class struggle and was committed to an analysis of power beyond the male/female binary of patriarchy. Cultural feminism also remained close to the larger leftist movement; however, it advocated a "new femininity" that highlighted women's differences from men as more peace-loving and nurturing. This feminism believed that women's innate cultural values (which are fostered and developed in women-only spaces) are natural (i.e., biological) and are superior to patriarchy's destructive culture.[108] The last segment were the so-called radical feminists,[109] who were fiercely anti-essentialist and believed in an absolute equality between men and women that had to be reflected in a gender-egalitarian society.[110] While there existed much overlap between these three segments of the movement, the emerging polarization within the movement signaled a fracture that later would have large numbers of women retreating into a more private space of what Davis calls "politics of the kitchen table" and self-discovery. However, following the years of intense activism around reproductive rights, women's spaces, and women's health care, the damage experienced by women as a result of patriarchal values was increasingly recognized to be rooted in a violence inherent in patriarchal culture—a recognition that would dominate the autonomous women's movement's theoretical and political focus in the second half of the 1970s and into the 1980s.

### The Campaign against Violence against Women: 1976–81

Beginning in 1974, with the third issue of the feminist publication *Frauenzeitung* focusing on rape, sexual violence moved to the center of a new feminist debate in West Germany.[111] With the publication in the United States in 1975 of Susan Brownmiller's analysis of rape as a systemic act of male violence against women, *Against Our Will*, West German feminists extended their own analysis of rape to view sexual violence not as acts of individual men against individual women but as exertions of systemic power by one privileged social group over another vulnerable, oppressed social group. The important recognition that cultural acceptance of sexual crimes contributes to their persistence and that male violence against women reflects existing social power structures was at the core of the emerging paradigm of gendered violence that cast violence as inherently male, and its cultural manifestation as masculine.

The already existing association of violence with masculinity that underlay much of West Germany's social order, including state institutions such as the military (there were no women in the West German Bundeswehr in the 1960s and 1970s), was framed as political by the emerging feminist movement. An unprecedented campaign against violence against women during the 1970s and 1980s forced public discourse into a recognition of the existence of routine violence against women; feminists were declaring that a war was being waged against women with "everyday violence."[112] As feminist activist Anna Dorethea Brockmann describes it, "the war is waged daily against us [women]"[113] by men and a male-run state. Male violence against women—including not only domestic and sexual violence but sexual harassment as well—was understood not to be the pathological behavior of individual men but a tool of social control to maintain patriarchal power structures.

While the movement against domestic violence had taken root in countries like the UK, the United States, and the Netherlands in the first half of the 1970s, it was the feminist-initiated International Tribunal on Crimes Against Women, which was held in Brussels in March 1976, that created a forum that facilitated the newly forming *Frauenhausbewegung* (battered women's shelter movement) in the FRG. It concretized the gendered theory of violence underlying much of the women's movement's early activism around sexual and domestic violence against women:

> [Domestic] abuse [i.e., violence] is part of a continuum of women's oppression and exploitation and [. . .] battered women's shelters are part of the struggle against this oppression, not an attempted solution to a circumscribed social problem. [. . .] Abuse within marriage [. . .] is a structural part of a violence against women that runs through the entire society, a violence that has become even more a principle of this society, not an aberration.[114]

The sexual aggression and male violence that every woman encounters in a patriarchal society became the basis for a shared standpoint among women. Thus, the argument went, female social workers, medical personnel, and activists could not only sympathize with the victims of domestic and sexual violence they might meet but could actually politicize that shared experience, as it pointed to a structural, not a personal, problem. The first shelter for battered women was opened in 1976 in Berlin.[115]

Rape was a second instance of gendered violence of which the autonomous women's movement worked to promote awareness. Marital rape was not punishable under the law, and rape victims often were blamed for the assault because of presumed secret sexual pathologies and/or indecent clothing and behavior that provoked the attack.[116] Feminists organized to create rape hotlines and support networks for rape victims as well as court support for them. In March 1977, a protest in Berlin following the death of a young woman who was raped put the topic of sexual violence on both the women's movement's and mainstream society's radar. The understanding of rampant occurrence of violence against women as fundamentally part of the social fabric resulted in the feminist charge that *every* man was implicated in this gendered structure and that the campaign against violence against women could not be directed just at media outlets and state institutions: "Because every man[—]the husband, father and also the brother[—]is to be seen as a potential rapist."[117] Debates about the inherent violence of men (Was it natural/biological? Socialized?) were accompanied by debates about women's relationship to violent resistance within this culture of violence. "Take back the night" initiatives, such as the feminist protests on Walpurgisnacht, on April 30, 1977 (traditionally the night that witches celebrated with the "dance into the May"),[118] aimed to empower women within the discourse of sexual violence. Feminists dedicated this night, which folklore associates with dangerous, outlaw women, to feminist protests against violence against women. They aimed to mobilize the witches' spirit of empowerment and the collective rejection of victimhood, instead celebrating women's strength and resistance.[119] The question of how to overcome fear and the actual threat present in daily life also raised questions of vigilantism: in addition to the self-defense training that many women's centers offered, some women's groups targeted men they believed participated in the culture of violence (such as leftist attorneys who defended rapists),[120] bringing to the forefront the debate around violence as a feminist political tool.

The violence-against-women paradigm positions women as victims (and resisters) of male violence, and male violence in turn as a major structuring force in society. Theorizing violence as male/masculine grew from the startling and upsetting realization that sexual and domestic violence against women was taking place everywhere and that it was behavior sanctioned by society, its legal system, and its law enforcement system. It demanded radical (social and political) changes within gender relations for any true system of justice to be attainable.[121] Feminists argued that every woman is physically and emotionally imprisoned and violated by this force; she is alienated from her body, which has become the battleground for patriarchal power: "Male violence has settled within my body, has broken my voice, constrained my movements, has blinded my imagination: the female body as microphysics of patriarchal violence, faceless identity, formless history, invisible labor, called love."[122] This theoretical model impacted feminist debates on violence as a political tool in two ways: one was the issue of a woman's right (and need) to defend herself (and other women) against male violence, by force if necessary, and the other was the larger question raised through the *Gewaltdebatte* within the Left, of whether (revolutionary) political violence is not a masculine response to a patriarchal system that inherently upholds the destructive role of masculine violence. It was especially the latter debate that had feminists turning against the radical Left and its at times militant stance.

Beginning in 1976, activists in the autonomous women's movement were debating the increasing *Feminismusverdacht* (charge/accusation of feminism) by the state and the media that linked women's liberation to terrorism. The actions of the female members of the RAF and Movement 2nd June evoked historical analogies between militant labor activists and Russian *Flintenweiber* (gun broads/gun molls) who threatened a German social order, and conservative media tapped into these old resentments.[123] Many women activists felt they had to distance themselves from the stereotype of the rabid, radical, man-hating feminist, often by evoking the cultural-feminist concept of the peace-loving and maternal woman who rejects violence as a destructive product of patriarchy. This attempt to distance oneself from the violence of underground groups has to be seen in the larger context of the *Abgrenzungsdebatte* (exclusion/demarcation debate) taking place in West Germany at the time, as the state was increasing its repression of any leftist activism, and conservative media forced public intellectuals to distance themselves from the action of the RAF.[124] While many women organized in solidarity with RAF prisoners and their hunger strike, and expressed agreement with militant feminists such as the Red Zora, others were reluctant to view this as feminist political work, despite the terrorists' identities as women.

In December of 1979, NATO's Dual Track policy was announced, launching the (new) peace movement. The focus on a perceived impending nuclear holocaust and bilateral disarmament as the solution to that threat mobilized large numbers of Germans and impacted the autonomous women's movement. Many feminists began organizing peace protests in their localities, and women's centers throughout the republic held informational and protest events. While the so-called women's peace movement[125] usually is understood as a part of the general peace movement, it is useful to distinguish between these two groups in terms of how gender was conceptualized and used as a political tool. The peace movement shared with the women's peace movement a "joint [. . .] objective of peace politics."[126] The approach of the women's peace movement, although not always feminist, as Karola Maltry discusses in *Die neue Frauenfriedensbewegung* (The New Women's Peace Movement), nevertheless rested on the "conscious reference to a female gender identity in explaining individual involvement in the peace movement and/ or in the formulation of peace-political demands and objectives."[127] In addition, "women's peace activities that consciously referenced gender took place in separate political activist structures."[128] Reflecting this referencing of gender identity as the base for one's peace activism while not offering an explicit feminist analysis is the 1980 manifesto of Women for Peace (Kvinder for Fred). Women for Peace was formed by a group of Danish women who voiced their fear and despair in the face of the arms race between the two superpowers. That same year, the Berlin Women's Group (Berliner Frauengruppe), in their call to action titled "Anstiftung der Frauen zum Frieden" (Women's Incitement for Peace), expanded the original Women for Peace manifesto to include a feminist statement against male militarism, situating a women's peace movement within the context of both an autonomous women's movement's critique of patriarchal violence and a peace movement that was mobilizing around the fear of a nuclear war.[129] In turn, the criticism of a masculine culture that valorizes conquest and risk voiced by the women's movement resonated with the growing peace movement, which integrated the notion of feminine nonviolence into its movement rhetoric.[130]

A variety of feminist groups applied the analysis of violence against women to their politics, mirroring the heterogeneous makeup of the autonomous women's movement: grass-roots antipornography and antiprostitution campaigns thematized (sexual) violence against women in similar ways, as did liberal feminist attempts to influence legislation around sexual harassment in the workplace and marital rape laws. Within the larger political and theoretical campaign against violence against women, women were positioned as victims of violence, and men as perpetrators within a misogynist culture permissive of violence in general, and violence against women in particular. Examples of manifestations of this violent social order included the commercialization and thus objectification of women's sexuality and domestic violence with women and children as targets of physical, emotional, and sexual abuse in a private sphere protected by the state. They were further extended to masculine state formations such as the legal system, law enforcement, the military, and war. The alignment of violence with masculinity/men resulted in the logical association of women/femininity with nonviolence. The figure of the mother thereby emerged as embodiment of peaceful politics and resistance.[131] However, since the early 1970s, a number of feminists who maintained the perspective that violence is a legitimate means of feminist resistance continuously challenged the truism of women's nonviolence that was gaining an increasingly strong foothold in feminist activist circles.

## Militant Feminisms: Violence as Feminist Resistance

By 1981, in the context of a strong peace movement protesting the nuclear arms race, Sybille Plogstedt asked in an article for the nationally circulated (cultural) feminist journal *Courage*, "Has violence arrived in the Women's Movement?"—calling into question (and judging) the role of violence as it was adopted by some militant feminists and the leftist political scene overall.[132] Her criticism was countered by Helga Braun's response in the small local feminist publication *Hamburger Frauenzeitung* (Hamburg's Women's Paper) with the question, "Has the exclusion/demarcation debate arrived in the Women's Movement?"[133] Their opposing positions represent points of disagreement that existed throughout the heterogeneous and decentralized autonomous women's movement: one declared militant activism and the (male) Left as romanticizing violence and as participating in excesses of destruction instead of effectively organizing; the other accused that critique of being complicit with mainstream society's and the state's attempts to marginalize leftist activists and to voice an authoritarian and judgmental definition of what constitutes feminist politics.

Even before the autonomous women's movement gained momentum and formed a mass movement, militant women constituted feminist voices from within the Left. While not represented widely in the radical movement publication *Agit 883*, the Women's Liberation Front[134] in various issues offered a militant feminist analysis of oppression and the politics of the New Left. Small, militant formations like this, however, were short-lived, and their actions usually were limited to low-level, symbolic violence aimed at drawing attention to the liberation of women as part of the revolutionary struggle. Meanwhile, armed underground groups forming after 1970, such as the RAF and Movement 2nd June, did not propagate feminist analyses but instead framed their violent actions as part of a leftist revolutionary struggle that viewed women's oppression as a "secondary contradiction" produced by capitalism that would be resolved once the "primary contradiction"—class differences—was eliminated. Noticeably, though, in 1968, journalist Ulrike Meinhof, later founding member of the RAF, wrote one of her weekly columns in *konkret* in response to the feminist challenge that took place at the SDS conference in which she applauded women's political demands "on their own behalf."[135] The founding document of the RAF, "Die Rote Armee aufbauen," also authored by Meinhof in 1970, included references to women's oppression. However, this would be the last explicit reference to women's liberation in an RAF statement.

The one West German women-only armed group that explicitly attacked targets they viewed as oppressing women was the Red Zora. Initially the feminist contingent of the Revolutionary Cells that formed in 1973, the Red Zora split off into an autonomous feminist group in 1977 with the bombing of the Federal Medical Association as a patriarchal perpetrator against women. The Red Zora, whose members never went underground, maintained close ties to the radical leftist scene, and members usually are understood to have been active in the Autonomen movement.[136] Other militant feminist groups associated with the Autonomen also included Women against Imperialist Wars,[137] a group of women supportive of the RAF's general politics and of militant feminist actions, who self-identified as being a part of the autonomous women's movement despite criticizing its overall nonviolent politics.[138] These militant feminists understood violence to be a valid form of feminist resistance. In their view, male violence—both individual and state—necessitates a forceful response in order to break the cycle of male violence/female oppression: "As every act of violence against one woman creates an atmosphere of threat against all women, our actions contribute—even if they only aim against those individuals who are responsible—to the development of a new atmosphere: Resistance is possible!"[139] And while militant feminists seemed a minority within the autonomous women's movement, their arguments were taken seriously and were debated by many women wrestling with the question of political violence more generally.

The concept of violence against women as symptomatic of patriarchal dominance and female nonviolence as its binary opposite provided a powerful framework for feminist theorizing within both the women's movement and the peace movement. One of the consequences of this successful thematization of male-on-female violence as systemic is that since the late 1970s, feminist scholars have mainly interpreted women's resistance through analyzing women's nonviolent activism and the militarization of women's lives through examining masculinist cultures and states. This interpretation solidified an understanding of women's political work that clearly viewed violence as a product of patriarchy and defined it as a masculine quality. This in turn fostered the equation of feminist identity with pacifism.[140] So when analyzing the gender politics surrounding women in the RAF and Movement 2nd June, we need to understand the sequence in the development of feminist politics. First there was the "splitting-off" of an autonomous women's movement from the Left, which resulted in a historicization of the New Left essentially as an antifeminist (even antiwomen) movement. Following this, within the debate on political violence that emerged in the mid-1970s and was solidified in the early 1980s, cultural feminism gained significant influence in the women's movement. Its understanding of women as naturally different from men cast patriarchal violence as rooted in individual men and their aggressive nature, while radical feminists' analysis of patriarchal violence understood it to be based in the social construction of gender roles. The paradigm shift that refocused the autonomous women's movement onto patriarchal violence produced two main discursive phenomena:[141] one was the alignment of dominant gender ideology's notion of women as naturally nonviolent (which necessarily paints the female terrorist as deviant or insane) with a feminist analysis of power that declared women to be those who experience violence, rather than those who execute it within patriarchy. The second discursive development—which contradicts the previous one—centers around debates within the women's movement about the validity of the paradigm of patriarchal violence manifesting primarily through violence against women alone: many women activists understood patriarchy to be in complicated complicity with other systems, such as capitalism, and thus resisted the binary explanation of men (and by extension, the state) abusing resisting women. This last discursive strand actually produced positions that argued for (counter)violence to be a legitimate feminist means of resistance.

The question of whether political violence can be feminist, then, is not a new one but rather one that has been considered in feminist circles in various ways. The relationship of feminists to the New Left and its *Gewaltdebatte* (debate on violence) cannot easily be dismissed as one of disgusted women activists walking away from a sexist, male-dominated movement. Violence, though differently theorized by the New Left and in the autonomous women's movement, took a central role in both. The troubled discussions feminists had about how their oppression figured within existing analyses of power (and thus the contradictory understandings of violence that were debated within political circles) allow us to better understand the discursive effects women's participation in political violence had on social entities such as mainstream society, the state, the New Left and the autonomous women's movement (and their points of convergence), and to conceptualize their actions as feminist practices. Politically violent leftist women then represent a historical moment in which very different political and theoretical conceptualizations of violence (and resistance) intersect.

## "Between a Rock and a Hard Place"

### The "Betrayal" of Motherhood among the Women of the RAF and Movement 2nd June

There is [. . .] no one in the old society who experiences alienation [. . .] more directly than women. [. . .] for this reason, though, the dialectic of their situation also becomes clear—if, after the particular brutalities of their domestication [. . .] they even want *themselves*, to think *themselves*—they need to think radically *and* subversively: a content and a form that predestines them to illegality.

  ★ Gudrun Ensslin, 1976

Women find themselves between a rock and a hard place, caught between paid labor and family, more specifically: children—existing ones, expected ones, and those they once had.

  ★ Ulrike Meinhof, 1968

### Introduction

In the mid-1970s in West Berlin, a young woman, Karin,[1] entered a hospital to terminate her pregnancy.[2] She was able to have the procedure done legally under a recently reformed abortion law, and shortly after, she left the hospital. Unlike the average West German woman claiming her right to reproductive freedom, this young woman accessed the medical care with a forged health insurance card. Fearing arrest by the police, she returned to an illegally rented apartment to recover from the surgery. For her, the decision to terminate her pregnancy was not only personal (she had never wanted children) but also motivated by her political situation: living underground as part of a group that understood itself to be in armed struggle against a repressive state, she did not envision family life as a part of her immediate future. Motherhood, she felt, was strategically incongruent with revolutionary struggle. Other women who participated in political violence reached similar

73

conclusions. However, some had to choose between their existing chil
dren and a political life they believed would ultimately better the world.
For them, actively rescinding the role as mother was a necessary step in
their political development. Their choice counters several assumptions
about motherhood, namely, that once pregnant, a woman will embrace
her natural identity as mother and that, as mother, she will foreground
her children's needs above all else. Most importantly, the decisions of
these women regarding reproduction and family were framed by actions
of political violence that trouble common notions of mothers as nurturing and life giving.

It appears that because society views women and motherhood as
synonymous and motherhood is tied to the assumption of nonviolence,
the concepts of terrorism (violence) and women (mothers) can only be
imagined as irreconcilable. This chapter addresses the contradictions
that emerge when bringing three connected discourses to the current
debate on West German leftist terrorism, namely, an existing ideology
of motherhood, a set of feminist theories that conceptualize nonviolent
feminist politics as growing from "maternal ethics" or "maternal thinking," and the decisions of women in the RAF and the Movement 2nd
June to abandon their lives as mothers. These women's decisions either
to leave behind their children when going underground or to terminate
pregnancies challenge the ideological construction of motherhood as a
woman's primary identity, while also decoupling strategic violence from
a naturalized masculinity.

The crisis that female terrorists pose to our cultural understanding
of political violence builds on a long tradition of dissociating women
from (political) violence in German culture and Western thought in
general.[3] The contradiction that women's employment of violence
poses is usually resolved by declaring these women to be "unnatural,"
a sentiment cemented into German cultural tradition with Friedrich
Schiller's famous characterization from his 1799 ballad "The Song of
the Bell" (1799)—"then women to hyenas grow"[4]—which describes
French revolutionary women as crazed, immoral animals (hyenas).
Underlying the relegation of "natural" women to the private (nonpolitical and implicitly nonviolent) sphere is the definition of women *as*
mothers, since mothers are viewed as those who produce and take care
of life rather than destroy it. Because women are excluded from both

politics and the deliberate use of violence, those women who claim political space through violence are seen as inhuman. Hanna Hacker, in *Gewalt ist: keine Frau* (Violence Is: Not Woman) traces this phenomenon in the transgressive gender identity inhabited by "women" who committed public violence in fin-de-siècle France and Austria. The female soldiers, duel contestants, and murderers she examines became "inverts"—implying both a sexual and a gender transgression—in a culture that ascribed to them *Nicht-Weiblichkeit* (unfemininity) and status as *Nicht-Frauen* (nonwomen) on the basis of their violent behavior.[5] More than simply being declared unfeminine, they were effectively unreadable *as women*. This "degendering" (and "unmothering") consequence of female public violence manifests in the figure of the female terrorist who "represents, perhaps, the ultimate pariah of the modern world. She is viewed as possessing an identity that exists outside the limits of political and moral discourse."[6]

In the 1980s, feminist theorists countered this persistent *naturalized* dissociation of women from violence in their explorations of the connection among women, motherhood, and nonviolence. The emerging concept of maternal ethics tried to account for women's historical claim of motherhood as the basis for their political participation without resorting to essentialist arguments of mainstream ideologies of motherhood. The cultural disassociation of women (as mothers) from political violence in turn is undermined by women in the RAF and further complicated by some women's rejection of their role as caretakers of their families. The RAF women not only challenge patriarchal assumptions about gender and motherhood but also demand a reevaluation of the claim of maternal ethics as the basis of women's politics.

A high percentage of RAF and Movement 2nd June members were women,[7] a phenomenon that apparently troubled West Germans' understanding of gender roles and that generated debates.[8] As founding members, Ulrike Meinhof and Gudrun Ensslin became synonymous with the brutal actions of the RAF. Their involvement in political violence has been early on narrated by Stefan Aust in his influential journalistic study *Der Baader Meinhof Komplex*[9] and in recent years it has been the object of an increasing amount of scholarship. Yet, very little scholarship addresses the fact that Meinhof and Ensslin left children behind when they went underground. If this fact is discussed at all, it

serves mainly to emphasize the women's "unnatural" (gendered) behavior,[10] to highlight the pathological group mentality that forced RAF
members to sever all external ties, which in the end resulted in personal
tragedy,[11] or to read this choice to abandon their children as a product
of a tragic misjudgment and naïveté about the consequences of their
political actions.[12] Even less discussion occurs about reproduction and
revolutionary armed struggle in general—a vision of alternative families
is absent not only in RAF ideology but also from the historical analysis of that ideology. The examples of women who understood armed
struggle as their destiny and who experienced their own motherhood as
irreconcilable with this political path are useful for making sense of the
complicated triangular discursive juxtaposition of cultural expectations
of motherhood, feminist claims of maternal ethics, and women committing political violence. Reading and hearing about the decisions of
these particular women invites the following questions that connect the
three discursive strands: Do mainstream notions of motherhood converge with feminist theories on maternal ethics when analyzed in the
context of politically violent women, including mothers? If so, can maternal ethics still contribute to progressive feminist political theorizing?
Or do these women's political actions and maternal decisions demand
an expanded redefinition of motherhood in which primary caretaking
is not the behavioral foundation for women's politics?

Both published sources and personal interviews with former members of the RAF and Movement 2nd June provide a context for understanding RAF women's experiences regarding gender relations and
motherhood while living underground. This chapter focuses on the case
studies of Ulrike Meinhof and Gudrun Ensslin as examples of the clash
between theories of maternal politics and the actions of RAF women.
My analysis of published letters, interviews, and biographies conveys
how these women (as cultural figures and as political agents) resist an
automatic association of mothers (i.e., women) with nonviolence, com-
plicating the current debate about the decision of (female) RAF members to participate in political violence.

## 1950s Conservatism and Growing Feminist Resistance

The context of the social politics of motherhood in West Germany forms the backdrop of my analysis of women's decision to leave their children for armed struggle. Women during the 1970s decided to go underground in a distinct historical moment following the clashes between a post–World War II German state-natalism (and assumed heterosexuality) and a 1960s counterculture that challenged notions of traditional motherhood primarily through a critique of the nuclear family and heterosexuality. The repressive sexual politics of the 1950s that shaped the Federal Republic (FRG) helped establish the conditions for the new generation's pursuit of sexual (and political) revolution that, according to Dagmar Herzog in *Sex after Fascism*, "demolished the postfascist culture of sexual conservatism."[13] The time of political and social turmoil in the aftermath of 1968 was perceived as a rebellion of youth against conservative family values as much as against a post–World War II political system. The role that "family"—and thus woman's identity as mother—played in West German discourse is indicative of the traditional gender ideologies that prevailed prior to the upheavals of the 1960s.

Legislation in the 1950s sought to protect the nuclear family and propagated gender roles within a framework of Christian (hetero) sexual morality. As Robert Moeller explains in "Reconstructing the Family in Reconstruction Germany," the 1950s saw an increased gender polarization that prioritized the nuclear family with a woman's definitive identity being that of mother and a man's role being that of breadwinner.[14] Women's role as (married) mothers became central to the rebuilding of the nation, and the debate around family policy reflected the cementing of the ideological positioning of mothers in the home. Despite their economic and social contributions during the final war years and reconstruction, women once again were confined to the private sphere.[15] Conservatives and socialists alike were aiming their family policies at a consolidation of women's role as housewife and mother.[16] While social theorists agreed that women who worked for wages were working a "double shift,"[17] the aim was to enable mothers not to work for competitive wages but to stay at home—thus making the mother a central figure in the debate on family policy. A woman's right should be, as Moeller quotes officials in the Social Democratic

Party (SPD), "to be housewife and mother, [which] is not only a woman's natural obligation but of great social significance."[18] A woman's primary identity was seen as naturally that of mother, and the role of the state would guarantee her right to exercise that role within the bounds of the traditional family.[19]

In the course of the debate, any criticism of the concept of the "normal" West German family disappeared in a climate that understood gender differences and their implied heterosexual relations to be "natural" without interfering with the concept of political equality. Middle-class feminists as well as socialists agreed on women's ultimate desire to stay at home (a home she ideally shared with a man) and "endorsed motherhood as the epitome of womanhood."[20] Paradoxically, fundamentals of the FRG family policy and ideology that continued to lock women into their reproductive role as mothers resembled Aryan women's social status under the Nazis.[21] Thus motherhood was (re)constructed in relation to a new nationalism.[22]

The conflict of women's equality guaranteed in the new West German constitution, the Basic Law,[23] and the notion of her central role in the nuclear family, which relegated her to the private sphere, remained unresolved in the 1950s and dominated women's roles into the 1960s.[24] The sexual revolution that began in the mid-1960s and lasted until the early 1970s, and especially the emerging women's movement with its increasingly visible lesbian contingent, challenged the sexual morals underlying the social institution of the nuclear family and the gender roles on which it relied. Domestic motherhood, as the core of conservative family values that emphasized privacy as a civil right against the state, was challenged in its function of upholding traditional social structures and German nationalism. However, West German feminists never politicized motherhood in a way that forced the state to support alternative families, such as through lobbying for a social policy for public childcare. Instead, feminist activists within the New Left, suspicious of any state interference, launched the *Kinderladen*[25] initiative, starting in 1968 with the *Kinderladen* of the SDS's *Aktionsrat zur Befreiung der Frau*, its action council for the liberation of women.[26]

The socialist and autonomous *Kinderläden* propagated anti-authoritarian childrearing and believed in the dissolution of the patriarchal nuclear family as a major catalyst for social change. By 1969, this initiative had resulted in the founding of parent co-ops through-out more than thirty West German cities.[27] Initially run by feminists to enable women to leave the home and participate in political work, the movement soon came under the control of men. As a result, its focus shifted from liberating women from the customary responsibilities of motherhood through collective childrearing to a refiguration of parent-ing in an anti-authoritarian way that—as the theory held—would equip children with the psychological skills to resist fascist authoritarian social dynamics,[28] this in the belief that resisting authority at home would pre-dispose future generations to resist the authority of nationalism.[29] While the *Kinderladen* movement generally countered the 1950s gender polar-ization within the nuclear family, its lack of a consistent feminist vision effectively reinstated the mother as primary caretaker.

In the following years, women's mounting resistance to the misogyny and sexism in the sexual revolution and the New Left[30] resulted in the formation of a separate women's movement that, beginning in the 1970s, included a lesbian faction that declared heterosexuality to be at the core of patriarchal gender relations.[31] West German women's political orga-nizing never focused on public childcare.[32] The focus on alternative—i.e., nonfascist, liberated, and feminist—family formations was shaped by women's demand to be able to chose *not* to have children (the right to abortion) that dominated much of feminist organizing, on the one hand, and antiauthoritarian childrearing, on the other.[33] While abortion rights and lesbian rejection of heterosexual reproduction denaturalized motherhood as women's innate identity and the *Kinderladen* initiative questioned both the nuclear family and state-run childcare as competent parenting models, neither explicitly undermined the role of women as primary caretakers:

> For many feminists, [. . .] liberation meant freedom not only from the bonds of conservative family and motherhood ideology, but from fam-ily and motherhood altogether. For another strand of feminism that emerged at the end of the 1970s, autonomy meant the emancipation of mothers, the social and financial recognition of their mothering and car-ing work. Interestingly, however, [. . .] they seem to have accepted the dominant cultural construction of the incompatibility of motherhood with employment.[34]

The latter strand—a cultural feminism that reclaimed motherhood as women's primary difference from men—became prevalent in the context of a growing international peace movement in the 1970s and 1980s that presented peace as a feminine/female realm.[35] This feminist embrace of motherhood, critics observed, was derived from an old ideology of motherhood as much as it opposed the patriarchal contexts that produced it. The threat of a nuclear conflict and the increase in women's peace work formed the basis for a theory of maternal ethics that focused on women's predisposition to peaceful activism as emanating from their social and/or biological role as mothers.

## Women, Peace, and Maternal Ethics

Mothering, so the argument from within the women's peace movement[36] went, is central to women's social being and should be understood as the foundation for a peaceful resolution of the tensions of the Cold War: "Whoever brings life into the world has a special relationship to peace."[37] The metaphor of mothering/nurturing became central in the gendered rhetoric of the peace movement,[38] which in turn declared militarism to be masculine and explored the question of how gender shapes political positions in the arms race, and how masculinity and militarism are mutually dependent, whereas women's liberation is linked to an effective disarmament and antiwar movement.[39] This line of argument is explored in a series of writing on "maternal thinking" or "maternal ethics" in the 1980s that developed into a more general philosophical school of a feminist ethics of care[40] in the 1990s.[41]

Unlike traditional patriarchal reasoning, which denies women political subjectivity, these feminist theories see a mother's identity as prioritizing a superior ethics of care that becomes the basis for her politics. Sara Ruddick's concept of a "feminist maternal peace politics"[42] developed in her influential *Maternal Thinking: Toward a Politics of Peace*, is representative of a body of texts that expand the notion of women's political work as primarily nonviolent.[43] Deemphasizing the biological process of motherhood, Ruddick establishes the connection between women and nonviolence in terms of social practice. The daily practice of mothering—usually executed by women—creates a predisposition for (or at least an inclination to support) nonviolence, since "the contradiction between violence and maternal work is evident":[44] maternal work sustains life and attempts to protect from harm. Ruddick does not reduce women to mothers, nor does she claim that all mothers are necessarily peaceful. However, she views maternal practice as a means to produce skills—maternal abilities—that enable a peaceful resistance when coupled with a feminist analysis: "[M]others who acquire a feminist consciousness and engage in feminist politics are more likely to become more effectively non-violent and antimilitarist. By increasing mothers' powers to know, care and act, feminism actualizes the peacefulness latent in maternal practice."[45]

Ruddick takes pains not to essentialize women's bodies or identities and instead focuses on the social practice that produces certain ethics, a focus that allows for men acquiring maternal abilities as well and a conceptual move that becomes central to an inclusive ethics of care. Here Ruddick de-essentializes the role of mother and decouples it from women's bodies, a theoretical move that enables an inclusive feminist politics—and an appropriation of the historical role of mother by male activists in the peace movement. Feminist philosopher Virgina Held agrees, arguing that "mothering" men are essential to a successful broad adoption of morals of care.[46] Other writers have linked women and their motherhood much more closely to their physical experiences, and hence their claims are more fundamentally (and essentially) tied to women's bodies. Caroline Whitbeck in "The Maternal Instinct" locates women's difference in the *experience* of pregnancy and childbirth (not the biological disposition per se) and thus prioritizes biological motherhood in its epistemic singularity. The mother's vulnerability in the moment of birth enables her to identify with the infant in ways that the father cannot and fosters a more powerful attachment.[47] Thus, Whitbeck argues, the peaceful potential is at its most fruitful in biological mothers.

Ruddick's feminist appropriation of the activity of mothering, which historically has confined women's influence to the private sphere, and the declaration of this practice as a basis for politics catapult motherhood outside the realm of the private into the public, politicizing women's identity as mother. Accordingly, Held's insistence that a mother's private relationship to her child forms a more sustainable model for a general moral code than do traditionally public relationships (such as contractual ones) also politicizes motherhood.[48] Since Ruddick's for-

mulations of maternal politics, feminist discourse has extrapolated assumptions about maternal ethics to a broader concept of ethics of care
(derived from women's occupations/activities of care more generally, of
which maternal work is one of several, such as domestic labor, nursing,
and childcare provision, etc.). Within this discourse, the figure of the
mother still has powerful meaning; it thus informs an understanding
both of RAF women's actions within a historical moment and of current
debates about the meaning of those actions. So even though the concept
of maternal ethics since its introduction to feminist discourse has been
challenged and complicated, it provides us with an analytical framework
within which to discuss resistance to normative notions of motherhood
and attempts to reconceptualize women's relations to politics. If we accept the idea that the practice of mothering—of actively and consistently
caring for another person—develops peace-making skills, then how are
we to understand female terrorists' contradictory relationship to motherhood? It could be argued that these relationships represent no more
than a failed internalization (and failed *political explication*) of a maternal ethics. However, it seems necessary to explore whether they do not
more substantially challenge our presumptions about women that make
maternal ethics a compelling, but idealized, theory on women's affinity
with nonviolent politics.

An analysis of the RAF women's decisions enables a critical perspective both on public responses to "terrorist mothers" and on feminist
understandings of women's politics. When bringing concepts of motherhood and—by extension—"maternal ethics" to armed struggle, we are
faced with familiar discursive contradictions: as women, and especially
as mothers, female terrorists counter the logic of a maternal ethics. This
contradiction surfaces prominently in the lives of two founding members of the RAF, Gudrun Ensslin and Ulrike Meinhof, and their rejection
of their role as mothers. Ensslin left her infant son first with his father
and then with a foster family. Meinhof was rumored to have preferred
placing her seven-year-old twin daughters into a Palestinian orphanage
camp rather than leaving them with their father. This chapter's discussion of these cases draws on selected writings on and by Meinhof and
Ensslin to elucidate where discursive contradictions around women's
militant politics and motherhood occur.

## Armed Struggle and Motherhood

In armed struggle, living underground meant taking up an "illegal" existence: not using one's legal name, leasing apartments with false identities, robbing banks to finance political actions and sustain members of the group, and so on. Although the Movement 2nd June allowed members to move between both legal and illegal existences and maintained close ties to the leftist political scene, the RAF sharply differentiated between those two realms, and declared an underground life as the only way for the revolutionary subject to exist.[49] In fact, the RAF was absolute in its demand that members disconnect from anything "old" (family, friends), while, according to former member Heike, the doctrine of disconnect was more pragmatic than ideological in the Movement 2nd June. The primacy of practice over theory dominated both groups. This ideology foregrounded life underground and acts of political violence and left little room for envisioning alternative families as actively pursued in other cultural and political formations in the New Left, such as the *Kinderladen* movement. For the RAF and other armed groups, however, much of the motivation to commit political violence was driven by a sense of a failed revolution by the APO[50] in the aftermath of 1968. A need for "action," not talk, had shaped much of the violent rhetoric of the student movement and found its conclusion in armed struggle.[51] The idea of confrontation *as* social change that defined the armed struggle did not include a utopian vision of a new (revolutionary) family. However, the rejection of the nuclear family that reverberated throughout West Germany in the 1960s and that potentially offered alternative gender roles was echoed in the RAF's definition of the revolutionary subject as disconnected from conventional social relations: within armed struggle, so the directive went, traditional family structures were obsolete, and women's identities (as well as men's) were absorbed into a shared revolutionary identity.[52] In fact, as Barbara, a former member of the RAF, observes, the ratio of women in the RAF "only reflected the ratio of women in the general population." She goes on to point out that "[t]he demarcation line the RAF drew to society was total and [. . .] this general break with social values made change in gender roles possible." Similarly, Heike states that while the revolution could not be envisioned as gender-specific, women's participation in armed struggle was the prerequisite for any liberation from gender roles in the new society.

Karin mentions in her reflections that many women going underground must have been troubled by the political and often personal conviction that a truly revolutionary subjectivity is achieved through a complete rejection of both family and "bourgeois" traditions of family. The literature peripherally observes this about Meinhof,[53] and Alois Prinz, in his autobiography of Ulrike Meinhof, discusses how some men were affected by the loss of their families.[54] Karin recounts that a woman in the Movement 2nd June left her children, which was at times painful to her, even as her political motivation was so strong that it outweighed considerations for her family. Unlike in the United States, where women and men formed families with children while participating in armed actions,[55] children had no place in the West German underground. The conviction that children must be a part of any revolution's vision that Katharina de Fries (who was repeatedly arrested for membership in a terrorist organization and was a mother of five children) expressed was rare: "Without children, she could not imagine a better world. Later she could not understand that Ulrike Meinhof and Gudrun Ensslin gave up their children and went underground. If we are not able, she told herself, to change the world with our children, then we can't do it without them. [. . .] With the children, utopia became concrete."[56] Considering the absence of children in the underground scene, a radical political affiliation posed far-reaching questions to women, challenging a primary identity as (potential) mother. "Our visions of the future," Karin recalls, "were dominated by the assumption that we would eventually be arrested, so long-term family plans were not part of our immediate discussions of the future."

Thus the pregnancy of Karin while being underground posed more of a logistical than an ideological problem, and she solved it with a forged health insurance card. Reproduction here played a radically different role than in militant groups identifying as inner colonies of Western countries in the 1960s and '70s, most notably the Black Power movement in the United States, which encouraged reproduction as an act against racial genocide: "Babies for the revolution" was the motto that (again) defined women primarily as mothers of the (new) nation.[57] In the context of a postwar conservatism that did not challenge the basic premise championed by National Socialism of (Aryan) women as domestic guardians of the family and mothers of the nation,[58] revolutionary sentiment in West Germany's armed groups rejected reproduction as the basis for a revolutionary society, in part *because* of reproduction's racist significance for German nationalism. Instead of viewing the logistical constraints of underground life as limiting to women, Karin views underground women as having chosen revolutionary life as a real alternative to traditional roles and believes that many of her female comrades decided to join the armed struggle within a broader social context in which women resisted the confines of assigned gender roles. Revolutionary space as experienced by women in the RAF and Movement 2nd June appears as a political realm that was separate from woman's identity as mother and thus brought some relief from traditional gender roles.

Political empowerment—and, according to Karin, the sense of effecting change and participating in decision making, which was attractive to women in armed groups, who did not experience this in general society—is conceptualized in opposition to women's role as mothers. This sense of empowerment runs counter both to a maternal ethics that builds on the daily prioritization of the well-being of those in one's care and to an essentialized ideology of motherhood that defines women's space as the domestic, nonpolitical sphere. If women in radical leftist political spaces, such as Karin, define their politics as *absence* of motherhood, we need to reexamine and denaturalize our understanding of a woman's relationship to the identity of mother, as well as a mother's relationship to political violence. An analysis of Gudrun Ensslin's and Ulrike Meinhof's experiences offers a view into this reexamination.

In the summer of 1968, Gudrun Ensslin was in detention in the women's prison in Frankfurt-Preungesheim, awaiting her trial on charges of arson. The trial later that year was to be remembered as a major leftist political spectacle, laying the foundation for the formation two years later of the left-wing terrorist group RAF, whose militant activity would dominate the FRG's domestic political landscape for years to come.[59] Ensslin and her lover, Andreas Baader, would become known as the leaders of the terrorists. Accounts of the violent events in the following years would establish her as a cold-blooded strategist and a woman blindly devoted to her man (Baader), a woman who abandoned her fiancé and young son for a life underground. However, letters she wrote to Bernward Vesper,[60] the father of her child, in anticipation of her trial in 1968–69, convey complex emotions that surface in her responses to Vesper's attempts to regain her commitment to him by appealing to her responsibility to their child, Felix. Contradicting social conventions that view children as binding their parents together, her love for her child forms the basis for her liberation from Vesper. The intense emotions and expectations she experienced around her pregnancy and Felix's existence, she explains in a letter from August 17, 1968, set into stark relief the patterns she sees their relationship trapped in: "Felix . . . I only know that from the first moment on I have loved him unconditionally, and that he, before he was born, already had intensified a process, had exposed you and me [. . .] and has triggered actions and attitudes that opened our eyes about ourselves."[61] Instead of accepting Vesper's claim to her as the father of her child, Ensslin experiences motherhood as transformational in that it exposes a stifling relationship as irreconcilable.

On May 14, 1970, Andreas Baader, incarcerated for arson in Berlin, Tegel, met with the well-known journalist Ulrike Meinhof at the German Central Institute for Social Issues. Baader and Meinhof had requested the meeting to work on what they said was a collaborative research project on youth at risk, which seemed confirmed by the book contract Meinhof presented to the authorities (signed by a friend, the publisher Klaus Wagenbach). Instead, the "meeting" resulted in Baader being freed from prison, a plan devised and executed by several women, including Gudrun Ensslin. Baader's prison break and Meinhof's subsequent flight underground marked the beginning of the RAF. One week later, on May 22, a manifesto written by Meinhof that called for the building of a "Red Army" appeared in the left-radical movement publication *Agit 833*. The rest is history: Meinhof, together with others in the newly formed group, would engage in political violence until their arrests and subsequent incarceration, followed by political hunger strikes, the recruitment of subsequent "generations" of RAF members, and ultimately the suicide of several founding members in prison.[62]

Rarely mentioned in the recounting of these events are the desperate attempts of Meinhof during the two days after Baader's prison break to find a safe place for her two seven-year-old daughters, Regine and Bettina, while she went underground, and to prevent her husband from securing exclusive custody. Generally, Meinhof's decision to go underground is viewed as a rejection of her daughters and as indicative of her failing as a mother by giving in to the group's demands to sever all ties to her "bourgeois" background. However, these attempts also lend themselves to interpreting Meinhof as a mother who was trying to ensure the future well-being of her children and whose circumstances prevented her from taking care of them herself.

What might appear to be Ensslin's careless dismissal of her son and Meinhof's cowardly surrender to group pressure in her abandonment of her twin girls have invited condemnation of the women as pathological and ultimately as "unmotherly." This is reflected in public debates, such as in media coverage and in scholarship on the two women. The one-dimensional depiction of them as having denied their children and thereby betrayed motherhood is prevalent. This and the absence of any real discussion of the conflict that the loss of their children must have posed to the two terrorists and what this must have meant to their identities as mothers suggests the unease that the association of mothers and political violence evokes. This unease is grounded as much in a conservative gender value system as in a general rejection of political violence.

Ensslin and Meinhof were products of a society colored by a postwar conservatism and shaped by a Protestant faith that mandated political engagement.[63] Ensslin, the daughter of a pastor, grew up in a household with traditional gender roles, with a mother devoted to the upbringing of her seven children and her husband's calling. Meinhof, on the other hand, had lost both parents by the time she reached her early teens. She was influenced by her mother's presumed lover, Renate Riemek, who understood herself to be a substitute mother to the two sisters, Ulrike and Wienke, after their mother's death. Both Ensslin and Meinhof were estranged from their parental figures. However, Ensslin's parents complied with her wishes about her son's care,[64] while Riemek openly and publicly spoke against Meinhof's explicit provision for her daughters and instead sided with her ex-husband.[65]

The conflict that the two women faced in deciding to go underground and leave their children is evident in their writings. Both cases counter the claim of maternal ethics that motherhood, through its daily practice, positions women politically. Instead, Ensslin's identity as mother shifts from a traditional role to that of a more abstracted, disconnected parent, while Meinhof's actions are grounded in a feminist understanding of how motherhood is a patriarchal ideal, not women's preferred reality. Both saw their motherhood as being in conflict with their political actions and felt compelled to make an "either-or" decision. Motherhood, in both cases, is conceded to a separate world of radical politics.

## Gudrun Ensslin

In the letters she writes early in her incarceration, Ensslin expresses intense love for her son and seems committed to taking care of him after her trial and prison time. Her correspondence with the child's father and her former fiancé, Bernward Vesper, before and after her first trial in 1968–69 shows her to be agonizing over her expected role as mother.[66] Much of the correspondence revolves around the child, with Vesper at times desperately trying to recapture their romantic relationship through the boy. Throughout their correspondence, Ensslin rejects him as her partner. While Ensslin was imprisoned, Vesper took care of Felix, though his caregiving was interrupted quite erratically by his travels. After one of his trips that took him away from their son, Ensslin denied him access to Felix, whom she had placed with foster parents at that time.

According to the letters, during her first year in prison, Ensslin created a variety of drawings for Felix and knit and crocheted for him a continuous flow of gifts that attest to her constant thoughts of him.[67] At times she seems overwhelmed by her emotions for the boy and refutes Vesper's doubts about her commitment, emphatically claiming that she never desired to be separated from Felix, as she writes in a letter from December 22–23, 1968: "The photos [of Felix] are beautiful, words fail me. [. . .] But, for god's sake, stop reproaching me with sentences . . . and never (I *scream* the word) did I want separation from Felix."[68] Initially she seems determined to be united with her son after her release, despite her falling out with Vesper. She emphasizes that she does not want to separate Vesper from Felix, instead aiming for some arrangement of shared custody: "[W]hen I get out . . . I 'want' Felix terribly, but I don't want to take him away from you, once and for all, I *am* serious."[69] As she states in a letter dating from June 20, 1968, she envisions herself as a part of the boy's future life while resisting Vesper's insistence on a (re) union: "[A]m more and more certain that we will always find a way not to separate anyone from Felix; and one day he will understand that he has two sources of affection and two worlds."[70]

However, once released from prison she did not seek out her son, and by going underground and subsequently founding the RAF, she risked never seeing him again. This change of plans is already anticipated in her letter from May 10, 1969, written about a month before her provisional release, when she evades a clear answer about what her intentions are regarding Felix, making them contingent on practical circumstances: "You have not for one minute imagined my situation concretely [. . .], when I get out. *What* will I do, *how* will I live, *where* will I live, *how* will I earn money etc . . . fine, *I* will have to see about all this before I will be able to get closer with Felix—which I very much want to—you understand?"[71]

This reserved statement comes amidst a heated and bitter argument over Ensslin's refusal to sign a statement of marriage[72] that would in retrospect declare Felix the child of a legal union (and give him his father's last name), since she feared that with her criminal record any right to Felix would be transferred to the legal father.[73] Her emerging changed identity is of a mother who is not the primary caregiver, but who still maintains (legal) rights to her child: relinquishing her rights as legal mother to Felix never seemed to be an option for her. The dispute is about state-patriarchy as well as (mostly appropriated) class positions. In 1969, West German law required fathers to pay child support for their children with women to whom they were not married without granting them automatic custody, a situation Vesper must have been acutely aware of.[74] Despite his urging, Ensslin never agreed to marry him so he could achieve shared custody because she was worried that he, jealous of her relationship with Baader, would retaliate and, as she put it, use Felix to hurt her, as she voices in a letter from January 28, 1969.[75] In their conflict-ridden letters, Vesper charges Ensslin with displaying bourgeois sentiment in her insistence on maintaining legal custody of Felix while not actually taking care of him. In letters from the beginning of May and May 4, 1969, he alludes to Brecht's play *The Caucasian Chalk Circle*,[76] questioning her right to decide the future of her child, based on her refusal to provide daily maternal care.[77] On May 10, 1969, she furiously replies with the charge that his anger really is about her leaving *him*, not about her being a bad mother (*Rabenmutter*) to Felix.[78] She then cynically comments on the fact that his position as exploited proletariat in this drama is backed by his friends in the socialist *Kinderladen* collective who agree with him that the *state*, of all entities, should regulate their duties towards Felix through marriage.[79] That Ensslin then insists on Felix staying with a conservative family seems a paradox, and Gerd Koenen reads it not only as a rational attempt to find the most stable environment for the boy but also as a step towards denying her own feelings for her son by avoiding him and instead sending him away.[80] When Vesper again dropped the boy off with the foster family to travel in September 1969, Ensslin ordered the boy to stay with them and denied Vesper the right to retrieve him. Vesper continued his custody battle with the Youth Welfare Offices until his suicide in May 1971.

After the RAF May Offensive[81] in 1972 and the subsequent arrest of their leaders, Ensslin was awaiting her trial in a prison in Essen.[82] The letters Ensslin wrote to her sister, Christiane, during her 1972–73 incarceration are infused with concern about her son, now permanently placed with foster parents. It is striking that in those letters she communicates a worry for her son that apparently never ceases, even though she does not access the conventional identity of mother as primary caregiver. In contrast, her position is that of an absent parent who tries to secure her child's safety through other people. In December of 1972, Ensslin asks her sister to look after Felix, while in a letter of July of that same year she is unsure whether the sister even knows anything about him: "Additionally maybe 2 [photos] of Felix. Felix is not a RAF member, Felix is my son; do you know anything about him?"[83]—although it is likely that the information that he is "not a RAF member" was written for the benefit of prison authorities censoring her letters. Embattled by the credo of disconnecting from all family ties, she nevertheless expresses the hope that her sister will foster a good relationship with Felix. Worried that Christiane will only interact with him out of duty, her plea is both defensive and urgent: "But be careful that you don't fall into the bullshit social worker-trap [. . .] if you aren't doing it *for yourself*, let it be, do you understand—[Felix] can shit on a charitable aunt."[84] Committed to the RAF in all of her actions and tying her subjectivity to the group's politics, she nevertheless is anxious about the vulnerability of her son and his ability to forge authentic relationships with her family. Meanwhile, the verdict of state officials examining her psychological state while in prison in 1973 was that she simply stopped caring for her son because her politics became more important to her: Ensslin "prioritized the 'political-revolutionary' objective over her affective bond with her own child."[85] Her pathology here is her transference of affection and care from natural object (her child) to one that not only is outside her ascribed role as mother (politics) but also is violent (terrorism).

The underlying implication—that her motherhood could have saved her from becoming a terrorist had Ensslin embraced it—is escalated with Koenen's claim that her obsession in the end was not with politics, but with Andreas Baader. Her rejection of motherhood (and thus a peaceful existence) is further perverted by her supposed overidentification with her lover and by her desire for union with him and his violent project. According to Koenen, this erotic—and therefore narcissistic—motivation stifled her original strong wish to reunite with her son.[86] So Ensslin's alleged identification with her adult lover is read as a loss of authentic subjectivity, her refusal to identify through her son as mother as a rejection of her true subjectivity. Koenen cites the remark by Ensslin's younger sister Ruth that Gudrun's first step at self-assertion, at saying "I," should have been her refusal in the summer of 1969 to participate in the underground activities "without her child."[87] Either way, there is no imagining her subjectivity outside of her relationship to lover or son. Koenen slips into accusatory style when he writes that instead, Ensslin joins Baader to lead a "Bohemian" life, rejecting the "banality of everyday life."[88] It seems that her refusal of motherhood points as much to her transgression as do her violent political means, her narrative becoming the story of a woman misguided by passion, not politics.

This analysis does not account for the criticism of patriarchal expectations of women that Ensslin expressed in some of her writing in *das info*, letters that circulated among RAF members in various prisons.[89] She clearly believed that capitalism and patriarchy account for each other[90] and that women particularly are affected by this combination, as becomes apparent in a letter she wrote in 1976: "there is [. . .] no one in the old society who experiences alienation [. . .] more directly than women."[91] She also believed that women's social position creates a specific ability for collective politics that men at times lack, while women exhibit a great capacity to think and act as a group: "to truly think and act as a collective [. . .] is where women are ahead of guys."[92] Most striking in this context, though, is that a woman's role in the family—the smallest economic unit of capitalist society—is at the center of her alienation.[93] Ensslin comes to the stunning conclusion that this predisposes women to be radical thinkers and ultimately to become underground guerrillas if they ever want to achieve an authentic self: "for this reason, though, the dialectic of their situation also becomes clear—if, after the particular brutalities of their domestication [. . .] they even want *themselves*, to think *themselves*—they need to think radically *and* subversively: a content and a form that predestines them to illegality."[94] This directly counters the notion of a maternal thinking that enables peacemaking and instead insists that the form women's oppression takes should logically lead to *armed* resistance. It also counters the streak of tragic passion and misplaced affection that dominates the discourse on her actions, and instead it foregrounds a clear—if controversial— linking of women's social position with the political choices they make— including those she made.

## Ulrike Meinhof

When following the premise of maternal thinking that daily practice (caregiving) forms an individual's political ethics, one might argue that since Ensslin was separated from her son when he was only eight months old, she did not fully internalize the attitude and skills produced by maternal practice. Meinhof, however, left her twin daughters after being their primary caregiver for seven years. Within the logic of maternal thinking, the obvious conflict she felt over leaving the girls and the fact that she sought contact with them while she was in prison were rooted in her long experience of taking care of her daughters. Her difficulties in separating from them, as well as her reportedly severe depressions during her time underground, would then point to an inner turmoil created by the contradiction between violence and her maternal ethics. This turmoil can be traced in the letters of *das info*, in which the group repeatedly demands that Meinhof completely disconnect from her past and ultimately seems to brand her a revolutionary failure.[95]

While Meinhof clearly had difficulties reconciling the demand for complete separation from ties outside the revolutionary struggle with her desire to see her daughters, she did not simply fall prey to the schizophrenic power fantasy and masochistic overidentification that are frequently attributed to her decision to join the armed struggle—and that can easily be associated with a mother leaving her children. Instead, her experiences of motherhood and of the limits primary caregiving set on her political engagements formed the background to her decision. Considering the early engagement with feminist thought that we encounter in Meinhof's writing, this seems an obvious conclusion. Most famously, in "Die Frauen im SDS oder in eigener Sache" (Women in the SDS: Acting on Their Own Behalf, 1968), she characterized the emerging autonomous women's movement, triggered by open conflicts between SDS men and women,[96] as a truly authentic political formation, since women were fighting for their own cause (not for that of a collective—and to middle-class students often abstract—proletariat). Her feminist analysis can also be traced in the early RAF statements she composed, even though a gendered analysis cannot be found in her later texts. As Sarah Colvin notes in *Ulrike Meinhof and West German Terrorism*, Meinhof's engagement with feminist ideas decreased as her time in the RAF progressed, and as her reality shifted: "In prison she is relieved of the problem of taking care of her twin daughters, and as her personal experience of the domestic limitations on women recedes, so does her empathy with anyone affected by those limitations. Instead her concern is for 'freedom' and 'humanity'; abstract notions more relevant to the situation of the imprisoned RAF."[97]

However, at the time of her going underground, in her writing Meinhof was engaging with feminist concerns. Two years before she cofounded the RAF, she articulated a feminist analysis of the way patriarchal ideology furthers capitalism in her essay "Falsches Bewußtsein" (False Consciousness), which appeared in a feminist publication in 1968. The text entails a sharp criticism of the gender conservatism of her time and of the Social Democrats' failure to pass progressive legislation. In accordance with voices in the emerging autonomous women's movement but maintaining a strong Marxist framework, she argues that the state is invested in patriarchal structures—that under the new Basic Law, bourgeois equality (*Gleichberechtigung*), which furthers capitalism, has supplanted socialist liberation (*Emanzipation*), thus weakening women's chances of actual emancipation. Women, she argues, are caught in the dilemma between working for a wage and taking care of their children, which results in unfair work burdens and an inevitable sense of failure. Industrialization has created the need for female workers without accounting for the reproductive work women are doing. Simultaneously, Meinhof points out, mothers' work[98] is defamed by the myth that it destabilizes families and robs children (and husbands) of their domestic center and thus threatens the social order. Consequently, most West Germans reject women working outside the home. Mothers end up being "blackmailed"[99] and, without receiving any real social support, accept this rejection. Meinhof emphasizes the emotional work behind these decisions, pointing out that women's complicity is based not on their weakness but on their humanity, their readiness to consider their children's needs—a point on which they can be pressured into giving up other goals: "This way women are blackmailed with their children, and it might be their humaness that allows them to be blackmailed with their children, the fact that they—as a matter of course—accept the demand to be primarily there for their children."[100] So women find themselves caught between a rock and a hard place: between economic realities and the social myth that their absence from their families damages the social fabric. These contradictory demands that control and limit women's choices rest on an ideology of motherhood that far exceeds the immediate realities of raising small children. This ideology has broad implications for reproductive rights, career plans, and relationship choices for women: "Women find themselves between a rock and hard place, caught between paid labor and family, more specifically: children—existing ones, expected ones and those they once had."[101]

Here Meinhof argues that the ideology of motherhood as a woman's natural destiny makes plausible the myth of social disorder being caused by working mothers. Having internalized the "idealization of their role as mothers,"[102] women are convinced that they only work—participate in public life—for their families, not noticing how they are really following the laws of capitalism that make it impossible for them to stay home and follow their "nature." Since they do not identify as "real" workers, Meinhof points out, women do not organize the way men do as "breadwinners" and are severely discriminated against as wage earners. Middle-class, well-educated women, on the other hand, while having more resources to afford childcare, find themselves in the same dilemma as working mothers: if they do not find fulfillment (and economic sustainability) through housework and motherhood, they feel social pressure.[103] Considering the RAF's Marxist roots, it is significant that Meinhof claims that concepts of motherhood cross class boundaries. Mothers—*all* mothers—must be blamed for working outside the home, so as to conceal the failure of those in power to contribute to a solution to the problem. Meinhof's central feminist argument is that liberation from capitalist exploitation can happen only in conjunction with the liberation of women from patriarchal ideology. This is prevented by women's internalization of this ideology, regarding which an irritated Meinhof observes, "Protest is overdue. It's not happening."[104] Motherhood then becomes an identity of irreconcilable contradictions and impossible demands.

Some of this dilemma is reflected in Meinhof's biography: balancing the needs of her two daughters with her career as a journalist, she became involved with the student movement in West Berlin.[105] She left her husband, Klaus Röhl, not primarily (as commonly is agreed upon) because he persistently cheated on her, but also because she could not reconcile her political work with his. As Jutta Ditfurth quotes Peter Coulmas, the husband of one of Röhl's lovers, Meinhof's passion at the time was politics, not men: "Ulrike's problems during this time is not the man or a different man or any man, but politics. [. . .] Her 'engagement' [. . .] that is, the concern and activism, were so strong, that the man did not even exist."[106] In a letter to Peter Coulmas, Meinhof writes about her move from Hamburg to Berlin without Röhl, saying that she finds the decision liberating.[107] She took the girls with her, making them part of her new life in the radical political scene in West Berlin.

However, her conflict between public and private realms recurred in West Berlin. A single mother, Meinhof unsuccessfully sought to live with families with children in order to share childcare.[108] Sending Regine and Bettina to an anti-authoritarian kindergarten for part of the day, she juggled her journalistic and political work with their care the rest of the time, with the help of friends.[109] In an interview with filmmaker Helma Sanders in 1970, months before she went underground, she voiced some of her criticism of the separation of public and private that renders women apolitical in the traditional sense. In this interview, she speaks to the particular dilemma in which women—mothers—find themselves. She acknowledges that children need a stable family, and that men have their wives to see to that, whereas a politically active woman does not have a wife to take care of her children, and thus is faced with a problem:

> From the point of view of the children's needs, the family [. . .] is necessary, indispensable as a stable place with stable human relationships. [. . .] Of course, many things are easier if you're a man, and you have a wife to look after the children. [. . .] If you're a woman, so that you don't have a wife to do all that for you, then you have to do everything yourself—it's terribly difficult.[110]

She continues, "Thus the problem of all politically active women is—including my own—that they on the one hand do socially necessary work. [. . .] But on the other hand they helplessly sit around with their children just as much as all the other women."[111] In addition to criticizing the oppressive effect that the separation of public and private exerts on women through their motherhood (you either have a private *or* a public life), she also points to the limitations of politics that discount the private realm, and she counters that view with the claim that political work detached from "private life" is in fact not sustainable: "One could say the central oppression of woman is that her private life as private life is contrasted to any political life. Whereas one could turn this around and say that where political work is unrelated to private life, it is not right, it cannot be seen through."[112]

While Meinhof demands that politics integrate what Ruddick later identified as maternal thinking, Meinhof's denunciation of maternal practice for keeping women away from the established political sphere might appear to take precedence in her thinking. Yet nothing seems to have prepared her for the emotional conflict that her decision to go underground triggered when her husband initiated a custody battle as soon as there was a warrant for her arrest. Röhl catered to conservative disapproval of the New Left's alternative visions of family in his attempts to gain exclusive custody of the twins. He presented Meinhof's failure as mother as a direct result of her left-political engagement and her rejection of sexual conventions.[113] The courts reacted swiftly and granted him temporary custody.

Meinhof had always intended for her twins to be raised by her sister if something should happen to her.[114] While wanted by the police, she took considerable risks during the two days after freeing Baader to meet with her attorneys in order to find a way to convince her ex-husband of this solution. Family members supported her in this, but without success. Her frantic negotiations—while underground and on the run from the police—seemed as much driven by her experience of loss as by an unstated fear of leaving the girls to be raised by their father[115]—a point that was also reiterated in the interview with Barbara. Meinhof confessed in a letter to her attorney that she did not get divorced *despite* the children, but *because* of them, to protect them from their father.[116] When the courts gave her ex-husband temporary custody, she decided to hide Regine and Bettina until she could secure her sister's custody of the twins through the courts. As a temporary solution, she sent them to a village in Sicily, where they were taken care of by leftist activists. The rumor that she had plans to send the twins to a Palestinian orphanage camp in Jordan is disputed today; it may never have been her intention to have them stay anywhere but with her sister.[117] In case she lost in the courts, the alternatives were sending them to friends or to East Germany. The plan was for Meinhof to retrieve the children from Italy and keep them underground until a solution was found.[118] The court did reverse its initial decision and Meinhof was given custody, whereupon her sister Wienke Meinhof began preparing for their arrival.[119] Before Meinhof's sister could organize their return, however, journalist Stefan Aust heard of their whereabouts and brought them to Röhl.[120] The courts never rectified that situation—Meinhof still had legal custody—and the daughters were raised by their father.[121] Though the situation was legally incorrect, her status as "enemy of the state" nullified her status as mother and any rights tied to it. Meinhof's actions point to the fact that the safety of her daughters was very much on her mind and that she attempted to ensure their well-being while also committing to armed struggle. It turned out that the two goals were irreconcilable.

After her arrest in 1972, Meinhof was in contact with her daughters, who later that year (they were then ten years old) also began visiting her in prison. In the early years of her incarceration, her letters to the twins profess her emotional commitment to them, and encourage them to be angry, not sad, about their separation, thus attempting to make some agency accessible to them: "Hello there, little ones! [. . .] [G]rit your teeth. And don't think you have to be sad because you have a Mummy in prison. It's much better to be angry than sad. Oh, I'll be so glad to see you, so very glad."[122] At their first visit she was finally face to face with them after two and a half years and seemingly was overjoyed as well as overwhelmed with her emotions.[123] The contact with the twins cemented Meinhof's continuous identity as their mother and attests that they were at the center of her thoughts. Her desire to let them know that seemed as strong as her need to feel their presence in her life in prison: "I've been thinking a lot about you two. . . . And visit me! And write—come on! Or draw something for me, ok? I think it's time I get another picture. The ones I have I know by heart."[124] After her transfer to Stammheim and the ensuing series of extreme hunger strikes, the twins never heard from their mother again. Although she was no longer actively engaged in maternal practice, Meinhof's identity as mother did not cease (especially prior to her transfer to Stammheim) and she clearly recognized the central role of a mother in her twins' lives: "Both of you. Your Mummy."[125] However, as dissatisfying as personal and political relationships were in the context of their revolutionary activity, the act of embracing political violence and Meinhof's subsequent "betrayal" of motherhood, which displays a clear lack of maternal ethics, force a recasting of feminist assumptions about maternal practices that claim to produce specific politics.

The cultural association of women with motherhood is central to the unease women's participation in political violence evokes, and therefore Ensslin's and Meinhof's roles as mothers are critical to our understanding of them. How much of their decision to leave their children was founded on a (feminist) rejection of the expected role of mother? Meinhof's writing gives a clear indication that she thought about these issues from a feminist perspective. She believed that women's political work affects them directly (unlike much of the political work of the Left) and that the private is, in fact, political.[126] While Ensslin's writing avoids an overtly feminist rhetoric, she nevertheless clearly links socialization and motherhood within capitalism with women's (political) oppression. Reports from a former RAF member, Peter Homann, state that Ensslin responded to his concerns about Meinhof leaving her twins with the challenge that he was hindering women from liberating themselves: "You want to keep the cunts from their liberation."[127] This expresses a clear understanding that rejecting motherhood is part of women's liberation as revolutionary subjects.

Read in the context of maternal ethics, Ensslin's and Meinhof's writings seem to evince a correlation between maternal practice, i.e., the act of mothering, and their emotional conflict about leaving their children. It appears to be necessary to be engaged in the act of mothering in order to experience patriarchal limitations imposed on women and thus to emphasize those limitations in theorizing about liberation (as seen in the experiential origin of the feminist observation that "the personal is political"). The longer Ensslin and Meinhof did not practice maternal care, the less they engaged with feminist ideas around motherhood and gender in their writings. However, to claim that this inevitably points to a correlation between maternal practice and maternal ethics is not logical: while both women experienced emotional turmoil over their decisions, they *did* leave their children and engaged in violent politics *while they were actively mothering*. Maternal practice as the foundation for (feminist) peace politics failed. Instead, Ensslin's and Meinhof's early politics—which clearly included aspects of feminist reasoning—turned violent. Even if a discernable feminist motivation remains elusive, their rejection of motherhood can be understood as a *feminist practice*— especially considering the discursive effects it triggers to the present day.

Evaluations of the women's actions usually do not consider these complicated emotional and theoretical struggles that underlay the RAF women's politics. Writings about Ensslin freeze her into the image of "nonmother"; she is reduced to the enigmatic woman, the sphinx-like icon of the RAF period,[128] with an underlying sexual devotion to her man that drives her extreme political actions. Armed struggle, so the musing goes, seems to have entailed an erotic component for her.[129] Her son, some have suggested, was nothing but a burden to her.[130] She is "de-mothered" in a particularly gendered way, and the figure of the violent mother fades to make place for a cold and calculated fanatic. Congruent with mainstream notions about motherhood, when evaluated in the context of feminist theories on maternal ethics, Ensslin's behavior is not maternal. Hence, she technically does not classify as a mother, or rather, she exemplifies a "bad" mother and thus her emotional struggle with her decision becomes invisible and irrelevant. Instead, images that circulated in the media, such as the newsmagazine *Der Spiegel*, emphasized the sexualized icon—the femme fatale—that contrasted with earlier photos of a more "authentic" Ensslin as mother (figures 2.1 and 2.2).[131] These images leave invisible the activist Gudrun Ensslin as she emerges in the letters published by her sister and brother, who include photos of her taken in prison (see figures 2.3 and 2.4).[132] These images, which show Ensslin devoid of any gendered markers of motherhood or sexual seduction, together with her letters, form impressions of "Gudrun Ensslin's humanness"[133] that are absent in mainstream media representation and most scholarship.

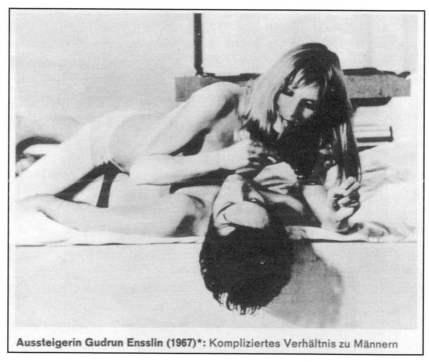

**Aussteigerin Gudrun Ensslin (1967)\*:** Kompliziertes Verhältnis zu Männern

Figure 2.1. Stills like this from a film made in the early 1960s were regularly circulated in media reports on Ensslin. Their focus on Ensslin's naked body and sexuality, which were unrelated to any RAF actions, effectively sexualized her politics. (*Der Spiegel*)

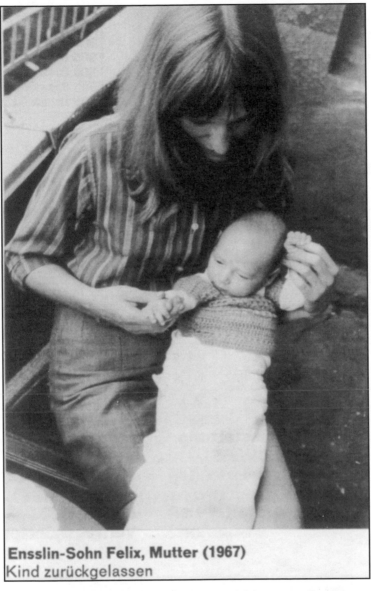

**Ensslin-Sohn Felix, Mutter (1967)**
Kind zurückgelassen

Figure 2.2. This (rare) 1967 photo of Ensslin with her son, Felix, often was placed in media reports in contrast to sexualized or defeminized images of her. The image served to present her motherhood as a natural, "authentic" state of being that she traded in for a deviant, violent existence. (*Der Spiegel*)

Figure 2.3. Photos taken of Ensslin inside the Stuttgart-Stammheim prison resist the media's image selections, which present her political development as a good daughter gone bad. Instead, they offer a rare glimpse of Ensslin's personality without gendering or sexualizing her. (*Gudrun Ensslin*, Ensslin and Ensslin, eds.)

Figure 2.4. Pictures taken of Ensslin in prison by fellow inmates were reprinted with her letters to her siblings. Particularly in conjunction with her letters, these photos present an unusual perspective on Ensslin's "humanness" that is absent in mainstream media coverage. (*Gudrun Ensslin*, Ensslin and Ensslin, eds.)

Meinhof, on the other hand, is locked into the image of a tragically misguided intellectual, a *Vorzeigelinke* (model lefty) gone bad and ultimately bullied into killing herself.[134] Her major crime was abandoning her daughters for a foolish and violent project when she should have known better. Rarely is her criticism of patriarchal structures taken into account in attempts to understand her actions, even though such criticism offers insight into her relationship to motherhood as an institution. Here media images trace the descent from success and respectability into criminality and ultimately madness through a deteriorating femininity: Meinhof as successful journalist (sophisticated and attractive—see figure 2.5) and particularly as mother (soft, nurturing, and loving—see figure 2.6)[135] contrasts with the hard and masculinized Meinhof photographed in the prison yard (see figure 2.7). Ultimately, neither woman was able to reconcile this conflict between motherhood as institution and her maternal emotions. Both women committed suicide; they hanged themselves about one and a half years apart in the same cell, at the same window.[136] Underneath the political furor and social trauma their deaths caused lay a final disavowal of their children. They left them not merely without mothers, but without answers. Whether to read their suicides as final acts of political resistance or of personal desperation remains a matter of speculation. However, it is obvious that their experiences as mothers did not provide them with ethics that prohibited violence or the risking of their children's well-being and that their identities as mothers did not prevent them from ending their lives. Ultimately, women in armed struggle resist the automatic conception of mothers (women) as nonviolent and instead bring into relief a cultural inability to approach the phenomenon of female terrorists with children outside the context of mothers gone bad. Their "betrayal" of motherhood and their claiming of political space through violence destabilize naturalized assumptions about women's primary identity as mother—and of mothers as nonviolent. These acts call for a reconsideration both of women's politics as founded in maternal thinking and of the forms motherhood can take.

**Aussteigerinnen Ulrike Meinhof (1967),**

Figure 2.5. This image shows Meinhof at the height of her career as a well-known journalist. Her polished, feminine appearance, coupled with her professional competence, represented acceptable political opposition. (*Der Spiegel*)

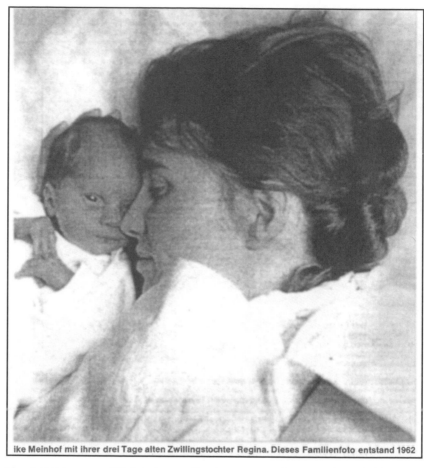

ike Meinhof mit ihrer drei Tage alten Zwillingstochter Regina. Dieses Familienfoto entstand 1962

Figure 2.6. Images of Meinhof as mother in reports on her terrorist activities emphasized her gendered transgression. Her "natural" role as mother is lost to an irrational and violent role as terrorist. (*Stern*)

Figure 2.7. The media visually narrated Meinhof's "fall from grace" with contrasting images. As prisoner she here is degendered and unmothered. (*Der Spiegel*)

# "Terrorist Girls" and "Wild Furies"

## Feminist Responses to Media Representations of Women Terrorists during the "German Autumn" of 1977

The result of violence against women is that women also employ violence.

⋆ Anonymous, "Frauen und Gewalt," 1977

This "call to action" [for women to pull out of political conflict] rather is aimed at getting us back to where those in power wanted us in the first place!

⋆ Anonymous, "Frauenbewegung seit 'Deutschland im Herbst,'" 1978

When the fight against terrorism suddenly degenerates into a fight against emancipation, when female suspects are persecuted and branded not only for their delinquencies but beyond that as insubordinate women, then this persecution is also aimed at myself and at my efforts for change. [. . .] If the rejection of violence, the horror at a group who wants to destroy itself and our society, is at the same time turned into a rejection of active women, into a surrendering of protest and necessary rage, then I am paralyzed by this conflict between two affinities.

⋆ Susanne von Paczensky, 1978

## Introduction

After three members of the Red Army Faction (RAF), two women and a man,[1] entered the house of Dresdner Bank CEO Jürgen Ponto on July 30, 1977, and shot him in what usually is understood to have been a failed kidnapping attempt, the incident became one of a series of events foreshadowing the dramatic climax of the German Autumn.[2] The confrontation between the state and the RAF escalated dramatically that year. Significantly, media coverage of the Ponto murder focused mainly on Susanne Albrecht's "deviant" behavior, rather than the brutal shooting. Albrecht, the sister of the banker's goddaughter, provided the terrorists with access to the house, famously bringing flowers when ringing the doorbell. By highlighting the stereotypical feminine deceit that allowed the RAF to enter the house, mainstream media created a highly gendered representation of the terrorist action. Unlike other incidents, where images of the victims of terrorist attacks became icons for helplessness and fear, gender transgression became the marker of the intense brutality of the Ponto murder: "In this case, the cruelty is not constructed through open brutality, but in a stereotypical way through the underhandedness [backstabbing] of the female perpetrator with the flower bouquet."[3] In turn, a feminist outcry against sexist portrayals of female terrorists that suggested that "the farewell to the kitchen indicates the direct path to prison"[4] reverberated through the print subculture of movement publications.

In the social drama that had been unfolding during the RAF's activities, the "murderous girls"[5] of the RAF and other groups such as the Movement 2nd June created moments of destabilization of gender conventions that posed an acute threat to the nation: a deviance (violent female actors) within an already deviant framework (terrorism). This troubling of gender norms became a key element in the West German public's imagination, as is demonstrated in the excessive press coverage of women active in left-wing militant groups in the 1970s and early 1980s. This excess reveals gender as a part of the mechanisms that shaped public debate on the RAF and that resulted in the exclusion/demarcation (*Abgrenzung*) of those of the political Left—not only within public discourse, but from the nation-community (*Gemeinschaft*) as such.[6] Female terrorists thus symbolized not only the gender transgressions of female criminals but also a perversion of women's relationship to the nation (state) because of the politicized framework of their violent actions. As Clare Bielby argues in "Attacking the Body Politic: The *Terroristin* in 1970s German Media," the "German media [. . .] posits violent female terrorists as a direct threat to the body-politic of the nation and as the 'unnatural' abject other of sanctioned, 'natural' and pure German womanhood."[7]

Simultaneously dismissed as "terrorist girls" and demonized as "wild furies"[8] in the West German press, these women inspired a gendered discourse that reflected a cultural unease about women participating in political violence. The media coverage in turn elicited responses from feminist movement publications that resisted what Uta Klein in "Kriminalität, Geschlecht, und Medienöffentlichkeit" (Crime, Gender, and Media Public) refers to as *Alltagstheorien*, everyday or commonsense theories on the "nature" of women's relationship to criminal violence propagated by mass media. According to Klein, popular *Alltagstheorien* build on pseudoscientific theories long proven scientifically obsolete, whose basic patterns can be summarized as follows: "A woman's delinquency and nondelinquency are explained with *biological characteristics* of women and always have something to do with *sexuality.*"[9] These *Alltagstheorien* that circulate through various media of public debate position a female terrorist's gender as registering outside the categories of intelligibility—she becomes what Hanna Hacker terms "nonwoman" or "non–femininity/femaleness."[10] On the basis of her violent behavior, "nonwoman" symbolizes a gender (and sexual) transgression beyond simply enacted masculinity and instead represents a gender outside the "normal" manifestations of man and woman.[11] This crisis of intelligibility produces what Judith Butler has termed "gender trouble"—the disclosure of gender as performative and as reproduced ritualistically, not as natural. Significantly, "nonwoman's" threat to heteronormativity and its patriarchal gender norms significantly poses a threat to the German nation itself: it relies on women's identities and social role as mothers to reproduce itself, and motherhood seemingly is foreclosed in the presence of "nonwomen."

In this chapter, I not only examine mainstream or mass media's general casting of politically violent women as inherently (gender) deviant but also focus on feminist responses to these theories and the ensuing debates as productive sites for thinking about feminist politics in this context.[12] I will show how different *Alltagstheorien* on female terrorists we find in West German media publications in the 1970s and 1980s served as a springboard for West German feminist activists to examine arguments about violence as a legitimate means in their own political communities.[13] The emphasis here is on three types of publications that discussed women and political violence: corporate print media, cross-regional feminist periodicals, and small local feminist newsletters. The mass media here serves as the primary source for looking at the mainstream debate, so I am focusing my discussion on *Der Spiegel*, West Germany's main left-leaning news magazine. In terms of readership and political position within the *Abgrenzungs* (exclusion/demarcation) debate that structured the discourse on terrorism by 1977, its coverage is of particular interest. Further, I am differentiating between two kinds of feminist movement publications responding to media coverage. First are the larger, regularly published magazines distributed nationally through newsstands and/or bookstores and so-called Infoshops (*Infoläden*), such as *Emma, Courage*, and *Die Schwarze Botin*. The second group of movement publications consisted of short-lived newsletters and journals put out by local women's initiatives, especially the women's centers (*Frauenzentren*) that were established throughout West Germany in the 1970s. These publications often display more radical positions than the nationally distributed ones and are the object of the main textual analysis in this chapter.

This chapter seeks to illuminate the feminist discourse that was triggered by the at times blatantly sexist representation of female terrorists in the West German press. In pursuit of this aim, I analyze images and news coverage of female terrorists in the newsmagazine *Der Spiegel* to contextualize the *Alltagstheorien* the magazine propagated in an article covering the Ponto murder in 1977. I then examine the responses this and other articles elicited from feminist movement publications and the implications these responses have for feminist understandings of political violence more generally. What emerges is a diversity of positions articulated in these debates, ranging from understanding leftist political violence as actively harming women's causes to outright support of revolutionary violence as feminist politics. This diversity challenges the assumption that there is *one* feminist understanding of violence as a political means. This in turns disallows the identification of a sole feminist subject position that—while condemning sexist portrayals of female terrorists in the media—clearly distances itself from any use of political violence. Instead, we are offered several readings of terrorist women's actions as *feminist practices*, even if they are not claiming them as such.

## Women's Politics as Nonviolent: Feminist Renditions of the Peaceful Sex

The debates that took place in West German movement publications illuminate the way Western feminists categorized more broadly have struggled to define women's relationship to political violence.[14] Traditionally, Western feminists in the second half of the twentieth century have explored this relationship primarily in two ways: one set of theories takes the position that women's activism typically is nonviolent and that violence contradicts feminism's principles, and the other rejects the naturalization of women as peaceful. The first position emerged from the cultural feminist understanding of women's political work in the 1970s—informed by the campaign against violence against women—that was cemented during a growing peace movement and the mobilization for disarmament in the 1980s.[15] This in turn fostered the equation of feminist identity with pacifism.[16] The 1980s peace movement gradually adopted "feminist ideological frames,"[17] producing a rhetoric that allocates peace as a "naturally" female trait.[18] Statements such as those expressed by peace activist Helen Caldicott, who said, "'[T]here are no Communist babies; there are no capitalist babies. A baby is a baby is a baby'" had the effect, as David Meyer and Nancy Whittier point out, of "promot[ing] an analysis of militarism rooted in a feminist critique of patriarchy."[19] Within a growing feminist debate on how women's "feminine" qualities could be understood as a source of "good" power that opposes "masculine"-defined "bad" power,[20] war and destruction were viewed as results of patriarchal rule.[21] By the early 1980s, as Gilda Zwerman observes, "a new ideological position was consolidated: strategies for political change that included violence do not serve the interest of women, mothers, or feminism."[22] Consequently, the embracing of nonviolence as women's distinct political disposition became naturalized and women's political work became synonymous with pacifism. This approach was further developed in feminist social movement history and theory in the 1990s,[23] in which women's relationship to political violence is primarily explored through their experiences of militarism, state terrorism, and imperialism either as victimized or as corrupted by patriarchal power.[24]

Within the debate on political violence that emerged in the mid-1970s, cultural feminism, also referred to as "gynocentric feminism,"[25] gained significant influence on the basis of its theoretical affinities to the anti–violence-against-women paradigm, which, especially in West Germany, would later trigger painful discussions of women's roles as victims and/or as perpetrators in the context of National Socialism. Cultural feminism conceptualizes women—primarily due to their role as actual and/or potential mothers—as nonviolent. In its earlier manifestations, cultural feminism situated feminist nonviolence within an essentialist framework; that is, women as life givers are inclined to be naturally/psychologically opposed to violence.[26] Responding to critiques of reproducing patriarchal constructions of motherhood and other naturalized norms of womanhood, feminist scholars since the mid-1980s have countered this biological essentialism with a gynocentric understanding of women's activism as rooted in social roles such as primary caretakers and socially conscious citizens.[27]

The second and opposing set of theories about women and political violence—mainly developed in activist literature—contradicts the naturalization of women's activism as peaceful. Some of these theories examine how political violence in specific contexts (such as colonialisms) can serve feminist ends and point to factors other than gender that drive women's political decisions. Others do not view feminist work as separate from leftist activism as a whole.[28] In scholarly work, this approach finds most resonance in research on anticolonial nationalist movements in the "Third World."[29] However, in the pre-9/11 decades following 1970s armed struggle in Western industrialized nations, definitions of women's political strategies as nonviolent became the feminist norm.[30]

Many of the feminist positions on political violence developed in the decades following the German Autumn of 1977 have made invisible the complex debates taking place in the 1970s. Women's participation in the RAF and in revolutionary groups throughout Europe and the United States was extensively debated in the 1970s and 1980s.[31] However, in later historical accounts and within a broader cultural memory of women's political activism, these women's controversial political actions increasingly are viewed as contradicting a feminist worldview, or are simply not part of the account.[32] The troubling result of this evolving invisibility is the emergence of a normative feminist subject position that distances (*abgrenzen*) itself from any patriarchal violence and marginalizes diverging feminist practices.[33]

It does not seem possible to reconcile this nonviolent feminist subject with the actions of politically militant women in the 1970s and '80s. The latter simply did not correspond with these prevalent perceptions of women's political participation. Not only did militant women trouble naturalized gender norms in the greater population, but the media conjured the myth of the female terrorist as "the foil to the 'proper' German woman and mother."[34] These militants also challenged feminist truth-effects of pacifist political methods as women's most natural political strategy. To facilitate a more comprehensive understanding of this tension among feminist thought, mainstream gender norms, and women's violent actions, I examine how political violence was understood in West German feminist debates as found in 1970s radical movement publications *before* women's activism was naturalized as nonviolent. These debates were greatly influenced and often triggered by media coverage, and need to be understood as taking place in the context of a larger public debate on women and political violence as it was occurring in West Germany.

## RAF Women, the Media, and Public Imagination

Considering the media's central role in shaping and facilitating public debates and channeling anxieties and fears, the triangular nodes of representation of women's political work—in mainstream print media, in publications of the autonomous women's movement,[35] and in radical leftist feminist publications—highlight how gender is a structuring force in public debates on terrorism and the threat the autonomous women's movement posed to mainstream culture. Initially, media coverage of left-wing terrorism printed a diversity of opinions—especially in early discussions of the RAF—that clearly marked political positions. By 1977, this diversity was leveled to become more homogenous as the discursive, political, and social *Abgrenzung* (exclusion/demarcation) of anyone left-leaning was solidified.[36]

The following outline of discourses on media and female terrorists understands print mass media[37] in general as both producing and reproducing discourse (by relating "facts" and the state's reactions and measures and through op eds) and thus as shaping public opinion at the same time as they provide a forum for public debate (through genres such as the letter to the editor). In the case of the RAF in particular, terrorism was a topic that sold copies for the print media at the same time as it was used by terrorists to make visible their cause and actions (terrorism as communicated by media) and to negotiate with the state. Simultaneously, according to Dominique Grisard in *Gendering Terror*, the media's incessant featuring of "terrorism experts" (and journalists authoring books on terrorism, presented as "experts") actually contributed to the production of left-wing terrorism as a phenomenon. The state used the media to control information and the way it was portrayed; for example, the construction of the RAF as a national security risk that justified the expansion of surveillance and regulations would not have been possible without the media. Finally, the media also influenced policy making. Media discourses thus are not simply vehicles for ideology dissemination but instead are "sites of ideological debates."[38] However, these debates are infused with power structures and have concrete political dimensions: "In the frame of a modern 'media democracy' the distinction between a political and a media apparatus is barely sustainable. Rather, the media, in particular news media, are the determining authority of political discourse."[39]

## Terrorist Communication and the News Value of Fear: The RAF and the Media

Understanding terrorism as a form of communication has a long history, going back to the term attributed to Russian anarchists Bakunin and Kropotkin: "propaganda of the deed."[40] In the 1960s and 1970s, revolutionary movements viewed not only the terrorist deed as propaganda for their cause but also mass media's dissemination of information and images *about* the act.[41] In his widely read *Mini-Manual of the Urban Guerilla* (1969), Brazilian radical Carlos Marighella emphasizes the importance not only of the violent act communicating a political message but also of the act being conveyed—mediated—by mass media. This is interpreted by the RAF in the German context to include reaching the widest audience possible and forcing the state to deal with the issue: urban guerilla activities "carried out with specific objectives and aims in mind, inevitably become propaganda material for the mass communication system."[42] The RAF and Movement 2nd June recognized the role the media plays in disseminating information and images of terrorist attacks, in the case of the RAF not the least because of Ulrike Meinhof's profession as a journalist. They were conscious as well of the necessity of *convincing* various elements of the German public through their communicative acts (i.e., terrorism): they sought to convince the Left of the urgency of moving from opposition to guerilla warfare; the broader mainstream of the state's latent fascist nature; state officials of the imminent danger the RAF posed to the state; and the mass media of the importance of the RAF as a voice in discourse.[43] In short, as Hanno Balz observes, media became an important factor in the RAF's strategic planning: "[The RAF's] plan consists of symbolic politics as well as an explicit form of public relations, such as the sending out of *communiqués* to international news agencies."[44]

However, rooted in the Left's general criticism of the "bourgeois" press, the RAF's relationship to public media was at best ambivalent: although the group relied on the media for communication with the state and the public as a "mass media conveyor of their messages"[45] and to make the group part of the West German political landscape,[46] it simultaneously dismissed mass media as generally propagating fascist ideology and as catering to the state's interests.[47] In turn, a story on the terrorists always boosted press sales,[48] so the terrorists' demands that media publish statements and kidnapping stipulations mostly were heeded by journalists and editors. The RAF thus was successful in establishing its presence within public discourse, which perhaps is most significant in the group's construction of itself as an actual counterforce to the state: "In the end, hegemonic discourse [. . .] at times serves basically as an amplifier for the RAF, whose clearest marker of superiority is the ability, through their initiative, to force a reaction from the voices within discourses as well as political institutions."[49] While the RAF ultimately failed to control the representations of their actions and beliefs in the media and their influence on hegemonic discourse waned, their performative and discursive strategies ensured some presence within the debate, even if less and less a corrective one. They managed at times to place certain topics on the news agenda, especially at those moments when the group could present itself as victim of state repression, as the case of politicized prison conditions demonstrates.[50]

Since the inception of the group, the RAF had been openly hostile towards the Springer press, one of West Germany's largest publishing houses that produces Germany's most notorious tabloids. The RAF's anti-Springer stance stood in the tradition of the 1960s student movement's "Enteignet [Disown] Springer" campaign, which charged the media giant with feeding malicious right-leaning propaganda to the German public. During that period, Jürgen Habermas's notion of "the public sphere" as an instance of democratic control against the state was influential in student circles. Thus the rationale underlying the anti-Springer campaign was "manipulation theory," which assumes a true political interest within the public that needs to be freed from willful manipulation by external forces.[51] The "Enteignet Springer" campaign was one aspect in the 1968 movement's broader attempts at establishing "alternative" public spheres, in which hegemonic discourse was challenged and its underlying national values questioned.[52] Taking the campaign to a controversial extreme, the RAF bombed the main Springer building in Hamburg in 1972, injuring several workers.[53]

Without question, the media granted the RAF visibility by reporting certain events and circulating images. The foci and interpretation of these events varied radically, depending on the particular medium's position on the political spectrum. How far the media's role extended from reporting to *shaping* public opinion is much more difficult to determine. As Balz emphasizes in "Der 'Sympathisanten'-Diskurs im Deutschen Herbst" (The "Sympathizers" Discourse during the German Autumn), "*published* opinion is not necessarily congruent with *public* opinion."[54] While the media defines issues as newsworthy, thereby strongly influencing public debate and emotions triggered by events, it also at times counters prevalent public opinion, creating spaces for the discourse on events to shift. In the case of the RAF, we should be cautious then about understanding media analysis as public opinion, even as we accept the impact of media discourse on political decisions,[55] which in the case of the state's reliance on the media was considerable.

The most consequential development in the media coverage of left-wing terrorism was the increasing *Abrenzung* (exclusion/demarcation) of (and from) anything that might be construed as (radical) leftist after

1972, accompanied by legislative and law-enforcement efforts to limit the legality of leftist activism.[56] Balz argues that on the surface, the escalation in the coverage towards a shut-down of any real oppositional opinions could be understood as the mercenary chase after the "terrorism story," which generated revenue by drawing on fear, threat, and outrage. He cautions, however, that in terms of ideologies inscribed in the discourse, a "struggle over minds" took place at the core of the debate,[57] with the entire Left and its place in German politics at stake, steering questions of social inclusion and exclusion. In the end, Balz concludes, the discursive meaning making centered less on the RAF than on West German society itself: "It's safe to say that between 1970 and 1977 the society of the Federal Republic projected an image of itself not in a debate *with* the RAF [as external element] but in a debate *through/about* the RAF"[58]—as an element that generates ideas in society's midst that need to be exorcized at whatever cost in the name of national and civil society's democratic values.

The *Feminismusverdacht* (charge/accusation of feminism) voiced by state officials and media in the discussion of terrorism was a central component of the *Abgrenzung* that took place, both in terms of social anxieties that triggered the need for reigning in gender transgressions in general and in terms of legal efforts to limit the influence of leftist feminists on social and political developments. "The debate on left-wing terrorism," argues Vojin Saša Vukadinović, needs to be understood as "a decidedly political intervention against feminism."[59] Fantasies of gender-gone-wrong and misogynist readings of women's demands for social change that conflated feminism with terrorism in the mass media led to the perpetuation of *Alltagstheorien* about the "nature" of women and played a crucial role in shaping public debate, which becomes visible in the responses the coverage of RAF women generated in movement publications as well as in scholarly work.

## "Terrorist Girls" and "Wild Furies": Gender Discourse and Cultural Anxiety in the Media Representation of Terrorist Women

The representation of women in the RAF and Movement 2nd June is characterized by a moral outrage and condemnation that points to meanings their actions held that went far beyond simply constituting criminal acts. The extreme reactions female terrorists generated are congruent with a general unease that surfaces in media representations of women committing violence.[60] In the 1970s and early 1980s, sexuality and reproduction were the main tropes through which terrorism was rendered *through* the female body, so to speak. In print, RAF women and those active in the Movement 2nd June were locked into a limited range of images that speak to patriarchal fears and fantasies regarding women's relationship to community and nation: as dangerous objects of sexual desire (*Terroristen-Mädchen* [terrorist girls]) they tantalize, as failed mothers they shock, as lesbians they disgust, and as women who claim "subject status through a weapon"[61] they horrify. This does not mean that RAF men were not pathologized in public discourse. At times, their deviance was framed in terms of sexual (and, implicitly, gender) transgression, such as when Andreas Baader's political activities were analyzed in relation to the fact that he was "spoilt" by a women-only household in his childhood, his bisexual practices, and his (presumed) sexual relations with RAF women.[62] My point is that while terrorism as a political strategy is considered deviant to begin with, the public discussion of women within that practice is gendered and sexualized in ways that the discussion of men is not.

The women are less often depicted as *acting* as terrorists than as *embodying* political violence. The RAF, then, is feminized in its threat to the state and society, and its irrational politics is contrasted with a rational masculine state and authorities that shield the nation from the devastating threat of gendered perversion. The RAF (and, by extension, all violent politics) as feminine entity is eerily mirrored in the actual roles of those involved in the conflict—a mirroring that produces an area of tension for many feminists. Reflecting on the gender politics underlying the escalation of violence in the fall of 1977, journalist and editor Susanne von Paczensky observes in her preface to *Frauen und Terror* (Women and Terror) the gendered division of labor apparent in the state's execution of power and in sites of cultural authority as it is presented in the media, a phenomenon that the terrorists undermine:

> Everybody who publicly, visibly dealt with terrorism—the crisis staff, the investigative bodies, [from] the rescue team to the serious experts, who [. . .] discussed the backgrounds and consequences of the events—

all were men. [. . .] But the affected—from the hostages in the [hijacked plane] *Landshut* and their kidnappers, the RAF prisoners whose release was to be obtained, to the figure that commonly is referred to as "the man on the street"—the affected were predominantly women. [. . .] After the violent acts of 1977 it became clear just how unusual the gendered division among the terrorists is.[63]

A year later, she notes, little had changed: "The smooth faces of girls look out from the wanted posters, but their persecutors and those studying them and even their attorneys are men."[64] Paczensky's observation addresses an inherent dilemma female terrorists pose to feminist politics: while their violence is destructive, morally indefensible to most, and politically ineffective, their presence and actions *do* threaten the existing gender order, which is reflected in the (masculine/male) state apparatus's severe response, and which includes the conscious creation of a narrative that links feminism with terrorism. While the hyperbolic representation of female terrorists by media and state officials was systematic and unrealistic, it might be useful to view it as a panicked measure in response to the actual undermining of power organized along gendered lines by women in the RAF and Movement 2nd June. In other words, while these women might not constitute feminist subjects, they engaged in feminist practices whose discursive effects were immediate and concrete.

Two major points in media coverage of female terrorists emerge that are relevant to this analysis. First is the *Feminismusverdacht*, which was openly voiced as early as February 1971 (less than a year after the RAF became active) in a *Der Spiegel* interview with Günther Nollau, who was at the time manager of the Department of Public Safety in the Ministry of the Interior and later president of the Bundesamt für Verfassungsschutz (the West German equivalent to a combination of the American CIA and FBI). Nollau detected "something irrational" in the high number of "girls" participating in political violence and was wondering if "maybe this is an excess of women's emancipation that becomes apparent here."[65] The media (re)produced this *Feminismusverdacht* continuously in its coverage, as Irene Bandhauer-Schöffmann argues: "On the one hand the life of women underground was presented as an experience of emancipation, on the other hand the equation was set up that feminist rebellion against patriarchal structure was the true political origin of terrorism and female terrorists embody a perverse, excessive emancipation."[66] This linking of feminism with terrorism would develop into a systematic investigation (and persecution) of feminist activists by the state as well as a social backlash against "uppity" (i.e., "emancipated") women's gender transgressions in general. The second aspect is the blatant "sexualization and pornographization"[67] of left-wing terrorism through the pathologizing of its female executors. The extreme juxtaposition of maternal images of especially Gudrun Ensslin and Ulrike Meinhof prior to their lives underground with subsequently sexualized images and descriptions of heterosexually unbound women and/or crazy lesbians projected cultural fantasies of both sexual desire and violent abjection.[68] Both these aspects created narratives of irrationality and unnatural gender perversion that depoliticized armed women's actions and ignited debates in feminist communities about how to understand the relationship between these women's challenges, which aroused such widespread fear and hatred, and feminist politics that broadly reject political violence.

These two aspects can be found in the RAF coverage in *Der Spiegel*, Germany's most prominent weekly news magazine. *Der Spiegel* is known for its "story" format, which garners the reader's interest in an issue not only through traditional presentations of a coverage's news value but by "packaging" it in a context that often personalizes and narrates the events and often serializes them: "The story comments while it narrates the facts."[69] This format often demands a political position of the writer, even if voiced indirectly. Many articles in *Der Spiegel* are published without the writer's name, which contributes to a universalizing effect of the narrated event. A clear leftist voice in the postwar media landscape,[70] *Der Spiegel* in the 1970s considered itself the direct opposite to the Springer-dominated tabloids, especially the notoriously right-wing *Bild*. By the mid-1970s, its reach in particular with educated middle-class readers was impressive,[71] which is relevant because it overlaps with the demographic of feminist activists in the autonomous women's movement: "As early as 1970 it reached close to a quarter of the entire population above 14 years."[72] Despite an editorial adjustment towards a more centrist position in the early 1970s,[73] the news magazine still was considered a major influence on left-leaning Germans, and its shift away from the radical leftists also needs to be attributed to the overall *Abgrenzung* that was economically driven (in terms of advertisements) as much as politically.[74] For this analysis, *Der Spiegel*—as the undisputed "opinion leader"[75] in the left-leaning portion of the population—is particularly interesting. *Der Spiegel* reports often synthesize concerns voiced in the larger media, including those in the tabloids and in the conservative daily press. Images and ideas regarding RAF women that were circulated by *Der Spiegel* thus make visible some of the *Alltagstheorien* held on the nature of women. This becomes particularly evident in feminist responses to the magazine's coverage of the Ponto murder.

*Der Spiegel*'s coverage of RAF women suggests that in terms of the German public imagination, the face of the RAF has always been primarily female. Like other print media, *Der Spiegel* frequently reprinted images of RAF founders Meinhof and Ensslin (both "good" daughters turned "bad"), no doubt because they tapped into the cultural paradoxes these women represented. The danger these women pose, the images suggest, derives not only from their violent terrorist actions but from their rejection of traditional roles as wives and mothers.[76] Meinhof is portrayed as an accomplished journalist (revered by the Left and viewed as unduly emancipated by the Right) turned crazed outlaw,[77] her social descent marked by a loss of feminine appearance.[78] Ensslin is portrayed as a mother, fiancée, and pastor's daughter turned terrorist and sexual seductress or sexual servant to Andreas Baader. Still shots of a close-to-naked Ensslin taken from a small, avant-garde porn movie before her time in the RAF[79] circulated widely and consistently in the media, reducing the RAF's political agenda to sexual spectacle. Bielby observes that "Gudrun Ensslin's whole life, identity and female body are sexualized and 'pornographized.'"[80] These two women—German bourgeois society's "fallen angels"[81]—become emblematic of left-wing terrorism, much more so than their male counterparts. Their transgression is from object of desire to subject of violence, from maternal figure to *femme fatale*—a troubling of sex and gender firmly located in bodies that evade discipline. This initial evasion is punished with images of distortion and alienation once they are captured by the police, the display of their bodies *being disciplined* serving as contrast to a proper femininity (see figure 3.1).[82]

Ulrike Meinhof

Polizeiphotos von RAF-Aktivisten

„Wie wilde Furien"

Figure 3.1. After Meinhof's arrest in 1972, images of her resisting being paraded by police depict her as irrational and deranged. Devoid of feminine markers, she is presented as "unwoman." (*Der Spiegel*)

In 1976, four women—Juliane Plambek, Inge Viett, Gabriele Rollnik from the Movement 2nd June, and Monika Berberich from the RAF— broke out of prison in West Berlin. The incident made the cover of *Der Spiegel*, which read "Ausbruch der Frauen: Die Terroristen machen mobil" (The Women's Prison Break: The Terrorists Are Mobilizing).[83] The cover sensationalizes the event with the image of a knotted sheet hanging down a brick wall that dominates the cover, with the photos of the four escapees printed at the top of the page. The article conveys an almost erotic charge concerning these empowered women while contributing to the general perception of them as violating more than their prison sentence (see figure 3.2). In its reporting on the escape of the "Berlin lady-quartet,"[84] desire and fear/abjection create a tense polarity. Erotic associations invite a pleasurable disruption of prisons as all-powerful institutions of discipline: women's legs dangling out of

Figure 3.2. The prison break of four women in 1976 triggered an increasingly gendered media coverage that in turn feminized the discourse on terrorism. With the headline "The Women's Prison Break: The Terrorists Are Mobilizing," the newspaper warned German citizens of the gendered threat. (*Der Spiegel*)

Figure 3.3. Sexualized images like this—that had no relation to the report on four women's escape from prison—framed terrorism as inherently female. (*Der Spiegel*)

prison windows tantalize the reader (imprisoned dangerous women are projected as unattainable objects of desire, while the photo was actually reportedly taken during a protest of women prisoners—see figure 3.3). Images of women with guns not related to the actual event emphasize the lethal potential of armed women beyond the context of the prison break: one is a woman identified by the caption as Gabriele Kröcher-Tiedemann[85] threatening a man with a gun, and the other is the Palestinian guerilla Leila Chalid brandishing an assault weapon (see figure 3.4).[86] By 1981, a wanted poster distributed throughout the country suggests the extent to which women were associated with left-wing terrorism in West Germany: the poster shows that ten of fifteen terrorists wanted by the police were women (see figure 3.5).[87]

Media coverage was central in the reporting on, understanding of, and—in combination with the state and the terrorists themselves—actual production of terrorism as a phenomenon, including the *Feminismusverdacht*, which charged women's liberation with inciting violence.[88] These discourses featured a variety of actors, and while mass print media such as *Der Spiegel* drowned out many of the diverging voices—the number of issues of movement publications circulating was minimal in comparison and larger media outlets generally ignored movement publications—debates *within* feminist political subcultures did take place. Knowing about them enables a more comprehensive understanding of how political violence has been theorized outside a sexist mainstream public space and within contentious feminist communities. The debate on women's participation in armed struggle is reflected within movement publications, in which many responded to what activists viewed as sexist media coverage. A close reading of original publications in direct response to specific mainstream media's depiction of militant women illuminates the gendered relationship between ideology and political strategy and how that relationship was debated among feminist activists. A dialogue emerged among feminists from the autonomous women's movement, mainstream culture's "opinion leader"—the media—and radical feminist political activists, in which these groups debated how terrorist acts constituted a violent disruption of both the social contract and gender prescriptions. Socialist and anarchist feminists challenged universal ideas about gender that they believed to be underlying an emerging cultural feminism, with some claiming violent political activism as legitimate feminist practice.

Terroristinnen Gabriele Kröcher-Tiedemann, Leila Chalid: "Sie agieren als Prellbock"

Figure 3.4. Pictures of armed women next to the report on the prison break amplified the sense of danger the escaped terrorist women posed. (*Der Spiegel*)

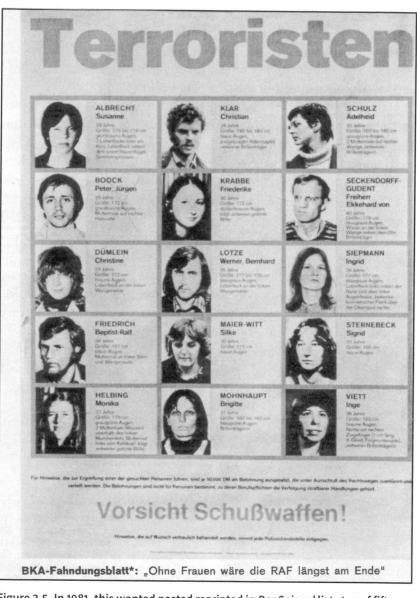

Figure 3.5. In 1981, this wanted posted reprinted in *Der Spiegel* lists ten of fifteen terrorists as women. The face of West German terrorism at this point was female.

## Women and Political Violence: The Debate in Feminist Movement Publications

Social movement archives throughout Germany as well as in Amsterdam house immense collections of informal feminist publications produced since the 1970s that were generated by activists of feminist networks and groups strewn across the republic.[89] There are literally hundreds of pamphlets and dozens of women's centers' newsletters that speak to issues that concerned feminist grass-roots organizations and local politics. The circulation was mostly small and local; at times, though, a local women's center or group published statements or discussion papers that ended up being reprinted and distributed further. An initial survey reveals that movement publications responded to the media's interpretations of women's role in armed struggle in the mid-1970s. Feminists debated women's relationship to political violence, especially in the context of an emerging criticism of violence against women that formed the major theoretical paradigm in the 1970s. Nationally established feminist journals such as *Emma, Courage, AUF!* and *Die Schwarze Botin* commented on mass media coverage, and the small local newsletters in turn responded to *both* mainstream media and the more widely circulated feminist press.

In 1977, *Der Spiegel* printed an article on female terrorists that sparked a discussion about women and political violence in West Germany, as well as feminist analyses of the armed struggle in movement publications. *Der Spiegel*'s reporting is of particular value to my analysis since it delineates *other* media's framing of the debate by frequently quoting other sources (including those of the Springer publishing house). Its report on women's participation in political violence presents a layered discussion of gender and of female terrorists' failure to perform femininity; the author uses the rhetorical strategy of first quoting extreme statements by officials or the media, and then contextualizing them. So while the simplified "hysterical" positions articulated in the article might not be *Der Spiegel*'s, the text consolidates the major concerns voiced in the media and in "expert" publications and makes them accessible in one lengthy discussion. When analyzing the feminist debates triggered by this coverage, we see complex positions developing that are not reflected in many later feminist writings on armed struggle. Positions voiced within fringe movement publications often do not find their way into research on feminist movements; thus I am particularly interested in small, grass-roots publications. The debates that my analysis makes visible challenge the prevailing view that women who engage in political violence are seduced into it and that they lack a feminist consciousness and/or any political position outside their relationship with men. They situate the media coverage of terrorist women clearly into the broader gender discourse that perceived the autonomous women's movement as a threat to the West German society and nation. A description of the cover story on female terrorists in *Der Spiegel* following the Ponto murder contextualizes the following analysis of feminist critiques of said coverage.

## August 1977: *Der Spiegel* and the Irrationality of Women in Armed Struggle

Following the events of the Ponto killing, the August 8, 1977, edition of *Der Spiegel* featured a cover story on the topic of women and violence that, as Vukadinović argues, marked the "triumphant entry of the anti-feminist RAF debates into the landscape of West German print media."[90] As shown in figure 3.6, the magazine placed Susanne Albrecht's picture on its blood-red cover,[91] evoking the tension—printed in bold on the title page—that plagued the nation: "Terroristinnen: Frauen und Gewalt" (Female Terrorists: Women and Violence).

In its coverage of the murder, *Der Spiegel*'s provocative lead-in to the story—titled "Frauen im Untergrund: 'Etwas Irrationales'" (Women Living Underground: "Somehow Irrational"), quoting Günther Nollau— sets the tone of the article, which draws on several other print sources in its commentary on both the media's and officials' responses to the murder. While the unnamed authors of *Der Spiegel* rhetorically distance themselves from some of the most outrageously sexist comments they cite, the strategic use of those comments in staging the journalists' (often more moderate) position enables the magazine to highlight gendered responses while itself maintaining a more moderately gendered language. Much of the replication of conservative gendered positions that occurs in the article derives from the authors' choice of sources, which include "experts" (on terrorism and/or on women), such as sociologists, crimi-

**C 7007 CX**
**Nr. 33**
**31. Jahrgang · DM 2,50**
**8. August 1977**

# DER SPIEGEL

## Die Terroristinnen

# *Frauen und Gewalt*

Figure 3.6. The headline "Women and Violence" front-staged the cultural paradox—death in the shape of a young girl—as central to the debate on terrorism. (*Der Spiegel*)

nologists, and psychoanalysts as well as other print media. The parading of "terrorism experts" and "women's experts" and the making visible of their pseudoscientific and political debates that previously had not been consumed by a mass audience thus effectively legitimizes existing *Alltagstheorien* about "natural" femininity and its aberrations: "The anonymous writers of the [*Der Spiegel*] article functioned as coordinating point between the quoted scientists and the readers."[92]

The second source of reference for the *Der Spiegel* article is other print media, including those of the Springer press, such as *Die Welt*. The article features images of the women wanted in connection with the Ponto murder, pictures of other armed women active in international organizations, as well as sexualized pop-culture images of violent women, such as a film still of *Viva Maria* with Brigitte Bardot and Jeanne Moreau. Strikingly, the twelve-page article is framed by two pictures of women affected by the Ponto murder that starkly contrast with the images of the terrorist women: on the first page is displayed the widow, Ignes Ponto, with son and daughter, her mourning pose juxtaposed with images of the four wanted women on the opposite page.[93] The article closes with a picture of Ignes Ponto heavily veiled at her husband's grave, flanked by two men, one of whom is Helmut Schmidt, the chancellor of West Germany in the German Autumn. The images of the wife and daughter of the murdered man supported by representatives of the state (see figure 3.7) serve as antithesis to those of the violent women, as mother (daughter) of the nation versus daughters who are out to destroy it. This juxtaposition reflects a general tendency in the media coverage of female terrorists to offer women in traditional roles to the reader for identification[94] and as point of reference as to what constitutes "normal."[95]

The writers of the *Der Spiegel* article consistently refer to women in the leftist terror scene using the diminutive term "girls."[96] This emphasizes a general tendency to frame women as (political) minors, despite the fact that there was a clear majority of women wanted by the police in relation to terrorist activities and that these women often led the groups efficiently and ruthlessly. The article emphasizes the destabilizing nature of their leadership by describing it as "macabre" and frames it in (perverted) sexual terms: these women "descended with self-destructive lust into the dark depths of blood and thunder."[97] The public, both "men and women," claim the journalists, is puzzled as to what prompts these "girls"

Trauerakt für Ponto: „Gewaltsamer Tod in Gestalt eines Mädchens"

Figure 3.7. At her husband's funeral, Ignes Ponto is being supported in her grief by state representatives. Her figure is contrasted sharply with the images of the young terrorist women whose actions betrayed both their class and their nation. (*Der Spiegel*)

to "act against their traditional role" as the fair sex, "the beautiful, the decent, the fair,"[98] highlighting the transgression of gender expectations as the main marker of the terrorists' deviance.

At the time of the Ponto killing, terrorist acts in West Germany were mainly focused on freeing political prisoners; it was a period characterized by the kidnapping and/or killing of individuals who represented the state system and who would be exchanged for prisoners.[99] The article's reprinting of pictures of RAF women wanted in connection with the Ponto killing makes their involvement tangible: the images of Susanne Albrecht, Sigrid Sternebeck, Silke Maier-Witt, and Adelheid Schulz give faces to the elusive RAF, coding it unambiguously as female (see figure 3.8).[100] Referring to the RAF's stated challenge to the middle class, the *Der Spiegel* authors subtly shift from the RAF's general goal (to upset

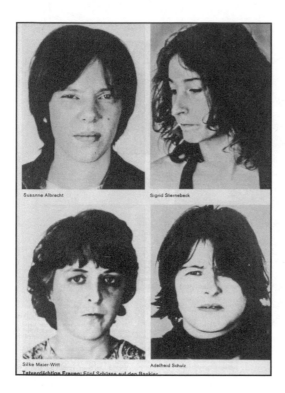

Figure 3.8. The photos of terrorist women—in the absence of any male terrorists depicted in *Der Spiegel* article—code the RAF as female. (*Der Spiegel*)

social relations by destabilizing the middle-class privileged position) to a gendered image of armed *women*, playing on (and evoking) the double threat RAF women posed. The journalists write, "[These women] could not have made it clearer to the middle-class, comfortable West Germans who is pulling the trigger now,"[101] leaving the reader to wonder whether it is the RAF posing the threat, or women. The highly gendered condemnation of the deception that made the attack possible enhances the violence of the crime: Susanne Albrecht, the daughter of friends of the house, brings flowers when ringing the doorbell. Womanly innocence here is deceit, and hence deadly. A manifestation of "the extreme limit of human perversion,"[102] *Der Spiegel* quotes the daily newspaper *Die Welt*: "Must 'every citizen' reckon that one of these days 'he'll be confronted with death in the shape of a young girl?'"[103] The shattering of the near-universal symbol of innocence in Albrecht's behavior evoked particular outrage, which makes visible the unease felt—maybe understandably—by West Germans at this explosion of gendered cultural expectations. The ultimate cultural paradox of a young girl as a figure of violent death—the abnormal performance of femininity—is at the root of the sense of "irrationality" (unrealness) articulated by Nollau[104] that was echoed throughout the public debate. The *Der Spiegel* article further highlights the deviance implicit in the manipulations of gendered expectations with images such as the "Baby-Bomb" (a woman disguising explosives as her pregnant belly), which relies on the cultural perception of pregnant women as mothers and thus peaceful (see figure 3.9).[105] Bielby reminds us of the centrality of reproduction in the RAF debates and how the employment of normative femininity serves both as political strategy and as rhetorical and visual device to discredit political motivation: "[T]he 'Baby-Bomb' image styles the female terrorists as constituting a symbolic attack on the female body, motherhood, 'nature'

**Kampfmittel Baby-Bombe, Tarnung***
„Klasse, einfach besser als Männer"

Figure 3.9. The "Baby-Bomb" as symbol for the terrorists' manipulation of "natural" gender expectations. (*Der Spiegel*)

and the 'natural' itself. It is the absolute illustration of the 'paradox' of women taking, rather than giving, life."[106] Beyond challenging women's social roles, this non-normative gender performance risks more than simply male discontent: "Furthermore, [. . .] the female terrorist is being figured as a direct threat not only to the female spaces of femininity, motherhood, the family and 'Heim und Herd' [hearth and home], but also to the nation."[107] The *Der Spiegel* article does not provide any context other than that the photo of the "Baby-Bomb" displays a reconstruction of a camouflage device for a law-enforcement demonstration—the author gives no indication as to whether it actually ever was employed by the RAF.

After explaining the extent of women's participation in the radical scene (and making the point that many of these women were "man enough"[108] to lead), the article speculates on *reasons* for women turning into terrorists. The phenomenon is termed a particular sort of "girl-militancy."[109] The author discusses two prevalent explanations given by "experts." The first one is sexual dependency (even though, the author admits, it is at times unclear who is dependent on whom), which defines women's political violence as acts of desperate lovers, not as expressions of political agency. This corresponds with the general media coverage's emphasis on sexual excess and perversion (such as lesbianism) as defining women's life underground.[110] The voyeuristic speculations as to whether terrorist women were lesbians is linked to the second reason given for women's violent political activism, which is located within women's liberation. Here, terrorist violence is an "excess of emancipation [women's liberation]" (the by-now-famous remark by Nollau). *Der Spiegel* refers to the *Feminismusverdacht* by evoking the lurking connection between the rejection of conventional gender roles and violence: with the gun as its primary weapon, female terrorism symbolizes the "dark side of the movement for full equality," *Der Spiegel* says, quoting U.S. sociologist Freda Adler.[111] According to sociologist Erwin Scheuch, women in terrorist groups can only imagine themselves as completely liberated by claiming extreme hardness and the gun—the ultimate symbol for masculinity—as theirs. As "female supermen"[112] they carry their "gun in the beauty-bag,"[113] which symbolizes the ultimate break with rejected femininity and thus connects feminist demands for the end of patriarchal oppression to political

Kampfmittel Pistole, Tarnung*: „Vorsicht, Eigensicherung beachten"

Figure 3.10. The female terrorist's gun in the beauty bag symbolizes the exchange of femininity for masculine violence. (*Der Spiegel*)

violence; the replacement of feminine accessories, especially make-up, which objectifies women as sexually desirable, with weapons is a violent reach for subjectivity. Positioned underneath the "Baby-Bomb" image, a photo of a woman's handbag emptied to show a gun, two clips, a bullet, sunglasses, and a wallet visualizes the threat of this "break with femininity" (see figure 3.10). The terrorists' "unnatural" performance of femininity—the norm of which is imagined as irrational, emotional, nervous, and soft—is further enhanced through the evoked image of RAF leader Gudrun Ensslin as "'relaxed, calm, controlled, extremely cool'" by a former RAF member, who remembers her as having "'nerves of steel.'"[114] The majority of "experts" consulted in the article (psychologists, criminologists, sociologists, and law-enforcement officers) depoliticize the actions of female terrorists, and instead try to find individual and psychological reasons for them—or declare them to be the results of unnatural gender identities. Much of their reasoning seems to rely on *Alltagstheorien*—assumptions based on pseudoscientific "knowledge" that attain commonsense status. The link to feminism, the claim that these women's own sense of identity was as emancipated females, underlies the entire article and—as Vukadinović reminds us—remains extremely problematic not the least because a definition of "emancipation" is never provided, and the term can thus be flexibly applied without a need to justify the application.[115]

The gendered stereotypes the article employs are aided by other traditional *Feindbilder* (concepts of an enemy) that draw on historic conflicts in Germany: the image of the *rotes Flintenweib* (the red gun broad/gun moll), in Nazi mythology evokes communist women in the street fights of the Weimar Republic and partisan fighters—"Jewish gun broads"—particularly in the Second World War that are found in reports of soldiers in the Wehrmacht confronted with female resistance fighters and female soldiers of the Red Army.[116] The explicitly classed image of the armed female fighter as aberrant is incessantly pondered in relation to the "fallen" upper-class daughters such as Susanne Albrecht, daughter of a successful attorney, who betrays not only her nation but her own ruling class: the *Der Spiegel* article features an insert taking up more than a page that gives a psychoanalytic reading of upper-class daughters' rebellion against their fathers.[117]

The authors of the *Der Spiegel* article succeed in maintaining a certain rhetorical distance from the at times sexist and misogynist overtones of other media coverage. Nevertheless, the journalists treat female terrorists as "unnatural" with highly (and often derogatory) gendered word choices, such as the terms "gun broad"[118] and "broad violence,"[119] and the more subtle statement of agreement with the "excess of emancipation": "That might well be the case."[120] The tone of the article becomes more neutral after the initial three to four pages on "girl-militancy" as the report moves into the actual reconstruction of the crime, only to conclude with the highly gendered (and classed) reflection that points to gender performativity's power as social coding: "The upper-class daughter one day as political killer—that is a nightmare become real. From its niches in the industrialized society, such a camouflaged murder system can unsuspectedly strike, barely to be parried."[121] The class-betraying, unnaturally gendered daughter who kills for political reasons is the matured image of the young girl bringing death to unsuspecting citizens. Both figures rely on normative femininity to be intelligible in public discourse, something feminists responding to the *Der Spiegel* article point out quite clearly.

## Women and Violence or Violence and Women: Feminist Responses to Mass Media's Construction of "Unnatural Women"

The article on women and violence published in *Der Spiegel* generated criticism by some members of its readership, which was voiced in letters to the editor that appeared in the *Der Spiegel* edition published two weeks after the cover story.[122] These letters offer an astute reading of the gender politics of the article by a number of its female audience members. And while this specific article is only one of many on RAF women, responses in leftist feminist movement circles were immediate. It appears that feminist activists within a broader political subculture critical of the "bourgeois" media perceived the newsmagazine as a major voice in German culture and attributed considerable influence to its coverage. In their responses, authors of movement publications took issue with what they viewed as the sexism and conservatism underlying the mass media's treatment of the topic.

The cross-regionally circulated feminist publications in the German-speaking countries, *Emma, Die Schwarze Botin*, and *Courage* in West Germany and *AUF!* in Austria, all debated the media representations of female terrorists generally, and the *Feminismusverdacht* in particular. The state's overzealous reach towards women and feminist groups was a main consequence of the constructed link between feminism and terrorism and was discussed in the alternative feminist media. As Irene Bandhauer-Schöffmann notes in her study of the four magazines, "The harassment against women during the search for terrorists in the FRG took up much space in the women's periodicals."[123] Each of the four represented certain theoretical positions within the broader autonomous women's movement. *Die Schwarze Botin* (The Black Female Messenger)[124] was a radical anarcha-feminist publication issued in West Berlin whose feminist politics were based in a general radical critique of existing power relations and were highly suspicious of any essentialized identity of "woman" as peace-loving and nurturing.[125] *Courage* was associated with left-socialist-leaning as well as cultural feminists,[126] while *Emma* represented the part of the autonomous women's movement that appealed most broadly to women who were not necessarily activists but were concerned with women's issues.[127] The Austrian *AUF!* (Let's Go!)[128] also entered the debate in the late 1970s, even though Austria was differently affected by the terrorism debates as they took place in Germany. None of the periodicals actually propones political violence directly or views the RAF and Movement 2nd June as having feminist politics—to the contrary, all are skeptical of RAF men and the organization's extremely hierarchical structure.[129] However, the nuances are in the details: the degree and reasoning with which violence was rejected as a political means vary. The editors of *Die Schwarze Botin* viewed the RAF's politics as misguided less because of its use of violence than because they thought it naïve to believe one could target power that precisely, and instead pointed, in Foucauldian terms, to the complexity of how power functions. Overall, the magazine rejected the new politics of motherhood and its assumptions of peacefulness, and harshly criticized *Courage* for appealing to those ideas to express the alienation and horror the RAF's actions evoked in many women/feminists.[130]

Overall, *Courage* and *Emma* took the strongest positions against the conflation of terrorism with feminism and clearly viewed terrorism as *not* liberating, and *AUF!* declared its support for those politics that end the cycle of violence.[131] *Emma* did point to the fact that life underground might feel liberating because a woman's life generally is oppressive,[132] and *Courage* at times voiced strong admiration for Ulrike Meinhof.[133] *AUF!*, while never writing of terrorism as a legitimate political means, showed impatience with the state's and the public's attention to the RAF's attack on privileged men, while women, so the periodical's argument went, experience actual violence or fear of it every day.[134] All four periodicals condemned the criminalization of women's nontraditional gendered behavior by law enforcement and its demonization by media and political discourses.

Small feminist movement publications, while not reaching the wide readership the larger feminist publications did (a readership that, compared to that of the corporate media, was still small), provide insight into how women in their own local activist communities thought about these issues. In these texts, we can find the arguments of a debate within the multifaceted autonomous women's movement that demonstrate the complicated relationship feminist activists had to political violence. Two documents in particular represent distinct positions in the discussion: one in a Swiss-based radical publication that discusses the *Der Spiegel* article from a perspective generally supportive of armed struggle and political violence as a legitimate feminist means, and the other a publication of the socialist "Weiberplenum" (Broads' Plenum) in West Berlin in 1978, *Frauen gegen den Strom II* (Women against the Tide), which, while condemning armed struggle, refutes both the demonization and the dismissal of women who employ political violence and is critical of an emerging cultural feminism. I focus on these two publications because of their detailed analysis of media coverage and of the *Der Spiegel* article.[135] While one originated in Switzerland, not West Germany, its discussion of the events can be understood as part of the debates of left-wing political groups in German-speaking Europe, excluding East Germany. On the one hand, both publications, as different as their responses are in terms of their overall feminist positions, protest the conflation of women's liberation with political violence. On the other hand, they point out the more basic cultural fear of women stepping out of line—in any way—that manifests in *Alltagstheorien* on women and violence. I will begin with a discussion of the article published in *Dokumentation zur Situation in der BRD und zum Verhältnis BRD-Schweiz* (Documentation on the Situation in the BRD and on the Relationship of BRD to Switzerland) in Zürich in 1977, "Frauen und Gewalt oder Gewalt und Frauen" (Women and Violence or Violence and Women). The second article discussed, "Terrorismus, der Exzeß der Emanzipation" (Terrorism, the Excess of Emancipation), was published in *Frauen gegen den Strom II*, in which the third article of relevance here is also printed: "Frauenbewegung seit 'Deutschland im Herbst'" (Women's Movement since "Germany in Autumn"). The author of the third article in turn criticizes a "call to action" reprinted in *Emma*.

The article "Frauen und Gewalt oder Gewalt und Frauen" comes out of a left-radical, anti-imperialist, activist context. It discusses the *Der Spiegel* article in detail, giving quotes and commenting on them. Its main issue is with the construction of women who do not adhere to traditional roles as deviant and "unnatural"—women using political violence are then nothing but an example of aberrant women. Those in power, claims the anonymous author, cannot otherwise explain a phenomenon that contradicts their historical experience; they are blind to the reality that "the result of violence against women is that women also employ violence."[136] Instead of viewing violent women as unnatural, the article "Frauen und Gewalt oder Gewalt und Frauen" proclaims that political violence employed by women is a product of the violence experienced at the hands of the state—they are *resisting*, not randomly turning violent. This was a contentious argument within the autonomous women's movement at the time. Feminists in the 1970s had begun to politically organize around the theoretical claim that women *experience* violence on a daily basis at the hands of a patriarchal system and sexist men. Nonviolence as the main expression of women's politics was an important strategic positioning that was threatened by the notion of counterviolence, which was nevertheless popular with many women.[137] Within the politics of against-violence-against-women campaigns, the construction of armed women as *countering violence* and self-defending against a male state seemed counterproductive to many.

It is important to point out that the text's feminist criticism is firmly rooted in a radical anti-imperialist context that views the monopoly of violence that the state holds in a democracy as illegitimate and counterviolence as an important part of resistance. Mainstream culture's understanding of Susanne Albrecht's "deception" as "perversion of humanity" is countered with the observation that Ponto's role in the exploitation of Third World countries by industrialized nations is understood by anti-imperialist groups as "perversion." The author employs an international revolutionary position to challenge the basic moral values of postwar West German society, of which traditional, patriarchal gender roles are just one aspect.

The article points out the underlying sexism in *Der Spiegel*'s comments on women being "man enough" to lead radical groups. The newsmagazine's inquiry into why women partake in political violence is then itself based on the assumption that political activism (and violence) is masculine. The depiction of violent women as "unnatural" and "irrational," the author insists, is aimed at creating the impression that "those women, who do not shy away from employing violence in order to fight for a more humane life for themselves and others, are not quite normal, and need not be taken seriously as a political force."[138] So instead of acknowledging that women's militancy has become a necessary premise for liberation, society views it as an "excess of emancipation"[139]—the writer here directly quoting Nollau's by then infamous statement. The article concludes that the depoliticization of violent acts committed by women reflects society's inability to conceptualize women as independent thinkers, as their acts are reduced to self-serving motives and pathologies. This further allows those in power to deny that they are dealing with a political opponent by characterizing female militants as random, crazy women: "They still don't want to face the fact that they are dealing with a political opponent whose goal it is to achieve a more humane life and who is willing to risk his [sic] own life in the process."[140] The overall feminist position in this article declares women's participation in armed struggle to be a response to oppression and a necessity in the overarching goal of worldwide revolution. This is evidence for a militant presence in the discourse that claimed violence as feminist practice.

The socialist feminist publication *Frauen gegen den Strom*, unlike the previously discussed *Dokumentation*, originated in one of the centers of the autonomous women's liberation movement; it was published by the "Weiberplenum" (Broads' Plenum) in Berlin, a well-known local feminist group. The printed issue in question consists of five parts, one of which is dedicated to women and armed struggle and has four contributions. In the article "Terrorismus, der Exzeß der Emanzipation" (Terrorism, the Excess of Emancipation), the author gives an analysis of mass media's coverage of women in armed struggle and points out the continuous attempts to depoliticize violent acts committed by women. Print media the author discusses include *Bild* and *Welt* (both Springer publications) and the magazines *Stern*, *Quick*, and *Der Spiegel*. The anonymous author traces recurrent themes in the coverage that obscure the "real reasons"[141] for women resorting to violence as a political means, framing the article's discussion with an underlying assumption that there *are* "real" reasons for these women to participate in political violence.

Sexuality, states the article, is a favorite issue in the media; female terrorists are declared lesbians with no other desires than to "be" men by wielding guns, or to have developed pathological lesbian desires during their time in gender-segregated prison.[142] The author is reacting to a tendency in the press to hypersexualize female terrorists and to link lesbianism as "deviant" sexuality with "deviant" politics. Typical of this is the tabloid *Bild-Berlin*'s quoting of a psychologist after the escape of the four women from prison in 1976, which the feminist journal *Courage* reprinted in a parody of the newspaper's coverage: "Women, who have been imprisoned for years, gravitate towards lesbian contacts. A hug, some stroking and maybe a motherly kiss already affect some women like an explosion of intoxicating desire."[143] By placing caricatures of terrorist women as converging with lesbian stereotypes (the pistol-wielding woman, the female savage, etc.) next to the news text, the authors in *Courage* problematize the way *Bild*'s coverage draws on, and feeds off, the public's illicit sexual fantasies, and how it criminalizes lesbian identity ("It is definitely possible that the escapees are being hidden by lesbians."),[144] while at the same time it frames lesbian desire as deviant and deceitful (see figure 3.11). This is reflected in the speculation that RAF founder Gudrun Ensslin, the "ice-cold seductress,"[145] seduced not only men but also women into terrorism.

The result, observes the article in *Frauen gegen den Strom*, is a homophobic equation of female terrorists with lesbian identity, both of which represent a threat to the status quo, as if "unnatural" sexual desire leads to violence, or a violent woman is only conceivable if she is known to have deviant sexual preferences. The author points out that if they are not constructed as wanna-be-men lesbians, female terrorists are "explained" in further contradictory ways. The *Der Spiegel* article depicts them as sexually dependent on men who seduce them into committing terrorist acts, or alternately as dangerous seducers of men. Family is also a theme through which women are pathologized. The author is concerned about the characterization of female terrorists as having distant fathers they desperately hate and want to hurt through their rebellion, or mothers who neglected their duties in bringing up their daughters properly.[146]

The author speculates that the evocation of "Home and Stove Ideology,"[147] which implies that mothers need to pay more attention to what their daughters are doing and that they can do that best by staying home, is no coincidence in the late 1970s when unemployment rates were staggering. In accordance with an obsession with women's role as mothers within the debate on women and political violence, these women are declared to "negate deliberately everything that defines female/feminine nature," [148] as the author quotes a female politician. This "negation of female/feminine nature" then is extended to all women who do not adhere to traditional roles—and all are destined to turn into terrorists: "The farewell to the kitchen indicates the direct path to prison."[149] The assumption that a rejection of any assigned gender roles (such as mother) leads to terrorism, the article concludes, together with the tendency to

Figure 3.11. *Courage*'s caricatures next to actual *Bild* news text problematize homophobic media coverage that criminalizes lesbian sexuality. The article discusses the state's conflation of feminism with terrorism. (*Courage*, HIS)

construct women's biology as predestined for psychosis, effectively declares efforts of women's liberation to be criminal. The overall image that "women who resist are crazy"[150] results in a psychopathologizing of militant women that "completely deflects from their political motives,"[151] echoing the characterization of female terrorists as "wild furies" in the *Der Spiegel* article. Here, the main criticism again is of a conflation of terrorism with women's liberation, on the one hand, and sexist *Alltag-*

*stheorien* on the "nature" of women that deny their political agency, on the other. Also noteworthy is the insistence on viewing RAF and other terrorist women's actions as *political*, even if the author disagrees with their political measures.

While the first movement publication clearly situates women's political violence in relation to necessary *revolutionary* violence, *Frauen gegen den Strom* takes a more complicated—and troubled—standpoint that voices feminist objections to stereotypes at the same time as it questions violence as a political means. While in a second article in the section on women and terrorism *Frauen gegen den Strom* rejects the armed struggle's "strategy and tactic [as] damaging to the development of leftist politics,"[152] like many other feminist grass-roots groups they declare solidarity with the political prisoners. In this second article, "Frauenbewegung seit 'Deutschland im Herbst'" (Women's Movement since "Germany in Autumn"), the author recounts the debate within several factions of the autonomous women's movement about how to achieve liberation. The article relates the concern of leftist, socialist/anarchist feminists in face of a growing tendency of some feminists to retreat into "self-awareness and experience"[153] and to view individual empowerment as the only means to achieve women's liberation. These politics of retreat from "male-defined politics" and a claiming of women's "culture" as separate from larger society are connected to the "Neue Mütterlichkeit" (new maternity or motherhood)[154] that allowed a new essentialist women's standpoint to dominate the larger women's movement.

The author of "Frauenbewegung seit 'Deutschland im Herbst'" speaks of one particular "call to action" formulated by women in Frankfurt in October 1977 during the aftermath of the German Autumn that was widely circulated in feminist circles. It is titled "Aufruf an alle Frauen zur Erfindung des Glücks" (Call to All Women for the Invention of Happiness). The text reprinted in *Emma* is superimposed on a photo of a happily smiling woman, who is forming the yoni symbol while raising her hands to the sky (see figure 3.12).[155] The image connotes peacefulness and joy. In the first sentence of this call, women are asked to reject patriarchal violence, and as the "mothers, the daughters, the women of this country demand to be released from the nation that brings forth nothing but unhappiness"[156] and instead to insist on their right to

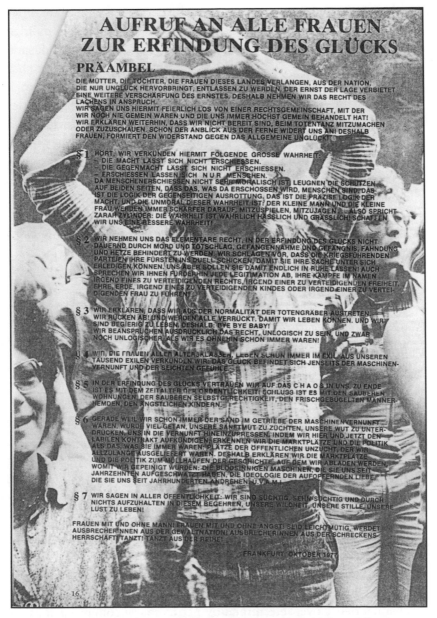

**AUFRUF AN ALLE FRAUEN ZUR ERFINDUNG DES GLÜCKS**

**PRÄAMBEL**

DIE MÜTTER, DIE TÖCHTER, DIE FRAUEN DIESES LANDES VERLANGEN, AUS DER NATION, DIE NUR UNGLÜCK HERVORBRINGT, ENTLASSEN ZU WERDEN. DER ERNST DER LAGE VERBIETET EINE WEITERE VERSCHÄRFUNG DES ERNSTES. DESHALB NEHMEN WIR DAS RECHT DES LACHENS IN ANSPRUCH.
WIR SAGEN UNS HIERMIT FEIERLICH LOS VON EINER RECHTSGEMEINSCHAFT, MIT DER WIR NOCH NIE GEMEIN WAREN UND DIE UNS IMMER HÖCHST GEMEIN BEHANDELT HAT!
WIR ERKLÄREN WEITERHIN, DASS WIR NICHT BEREIT SIND, BEIM TOTENTANZ MITZUMACHEN ODER ZUZUSCHAUEN. SCHON DER ANBLICK AUS DER FERNE WIDERT UNS AN! DESHALB FRAUEN, FORMIERT DEN WIDERSTAND GEGEN DAS ALLGEMEINE UNGLÜCK!

§ 1  HÖRT, WIR VERKÜNDEN HIERMIT FOLGENDE GROSSE WAHRHEIT:
– DIE MACHT LÄSST SICH NICHT ERSCHIESSEN.
– DIE GEGENMACHT LÄSST SICH NICHT ERSCHIESSEN.
– ERSCHIESSEN LASSEN SICH  N U R  MENSCHEN.
DA MENSCHENERSCHIESSEN NICHT SEHR MORALISCH IST, LEUGNEN DIE SCHÜTZEN AUF BEIDEN SEITEN, DASS DAS, WAS DA ERSCHOSSEN WIRD, MENSCHEN SIND; DAS IST DIE LOGIK DER GEGENSEITIGEN AUSROTTUNG, DAS IST DIE PRÄZISE LOGIK DER MACHT, UND DIE UNMORAL DIESER WAHRHEIT IST! DER KLEINE MANN UND DIE KLEINE FRAU WERDEN IMMER SCHÄRFER DARAUF, MITZUSPIELEN, MITZUJAGEN . . . ALSO SPRICHT ZARAH ZYLINDER: DIE WAHRHEIT IST WAHRLICH HÄSSLICH UND GRÄSSLICH! SCHAFFEN WIR UNS EINE BESSERE WAHRHEIT!

§ 2  WIR NEHMEN UNS DAS ELEMENTARE RECHT, IN DER ERFINDUNG DES GLÜCKS NICHT DAUERND DURCH MORD UND TOTSCHLAG, GEFANGENNAHME UND GEFÄNGNIS, FAHNDUNG UND HETZE BEHINDERT ZU WERDEN. WIR SCHLAGEN VOR, DASS DIE KRIEGSFÜHRENDEN PARTEIEN IHRE FÜRSTEN INS DUELL SCHICKEN, DAMIT SIE IHRE SACHE UNTER SICH ERLEDIGEN KÖNNEN. UNS ABER SOLLEN SIE DAMIT ENDLICH IN RUHE LASSEN! AUCH SPRECHEN WIR IHNEN FÜRDERHIN JEDE LEGITIMATION AB, IHRE KÄMPFE IM NAMEN IRGEND EINES ZU VERTEIDIGENDEN RECHTS, IRGEND EINER ZU VERTEIDIGENDEN FREIHEIT, EHRE, ERDE, IRGEND EINES ZU VERTEIDIGENDEN KINDES ODER IRGEND EINER ZU VERTEI-DIGENDEN FRAU ZU FÜHREN!

§ 3  WIR ERKLÄREN, DASS WIR AUS DER NORMALITÄT DER TOTENGRÄBER AUSTRETEN. WIR RÜCKEN AB! UND WERDEN ALLE VERRÜCKT. DAMIT WIR LEBEN KÖNNEN. UND WIR SIND BEGIERIG ZU LEBEN, DESHALB: BYE BYE BABY!
WIR BEANSPRUCHEN AUSDRÜCKLICH DAS RECHT, UNLOGISCH ZU SEIN, UND ZWAR NOCH UNLOGISCHER, ALS WIR ES OHNEHIN SCHON IMMER WAREN!

§ 4  WIR, DIE FRAUEN ALLER ALTERSKLASSEN, LEBEN SCHON IMMER IM EXIL. AUS UNSEREN TAUSEND EXILEN VERKÜNDEN WIR: DAS GLÜCK BEFINDET SICH JENSEITS DER MASCHINEN-VERNUNFT UND DER SEICHTEN GEFÜHLE.

§ 5  IN DER ERFINDUNG DES GLÜCKS VERTRAUEN WIR AUF DAS C H A O S IN UNS. ZU ENDE IST ES MIT DEM ZEITALTER DER ORDENTLICHKEIT! SCHLUSS IST ES MIT DEN SAUBEREN WOHNUNGEN, DER SAUBEREN SELBSTGERECHTIGKEIT, DEN FRISCHGEBÜGELTEN MÄNNER-HEMDEN, DEN ÄNGSTLICHEN KINDERN.

§ 6  GERADE WEIL WIR SCHON IMMER DER SAND IM GETRIEBE DER MASCHINENVERNUNFT WAREN, WURDE VIEL GETAN, UNSERE SANFTMUT ZU ZÜCHTEN, UNSERE WUT ZU UNTER-DRÜCKEN, UNS IN DIE VERNUNFT HINEINZUPRESSEN. INDEM WIR HIER UND JETZT DEN LABILEN KONTRAKT AUFKÜNDIGEN, ERKENNEN WIR DIE MARKTPLÄTZE UND DIE POLITIK ALS DAS, WAS SIE IMMER WAREN: PLÄTZE DER ÖFFENTLICHEN UNZUCHT, DER WIR ALLZULANGE AUSGELIEFERT WAREN. DESHALB ERKLÄREN WIR DIE MARKTPLÄTZE UND DIE POLITIK ZUM MÜLLHAUFEN DER GESCHICHTE, AUF DEM WIR ABLADEN WERDEN, WOMIT WIR GEPEINIGT WURDEN: DIE BLÖDSINNIGEN MASCHINEN, DIE SIE UNS SEIT JAHRZEHNTEN AUFGESCHWATZT HABEN, DIE IDEOLOGIE DER AUFOPFERNDEN LIEBE, DIE SIE UNS SEIT JAHRHUNDERTEN ANDREHEN, U.V.A.M.!

§ 7  WIR SAGEN IN ALLER ÖFFENTLICHKEIT: WIR SIND SÜCHTIG, SEHN-SÜCHTIG UND DURCH NICHTS AUFZUHALTEN IN DIESEM BEGEHREN, UNSERE WILDHEIT, UNSERE STILLE, UNSERE LUST ZU LEBEN!

FRAUEN MIT UND OHNE MANN! FRAUEN MIT UND OHNE ANGST! SEID LEICHTMÜTIG, WERDET AUSBRECHERINNEN AUS DER GEWALTNATION! AUSBRECHERINNEN AUS DER SCHRECKENS-HERRSCHAFT! TANZT! TANZT AUS DER REIHE!

FRANKFURT, OKTOBER 1977

16

Figure 3.12. In 1977, this call to action was distributed in feminist publications. It naturalizes women's peacefulness and codes feminist politics as separate from both the radical Left and mainstream society/the state. (*Emma*, APO-Archiv, Ordner: Frauenbewegung)

laughter. In the authors' view, by resorting to their "female" qualities of peace and nonviolence, women stand outside of power and politics: "We, women of all ages, always already live in exile. From our thousand exiles we announce: happiness lies beyond machine-reason and shallow emotions."[157] They declare public space as patriarchal, the politics it produces as useless: "Therefore we declare the market place and politics to be the garbage dump of history, where we will unload that with which we have been tormented."[158] The call imperatively demands that women remove themselves from patriarchal destruction and despair (terrorism and state repression): "[B]e light-hearted, become escapees from the nation of violence, escapees from the reign of terror. Dance, dance out of line!"[159]

Responding to this call, the author in *Frauen gegen den Strom* declares this to be a dangerously naïve and apolitical position. She writes,

> Our "happiness" is not independent from social power relations, to whose change we want and have to contribute actively. And *how* are we to "dance out of line" when we are denied our basic rights every day and the repression against us continuously intensifies? Supposedly only if we wear blinders! This "call to action" rather is aimed at getting us back to where those in power wanted us in the first place![160]

The author views the "peaceful" feminist position not only as unrealistic and apolitical but also as ignorant of women's participation in oppression and of the complex interrelations of global capitalism, imperialism, and patriarchy. Instead of viewing women's political concerns as separate from others', the author in *Frauen gegen den Strom* criticizes the naturalization of women as peaceful and of their activism as nonviolent (and as *outside* of violence) as reproducing many of the assumptions about women's nature found in mainstream media.

The article not only thematizes the need to challenge sexist representations but also cautions readers to be wary of feminists resorting to characteristics overdetermined by patriarchal ideology, such as an essentialist womanhood derived from an identity as mother and a resulting inherent peacefulness. Both mainstream gender ideology and cultural feminism speak to the need to *explain* women's engagement with political violence—while men's terrorist activities are condemned as morally wrong political choices, they do not warrant the same cultural and psychological investigation women's violence does.

This discursive need to turn to universal notions about the female gender for explanations is cleverly captured in a sarcastic pamphlet beginning with "Ihr Weg zum Terrorimus ist vorgezeichnet, denn . . ." ("Her Path to Terrorism Is Predetermined, Since . . ."),[161] which quotes media headlines beneath the photo of a smiling young woman (see figure 3.13):

> Her path to terrorism is predetermined, since . . .
> . . . she is at times aggressive (*Bild*)
> . . . she is from a good/respected family (*Stern*)
> . . . she is thin and small-boned (*Stern*)
> . . . she has a confident demeanor (*Bild*)
> . . . her toilet is frequently flushed (*Bild*)[162]
> . . . students get caught up in these things more easily (*Spiegel*).[163]

The pamphlet makes visible the cultural paradox that has mainstream culture resort to *Alltagstheorien* about women's "nature" and that a diverse range of feminist voices responded to. The position of cultural feminists—that women need to remove themselves from violent conflicts that are not theirs—is criticized from within the autonomous women's movement as naïve and self-serving. The danger, according to the argument, is that a claiming of "female values" depoliticizes women's agency as much as traditional gender roles do.

My analysis of small feminist movement publications complicates the notion of a universal feminist political subjectivity by insisting on historical specificities of women's activism. However, some contradictions emerge in these responses to the media's framing of women and violence that pose a dilemma for feminists, which Paczensky addresses as follows:

> When the fight against terrorism suddenly degenerates into a fight against emancipation, when female suspects are persecuted and branded not only for their delinquencies but beyond that as insubordinate women, then this persecution is also aimed at myself and at my efforts for change. [. . .] If the rejection of violence, the horror at a group who wants to de-

Figure 3.13. This pamphlet highlights the cultural compulsion to explain (and contain) women's participation in violent politics. The absurd accusations de facto criminalize women's existence. (Anonymous, APO-Archiv, Ordner: Frauenbewegung)

stroy itself and our society, is at the same time turned into a rejection of active women, into a surrendering of protest and necessary rage, then I am paralyzed by this conflict between two affinities.[164]

Furthermore, feminist outrage at the assumption that terrorism is an "excess of emancipation" leaves unanswered the troubling question of why revolutionary spaces seem to allow women greater participation than most other social arenas—after all, the percentage of women in the RAF only reflects their proportion in the wider population. A rejection of *Alltagstheorien* that explain female delinquency with either a natural disposition for deviance or with "nonfemaleness" at the same time should entail an analysis of *Alltagstheorien* on masculinity and the naturalization of male violence.[165] "It is not enough to disclaim the connection between terror and emancipation; for the sake of our own conflicting loyalty we need to examine [this connection] thoroughly and conscientiously."[166] In their justifiable indignation at the sexist portrayal of RAF women, West German feminist movement publications (and the autonomous women's movement in general), while pointing out the contradictions inherent in *Alltagstheorien* on women, at times fail to thoroughly engage with these underlying contradictions and their implications for feminist politics. Some implications include conflicting theories of gendered political subjectivity and the need to conceptualize women's political decisions as geared *towards* liberation and not as based in a feminist subjectivity constructed *through* liberation. While the violent politics of the RAF pose moral questions, the fact that they were executed through gendered transgressions makes them a threat to the existing gender order—and evokes the necessity to examine them as feminist practices.

# The Gendered Politics of Starving

## (State) Power and the Body as Locus of Political Subjectivities in the RAF Hunger Strikes

Against their terrorist program there certainly exists only one thing—to fight and to attack even from the most extreme defensive position, that of isolation, with what they cannot take from us without killing us: our collective consciousness and our will to win. It is a question of power.

⋆ "Hungerstreik-Erklärung [Hunger Strike Statement] vom Dezember 1984"

## Introduction

In 1981, four women in a Berlin prison participated in a hunger strike organized by forty prisoners throughout West German prisons.[1] When some of them were so weakened by their starvation that their lives were threatened, the medical director of the facility had them brought to the hospital tract of the prison and ensured that they had direct contact with each other as their health was monitored by the medical staff. Karin, one of the women on hunger strike, remembers how the proximity of the other inmates during this time strengthened her in her resolve to continue with the strike and how appreciative they were of the doctor's orders, which were in direct violation of prison regulations.[2] Most importantly, the physician refused to force-feed the prisoners, against the directives of prison authorities and politicians in the justice department. The prisoners interpreted the physician's decision as a demonstration of his respect for their integrity and rights as his medical patients who were refusing a medical treatment. The decision to, as Karin frames it, "use one's own body as weapon" against the state was driven by a sense that—locked away from the public eye—the prisoners were targets of the state, whose aim was to destroy them as individuals and as a political group through imposing intolerable conditions of detention. As Karin explains, "So we thought, we'll turn this around. If you [the state] want people dead, we'll give that to you—but *publicly*, officially this will go on your account." The four women survived the strike (one of several they participated in), even though some experienced physical damage as a result, such as temporary partial blindness and other irreparable injuries. The physician, Volker Leschhorn, who seemingly defied the pressures of his political superiors and public opinion by adhering to his code of medical ethics, later committed suicide. He was charged with undermining official policy on how to treat political prisoners on hunger strike and with that the interest of the state. However, he had the full professional support of other Berlin physicians and colleagues who evaluated his actions not only as in accord with (international) medical standards but as more effective in preventing harm and escalation. When considering his suicide in the light of the intense debates among RAF prisoners, state officials, and the medical staff of prisons on the politics of force-feeding—debates that were discussed and evaluated in public opinions in the media and at political events—one could argue that he was escaping the humiliation and isolation he experienced from colleagues and administrators after the 1981 strike.[3]

The four female prisoners during the hunger strike of 1981 were all RAF members, and some were also former members of Movement 2nd June. They utilized their bodies, hidden as they were from the public behind prison walls, to exert and develop political agency. Their enemy, the "state," was mostly conceived by them as a homogeneous entity that utilized its institutional apparatus to persecute RAF prisoners, when in reality the state appears multilayered in its contradictory institutional manifestations: politicians, law enforcement, the judicial arm, prison directors, wardens, and the medical staff of the prisons, though all committed to national security, define the prisoner and her/his body in their relationship to the state differently. The physician's actions as those of a state representative, though most likely driven by his medical ethics and not by attempts to enable the prisoners' politicization of their position, nevertheless allowed the prisoners to frame the body as an extension of the prisoner's political subjectivity that should not be violated and appropriated by the state through force-feeding. His refusal to force-feed the women against the orders of his nonmedical superiors thus made him complicit in their politicization of their bodies.

In turn, the doctor's decision to prioritize his medical concerns over the state's broader interests made it impossible for him to continue his work professionally (they relegated him to a desk job) and in retrospect he is depicted as having despaired over his expulsion from liberal society as a civil servant.[4] His case became representative of the conflict among the state, prisoners, the public, and medical professionals in which control over the body became the central point of contention. The role the body plays in this conflict between prisoners and the state is significant—so significant that it destabilizes the claim of a rational, universal political subjectivity *outside* the body. This destabilization carries gendered implications: historically, the (white) male body signaled an ability to reason separately from physical existence, while the female body stood for an embodied subjectivity that barred access to reason, and thus to political subjectivity. A foregrounding of the body in political conflict thus implies a feminization of political subjectivity. The second significance of this narrative lies in the hunger strike as a means of using the body in a political conflict and follows the first: self-starvation is, in a Western context (as well as many others), associated with femininity, initially seen in religious fasting and most recently with the anorexic and/or dieting woman. The prison hunger strike is a politicization of that feminized subject position.

Considering the gendered constellations of body, political activism and subjectivity, state and public discourse, the politicization of voluntary starvation, and the way feminist theories have conceptualized the body's relationship to politics, I argue that we need to understand hunger strikes as feminist political gestures. Hunger strikes foreground the body as locus for political subjectivity and undermine the liberal concept of reason—i.e., the mind—as the basis for political participation. The general nature of hunger strikes as conducive to feminist theorizing is brought into particular relief with the RAF hunger strikes: the RAF's threat to German society and national security was presented by both state and public discourses as a female one (with 50 percent of RAF members being women), as a feminized one (the group's violent politics mirroring an irrational and insane mind), and as one emanating from the liberation demands of the autonomous women's movement (as an "excess" of women's emancipation).[5] Finally, in the case of RAF *women*, these dynamics are intensified, since they already lived in the social system as women, which informs their prison experiences and those of the hunger strikes. The main question pursued in this chapter is not whether RAF women (or men) participating in the hunger strikes identified as feminist subjects, or whether their demands included issues marked as "women's," but instead whether their practice of using the body in their bargaining with the state opens up the possibility for an alternative subject position that allows for collectivity that undermines the gendered politics of the autonomous liberal subject.

### The RAF, Hunger Strikes, and Feminist Theory

Until very recently, the meaning of the RAF hunger strikes has not been the object of serious study in the debate on the history of the RAF and other terrorist groups. The hunger strike phenomenon was viewed mainly as a manipulative, narcissistic spectacle that protested the consequences (conditions of detention) brought upon the prisoners by their own actions (terrorism).[6] The depoliticization of the hunger strikes denies them the quality of "real" political acts and instead paints them as simply a continuation of terrorist means—this time from behind prison walls. While the hunger strikes' power to generate support from outside has been acknowledged, their meaning as political strategy and as raising legitimate political concerns has only lately been considered more closely.[7] I argue that a gendered analysis of the RAF hunger strikes in fact offers an opportunity to reconceptualize political hunger strikes outside a frame of "we don't like their politics therefore hunger strikes cannot be seen as political" that dominates German engagement with the RAF hunger strikes by focusing on political subjectivity as it is produced in a collective identity/action *through the body*.

In their official statement on the RAF's eighth hunger strike in February 1981, the left-wing militant group declared that "after years of isolation from one another and excluded from all shared political process and the world outside, we are determined to break through the separation with our only effective measure—the collective unlimited hunger strike—and to fight for the conditions for a collective learning and work process, so that we can survive as humans."[8] Thus the political dimension of the RAF's hunger strikes manifests as a desperate last measure, as well as a collective action. By the mid-1970s, the successful politicization of the hunger strikes was central to the group's survival inside and outside of the prisons—it would dominate much of radical left activism into the late 1980s. Self-identifying as political prisoners, the RAF organized hunger strikes to protest solitary confinement, "information shutdown," and other conditions of detention. At times, the state responded with violent force-feeding of the prisoners on strike. Once the prisoner's life was in imminent danger, force-feeding of hunger strikers was interpreted by the criminal justice system as mandatory on the basis of (West) German law, which makes the state accountable for its prisoners' physical condition.[9] However, this practice was highly controversial. The ambiguity of the legal situation was underscored by medical professionals as well as ethicists and human rights activists, who denounced the practice as inhumane and as a violation of human rights. Two prisoners died of starvation and complications induced by force-feeding during the fifteen-year span of political hunger strikes in West Germany.[10]

A large number of the prisoners who participated in the strikes in prisons across West Germany (ranging from thirty-five to one hundred prisoners at a time) were women. Together with male prisoners, they organized hunger strikes in their facilities and politicized their actions by using their bodies as tools for negotiations with the state. This chapter explores the implications of these West German women's act of starving for their political agency in the context of a feminist discourse on the body. More specifically, since any hunger strike intensely involves the body by expressing political agency in corporeal terms, I am interested in the connections (and divergences) between feminist theories that have critically delineated a woman's assumed subjectivity as connected to her body in patriarchy's political order, on the one hand, and the starving prisoner, on the other. How does a feminist focus on the body shift a liberal/enlightened political subjectivity towards a more radical, collective identity in the context of the collective hunger strike that uses bodies to assert a politicized presence?

The RAF's political actions generated a great deal of gendered (and sexualized) media coverage—female RAF members troubled prevalent assumptions about the gender of violence and the terrorist group was conceptualized as a particularly *female* threat.[11] Interestingly, there does not seem to be a focus on women within media discussions of the hunger strikes. On the contrary, mainstream media focused on male prisoners on hunger strike (propelled also by the fact that the two prisoners who died in the context of hunger strikes were men), both in imagery and in general coverage.[12] Conservative media dismissed RAF prisoners as cowardly blackmailers of the state and attempted to discredit prisoners on hunger strike, while the liberal press was concerned about human rights violations, such as in the force-feeding following the second hunger strike. Leftist activists used hunger strikes to mobilize solidarity and visibility for the RAF by referring to the prisoners as victims of state abuse. Throughout this political and public discourse, women who were using their bodies as political tools were barely commented on *as women* by the press, by activists, or in scholarship, nor is the gendered nature of the political hunger strike discussed.[13] Despite this, prisoners on hunger strike were consistently feminized in their treatment and handling by the West German state, in a manner that echoed conventional medical treatment of women with hysterical conditions and/or eating disorders. This curious dynamic of invisible starving women and a feminization of the (male) prisoner on hunger strike (as coward/victim) is central to an understanding of the political meaning of hunger strikes.

A third factor within this gendered constellation (invisible female prisoners and the feminized starving body) is the lack of engagement within feminist scholarship with the political hunger strike and its significance for theorizing female political subjectivity.[14] Considering the body's impact on political subjectivity as it is theorized both in (male-dominated) Western philosophy as well as in feminist counterdiscourses, it appears that a feminist analysis of the practice of hunger strike as a political act is sorely needed. However, while the body features prominently in feminist criticisms of classical political theory, particularly in relation to liberalism, the employment of the body in the political act of hunger striking has not been incorporated into a feminist conceptualization of political resistance. This is the case for RAF scholarship in particular and feminist studies more broadly, with important exceptions such as Begoña Aretxaga's work on IRA women.[15]

From this (gendered) silence surrounding the RAF hunger strikes arises the specter of liberal politics of the body, in which mind and body are situated as two conflicting entities of human existence. Here the female body (erased in liberal thought as a threat of excess that might annihilate the political mind) is evoked in a strategic gesture of resistance against the state. For me, a feminist scholar interested in a cultural and historical understanding of women's participation in the RAF, the important question that arises is how the utilization of the (feminized) body as the site of resistance disrupts the liberal (political) subject that dominates discussion on political violence in the context of the RAF[16] by making visible a major contradiction in Enlightenment discourse: the mind's elevation from the body as constitutive of political subjectivity, while the mind effectively relies on the body for its existence. Thus my focus is twofold: one is on hunger strikes as signifying a female (or, rather, feminized) political subject position in general inhabited by both women and men (the practice as a feminized trope), the other on women participating in hunger strikes in particular (female political subjectivity in the context of hunger strikes). After a brief discussion of hunger strikes as a political strategy, I provide some background information on the RAF strikes in particular, the way public discourse and the state framed the hunger strikes, and how that framing was implicitly gendered. I then introduce the way feminist (liberal) thought challenges the body as limitation as declared by patriarchal authority. Finally, I then examine how these gendered concepts of embodied political subjectivity apply to the RAF hunger strikes and the implications that arise for feminist political thought on the body and violence.

In my placement of feminist political theories on the body in conversation with the phenomenon of the RAF's strategic utilization of the body and the state's/public's responses to it, I draw from published sources (autobiographical accounts and the extensive clandestine information exchange system that enabled the RAF to coordinate the early strikes and to secure group coherence: a set of letters smuggled through the prison system during the early hunger strikes [1973–77], which is generally referred to and has been published as *das info*). I use social and historical studies of the RAF, movement publications on hunger strikes, including the official hunger strike statements addressed to the state and the public, which were circulated in the leftist political scene and are collected in a variety of archives. I also consider news coverage, state documents (counterterrorism units' reports and prison officials' letters) as well as attorney's letters, and personal interviews with three women who participated in several hunger strikes and were incarcerated between eleven and eighteen years.

## Hunger Strikes as Political Strategy

In *The Hunger Artists*, Maud Ellmann observes that the meaning of hunger is cultural, that despite its physical root its significance for the afflicted is always situational, referencing Foucault's notion of the body as inscribed through discourse: "[H]unger exemplifies the fact that the body is determined by its culture, because the meanings of starvation differ so profoundly according to the social contexts in which it is endured."[17] Voluntary starvation thus serves a variety of goals: often it is associated with religious and spiritual fasting, which is understood as a means of cleansing and preparation for spiritual quests. In contemporary Western culture, the refusal of food is most commonly associated with eating disorders, in particular anorexia nervosa. These two forms of fasting—religious and anorexic—together with the public starving of hunger artists, are often examined in relation to each other, with a historical continuity in the fact that the majority of those engaging in the fasting practices tend to be women.[18] The political hunger strike is rarely part of this "taxonomy of self-starvation."[19] However, the organized hunger strike as part of the political landscape of state repression and resistance is significant; a corporeal manifestation of political subjectivity, it is separate from "ascetic forms of self-starvation."[20] Hunger strikes are associated with historical figures such as Gandhi, who employed them as powerful forms of symbolic political protest. Historically, political groups of women have also resorted to hunger strikes, such as British, Irish and U.S. suffragettes protesting their imprisonment and exclusion from political participation. Generally, hunger strikes are viewed as a passive/nonviolent form of resistance, and have been "feminized" accordingly, especially in colonial settings (e.g., India and South Africa) and of course in the case of the suffragettes. The gendered meaning of hunger strikes here is not reduced to the reading of the practice as feminine or masculine in Western reception, but also manifests in the practices of hunger/fasting within colonized cultures. As Ellmann points out, "Gandhi [. . .] learned to fast from his devout mother, and his hunger strikes against the British raj owed much of their effect to their roots in feminine religious practices."[21] On the other hand, the construction by the public and the state of hunger-striking suffragettes as hysterical women who needed to be force-fed for their own good[22] was countered by a feminist reading of force-feeding as rape and as a symptom of the patriarchal state that denied them the vote. Both readings solidify the feminized subject as the agent of the hunger strike.

This feminization of hunger strikes builds on a gendered ideology that associates violence with masculinity (the state with its monopoly of violence here is clearly masculine, with police and military as its armed enforcers), and more specifically—this in particular in a colonial or racial-apartheid context—with a *white* masculinity. The association of masculinity with violence creates a paradox that is at the center of liberal political discourse and its narrative of progress: while nonviolent resistance in liberal discourse is debated as the only form of acceptable dissent (civil disobedience), at the same time (male) activists who employ nonviolent resistance against the state/society are feminized, i.e., declared nonthreatening and infantile in a normative gendered framework.[23] Simultaneously, any violent political activism that challenges the liberal (democratic) state outside its authorized means (public debates, elections, etc.) is viewed as irrational, cowardly, backward and—as I argue—feminine by association.[24] The group prison hunger strike as a political strategy that refuses accepted forms of civil discourse falls into this category.[25]

In recent history, self-starvation has been employed as a political strategy by *state prisoners* in various countries and contexts—including apartheid South Africa, British-occupied Northern Ireland, Israel, and preunification West Germany as well as postunification Germany, Turkey, and the U.S. Navy's prison complex in Guantanamo Bay, Cuba. Usually considered a desperate last measure, which aims at forcing the state to negotiate prison conditions or to protest trials and other judicial procedures, hunger strikes are often organized by prisoners who are incarcerated for criminalized political affiliations and/or actions. For a hunger strike to have successful results, it needs publicity through media and active support through local and international networks outside of prisons. Otherwise, the hunger strike remains invisible and negotiations with the state lack pressure, since its authority is not monitored from the outside. In order for the strike to be readable as protest, a "declaration of intention,"[26] usually a hunger strike statement, is published in the media and/or circulated in supportive political movements that subsequently become mobilized.[27] Media coverage and public debate force the state to publicly respond to the protest. *Visibility* of the starving body is key: it is not the starving itself, but the "spectacle of their starvation"[28] that effectively challenges the state during a hunger strike.

Depending on the legal framework their judicial system prescribes, states often respond with force-feeding of starving prisoners. This violent procedure (which generally takes place under strong opposition of the prisoner) is both ethically controversial, as it interferes with the prisoner's self-determination, and medically dangerous, as the starved body is volatile and its reaction to nutrition unpredictable.[29] Force-feeding is often viewed by those opposing the state as a logical extension of the state's unlimited control of, and access to, the political prisoner. Confronted with the threat of prisoners publicly dying while under its control, the state is forced to account for its response to the prisoners' demands—a requirement often amplified by international pressure. Ultimately, the hunger strike as a political strategy does not defy but instead relies on state power over the body for effectiveness and on an effacement of individual liberal autonomy: "Because its secret is to overpower the oppressive with the spectacle of disempowerment, a hunger strike is an ingenious way of *playing* hierarchical relations rather than abnegating their authority."[30] Political hunger strikes thus both limit and make transparent the state's absolute power over incarcerated citizens and their bodies.

## The RAF Hunger Strikes: 1973–89

The role of the body in the politics surrounding the RAF's conflict with the state is clearly outlined in Hanno Balz's analysis of what he describes as "*Körperdiskurse*" (discourses of the body) in *Von Terroristen, Sympathisanten, und dem Starken Staat*: "The hunger strike becomes a weapon in the struggle for the public sphere [*Öffentlichkeit*]. The boundary of this life-threatening, existential confrontation thereby runs along and through the body of the prisoner."[31] Of particular interest here is the symbolic force ascribed to the body, its power to install meaning into negotiations of the state and German society with the RAF, and the Left at large. The corporeality of the RAF's politics constituted a major aspect of the threat the group posed—it challenged the rational and commonsense framework of a democratic nation-state in particularly gendered ways, partly because of the number of women active in the RAF. The RAF was openly associated with women's emancipation efforts (*Feminismusverdacht*), and therefore the group symbolized a feminine entity, whose violence was characterized by chaos, irrationality, neurosis, and destruction aimed at destabilizing a state and social order whose violence was seen to serve a masculine rationality, order, and social stability.[32] Julia Kristeva's concept of the abject, which she conceptually links with the maternal, the feminine, explains the fundamentally gendered threat the RAF posed. As Clare Bielby discusses in *Women in Print*, the crimes of the RAF became, in Kristeva's term, the abject of German decency, representing that aspect of the phenomenon that "disturbs identity, system, order."[33] The hunger strikes foreground certain aspects of the intolerability of the abject the RAF represents, both in the particularity of the terrorist strategies of violence and in their using of their bodies as weapons against the state. The willful risking of the body for political gain demanded by the hunger strike implies a perversion of human nature:

> Any crime, because it draws attention to the fragility of the law, is abject, but premeditated crime, cunning murder, hypocritical revenge are even more so because they heighten the display of such fragility. [. . .] Abjection [. . .] is immoral, sinister, scheming, and shady: a terror that dissembles, a hatred that smiles, a *passion that uses the body for barter instead of inflaming it*, a debtor who sells you up, a friend who stabs you.[34]

The centrality of the corporeal and in particular the looming threat of the corpse resulting from the hunger strikes instills expulsion, separation into political process beyond the bounds of rationality (or rather, the symbolic): "The corpse, seen without God and outside of science, is the utmost of abjection. It is death infecting life."[35] In the discourses of the body that emerged around the meaning of the RAF hunger strikes, we encounter the specter of the abject that keeps threatening the cohesion of the social contract—the state and much public opinion responded with abjection of the RAF, while activists at time strategically employed mechanisms that triggered this abjection to make visible its inherent violence.

The media played an important role in facilitating public debate and state responses; many news outlets also took positions in the discussion about the meaning of the hunger strikes. Aside from movement publications, which agitated and organized around the strikes, commercial print media functioned as a forum for a variety of voices, including journalists, experts, state officials, and citizens—letters to editors became important tools for exchanges on the topic. In terms of content, the medical debate on force-feeding, prison conditions, and events organized "outside" about the hunger strikes framed much of the discussion, while the actual demands of prisoners were mostly neglected. The RAF organized ten *unbefristet* (open-ended) hunger strikes between 1973 and 1989 (all pre–German unification).[36] The duration of the strikes ranged from 26 to 159 days, and the number of participating prisoners from 30 to 100 (the number of prisons involved was up to 40 at a time). Some of the strikes were limited to RAF members, though at times other leftist political prisoners joined the strikes, and some became RAF members while in prison. Demands mostly concerned conditions within prison, trial procedures, and the special status as political prisoners, which the West German state at times denied the group, while nevertheless treating them differently from other ("criminal" or, as politicized groups would call them, "social") detainees. Solitary confinement, in the name of national security, was one of the major controversies: particularly in the early 1970s, incarcerated RAF members were routinely kept in solitary confinement (including early on in sensory-deprived sections commonly referred to as the "dead tract") or later in very small groups (three to eight) in maximum security prisons. The denial of comprehensive social contact and interaction with people other than the wardens was criticized early on by psychologists and psychiatrists, who declared it potentially dangerous to the human disposition (nervous system) and mental health. A minimum of fifteen prisoners per group who were in daily social contact was recommended in order to secure mental and physical health.[37] Cells were also routinely under surveillance, which the state denied in many cases. Necessary medical treatment (surgeries and treatment of chronic ailments) were denied certain prisoners,[38] and information flow was heavily regulated.[39] While the hunger strikers demanded changes to these local conditions, they were also aiming to call attention to broader political concerns, which served to maintain a link between the RAF and general politics, and to express solidarity with the hunger strikes of leftist militant groups in prisons worldwide.[40]

The state met these demands occasionally and partially, often retracting concessions once the hunger strike ended and/or public awareness diminished.[41] Public response to the hunger strikes was split and varied according to the political moment of the strike. Ten strikes organized by the RAF took place in the span of fifteen years, so the political climate varied considerably with each strike. Balz, in his extensive study on media discourse on the RAF during the 1970s, focuses on the initial five hunger strikes, which took place leading up to the trial of the founding leaders of the RAF (the so-called first generation) and their imprisonment in the high-security prison Stammheim, built for them. He argues that the hunger strikes were a part of a campaign to further politicize the imprisoned terrorists. These early hunger strikes were accompanied by extensive activism outside the prisons, even though the domestic media took some time before it began covering the strikes.[42] The hunger strikes early on generated international interest, including a visit by French philosopher Jean-Paul Sartre to RAF leader Andreas Baader in prison during the third hunger strike in December 1974[43] and continuous observation by Amnesty International. The death of Holger Meins in 1974 sparked intense public debates, especially on force-feeding, that would frame the "discourses of the body" in the following years, which in turn would define the role of the body in the armed conflict of the RAF with the state. In the course of the fifteen years of RAF hunger strikes, leftist movement publications, activists and RAF members, commercial media outlets, and various representatives of the state would produce competing versions of the meaning of the hunger strikes, creating a complex discourse on the gendered body and its relationship to political subjectivity and expression.

## Besieged Bodies: Leftist Activists' Understanding of the Hunger Strikes

By the 1980s, the leftist radical political scene in West Germany had invested much of its energy in organizing for prisoners and supporting the hunger strikes, and many militant confrontations with the state/police occurred in this context (demonstrations, sabotage, etc.), which in turn gave state officials the opportunity to discredit the political message of the protesters. Thus the violent protests in Berlin in April 1981 during the eighth hunger strike following rumors that a prisoner had died (Sigurd Debus would actually be dead a week later) elicited a statement from Berlin's senator of justice, Gerhard Moritz Meyer, in an interview with the news magazine *Der Spiegel*, declaring the hunger strikes to be nothing but an excuse for excess and violence on the part of activists:

> We have to assume that in Berlin, as in many other large cities, we are dealing with several hundred people who are always willing to commit violence, and who use the RAF hunger strikes in particular as a reason to begin riots. And we also know that there was not only rioting taking place after the hunger-strike death of Holger Meins in 1974, but also assaults on people and objects.[44]

Effectively, the violent clashes between activists and police during the hunger strike in 1981 were publicly depoliticized.

In order for hunger strikes to be effective, they require a well-organized and politicized network *outside* of prisons to publicize and disseminate information about the prisoners' concerns as well as a solid *internal* network within prison walls.[45] The RAF was aware of the importance of publicizing the strikes and—starting with the second hunger strike—circulated official hunger strike declarations/statements (*Hungerstreikerklärungen*) that stated the goals and demands of the strike.[46] RAF activists understood the relevance of a political movement outside that supported and agitated around the demands and integrated the strike as part of their strategy, as the statement about the second hunger strike conveys: "Our hunger strike is thereby nothing less but our only opportunity of resistance in solidarity within isolation. Without power, the violence of the street, without the mobilization of antifascist citizens, who advocate for human rights and against torture, whose loyalty the pigs still depend on—[without these] our hunger strike does not alleviate our powerlessness."[47] The hunger strikes were used by RAF sympathizers to generate solidarity in the leftist political scene and also resulted in recruitment for the RAF,[48] and were geared towards appealing to larger media outlets for coverage, such as occurred when Sartre visited Baader in prison in December 1974.

Any mobilization of the public also relies on a recognizable history of starving (or the convincing fabrication of an imagined history) to which the hunger strikers can appeal; only then can they muster the public support necessary for negotiations with the state.[49] This means infusing the hunger strike with meaning outside its immediate political context and implicating both state and the public as its witness in the act: "It is [. . .] unconscious resources of guilt that hunger strikers also have to tap if they are to triumph in their death-defying gamble. Somehow they must persuade the people whom they fast against to take responsibility for their starvation."[50] The RAF and leftist activists outside followed this strategy to an extreme with a targeted employment of images of Holger Meins, who died during the third hunger strike and who, at the time of his death, was over six feet tall but only weighed about eighty-six pounds.[51] In postwar Germany, images of skeleton-thin Jewish prisoners in Nazi concentration camps that circulated after the end of the war and visually defined the meaning of hunger were eventually eclipsed by the German population's experience of hunger during and immediately after the war years,[52] and only became more visible again in the late 1950s and 1960s.[53] Displaying huge, blown-up images of the emaciated Meins on his deathbed during protests against the state's "murder" of the RAF member created a visual (and literal) analogy between starved prisoners of Auschwitz and Meins that resonated in particular with a generation that positioned its politics as directly opposing those of the previous generation under National Socialism.[54] In one instance, protesters placed Meins's autopsy photo (generally assumed to have been "leaked" by one of his attorneys), which displays his skeletal body directly next to the image of an emaciated concentration camp survivor. The RAF member's dead body, a "corpse, seen without God and outside of science"[55] next to the body of the camp survivor—still alive but alienating and shocking in its starved condition—provokes abjection.[56] Activists instrumentalized this psychic mechanism to point to what they viewed as the cruelty and overreaction on the side of the state to the threat Meins's "blackmailing of the state" (as it is stated on the poster) presented. Both male bodies appear emasculated, castrated[57]—their starved existences positioned outside of the sexual economy of desire and want, threatening through their proximity of death and dissolution, which pairs them with the feminine's constant threat of devouring the self. By creating a visual and rhetorical analogy between Meins and a camp survivor and thus triggering abjection in the viewer, the activists—intentionally or not—contribute to the feminization that the terrorist group and the meaning of its actions underwent in the course of the conflict among state, public, and RAF that is crucial in furthering our understanding of the hunger strikes.

Demonstrators thus evoked the ghost of the Holocaust as the nation's primary signifier of hunger (and the trigger for repulsion and abjection more so than for regret and compassion),[58] to the effect that leftist activists projected fascist treatment of prisoners onto the West German state. Birgit Hogefeldt, later convicted and incarcerated as a member of the RAF, wrote of her emotional response to these images, in which she links the political radicalization she experienced with their iconographic power: she responded as she did "because the emaciated human [i.e., the body of Holger Meins] has such resemblance with concentration camp prisoners, with the dead of Auschwitz."[59] The appropriation (and misuse) of the association of Nazi fascists starving Jewish prisoners with the West German state's treatment of RAF detainees was aimed at triggering public guilt and public implication in Meins's death specifically, and in the hunger strikes more broadly, and inadvertently participated in the gendering of the body of the hunger striking prisoners as the feminine abject. This strategy expanded from the visual to the rhetorical: keywords such as "*Vernichtungshaft*" (incarceration aimed at extermination), "*Isolationshaft*" (solitary confinement), and "*Isolationsfolter*" (torture through isolation) established associations with Nazi Germany that "allowed RAF prisoners to frame themselves as the victim of Nazi crimes."[60]

Next to aggressive attempts at publicizing and mobilizing outside of prisons and negotiating with the state via attorneys about their demands, prisoners stayed in contact during the strikes through *das info*. While the hunger strike statements served to rhetorically frame the strikes for the public, *das info* served primarily to construct meaning internally and to build a collective subjectivity for which the hunger strikes became central.[61] The binding—and at times destructive—mechanisms of *das info* for the group have been well documented,[62] as well as the reliance of the RAF on media and activists to disseminate their political messages.[63] However, *das info*, with its dual effect (as both destructive and constructive in terms of collective identity), ended in 1977 when it was intercepted by the state, and the group dynamics of the later hunger strikes shifted accordingly.

### From Cowardly Blackmail to Terrorist Strategy to Sanctioned Political Expression: Public Opinion and Media Coverage of the Hunger Strikes

The image of Holger Meins's dead body in 1974 was circulated in activist communities as a tool to incite moral outrage and justification, but in the corporate media the photo primarily established an ambivalence that reflected fluctuating attitudes towards hunger-striking prisoners more broadly. Dominique Grisard ascribes this uncertainty of reaction to ambiguous readings of the gendered meaning of the hunger-striking body: "This could be related to [. . .] the sight of a feminized body. Holger Meins' body image left the consumers of media with uncertainty as to the terrorist's status—was this the body of an enemy of the state, the body of a victim of state violence or both?"[64]

Media coverage reflects the way the general public was divided in its evaluation of the hunger strikes: a progressive leftist spectrum, though opposed to the RAF's political means, sympathized with many of its concerns in prison and demanded accountability from the state (especially prior to the German Autumn in 1977, when the violence escalated, and in 1989, when the hunger strike statement of the tenth strike[65] appealed to a broader audience and included gestures towards an exchange with all social groups).[66] News coverage of the very early hunger strikes primarily resulted in a silence around the demands of prisoners and in an erasure of the prisoners' subjectivity. Instead it was the state and its institutions as well as media discourse that defined the meaning of the hunger strikes until 1977.[67] Holger Meins's death in 1974 forced coverage of the hunger strikes by conservative media outlets, which otherwise were avoiding creating any public forum for discussion of the group's politics.[68] By the 1980s, the hunger strikes had long lost their potential to shock and engage on political grounds,[69] and the contested practice of force-feeding became the focus of much of the debate. Significantly, meeting prisoners' demands was nevertheless not seriously considered as a variable in the ethical dilemma around force-feeding. Examining news coverage, expert opinions, and letters to the editor in 1981, the year Sigurd Debus died, shows how public discourse on the later hunger strikes solidified around the question of force-feeding, while his death never reached the intensity of public reaction that Holger Meins's did.

The news magazine *Der Spiegel* ran a cover story on the RAF hunger strike in 1981 just weeks before Sigurd Debus died of what is assumed to have been the effects of force-feeding. The bulk of the cover story is dedicated to an interview with medical experts, all of whom problematize the government policies on force-feeding, foregrounding the medical debate that had been taking place in this politicized discourse since the earlier hunger strikes.[70] The printing of a detailed report by an RAF detainee, Karl-Heinz Dellwo, on his experience of being force-fed, created a powerful critique of the practice without the newsmagazine directly taking that position.[71] The strategic feminization of his tortured body in the narrative feeds into the gendered dynamics that underlie the media coverage of a feminized RAF embattled by a masculinized state: here the body is vulnerable in its struggle to resist the overpowering presence of the system, echoing associations of feminist critiques of sexual assault on the female body in particular.

While *Der Spiegel* focused on force-feeding in its report, in an article the previous week, the politically left-leaning daily newspaper *Frankfurter Rundschau* raised questions about prison conditions and was concerned about how much the hunger strikes were actually about prison conditions of the individual (which could be simply solved by integrating RAF prisoners into the larger prison population) rather than a strategy to force the state to place RAF prisoners together so that the struggle could be perpetuated from within prison walls.[72] In February of that year, at the beginning of the hunger strike, the *tageszeitung* (*taz*), a daily national newspaper established by leftist activists who had been politically socialized by the APO[73] and the larger new social movements of the 1970s, provided a space for a former RAF member to comment on prison conditions and the hunger strike.[74] Its left-leaning readership used the *taz* as a forum to debate to what degree radical activists needed to support the RAF, given that their political actions, including the hunger strikes, polarized positions. Discussions in the letters to the editor section include a critique of the RAF monopolizing solidarity efforts by leftist activists, while prison conditions for all detainees needed to be politicized. Evaluation of the RAF's political actions were thus debated—and contested—within the leftist activist scene. The centrist weekly newspaper, *Die Zeit*, printed discussions of a number of moderate voices demanding that the state compromise and de-escalate, while also voicing concern about the state maintaining its *Rechtsstaatlichkeit* (constitutionality) with its hardliner position during the negotiations with RAF prisoners.[75]

In contrast, conservative media outlets and citizens generally viewed the hunger strikes as a means for terrorists and criminals to blackmail a democratic state and its judicial system. Blackmail, as crimes go, connotes a particularly gendered deviance since cowardice and the exploitation of someone's weakness signal a feminine mindset, a thread that runs through conservative media coverage and that echoes pseudo-scientific theories on gender in criminology.[76] The Springer publishing house, with its multiple print media, especially its national tabloid *Bild*, generally discredited any leftist political action and demonized and sensationalized the RAF. Broader conservative media outlets (such as larger regional newspapers) often were more nuanced in their reports, but carried the same message.[77] For example, as part of the intense debates following the death of RAF core member Holger Meins in prison in November 1974, which sparked huge numbers of protests on the streets, the Bavarian right-wing newspaper *Deutsche Wochen-Zeitung* recommended that prisoners be allowed to starve to death, and not to force-feed them, which, the author claimed, only allows them to establish a political presence in the prisons by accusing the state of terrorizing them. According to this position, the hunger strikes were nothing but "fool's play" (*Narrenspiel*): "The aim is to simultaneously make the constitutional state and its order defunct and expose it to ridicule. Knowing that sympathizers high up will take their side, the terrorists are attempting to establish their political power within the prisons."[78] The

*Kieler Nachrichten*, a regional newspaper, echoed this suspicion seven years later, in April 1981, in its questioning of the hunger strike's political meaning beyond inciting more left-wing terror: "The recent acts of violence thus seem merely the prelude to a wave of terror that, after the death of a detainee, could heighten into a highly dangerous escalation."[79] This type of coverage intimates that hunger strikes are aimed at destablizing the country's security by igniting acts of violence and terror and that the state should deal with this accordingly.

These extreme positions represented a minority of Germans; nevertheless, overall the general public seemed minimally sympathetic towards prisoners who were endangered by the effects of prolonged hunger strikes, since they were thought to have brought their health condition onto themselves. The progressive-leaning newspaper *Frankfurter Rundschau* published the results of a representative survey in January 1975, conducted after the death of Holger Meins. The survey indicates that

> only twelve percent of citizens view it as a failure of government authorities that Holger Meins died of the results of a hunger strike while in pretrial detention. On the other hand, 78 percent are of the opinion that one cannot blame the authorities when a hunger strike ends fatally. [. . .] Five percent were undecided which opinion they should take, another five percent did not respond to the question.[80]

This majority thinking stood in stark contrast to the leftist activists, whose protests clearly charged the state with failure to negotiate.

Overall, media coverage of the hunger strikes does not evince the same explicitly gendered overtones as the coverage of the RAF in general. However, the emphasis on the use of the body against the state as "blackmail" and as cowardly politics marks the hunger strike as particularly abject as a practice and the RAF's politics, which instill a "passion that uses the body for barter,"[81] place them firmly outside rational discourse and accepted political measures. The force-feeding debate's obsession with determining the boundaries of the state's power over the body and the anxiety the lack of resolution evoked in media texts draws on gendered discourses of violation of the body that mirror the RAF's status as deviant feminine threat to German society.

## The Hunger Strikes as Defamation Campaign: The State's Perception and the Debate on Force-Feeding

One could argue that the centrality of the body for the assertion of control for both the RAF and the state genders the debate from the outset. Gender and sexuality are cultural references that structure political struggles and discourse; according to Foucault, the regulation and control of bodies ("biopower") is at the core of discursive power. This becomes visible in the German state's attempt to wrest control from the RAF prisoners during their hunger strikes: the medicalization of their situation (in particular the threat of force-feeding) effectively depoliticizes the negotiations by reducing the prisoners to their bodies' perceived health condition and decoupling them from any demands regarding prison conditions. The medicalization, in conjunction with the violence inherent in force-feeding, creates dynamics between prisoner and representatives of the state that historically are gendered in the female body as object of knowledge and of medicalized violence that is also replicated onto bodies of color during colonization and other racialized systemic violence (including violence against the poor). The violent nature of the medical procedure completed against the "patient's" will discloses its punitive and controlling character.

The discourse on the RAF hunger strikes between the different factions of citizens (activists, journalists, and the general public) and the state (political, judicial, and medical authorities) focused on two main issues, both of which are tied to questions about prison conditions: the (political) meaning of the hunger strikes and the controversial practice of force-feeding prisoners. Concerning the first, the RAF's construction of the hunger strikes as a last attempt to limit the state's (fascist) control over the individual and the group was countered by the state's understanding of the hunger strikes as based on nothing but the desire to agitate and politicize for the group's terrorist goals. Officials evaluated the hunger strikes as primarily a means to recruit from the leftist political scene outside as well as inside prison walls, not in terms of actual mistreatment by prison authorities. Protests of solitary confinement and other prison conditions were thus viewed as pseudo-legitimization aimed at obscuring the true goal of politicization and organizing.

This position can be traced to the period of the early hunger strikes, such as it is formulated in the so-called Klaus Report[82] of April 1974, whose claims impacted federal investigation and counterterrorism measures. The report gives insight into how state investigators early on cemented the view that complaints about prison conditions were actually utilized to obscure attempts to grow the RAF. It dismisses any accusation of the state overstepping its democratic and judicial mandate as a product of left-wing paranoia:

> [U]nderlying the protests against torture is not so much the necessity to protect the life and health of those supposedly tortured, but above all the intent to build the guerilla organization without being hindered. [. . .] And the human rights focus of Amnesty International [. . .] is given a political dimension towards armed struggle. To see solitary confinement and other security measures as "methods of testimony extortion" lacks any real basis and could be ascribed to the overexcited imagination and the suspicion of the RAF prisoners.[83]

Later that year, the Klaus Report's position was adopted by the German Federal Bureau of Criminal Investigation (Bunderskrimanlamt, BKA) in the publication of its *Dokumentation* (documentation) of the "Baader-Meinhof-Bande" (Baader-Meinhof Gang), which understood the hunger strike as having launched a "campaign against the justice system": "[I]n fact, the abolishment of solitary confinement is pursued only to politically influence fellow prisoners and rile them up with the goal to incite prison revolts—and not the least also to make possible a prison escape."[84] From then on, the state took the official position that the politicization of supposedly inhumane prison conditions was nothing but terrorist propaganda, aimed at mobilizing a sympathetic leftist political scene. This belief was continuously vocalized by state officials in the course of the fifteen-year period of the hunger strikes, such as the one in 1981 that resulted in the death of Sigurd Debus. When asked if he believed the inmates' demand to be placed in larger groups with other RAF prisoners (a constant point of contention) to be nothing but the old strategy of "hunger strike, that is, passivity inside, produces new followers, that is, activity outside," the Berlin senator for justice stated in the interview with *Der Spiegel*, "It is a really bad development that these hunger strikes produce an emotionally determined solidarity. I nevertheless still have to assume that this is a long-term planned and targeted action, aimed at the construction of a new central command of the RAF."[85]

The second topic that dominated the discourse was the practice of force-feeding. Since the second RAF hunger strike, the federal state's policy was to recommend force-feeding of prisoners on hunger strike. However, actual jurisdiction on this decision in Germany lies with the individual states and ultimately with the medical staff of the prisons; the RAF prisoners' experiences with force-feeding would thus vary depending on the state and the prison in which they were incarcerated. Local courts were able to rule on details of force-feedings in prison hospitals, including tying prisoners' hands after force-feeding, determining the timing of medical treatment and force-feeding, processing prisoners' individual appeals, etc. These local rulings maintained an inconsistent and therefore potentially negotiable judicial front within the political battle between state and RAF.[86] Following the controversial death of Holger Meins in 1974, the law was passed, or rather, as critics claim, "hastily cobbled together" and modified in 1977, to state that doctors have the right to force-feed once the prisoner's life is in danger, and have the obligation to do so when the prisoner is in immediate life-threatening danger or if it is assumed that his or her mental capacity is impaired.[87]

Despite the general mandate to force-feed, medical staff in prison hospitals were ambivalent. Aware of the controversy regarding the medical benefits of force-feeding, the media made public the debate between conflicting medical and state interests, engaging the public in the discourse. This became visible in the discussions that erupted in the aftermath of Holger Meins's death during the third RAF hunger strike in 1974. Thus *Die Zeit*, a major weekly news and culture newspaper, quoted the German Federal Chamber of Physicians (Bundesärztekammer) at length in their coverage of the force-feeding debate:

> The Federal Association of Physicians remains committed to the task of the physician to sustain and save human life using all means available to him. However, this obligation has its limits in the face of an unequivocal decision of an individual, based on free will, to reject medical treatment and to even resist it actively. No physician can be obligated to perform such a forced treatment.[88]

The author observes that one might argue that this position runs counter to general medical ethics in Germany, such as the prohibition of assisted suicide of disabled or terminally ill patients. However, quoting former president Gustav Heinemann, the journalist claims that the case might be more complicated than this simple comparison: what if a person wants to "employ his [sic] self-determined death as weapon, as expression of his [sic] freedom and self-determination, even in prison?"[89] Starvation as political expression or tactic then becomes a defendable right. This early counterstatement to official positions on hunger strikes is echoed in an open letter sent by eighty Dutch physicians to West German prison doctors during the later RAF hunger strike of 1981. The letter cites the World Medical Association's 1975 behavioral code for the treatment of patients during a hunger strike, which clearly condemns force-feeding. The letter represents an international concern—skeptical of what many thought to be the West German state's overreach—that viewed force-feeding not as a legitimate medical treatment but as a political measure aimed at breaking individual prisoners' resistance.[90]

As late as 1985—eleven years into the RAF hunger strikes—medical experts openly denounced the state's continued practice of force-feeding.[91] The vagueness of the law contributed to the continuation of the debate, as is foregrounded in a *Der Spiegel* article on force-feeding:

> It's up to the judgment of individual states how long they gamble with starving prisoners' lives. The law contains only vagueness: it allows the wardens to almost, even though not completely, let their prisoners starve to death. The boundary at which the doctors' right to feed the starvers [. . .] by force becomes an obligation, is set by Paragraph 101 in the penal law [*Strafvollzugsgesetz*]—when the detainee's life is in "absolute danger" or a free will on the side of the prisoner can no longer be assumed.[92]

It appears that overall, doctors do not like to force-feed, in particular when prisoners express clear opposition to the treatment. Accordingly, the author points out, in 1981 the justice department "had trouble finding enough physicians who would agree to the force-feeding of the starving prisoners."[93] Reasons given here focus on the "violation of the prisoner's dignity"[94] and the fact that force-feeding with a nasal tube is considered to be at times life-threatening.[95] The journalist points to the demand by reformers that force-feeding should only take place when the prisoner is no longer "master of his senses," i.e., "is out of his mind."[96] The author does not consider that the state has a third option in addition to its choices to force-feed or not to force-feed: to negotiate with prisoners to end the hunger strikes.[97]

The medical staff as both decision-making body and executor of the justice department's will makes visible a fissure in the construction of the state as homogenous entity. The debate and disagreement between medical experts and prosecutors of the judicial system instead points to the complicated discourses and relations between state institutions that would allow RAF prisoners to negotiate, manipulate, and use the emerging discontinuities within the state's positions on hunger strikes so as to limit the state's control over their bodies. The body is at the center of the discourse and the conflict itself, and while this is acknowledged by most scholars—see for example Balz's discussions of the *Körperdiskurse* (discourses of the body)—this body and/or its relationship to political subjectivity is rarely gendered beyond a theoretical nod towards the construction of bodies through references to Judith Butler's theory of performativity and Foucault's discursive subjectivity.[98] However, the diverging narratives of the meaning of the hunger strikes that were produced by activists, the media, and the state draw on gendered psychic anxieties and powers of the abject as well as on cultural norms of gendered behaviors and relations. Their competing stories attest to the force of the hunger strike as what Grisard reminds us is a central component in Foucault's theory of power: a "biopolitical intervention"[99] that, Grisard argues, is particularly gendered in its appeal and its tactic. "[The hunger strike] could [. . .] for all intents and purposes be interpreted as a 'feminine' act of violence against one's own body: as manipulation of others by inflicting violence against one's own body."[100] The gendered meaning of the body that is underlying the discourse on hunger strikes makes visible their potential as a feminist gesture challenging the masculinized, patriarchal liberal subject.

## The Feminized Body as Catalyst of a Political Subjectivity in the RAF Hunger Strikes

Within the precarious—and tense—negotiations between the RAF and the state, the RAF hunger strikes emerge as a moment in which the gendered relationship between state and prisoners becomes visible: first in the feminized position of a prisoner through her or his body (in which force-feeding is a direct violation of that body), and second in the political subjectivity of female prisoners that is constructed through the hunger strike and that is based on solidarity and a collective corporeality. I am arguing that the centrality of the feminized body in hunger strikes points to the limits of the liberal political subject. It introduces a radical political subjectivity that is grounded in a collective identity via a strategic employment of individual bodies against a shared enemy, the state. The inherently gendered meaning of the hunger strike and the challenge it poses with and through the body to a political system reliant on the patriarchal ordering of things make the RAF hunger strike a specifically feminist gesture.

Liberalism as a political project is tied to the Enlightenment and its philosophy of reason. The Enlightenment's conceptual separation of mind and body—"man's" ability to reason, heralded as constituting the political subject of representative democracy and symbolizing progress—in general terms is challenged by critics on two fronts: first, as a universally true philosophical assessment of human nature whose attributes and privileges stemming from this ability need to be extended to all; and second, as a faulty individualism whose emphasis on individual reason and the right to private property foregrounds values that pervert the basic human need for community and whose dismissal of emotions and affect erases central human traits. Echoing either critique, feminist thought has both demanded access to political and economic privileges denied women (and other groups) through the exclusive definition of the political subject as (white, bourgeois) male, and condemned what is viewed as a patriarchal value system and truth claim based on reason and supposed objectivity.

In German history, the most consequential disruption of liberalism's narrative of progress occurred through National Socialism and its focus on the racialized and gendered body. The race discourse underlying German fascism's nationalism emphasized the role of the gendered body for the nation—the individual's political subjectivity was irrelevant beyond his or her service to the *Volkskörper* (body of the people) as soldier, worker, or mother. Postwar West Germany's struggle to embrace a liberal democracy in conflict with much of the cultural influence and legacy of Nazi Germany is thematized in the RAF and its generation's evocation of the specter of fascism as underlying West Germany's economic recovery, its political status as the final border with the East in Cold War geopolitics, and its role as ally to the United States.[101] In the context of the RAF hunger strikes, a feminist analysis of liberalism and its disruption through fascism allows for the centrality of the body as gendered entity to become visible.

## Feminist Critiques of the Female Body as Limit of Political Subjectivity

If we understand the gendered (and racialized/classed) body to mark the subject in relation to political participation, the ways in which hunger strikes foreground embodied agency defy political exclusion based on the body. Feminists have argued that Western thought has constructed the female body as the ideological limit of political subjectivity, denying women access to political and social power on the basis of their sex/gender (and by extension, bodies of color, poor bodies, and weak bodies signify the same limit). This exclusion points to the "androcentric core"[102] of Western political theory. Accordingly, experiences of an individual's political subjectivity are inherently gendered, since the foundation of political subjectivity—the body—is conceptualized within a binary gender classification system of male or female. As Thomas Laqueur argues in *Making Sex*, the naturalization of sexual differences as located in the body took place in eighteenth-century science's turn from a one-sex model to a two-sex model.[103] The application of the two-sex model allowed for the exclusion of women from newly formulated civil rights and the social contract of liberal society during the Enlightenment and the French Revolution, effectively barring them from political participation: "Based on their gender/sex, women now were denied just *those* skills and characteristics that had been declared the foundation of universal human and citizen rights."[104] The "natural" body (as either male or female) forms the basis for the new social order: "[T]he existing bourgeois-patriarchal gender order and the sex-specific division of labor that is connected with it is explained by the biological nature of the sexes, in particular that of the woman."[105]

The exclusion from politics extended to bodies other than female: the working-class, those without property, along with all women were together defined in Kantian terms as "passive" citizens, while bourgeois men were considered "active" citizens.[106] Of course bodies of color inhabited noncitizen status and further complicated the universal claim of citizen rights formulated by the Enlightenment.[107] "Passive" citizens were represented by "active" ones—women by the men heading their household, who were seen as voluntarily submitting themselves to men's rule in public. What Claudia Honegger defines as the new "gender order" in *Die Ordnung der Geschlechter* (The Gender Order) was expressed in the public sphere in the concept of the *Staatsbürger*, the citizen, which corresponded with the establishment of the bourgeois private sphere in the social sector.[108] By restricting the state's influence in the private sphere, the "social contract" of liberal society ultimately rests on securing men's access to the bodies of (white) women, who are relegated to the private sphere; this is what Carol Pateman defines in *The Sexual Contract* as the sexual contract underlying the spatial and political division into public and private spheres.

The paradox of the universal claim of citizen equality and private domination was solved by means of various concepts, all of which rested on the supposed nature of the female body. One such concept was the argument for the natural inferiority of the woman and her inability to fight wars; another concept was the ideal of republican motherhood developed by Rousseau. This ideal reduced a woman's (political and social) role to that of reproducing the nation[109] within the norms of racialized and classed femininity. Motherhood as social and cultural function then ideologically served national expansion projects such as colonialism and wars. Ultimately, a woman's inability to reason aligns her with nature[110] and thus marks her as incapable of participating in political life. The *body* as a woman's limiting factor is therefore inevitably evoked by the political hunger strike's empathic *embodiment* of political agency.

This becomes obvious when gender as a structuring force within political theory and practice is understood as co-contructed by race, class, and sexuality. Within Enlightenment philosophy, nature—the body—is reason's opponent. Women, and those men "trapped" in the excess of their bodies (working-class men and men of color), cannot escape their corporeal nature and thus cannot overcome irrationality. White, bourgeois women are politically represented by their fathers, brothers, and husbands, and in the traditions of racial hygiene (e.g., in the eugenics movement of the nineteenth and early twentieth centuries)[111] have a clear assigned role as mothers of enlightened citizens within liberal nationalism and colonialism.[112] The gendered (and racialized/classed) body as the marker of a subject's political positioning is central when contemplating hunger strikes and their foregrounding of corporeal agency as a political gesture. This becomes particularly apparent in the context of the German cultural and social history of National Socialism, whose specter haunts public discourse on activism and politics in Germany and which was deliberately evoked by West German leftist radicals in their opposition to what they viewed as a fascist postwar state.[113]

While women in Germany gained political rights during the time of the Weimar Republic after World War I (usually understood as liberalism's attempt at constitutional democracy), including the right to vote and be elected to public office, this challenge to separate spheres for men and women was met with cultural and social anxiety and resentment.[114] Fear and hostility accompanied the increased visibility of the "new woman" of the progressive era, whom many viewed as a "moral crisis"[115] for German society.[116]

The rise of fascism in Germany (and the consequent failure of the democratic "experiment" of the Weimar Republic) and its virulent antiliberalism[117] repositioned the political subject in a nationalist and racist worldview. Much of the individual-rights ideology of liberalism was negated under fascism, in which National Socialism mandated the absolute subjugation of the individual (body) to the nation (and *its* body, the *Volkskörper*) and the relinquishment of any individual political agency to the fascist leader. Women's political positions and broadened social and cultural activities gained between the world wars were negated and liberalism's expanded umbrella replaced with the reassertion of "biological destiny" (as opposed to individual rationality and intellect) as defining roles for women (and men) within nationalism.[118] The body (repressed, medicalized, and disciplined in liberal society) was openly evaluated, shaped, punished, and exterminated in National Socialism. The role the body plays in German fascism—in particular regarding its significance for the Nazi obsession with "racially pure" reproduction— complicates the feminized embodied agency of the hunger strikes as they were taking place in the post-Nazi era of the early Federal Republic.

The defining function of the female body in liberal politics and society—critiqued and challenged by the liberal bourgeois as well as the socialist women's movement but nevertheless parts of their thinking— becomes solidified within the racist political framework of National Socialism: women are physically inclined to be emotional (i.e., irrational), thrive in a separate female sphere, and have no role in the male world of politics.[119] Women identifying with Nazi politics and ideology claimed those social areas they deemed feminine to be in their control, such as "social welfare, education, culture, health care, and community organization."[120] Women's uniquely reduced role in fascist Germany rested on the racist population policy of Nazi ideology that determined their place.[121] Inspired by *Blut und Boden* (blood and soil) ideology, which links racial purity to national identity, the state took control over reproduction.[122] Consequently, a woman's body (and by extension, a man's), because of its ability to reproduce, became the basis for the categorization of her political and social status and disclosed "women" as a non-homogenous group (i.e., as "Aryan," "asocial," "Jewish," etc.). National Socialism's political ideology not only idealized an "Aryan" femininity that embodies racial purity (while denying it political agency), but actively excluded and persecuted embodied femininity deemed "impure" and deviant.[123] The female body's reproductive function is thus both fascist promise (reproducing the nation, subject to pro-natal policies) and excessive threat (to the nation's racial "purity" and subject to anti-natal, genocidal policies).

Reproduction as the main area of characterization of woman's status also defined her social space, which was seen as absolutely separate from the public sphere of her male counterpart.[124] Social power was thus limited to within the domestic space and only within the bounds of an overall submission to male (patriarchal) authority.[125] The masculine sphere in German fascism emphasized economics (man as breadwinner) and militarism (man as soldier) as well as a broader "unity of men" (*Männerbund*) that, while violently homophobic, nevertheless celebrates a "man" culture separate from women's. However, unlike the male liberal (bourgeois, white) subject within a democratic system, this public sphere is not distinctly a *political* one and does not create a general identity as individual political subject—that is reserved for the leader and his party representatives.

A woman's body's ability to produce (racially pure) subjects of the fascist state guaranteed her a place in society; because the woman was seen as the "nation's racial conscience,"[126] control (and/or repression) of her body became a priority of the Nazi state. If she failed to meet the fascist ideal—i.e., if she was not racially appropriate, such as being Jewish, and/or evinced physical or mental ailments—she had no place in society. Antifascist political activity branded her as unnatural and thus as expendable to the nation. Racially "pure" women's biological destiny to be mothers was thus interpreted as a "natural" national duty to a superior race that found expression in her support of the institutions of the Fatherland.[127]

Within fascist ideology, a body's given ethnic, racial, or genetic origin condemns it not only to political disenfranchisement but to extermination and genocide. While the female body in fascism becomes the signifier for acceptance or rejection into the nationalist community, it shares with classic liberalism a rejection of the female political mind because it saw that mind as being enslaved by the body, which is challenged by feminist and anticolonial movements. After the Second World War, the West German constitution prescribed equality between men and women. Conservative legislation, however, enacted family policy that emphasized separate roles for men and women.[128] In postwar years, the West German state/nation as well as the German population publicly embraced the rhetoric and ideology of a liberal, democratic society, which included the reinstitution of the individual rational subject, as opposed to the irrational blind believer in fascism (or what was increasingly presented as the subject oppressed by a fascist regime). De-Nazification should have reeducated West German citizens to a liberal-democratic sensibility. However, the RAF and other groups partly derived their fury from their conviction that the West German state (and their parent generation), in fact, remained inherently fascist in beliefs if not in political structure. This latent and often invisible historical struggle of the German public in redefining political subjectivity from democratic to fascist to back-to-liberal terms—and the extent to which this process was gendered—underlies public responses to the RAF's hunger strikes and the role of the state.

While historically the political participation of women in democratic societies has been instituted through the right to vote, feminist critiques point to a continued conceptualization of the political subject as male, such as in the critical theory of the Frankfurt School. This tendency, argues Andrea Maihofer in *Geschlecht als Existenzweise* (Gender as Form of Existence), conveys "that power and gender are not simply added to the modern subject, but that they are immanently a part of it."[129] Modern bourgeois thinking, Maihofer continues, is fundamentally a patriarchal-hegemonial discourse, and consists of a normative idealization of the bourgeois man as "man."[130] Masculinity and political subjectivity thus constitute each other, while femininity is located outside political discourse.[131]

The binary of masculinity and femininity, while serving as a useful analytical point of reference, easily constitutes a theoretical trap that does not account for the way sexual difference is mediated by race, class, and other social categories. Much is owed to Foucault's theory of discursive power and its constitutive effect on the subject, and to Judith Butler's theory of gender performativity, in efforts to explain female political subjectivity in relation to the state. Along the lines of Gundula Ludwig's argument in "Performing Gender, Performing the State," the "led" or "governed" subject (based on Gramsci's theory of hegemony as constituting the subject's relationship to state power and Foucault's idea of governing as a modern mode or power, respectively) is not separate from the state (and its power). Unlike the political subject in classic liberal theory, the subject constitutes itself in and through social, cultural, and political practices sanctioned and defined by the state and its institutions, at the same time as the subjects' daily and repetitive enactment of those practices forms the *basis for the state*.[132] Gender as a norm—that, according to Butler, is performed so as to achieve intelligibility of one's subjectivity—is thereby not a manifestation of natural, biological differences that need to be interpreted in their relationship to politics and the state, but instead forms a constitutive category of subjectivity itself: gender, as subjectivity in general, does not predate the state. This understanding of subjectivity makes visible the inherent violence of nor-

mative gender and its centrality in forming the subject,[133] as the failure
to perform those norms results in denial of citizenship and subjectivity by the state, while a success cannot ever be "achieved" but needs to
be continuously pursued, with the risk of non-normative performance
looming.

The understanding of the subject as constructed in its interactions
with the state undermines the binary setup of liberal subject and state,
at the same time as it discloses the immanence of liberal ideals as constitutive for modern subjectivity—the state relies on the subject's enactment of an autonomous agent to be able to govern it; the state "leads"
its citizen to internalize certain agreed-upon values and beliefs to form
hegemonic thinking that allows for the appearance of consensus. This
resists a top-down power model and instead allows for the workings of
mechanisms of both self- and external "leading" (*Selbst- und Fremdfüh-
rung*),[134] which potentially can subvert and redefine hegemonic norms
and can create what Foucault has termed "counterdiscourses." The
center-staging of gender as a constitutive element of political subjectivity within this process foregrounds the body and regulatory apparatuses
aimed at normalizing it. The body does not entail inherent truths, but it
manifests truth claims that can be enacted or disrupted by its physical
presence.

The constitutive role of the body in the formation of the subject (as
well as its existence as a *constructed materiality*) in an analysis of subjectivity allows for the starving body to be viewed as part of political discourse: self-starving a body is an engagement with gendered norms and
normative ideas of citizenship and political participation. For example,
a growing commodification of the female body insists on its malleability
towards a normative ideal defined by race, class, age, and ability. As a result, feminists claim, a woman's body has become a cultural site she feels
she can (and needs to) control, or more specifically, can regain control
over.[135] This phenomenon is generally discussed within the context of
either eating disorders, normally considered a private or individual experience (anorexia nervosa), or religious fasting (whose root in Western
history is traced to medieval female saints), which established a religious agency outside the immediate self (holy anorexia).[136]

The subjectivity/personhood that emerges from this gendered relationship of body and power is derived from standpoints that devel-

opcd out of complex historical and social configurations. Race and class, as much as gender, inform the subject's relationship to her body, which manifests in various behaviors and social orders. Gendered self-starvation—the denial of nutrients to one's own body—ranges from dieting (normative feminine behavior) to dangerously starving (pathologized feminine behavior).[137] Eating disorders initially associated with young, white, middle-class women, such as anorexia nervosa and a general self-destructive politics of starving (as Susan Bordo analyzes in *Unbearable Weight*), dominate U.S. and German feminist debates. As recent feminist research shows, these disorders spread across racial and ethnic lines at an alarming rate. Other disorders that manifest across racial and class divides, such as excessive overeating or bulimia, are understood in relation to either historical developments, such as black women's lack of control over their bodies in a racist system, or in relation to personal histories, such as sexual abuse/assault.[138]

The politics of starving in feminist discourse seem to politicize women's acts of hungering primarily by making this private act public—and political in its relationship to public cultures of consumption (media representation of women's bodies) and sexual desire.[139] As emblematic of Foucault's "docile body," disciplined by norms and hegemonic ideals, the anorexic body appears as a caricature of normative gender and seems to speak "to us of the pathology and violence that lurks just around the edge, waiting at the horizon of 'normal' femininity."[140] Recalling the constitutive aspect of norms and regulations surrounding subjectivity, the anorexic violent control of her body can be understood as "embodied *protest*—unconscious, inchoate, and counterproductive protest without an effective language, voice, or politics—but protest nonetheless."[141]

The context of hunger strikes brings to the forefront the politics of starving and theoretical implications for gendered expressions of agency and subjectivity within a particularly oppressive political context: prison. This points to the limits of the comparison of anorexia and hunger strikes: if, as feminists argue, the body becomes a site of control in lieu of social and political power, and the (waning) female body *is* politicized subjectivity, then anorexia nervosa exerts agency in self-destructive ways with no political implications outside of the individual subject, while religious anorexia is a trajectory of spiritual (and with that often political) dissent. Traditionally, the act of starving takes place outside of the "political" realm, containing the empowerment exerted through control over the body within a personalized and/or spiritual space.[142]

An analysis of hunger strikes by political prisoners shifts this relationship between subjective control and the body towards a relationship between state control over the body and political resistance. Here the body might be seen as engaged in "discursive demonstrations"[143] that force corporeality into public political discourse. The context of politicized activism, state control and imprisonment, and—maybe most importantly—collective resistance redefines the politics of starvation in ways that are important when conceptualizing gendered body politics. The corporeal manifestation of political subjectivity brings us to the hunger strikes of the RAF women.

## Gendered Locations and Collective Identities: Political Subjectivities in RAF Women's Hunger Strikes

In the hunger strikes of RAF members generally and—in conceptual terms—in those of women in particular, we encounter subjectivity constituted through a collective corporeality on the one hand, and a feminized position of the hunger-striking prisoner on the other. The basis for a shared politicized identity existed prior to the strikes: the RAF mandated a collective identity—individual identities were submerged in a shared revolutionary consciousness. This notion was partly based in a Marxist doctrine of solidarity, but became especially central during the hunger strikes. Personal subjectivity was dissolved within the revolutionary collective. This in itself poses a threat to the autonomous liberal political subject that is defined by individual will. A feminist analysis that is oriented towards a skeptical perspective of liberal political theory and that incorporates the body into political existence genders this revolutionary subjectivity as inherently feminized and threatening.

The hunger strike as a collective political project destabilizes the image of an individual "docile" body protesting the hegemonial governing of its subjectivity—such as an anorexic quietly, privately, and individually starving her/himself. Instead, central to the RAF women's experience is the strength of the collective group experience and the ways in which the bonds some of them shared with the other women during their time of self-starvation defined their act to them. Since prisons are primarily gender-segregated spaces, women participating in hunger strikes often relied on other women for any immediate personal contact. This was particularly the case when prisoners were in small groups together. Personal accounts published later by women participating in the strikes relate experiences of support and solidarity, as well as of pressure and abuse within the women's network.[144] It appears that the aspect of physical and direct solidarity these women experienced enhanced the collective identity mandated by the RAF leadership that was ideologically created and enforced through *das info* during the earlier hunger strikes.

The narratives of the three women who participated in the RAF hunger strikes all recount that their actions gave them an immense sense of power and agency as political subjects and they felt that their actions were able to change the political system: the state was forced, however briefly, to change the material conditions of the prisoners' lives. For example, having felt "administered" (*verwaltet*) and thus dehumanized by prison staff and the justice system, Karin felt "restored as a subject" through their hunger strike, her dangerous confrontation with the state. "I didn't want to die," she says, "but I started out with the conviction that that is what I had to put at stake to achieve any improvements in my existence." The hunger strike furthered a sense of self also through its collective nature, she recalls: "It created a sense of connection and solidarity." Barbara spoke of being powerless (*ohnmächtig*) prior to a hunger strike, and stated that this political action provided her with an area of influence (*Einwirkungsmöglichkeit*) that enabled subjectivity: "[O]ne becomes a subject again." The hunger strike becomes a power equalizer with the state, which is forced to face a loss of control over the prisoner: "At least for several weeks at a time," Barbara recalls, "we were able to negotiate on the same level."

A second important variable must be examined for these women though: they all had an intense perception of their group's persecution by the state. The RAF viewed itself (and was treated by the system) as a threat to the state that resulted, so the RAF claimed, in the state's goal to destroy its members literally through mental and physical torture in prison. The RAF's political potency stemmed from the fact that its members were a threat to the state while imprisoned. From the eighth hunger strike statement (1981): "The fight doesn't end in prison, the goals do not change, only the means and the terrain on which the war continues to be fought between guerilla/state, and so the state responds once again in this situation: imprisoned and unarmed—to a collective hunger strike as to an armed attack."[145] As revolutionary subjects the hunger strikers experienced their treatment not as a personal trial but as a systematic attempt to eradicate them as a group, thereby preventing any true political opposition. Thus, they understood any individual persecution as being more about the RAF than about each separate member. The insistence on a subjectivity that is not defined by individuality but that exists only in relation to the group and its political goals (this is a particular type of *erasure* of personal subjectivity) enables the life-threatening and individually dangerous potential of the hunger strike to be experienced as political empowerment (this happened with an intensity that evoked comparisons of the RAF's internal logic as a group to those of religious/spiritual sects). So we encounter a combination of hunger strike as political strategy (in general) and hunger strike as creating a shared subjectivity (RAF-specific).[146]

The act of starving that takes place in a group's prison hunger strike politicizes hunger through collective action. Consequently, creating solidarity becomes one of the desired goals of a hunger strike at the same time as it forms the basis for it. Solidarity expressed through a shared hunger strike is at the heart of a collective political identity that defies a liberal autonomous subject,[147] as the statement about the eighth hunger strike states: solidarity "is the practical expression of every single person's awareness that individual and collective liberation is no contradiction, as the pathetic apologia for individual satisfaction claims, instead it is a dialectic relationship—just as it is impossible to separate liberation here from the liberation struggle of the peoples of the Third World."[148] Solidarity—subjectivity through collective political action—becomes the tool to achieve actual collectivity of prisoners behind walls, and the hunger strike is the mechanism to enforce it. From the ninth hunger strike statement: "Where domination functions through separation, differentiation, destruction of individuals to affect all and to paralyze the entire process, solidarity is a weapon. It is the first strong subjective political experience for anyone who begins fighting here, the core of revolutionary morals: solidarity as weapon—concrete, material, action out of one's own decision for this war."[149] The collective negates the separation of public and private as the basis for an autonomous individual subject and replaces it with solidarity across those social spaces. The state seemed aware of the power of the collective that drove the strikes: Barbara remembers that during a hunger strike in the mid-1980s, she was separated from fellow prisoners in an attempt to disrupt group coherence. However, the sense of solidarity at times creates complications for the prisoners' determination to continue the hunger strike, as the vulnerability of the fellow prisoner becomes a point of concern. Karin recalls that the hunger strikes "created a strong sense of togetherness [Zusammengehörigkeit]. But also of course one of worry, when one of the others is not doing well, and you are wondering what you can do about that."

How does this relate to feminist ideas of women as political subjects and their bodies? Maud Ellmann reminds us that "in order to interpret self-starvation it is necessary to explore the cultural milieu in which the ritual occurs."[150] The "cultural milieu" of the RAF hunger strikes is prison, a distinct and complicated social space, both materially and ideologically, that challenges liberal notions of the individual's relationship to the state. As social space, prisons echo some of the constellations feminists have identified to be particular to the female subject within liberalism.[151] *Female* RAF prisoners thus encountered a social positioning that mirrors their experiences as women in broader society: as state prisoners, the RAF women were part of neither the public nor the private sphere. Their personal space (their cell) was under the control of the state. Their movements and social interactions were both regulated (e.g., no prison labor for political prisoners) and monitored (in prison yard, with/without other prisoners), and any social contact with people outside of prison was censored (letters) and regulated and monitored (visitors). In prison, the division of private/public, personal/political is obsolete, echoing woman's position within the social/sexual contract. At the same time as there is no private sphere under the individual's control, the inside of a prison is not really part of any public/political space, since it is not accessible from the outside, and is difficult to permeate from the inside (either through movement or information). The prisoners' intense loss of control and their isolation from the public sphere result in them feeling that they have lost access even to their own subjectivity through the feminization of their body. Thus, as in the case of the RAF women (and men), many relied on political action to retain a sense of control—and of self. At this point employing a feminist framework for an analysis of the RAF hunger strikes illuminates how political subjectivity is produced through the body.

In this particular situation, the body is both the main contested site as well as tool since the state is responsible for its physical condition while it is under state control. In this context, a highly publicized hunger strike catapults the otherwise nonpublic/nonpolitical space of prison cell into the public arena.[152] Force-feeding denies prisoners the control they have fought hard to regain; the violent act sustaining the body by providing nutrition is also importantly an extension of control and a denial/erasure of the political subject and its demands: it "demolishes the ego."[153] Thereby, the symbolic meaning (and actual experience) of force-feeding is as an intensely sexualized practice: the violent entry of tubes into a resisting human body is haunted by sexual imagery of rape. This imagery in turn is gendered (as either masculine-on-feminine or masculine-on-masculine sexual violence) and finds its way into accounts of force-feeding by prisoners, such as in those of British and Irish suffragettes. In these narratives, force-feeding is experienced as intensely gendered in an already gendered conflict between male state (men refusing women the right to vote) and female activists (suffragettes), such as in Sylvia Pankhurst's writing:

> A man's hands were trying to force open my mouth; my breath was coming so fast that I felt as though I should suffocate. His fingers were striving to pull my lips apart—getting inside. [. . .] They were trying to get the tube down my throat, I was struggling madly to stiffen my muscles and close my throat. They got it down, I suppose, though I was unconscious of anything then save a mad revolt of struggling, for they said at last: "That's all!" and I vomited as the tube came up. They left me on the bed exhausted, gasping for breath and sobbing convulsively.[154]

The metaphor of rape to describe force-feeding of hunger-striking female prisoners (imprisoned for their demand of suffrage) is consciously utilized to highlight the gendered violence of their struggle for political rights. It also inserts the body squarely into the context of political rights and their violation. The disenfranchisement at the voting booth is disclosed as a violent and painful denial of an individual's human rights.[155]

When trying to understand the decision of an individual to engage in a dangerous and potentially deadly practice not only to express political subjectivity but also to force the state (and the public) to recognize it, we return to Ellmann's insistence that the meaning of hunger is always situational. This is central to the political hunger strike, whose collective identity in a group setting transforms the body into a political weapon. Through hunger—the threatening dissolution of the self's corporeality—the prisoner uses the body to establish a political presence that otherwise would be invisible behind prison walls. Thereby the potential self-destruction of the prisoner on hunger strike is directed towards an outside goal, which is on the one hand defined by the groups' common (political) identity, but on the other also has an immediate impact on the everyday life of the individual who is participating (improved conditions, etc.). Also, hunger strikes are not a self-sacrifice for an abstract and removed greater political aspiration (such as kamikaze or suicide bombings), since the *threat* of the body's demise becomes the tool, not the actual death.[156] Neither are they a sanctioned risk taken for a national "good" greater than the individual, such as military service; they are taking place in direct opposition to the nation-state. Instead, political hunger strikes combine the political principle with the individual's immediate relationship to control over his or her life (this includes general political demands, but mainly relates to demands that immediately affect prisoners' lives), thus creating a challenge to domination through the separation of public and private, similar to a feminist one.

In the hunger strikes of the RAF, the (female) body remains a *tool*; it is not *disciplined* in pursuit of empowered subjectivity through internal control by wresting it away from external pressures (as in the case of eating disorders). Instead, it is used to *remove* external control from the state and—upon failure of traditional political discourse—to make visible political power. So women participating in the hunger strike of 1973–74 declared in an open letter that was published by *Der Spiegel*, "When our writing is not heard, our bodies will also prove the cruelty that you commit against us every day."[157] This reflects Grisard's assertion in "Transversale Widerstandspraktiken?" (Transversal Practices of Resistance?) that the hunger strike as mode of resistance allows a disclosure of repressive aspects of the liberal-democratic state and its supposed humanitarian interest in the saving of life: "Viewed as such, the hunger strike is read simultaneously as violent act against the self *and against the state*."[158] In fact, the ultimate goal of the prisoner on hunger strike is the end of starvation—hunger is a political strategy towards a particular end, not a goal in itself. The hunger strike, signifying control over the body as last resort, provides political agency, and thereby resists woman's structural and ideological position within the patriarchal division of public and private. The body—usually the excess that prohibits political subjectivity—is ejected into the public and *instills* political agency. Importantly, starving in the context of the RAF hunger strikes is a (logical) political strategy, not merely a subject position. Further, it is a collective action, not an isolated struggle, in which the goal is the reclaiming of a political position outside of others' control over one's body. The feminization of the hunger-striking body by media and the state (and strategically by leftist activists) thereby makes visible the gendered concept of the liberal subject—which cannot include the hunger-striking prisoner—at the same time as the body's politicizing force points to its limits. The threat the hunger-striking body poses is constituted not the least through its *gendered* (and sexualized) meaning, and its strategic use consequently can be understood as a feminist gesture of political resistance.

## "We Women Are the Better Half of Humanity Anyway"

Revolutionary Politics, Feminism, and Memory
in the Writings of Female Terrorists

What could possibly make us women more equal to men than
a gun?

    ⋆ Anonymous, 1973

For liberation is a process that cannot be prescribed through
laws or decrees. It is a live process, a prolonged process. [. . .]
[O]nly when women force men to rethink, only when they *de
facto* stand "shoulder to shoulder" with men does a joint struggle become possible.

    ⋆ Gabriele Tiedemann, 1986

### Introduction

At a meeting of a women's group at the political collective Socialist Center, Berlin (Sozialistisches Zentrum, Berlin) in 1973, the issue of armed
struggle was discussed—yet again. A young woman raised her voice as
she asked the group, "What could possibly make us women more equal
to men than a gun?"[1] Heike[2] vividly remembers the response of the
women in the room as amused and dismissive: "Everybody laughed and
nobody took it seriously." Women had gathered to develop their self-
confidence, articulate a criticism of sexism, and find ways to advocate
for cultural and political change both within and outside of the New Left.
Violence was not openly approved of as an emancipatory means; the
rhetoric of an emerging awareness of extensive violence against women
by men, institutions, and the state only began dominating debates in
the autonomous women's movement beginning in the second half of
the 1970s,[3] at which time armed struggle was perceived as a problematic
masculine revolutionary concept. The opportunity to recruit for armed

resistance among the female activists did not seem to be taken in this feminist setting. "But then," Heike continues, "less than a year later I found myself to be part of the armed struggle. So something must have stuck that night." For her, being part of the women's movement was a "catalyst" for her embracing armed resistance against what she viewed as an oppressive and dangerous state. The intellectual and personal skills she acquired in the company of political women—confident presentation of her positions, theoretical back-up for her opinions, political strategizing and organizing—later helped her assert herself as a political subject in the mixed-gender constellation of the Movement 2nd June. "My desire to effect change was fulfilled in my work underground with the Movement 2nd June, it was the only choice for me. But I never would have arrived there without the women's movement." And while the Movement 2nd June never openly expressed feminist positions, after 1975 the group was dominated by women. Many of the group's dynamics, Heike reflects, were shaped by the solidarity between the women (furthered by a prison break of four women in 1976, of which three were members of the Movement 2nd June).[4] For Heike, having a feminist analysis of power was a central part of her identity as a revolutionary, but more important for her sense of overall liberation as a political subject was the experience of armed struggle. "Women's true liberation," she explains, "is facilitated through armed struggle."

Heike's political history, which includes her moving in spaces of both the emerging autonomous women's movement and of armed groups underground, makes visible a connection that rarely is accounted for in the literature on the RAF and Movement 2nd June: that of feminist politics and leftist armed women. Instead, research on left-wing terrorism in West Germany usually concludes that women in left-radical groups—with the exception of a few activists who employed violence as a means of political resistance for an explicit feminist agenda—distanced themselves politically from the autonomous women's movement and thus from the question of feminist politics.[5] This conclusion stems from the fact that although about 50 percent of members in illegally operating groups were women who experienced the social space of "revolutionary cells" as liberation from social restrictions (including those defined by gender roles), power relations between the genders were not publicly challenged in those spaces:[6] "The intervention against structural sexism is nowhere [in texts by and about the RAF] declared to be wrong or superfluous; however, the RAF never viewed it as an urgency that needed to be pursued, which is equal to assuming it to be politically irrelevant, especially in relation to the issued 'revolutionary' line."[7] However, women's groups within the autonomous women's movement discussed political violence quite extensively in the 1970s and in no way rejected its use unanimously. Some felt inspired by the RAF women's uncompromising stance against the state.[8] At the same time, women in armed groups shared political experiences with women's groups and were thinking about the role of gender in revolutionary politics. Later some would declare armed struggle to have liberated them from restrictive gendered expectations, to have made it possible for them to escape traditional roles of wife and mothers. In fact, to dismiss gender (or feminism) as irrelevant to terrorist women because of a lack of political address of the topic is to underestimate the influence of militant women on feminist activists and vice versa—it appears that armed women's proximity to feminist groups had made them very aware of gender as an oppressive force and they sought actively to integrate that awareness into their revolutionary politics. More importantly, this dismissal also means discounting gender as an organizing force *beyond* consciously politicizing it. Instead, the at times intense engagement that armed women had with feminist issues and politics—and that is conveyed in memoirs and letters—suggests that there existed a mutual influence between the different political groups of women that demands a reconsideration of what is understood to constitute feminist politics.

Heike's reflections demonstrate the at times complicated relationship many armed women had to feminism and the women's movement. Initially attracted to the narrative of female assertion within the broader leftist movement, many did not agree with the exclusive focus on patriarchal oppression and cultural feminism's subsequent retreat into "female spaces." Heike describes the impression she had in Berlin in 1973, years before that shift would define the women's movement: "People like Alice Schwarzer[9] seemed to be hijacking the feminist movement and dropping any concern with socialist politics and imperialist oppression on the way." This dispels the notion of "the" feminist movement opposing political violence, as well as the notion that politically violent women did not have a stake in defying gender oppression. The "messiness" of the way subcultures and political groups related to aspects of progressive and/or radical leftist politics, which defies a clear demarcation as to where feminist politics begin and where they end, manifests in the writing of former female terrorists. The published memoirs of former RAF members (some of whom also belonged to the Movement 2nd June) Gabriele Rollnik, Inge Viett, and Margrit Schiller and the unpublished prison letters by former Movement 2nd June member Gabriele Tiedemann all mirror this "messiness." In fact, the reflections that are found in their writings constitute feminist practices in their thinking about, and framing of, women's liberation that challenge prescribed gender norms as they existed both outside of and within the women's movement.

## Life Narratives and Armed Struggle: Political Memoirs and Letters from the RAF and Movement 2nd June

The phenomenon of "life narrative," a genre that is characterized by "self-referential writing"[10] and that includes autobiographies, letters, diaries, political memoirs, and published interviews plays a significant role in the historicization and evaluation of the RAF and other militant activists. These texts have served different functions for various participants in public debate (for readers and authors): at times the aim seems to be to exonerate the author from any responsibility for his or her actions, while other narratives read like political manifestos, defending political moments of the past, and still others are testimonies of remorse, trauma, and grief. Since the mid-1990s, texts of "remembering" one's experiences as a terrorist began hitting the book market in Germany, generating a process of "personalizing" the phenomenon of armed groups like the RAF and Movement 2nd June, and eventually adding the element of potential profit-making through the publication of extremely popular "ex-terrorist histories."[11] Only recently have accounts from the victims' families been published, contributing to the voices describing the impact of violent politics on people's lives.[12] Composed or narrated by known and convicted former activists, (auto)biographical accounts of activists' political development create a complicated landscape for cultural historians to navigate. This is particularly true when one tries to move the discussion beyond biographical and personalized approaches to West German terrorism in the context of the new social movements, on the one hand, and beyond the (historical) chronicling of violent events, court trials, and legislation around national security, on the other. These life narratives can be understood as countervoices to media coverage and scholarship on West German terrorism that add the complicated (and controversial) component of oral history (individual memory, testimony, and *Zeitzeugen* [witnesses of the time]) to the historicization of the RAF.

A fair number of these autobiographical texts relate in various forms the experiences of women who had been members of the Movement 2nd June and/or the RAF. Some were authored by the women themselves, such as the memoirs by Inge Viett (Movement 2nd June and RAF) and Margit Schiller (RAF) and Inge Viett's prison letters. Others are published interviews, such as those by Gabriele Rollnik (Movement 2nd June and RAF) and Irmgard Möller (RAF). Others were published posthumously, such as letters from prison by Gudrun Ensslin (RAF) and Ulrike Meinhof (RAF).[13] All, to various degrees, reflect the complicated relationship armed women had to the autonomous women's movement.

Scholarship on writing by former participants in armed struggle primarily focuses on these published political memoirs and/or essays.[14] This chapter foregrounds instead the unpublished prison letters written by a political prisoner to friends and activists "outside" in order to explore the relationship of women in armed struggle to feminism and the autonomous women's movement. It examines the engagement of a Movement 2nd June member, the German Gabriele Tiedemann (formerly Kröcher-Tiedemann),[15] with feminist debates in letters she wrote during the 1970s and 1980s while incarcerated in prisons in Switzerland.[16] In her discussions of women's emancipation as they are documented in her letters, Tiedemann's original understanding of feminism shifts from her denying its political relevance towards a broader acceptance of feminism as a liberationist movement. The exchange of letters between the incarcerated Tiedemann and activists "outside" is testimony to her changing political position: over time, she increasingly identified *as a woman* in relation to her political actions. Her letters comment on this shift and thus provide insight into the tensions that a gendered analysis created within radical leftist groups who subscribed to theories of armed struggle. Even if Tiedemann's political development should not lead to generalizations about women in the militant leftist political scene or about gender structures within radical groups, her case as she relates it in her writing nevertheless offers important insights. While the poststructural criticism of the notion of an authentic "experience" as the primary basis for historical analysis and feminist knowledge of women's history (this criticism understands the process of writing *as creating* experiences and positioning the subject, not as objectively "reporting" on an experience)[17] is taken into account here, so is June Purvis's wariness of a disembodied discourse. She argues in the case of writings by suffragettes that even if letters are not the person's experience but a representation of it, "it was a lived experience even if mediated through her material, social and interpersonal context—as well as the discourse of the day [and of today, one should add]. Thus any one prisoner's experience would be both 'subject to' and the 'subject of' such phenomena—something about which we cannot draw clear hard and fast distinctions."[18] Since Tiedemann assumed an active role in the group Movement 2nd June and was an activist engaged passionately with theories of social oppression, her reflections provide important indications of how the Left understood feminist politics, how a female militant activist expressed criticism of leftist ideologies, and how she found ways to connect feminism with revolutionary politics.

The chapter's explorations begin with a discussion of the ways in which female revolutionaries expressed positions on women's oppression in political memoirs, in particular in the three autobiographical texts by Gabriele Rollnik, *Keine Angst vor niemand: Über die Siebziger, die Bewegung 2. Juni und die RAF* (Not Afraid of Anybody: About the Seventies, the Movement 2nd June, and the RAF); Margit Schiller, *Es war ein harter Kampf um meine Erinnerung: Ein Lebensbericht aus der RAF* (translated as *Remembering the Armed Struggle: Life in Baader-Meinhof*); and Inge Viett, *Nie war ich furchtloser: Autobiographie* (Never Was I More Fearless: Autobiography). While this discussion in no way presents a comprehensive analysis of these life narratives, this section aims to offer some understanding of how these women thought (and wrote) about gendered and sexualized power in the context of revolutionary politics. Following a brief elaboration on how the relationship of subjectivity and writing as it is conceptualized theoretically applies to prison writing, the final and main part of the chapter analyzes three sets of letters that Tiedemann exchanged with two women and one man in the course of eight years that relate the transformation of her position towards feminist politics. This final part of the chapter draws on and makes visible sources that are not easily accessible (archived unpublished letters); its primary contribution to the gendered analysis of women and political violence is an intervention into the way both feminist and historical discourse more broadly present radical women's relationship to, and understanding of, feminism.

## (Alienated) Sisters in Arms: Reading the Relationship of Underground Women to Feminism

In the context of social movements and cultural history, the genre of autobiographical writing as source inhabits a controversial status. Unlike other types of fictional writing, the narrative "I" in autobiographical texts claims not only narrative truth but historical truth, which implies an access to aspects of reality a "nonwitnessing" literary text lacks. This history might be a personal one, whose connections to larger history are implicit and/or parallel. The autobiographical "truth" of a life is distinct from the information the reader is offered in a biography—in the former genre, the author presents a life "simultaneously from externalized and internal points of view"; the internal perspective tells the history of a self, a "history of self-observation" [19] that eludes the biographer. So autobiographical "truth" relates both to historical events more generally (those make the personal history relevant and referential to the reader) and to insights that are internal. The text engages the reader in an "intersubjective exchange [. . .] aimed at producing a shared understanding of the meaning of a life";[20] the reconstruction of a particular life is thus a collaborative effort between author and reader. "The complexity of autobiographical texts requires reading practices that reflect on the narrative tropes, sociocultural contexts, rhetorical aims, and narrative shifts within the historical or chronological trajectory of the text."[21]

Working with the complex, interconnected elements of personal and cultural memory, experience, identity, and temporality, political memoirs create and draw on cultural, political, and social contexts that are located in historical moments. A comprehensive "objective" reading or writing of history generally does not seem possible (past the obvious agreements on rough facts, such as the dates on which things occurred), and autobiographical writing further heats the debate by introducing *visible* and *obvious* markers of the way history is made and experienced by individuals, not just historians. Literary approaches to life narratives here are helpful, as they offer reading strategies that release the reader from determining levels and degrees of "truthfulness" of the text and instead allow for an engagement with ideas as they are being developed and expressed: "If we approach self-referential writing as an intersubjective process that occurs within the writer/reader pact, rather than a true-or-false story, the emphasis of reading shifts from assessing and verifying knowledge to observing processes of communicative exchange and understanding."[22] This applies in particular to letters, "a mode of directed, and dated, correspondence with a specific addressee,"[23] since they present an exchange between two writers addressed to a third party, the reader: "processes of communicative exchange and understanding" necessarily dominate a historical approach to how and what was discussed between the authors. More so than published memoirs, letters are "interactional modes of self-presentation,"[24] as the former do not function as means of communication within a relationship between two people. Letters might be less general or self-referential and instead be more communicative: "Letters become vehicles through which information is circulated, social roles enacted, relationships secured, often in a paradoxical mix of intimacy and formality."[25] In the context of prison, this process is also informed by censorship, which introduces a "silent" third party who, unlike the external reader of letters either published or archived, witnesses their communication in the moment, and whose power to potentially interrupt, disrupt, or modify the exchange creates a looming invisible ("silent") textual presence.

This intersubjective production of meaning offered by life narratives enables a reading of RAF and other terrorist women's relationship to feminist politics as individually experienced and as evolving, as well as inconsistent. What role did the women's movement play in the way women experienced their political development? How do they reflect on previous experiences concerning feminist politics from an evolved, changed position years later (as in the case of political memoirs) or in direct, temporally concrete conversations with another (as in the case of letters)?

## "Their Solidarity Is Natural and Fearless": Re-membering Gender and Power in Autobiographical Writings by Former Female Terrorists

The autobiographies and published interviews of former left-wing female terrorists in the German-speaking countries, such as those by the former RAF member Margrit Schiller and those of former members of the Movement 2nd June (and later of the RAF) Inge Viett and Gabriele Rollnik, provide insights into political convictions and cultural milieus, create models for the interpretation of female subjectivity within the context of terrorist movements, and today largely dominate the over-all understanding of female revolutionary experience. The complicated relationship that armed women had with feminist issues prioritized by the autonomous women's movement emerges as central in these auto-biographical writings in which the engagement with (and/or rejection of) feminist concerns shaped the authors' articulations as revolutionary subjects. In these texts, some narrators were active in the early women's movement before going underground (such as Rollnik) or participated in feminist direct actions (such as Viett). All narrators, while not explic-itly retelling experiences in women's political groups, offer a gendered analysis of the status quo in German society, and some (such as Schil-ler) later did political work with leftist women's groups. Significantly, the narratives do not support the prevalent perception (and claim) that gender and sexual relations were not discussed as political issues by members of the groups. Instead, the narratives suggest that women and men were conscious of gendered power and the social dynamics it cre-ates, including among activists.

As a student in Berlin, Gabriele Rollnik joined the Movement 2nd June in 1974 and was an active member until its dissolution in 1980, when she joined the RAF while imprisoned. She actively participated in several political actions, including the kidnappings of Berlin politician Peter Lorenz in 1975 (he was successfully exchanged for political prison-ers) and of the Austrian businessman Walter Palmers in 1977 (his release was negotiated in return for money to fund members underground). She was arrested in 1975, but broke out of prison ten months later, to be arrested again in 1978. During the fifteen years she was imprisoned, she joined the RAF and continued to politically organize from prison, including participating in hunger strikes. She was released in 1992. In 2003 she published an interview with Daniel Dubbe about her political experiences, including her time in prison, *Keine Angst vor niemand*.

Inge Viett escaped what she experienced as the repressive and anti-Semitic environment of her childhood in a rural village in northern Germany, whose static social order and prohibitive class and gender structures fundamentally shaped her radical leftist politics. She founded a cell of the Movement 2nd June in 1972, only to be arrested and imprisoned a few months later. After fifteen months in prison she escaped, and following her arrest in 1975 she again broke out of prison with three other women (including Rollnik).[26] She reluctantly joined the RAF in 1980 when the Movement 2nd June was weakened by the arrest of most of its members, but never agreed with what she felt to be their dogmatic, elitist, and unrealistic approach to confrontations with the state. After shooting and injuring a police officer in France in 1981, she decided to flee into the German Democratic Republic (GDR), where she lived with a new identity (as did other former RAF members) until arrested in 1990 after the demise of the GDR. She was released in 1997. Her memoir, *Nie war ich furchtloser*, was published in 1996.

Margrit Schiller was a student in Heidelberg and active in the Sozialistisches Patientenkollektiv (SPK),[27] the Socialist Patients' Collective, when she supported the RAF by letting members use her apartment starting in early 1971. Later that year she became a member of the RAF and went underground. She was arrested in 1971 and was placed in solitary confinement (in so-called dead tracts, isolated sensory-deprivation cells) for parts of her incarceration. She participated in political hunger strikes organized by the RAF before she was released in 1973. She again went underground after her release from prison and was arrested again in early 1974. She was incarcerated until 1979. In 2000 she published her memoir, which was translated in 2009 as *Remembering the Armed Struggle: Life in Baader-Meinhof*.

In all three memoirs, the story relates that early on the narrator had an awareness of gender as an important aspect of a repressive social order. Maybe more importantly, in each of the memoirs, the narrator is presented as conscious of—and enraged by—women's sexual, economic, and social oppression years before her involvement in armed struggle. In *Keine Angst vor niemand*, Rollnik's political opinions early on are

shaped by a feminist approach to understanding oppression: years before she would go underground, as a student at the Free University in
Berlin, she chose as a topic for her master's thesis "Women's Double
Burden in Family and Work Life."[28] In her narration of her time working in manufacturing prior to going underground in an attempt to both
experience and politicize workers, she became acutely aware of the gendered differences within the labor force: overall, men would hold better
paid positions and "women would also generally be paid less for the
same work."[29] Her general attitude in the published interview is openly
feminist, even as she is drawn to more broadly defined liberationist
politics.

In *Remembering the Armed Struggle*, Schiller paints a picture of violent sexual repression and emotional abuse as she recounts her mother's
corporeal punishments resulting from her fourth grade crush on a boy,
and her father's sexual threat and domination of her that fell short of actual physical sexual abuse. His contained but expressed desire for her in-
stilled a sense of male domination and fear in her that contextualizes her
reflections on gender and sexuality throughout the memoir: "He often
played a game with me: he pressed me very closely to his body to prove
that I couldn't defend myself if a man tried to rape me. [. . .] As far as he
was concerned, I was his possession and he was jealous of every male
person I had even the slightest contact with."[30] Early on in the memoir,
Schiller makes clear how already as a teenage woman she completely
rejected traditional family structures and their gendered roles, including that of mother, when she narrates telling her mother that she would
never have children.[31] Her awareness of how gendered and sexual power
impacted her life as a woman continued to develop in her work with political groups, where "male structures, male dominance were subjects we
discussed over and over again."[32] Throughout her memoir, "she employs
concepts of sexuality and gender and simultaneously resists a sexualizing of both her body and her political activity by drawing attention to
the sexual character of state violence,"[33] in particular in the scenes of her
arrests and in moments of incarceration and prison organizing.

Finally, in *Nie war ich furchtloser*, Viett, who (as Schiller does) weaves
her sexual identity as lesbian into her narrative, in her childhood and
youth experienced extreme physical, emotional, and sexual violence.
She views both the state (which placed her in an abusive foster home)

and the inherent violence of bigoted and ideologically corrupt villagers of the town where she grew up as representative of an overall cultural coarseness and cruelty that she escapes from in a politically militant urban environment in Berlin. The first part of her narrative, which tells of her life prior to going underground, is dominated by her experiencing and condemning the gender and sexual oppression that are inseparably tied to class. Recalling her two-month stripping stint in Hamburg's infamous red-light district, St. Pauli, she views women as "the raw material" of the entertainment industry, and their labor as analogous to the worker's: just as the worker does not experience the wealth he produces, Viett states, so the stripping woman is not entertained by her work.

> Nowhere else is the economic dependence of women so apparent, is the commodity status within gender relations so exposed, are lust and love so illusionary as in the entertainment ghettos of the cities. Established, run, and controlled by men. Women labor, produce for them. [. . .] "The oldest profession in the world," winks patriarchy, referring to its world, in which the century-old oppression and exploitation of women is justified as an anthropological fact.[34]

Viett's narrative creates a strong image of the entrapment that girls in lower social and economic strata of her generation must have experienced, and the story of her revolutionary struggle is haunted by her fear of becoming what she was "destined" to be, just as her sister did; she left school after seventh grade and started working as domestic help, was married by eighteen, and soon after become a mother. "She went the prescribed way, which also was destined to be mine."[35] Viett's early militant activism in particular is characterized by feminist concerns that are the target of street-militant actions.[36]

This awareness that the narrators (retrospectively) ascribe to their pre-underground personas is carried over into descriptions of their activist experiences. These activist experiences are clearly shaped by an awareness of gender oppression and social experience as women, which are narrated in relation to their political work. Schiller writes of how impressed she was by the open treatment and acceptance of lesbian sexuality in the RAF[37] and how discussions with female leaders of the group about women's structural position in society communicated their knowledge of the gendered nature of their threat as violent political women to the West German state and society: "Women who break out of the mold, who refuse to play their role or who even take up weapons are not allowed to exist. That's why they [state and media] hate us so much."[38] Later in the narrative, when she is imprisoned with "social" (i.e., not political) prisoners in a normal prison, Schiller frames these women's prison experiences within a critique of patriarchal social and judicial structures.[39]

Viett in particular expresses affinity and love for women throughout her narrative and an acute sense of a shared social standpoint, a political orientation that should not be reduced to her affinity with women based on sexual desire—she had close and strong political bonds with male comrades as well. However, she recounts repeatedly how women, on the basis of their (assumed) shared experiences, support and relate to other women. She recalls how after she broke out of prison, she found refuge in a women's housing collective whose inhabitants, though not political, as a group clothed, fed, and sheltered her without asking questions or making her feel like an imposition: "Their solidarity is natural and fearless."[40]

The experiences of the Movement 2nd June's gender politics, according to Viett and (to a lesser degree) Rollnik, were extremely empowering and affirmative for women. What male former members later jokingly described as men being oppressed by women and students being oppressed by working-class members,[41] Viett viewed as an essential characteristic of the group's dynamics. What was being witnessed here, she stated, was

> the vehement unfolding of our, the women's, independence, the comprehensive development of abilities in ways men were not used to from women. [. . .] That might have intimidated this or that comrade, who would be new in the group and was faced with a majority of decisive women. He would not be granted any advantage because of his role [as man].[42]

While Viett elaborates on women's solidarity in general and within her political work, Rollnik primarily speaks of learning of women's solidarity and particular social and emotional skills in her time in prison. She recalls how the limited number of political prisoners in any given group in prison often led to conflict and political disagreement, furthered by the intense dependence on only a few to affirm a sense of self in an otherwise isolating environment. Unlike a number of men's groups that openly quarreled and ended up in irreconcilable political differences, she states, her women's group resisted what she views as the state's strategic attempt to weaken the political work of prisoners: once the women noticed that things were getting out of hand, she recalls,

> From there on we let each other have more air to breathe. Not that it wasn't scarce already. [. . .] You are under such enormous threat and pressure from outside, that you are constantly checking: Are we all acting the right way all the time? [. . .] One observes oneself so intensely that things can quickly deteriorate. But once we realized what was happening, we could change our behavior. [. . .] We ended up not cutting each other down, instead we are still friends today.[43]

Rollnik attributes this successful pulling together of the group of female prisoners also to their ability to communicate and process conflict before it got out of hand. While she does not emphasize this as a gendered skill, she implies as much in remarking on the failure of men's groups to achieve similar results.

It is quite striking how all three narrators experienced (or later identified) their armed struggle (and their time in prison) as liberation from the destined path patriarchy had assigned them in specifically gendered forms; all reflect on how they escaped a "regular" life as wife and mother. Schiller displays actual shock at the proposal by a male friend who (apparently worriedly) observed her radicalization that they just "get married, finish of [sic] our studies together and then have children."[44] She is struck by how firm her resolve is to never take that route of conventional family life: "My other way, my new path in life was already closer. I didn't know where it would take me, it could end in prison or death, but, for the first time in my life, I had the feeling that I was living my life the way I wanted to."[45] Echoing this rejection of a traditional life, Rollnik's memoir ends with her answer to the interviewer's final statement that she also could have lived as a housewife with two children in small-town Germany, had she not followed her radical inclinations: "No, never as housewife. Despite all mistakes, it was better this way."[46] Finally, Viett, echoing an earlier memory of how her eventual violent resistance to her foster mother's physical beatings as a teenager was the only thing that held the woman's violence in check,[47] in narrating her first of two prison breaks, establishes an implicit claim that armed struggle—violent resistance—constitutes women's liberation from life's prison more broadly, that violent acts release women from fear and defeat:

> Women seldom break out [of prison]; they are used to suffering, waiting and hoping. Sometimes they try to stretch the parameters of their role, maybe succeed in shattering them, if their power is great enough. The prison of life they break open, sometimes, and arduously escape. This iron prison, however, made of steel, keys and concrete, this concentration of human power over being human or not being human, this raw bleak corner, into which the ruling class sweeps everyone who is not a match for their system, and also those for whom they themselves are not a match, this absolute power overwhelms women with a hopeless finality that kills any thoughts of eventually overcoming.[48]

None of the texts evinces a strict demarcation line between women's issues and the narrator's own politics (which dominates the scholarly debate on the RAF), and while they all seem to have disagreed with the autonomous women's movement's gesture of separating from the Left, all either began or ended their armed struggle with political work in women's groups.[49] However, it remains important to understand these texts as autobiographies that reflect in *retrospect* on female activists' relationship to feminist politics. While they create an impression that gender and sexual oppression were actually much more part of these women's overall leftist political positions than is usually implied, they do not create insight into how conflicting political positions and calls to some actions (and condemnations of others) were resolved (or remained unresolved) for them as they occurred. The prison letters by Gabriele Tiedemann, member of Movement 2nd June, allow some insight into what this process meant to her as a female revolutionary.

## Writing in a Total Institution: Prison Letters as "Underlife" Strategy of Resistance

The autobiographical publications by female terrorists constitute, as do the media coverage and state documents, an important part of the public discourse about the RAF and similar groups. The letters by Gabriele Tiedemann that form the basis for the rest of this analysis belong to a different type of text: in contrast to political memoirs, which publicly (re)construct political subjectivity, letters by leftist political prisoners transmit often fractured and/or fragmented insights of and into the self (*Eigen-Einsichten*). First, these personal letters are less self-contained reproductions of a political career than are political memoirs. This is principally the case because records in the form of letters do not process past events and opinions in retrospect, but rather mirror political opinions of the moment of writing and thus present a more partial (temporally bound) picture of political developments, one less mediated by following events. Second, the private correspondence addresses specific recipients, in contrast to the autobiographies, which are geared towards a broader audience and offer a less complex discussion of topics. In prison letters this aspect of the addressee is complicated by censorship through prison authorities whose "silent" readers have the power to interject into the dialogue. Finally, their communicative nature characterizes letters as cultural texts and as historical sources: their testimonies develop in direct exchange between two authors. Because of varying addressees who have individual relationships with the prisoner and who initiate different conversations within an exchange of letters, prison letters appear simultaneously dynamic and inconsistent as sources. For the interpretation of their content it is thus significant with whom Tiedemann corresponded. While published memoirs are edited, collaboratively produced texts (especially in the case of published interviews), letters are often viewed as being less mediated texts. However, it also needs to be kept in mind that the letters on hand cannot be interpreted in the same way as other private correspondence since they were subject to censorship.

Tiedemann's prison letters are unique in that they offer a basis for an increased understanding of the interrelation between feminist thinking and militant leftist politics. By the mid-1970s, the focus of much of leftist radical politics had shifted towards the fate of political prisoners. Accordingly, the movement for political prisoners had morphed into a well-organized element of the radical political landscape. To prevent the political isolation of prisoners through prison authorities, the radical Left initiated visitations of prisoners and contacts through letters (*Brief-kontakt*) to incarcerated activists. These multifarious contacts between activists "outside" and prisoners "inside" served to exchange information as well as to maintain political connections and to further coherence between the prison movement and the radical Left.[50] Letters in this context point to a political exchange as much as to prison as a space that shapes political experiences and positions.

Being locked up in prison brings home Foucault's notion of the subject produced by discursive power that, disguised as "treatment," in fact punishes the prisoner. Here the at times elusive idea of the subject produced and governed by institutions, systems of knowledge (discourse), and norms becomes concrete. Prison represents what Erving Goffman has termed a "total institution," "a place of residence and work where a large number of like-situated individuals, cut off from the wider society for an appreciable amount of time, together lead an enclosed, formally administered round of life."[51] The enforced state of that "round of life" manifests in the population of a total institution, in the "basic split between a large managed group, conveniently called inmates, and a small supervisory staff."[52] Communication and information across the boundary of those social groups are strictly limited and monitored, and staff regularly leave the institution (such as at the end of a work shift), while inmates always remain within its physical boundary.[53] However, Goffman's concept of a total institution with absolute social control accounts for various ways in which inmates react to their managed state. He refers to the *underlife* of the institution, a range of practices that people establish to distance themselves from the surrounding institution in everyday life. He further differentiates between *disruptive* and *contained* practices. Disruptive practices are defined by "the realistic intentions of the participants [. . .] to abandon the organization or radically alter its structure [. . .] leading to a rupture in the smooth operation of the organization";[54] contained practices are defined by participants not "introducing pressure for radical change and [. . .] can, in fact, have the obvious function of deflecting efforts that might otherwise be disruptive."[55] The total institution's apparently unforgivable social order thus is in fact rendered complex and multilayered through the human effort to maintain a sense of self while surviving its restrictions.

Echoing this tension between experiencing oppressive and suffocating social control and at times subtle ways of resisting it can be found in feminist literature on prisons. As Kay Warren points out, the concept of "boundary regulation as central to the prison's technology of control"[56] has been dominant in prison-rights literature. However, some challenge the absolute parameters of that concept and instead call for broadening "the terrain of analysis of penal powers and resistance."[57] Prisons then are viewed as institutions that produce social relations both distinct from and in relation to "outside." Consequently, prison walls—as spatial orders as well as conceptual limitations—do not guard separate worlds, but instead are viewed as permeable. As Begoña Aretxaga argues in her work on women prisoners in Northern Ireland, *Shattering Silence*, letters to and from people "outside" are a fundamental tool to permeate prison walls—socially, politically, and emotionally. As a constrained practice of underlife in Goffman's sense, communicating with others, breaching the isolation of the prison walls (as the symbolic and literal boundary of the institution), creates counterrealities to the totality of the prison experience. However, censorship—a condition for the permeability of the prison walls—adds to the *Fremdbestimmung* (heteronomy) of not only the author's life but also the writing of the self. The double role of the prison author becomes visible in the act of censoring in- and out-going letters: s/he is simultaneously the writing subject and the object of the disciplining authorities and methods.[58]

These dynamics become visible in the years of Tiedemann's correspondence with those "outside." Censorship always sets the parameters for the written correspondence as it is archived, which can be traced through the carbon copies of letters she sent and that she kept with her other papers: all letters were read and censored for content, and between 1979 and the end of 1985, no matter to whom she was writing, Tiedemann's letters were limited to two pages. Her communication thus was censored both in terms of content and in terms of form, a fact that clearly irritated her, as she communicates in a letter to a friend in September 1979: "what has contributed to my frustration, though, is the shitty regulation that i recently have to abide by, that i can only write

2 pages."[59] Weigel's observation that to many prisoners incarcerated for crimes unrelated to political activism writing is less political than a strategy of survival, for maintaining a sense of self, is relevant here. Tiedemann's letters (both in content and in the status they held for her) are located somewhere in between the political and the personal: in the beginning her writing is very political, and it often is strategically geared towards censorship; her later writing, in contrast, includes more personal letters that also coincide with a changing strategy of how to contest her prison conditions. Overall, her letters contribute to a sense that writing was an important part of her attempt to preserve a sense of (political) self, to stave off despair and a loss of subjectivity.

Writing from prison then becomes an "underlife strategy,"[60] an attempt to actively shape one's life in a total institution, as opposed to simply a survival strategy—the prisoner's self is constituted through incarceration and writing is a constant reconstitution of subjectivity in the face of total external control.[61] Imagining (and experiencing) prison walls as permeable becomes a powerful concept in this underlife strategy, and writing in the form of letters amplifies this strategy in terms of actually permeating walls that separate the self from others and make transformations of the self through the process of incarceration visible. The way Tiedemann understood and debated feminist politics is not simply interesting in terms of a broader discussion of leftist radical politics but also insightful because of how we—as the "fourth" reader of her letters (after the censor)—can trace the shifting importance of a feminist sensibility to her own sense of self as well as her previous politics, and how it relates to her revolutionary politics as feminist practice. The rest of the chapter is devoted to a reading of three sets of letters Tiedemann wrote in which she is exchanging and debating views on feminist politics.

## Gabriele Tiedemann's Prison Letters

### Biographical Notes

As a student at the Free University of Berlin, Gabriele Tiedemann (born 1951) was active in different radical political groups. After 1971–72 she was a member of the Movement 2nd June and lived underground, and was arrested in 1973, inter alia, for bank robberies that she allegedly participated in as a member of the group Rote Ruhr Armee (Red Ruhr Army).[62] During her arrest Tiedemann shot and injured a police officer, upon which she was convicted of attempted murder and sentenced to eight years of prison. In 1975, the Movement 2nd June kidnapped the Berlin politician Peter Lorenz and successfully forced the West German government to exchange six political prisoners for him, including Tiedemann (then Kröcher-Tiedemann), who thereupon was flown into Yemen. She is said to have participated in the hostage taking during the OPEC conference in Vienna later in 1975, an attack led by international terrorist Ilich Ramirez Sanchez ("Carlos"),[63] but based on lack of evidence she was never convicted. In 1977 she was involved in logistical aspects of the kidnapping of the Austrian millionaire Walter Palmers.[64] When she was arrested in 1977 at the Swiss-French border, she was caught in a shooting with the Swiss border police and subsequently was sentenced to fifteen years of prison. After she completed two-thirds of her sentence, Swiss authorities extradited Tiedemann to the FRG in 1987 to serve out the remaining time of her eight-year sentence, from which she had escaped in 1975 after the Movement 2nd June had kidnapped Peter Lorenz. Overall, Tiedemann was imprisoned for fifteen years and was released in 1991. A year later she fell ill with cancer and she died in 1995, at age forty-four.

During her detention, Tiedemann corresponded with a variety of pen pals: friends from before her arrest; women whom she befriended during her incarceration; and a few activists from the prisoner's movement, whom she did not know prior to their exchange of letters. All letters give insight into the specific political and personal debates that occupied Tiedemann during her time in prison, as well as into debates that were taking place in radical circles more broadly.

Already in her early prison letters, Tiedemann takes positions on the attempts of the autonomous women's movement, specifically the West German women's liberation movement, to politicize gender relations. The letters that convey her changing position regarding feminism's political significance were written in the time period of eight years (between 1978 and 1986), during which time Gabriele Tiedemann was detained in various Swiss prisons. Her correspondence with three people in particular (two women, referred to here as Caroline and Beate, and one man, Amin) form the basis for this analysis.[65]

### Letters #1: The Women's Movement as Nothing but a "Self-Liberation Group"

The first batch of letters analyzed here are addressed to Caroline,[66] an activist in the prisoner rights movement who prior to her contact with Tiedemann had already corresponded with Christian Möller, a German charged with terrorism who had been arrested with Tiedemann. She also had met Tiedemann's mother, Ingeborg Tiedemann, at events for relatives of political prisoners. It appears that through their letters Tiedemann developed a friendship with Caroline. The exchange took place in the course of four and a half years, from July 1978 until February 1983. During this time Tiedemann was incarcerated in prisons in Bern, Geneva, Lausanne, and Winterhur. In this phase of her imprisonment, Tiedemann (like many RAF prisoners) agitated for status as "political prisoner" and for the consolidation of political prisoners (*Zusammenlegung*). Among other things, she sued the Swiss government at the European Human Rights Court in 1978 (together with Christian Möller) and participated in four hunger strikes.[67] In addition to her struggle with authorities, she also discussed this and other political topics in letters with activists of the prisoners' movement.

Her letters with Caroline were primarily of political content. Initially they shared political beliefs, which diverged as their exchange continued. In their correspondence they discussed leftist political concerns such as prison conditions and hunger strikes, the relationship of the Left to the "guerilla" and the status of the RAF, general world politics such as U.S. foreign policy and imperialism, and economic topics such as international labor relations, unemployment, the economic restructuring of Europe (under the European Community, later the European Union), and the significance of oil in global economics and politics. The relatively short discussion of the women's movement was not of central significance—it was one of many topics they discussed. The last two years of their correspondence saw a noticeable increase in political tensions beginning to develop that seemed insurmountable and that eventually led to a termination of their contact.

In an early letter to Caroline, dated September 2, 1978, Tiedemann clearly speaks out against an autonomous women's movement: "i must say that i find the politics of many women's groups pretty shitty."[68] She condemns the prioritizing of women's oppression over what she (in the tradition of the Marxist Left) declares to be the primary contradiction, "that between capital and work/metropolis and third world."[69] Speaking from a classic Marxist position, she criticizes the traditional (bourgeois) women's movement for actually furthering the "main contradiction" (i.e., class differences) in that it demands equality for women with men without challenging the inequality *between men* (i.e., between classes). Therewith, argues Tiedemann, the autonomous women's movement supports bourgeois reform politics whose implications are reactionary: "the traditional movement for women's emancipation does not change the main contradiction; on the contrary, it stabilizes it. [. . .] if the goal consists of only stabilizing existing conditions, then such politics need to be fought as much as any social democratic ones."[70]

Tiedemann believed the "traditional" women's movement as well as the autonomous women's groups in the 1970s to be bourgeois endeavors that countered the class struggle. Here she expresses a position that was quite prevalent among women in radical leftist circles (including among women participating in armed struggle). As early as 1968, the journalist and later cofounding member of the RAF, Ulrike Meinhof, wrote that the (socialist) "demand for emancipation" of women has become the (social democratic) "claim of equality": "Emancipation means liberation through the transformation of social conditions. [. . .] The claim of equality does not question the social premise of inequality between people anymore [. . .] it only demands equality within inequality."[71] In an exchange of letters from September 1978, Tiedemann dismisses the efforts on the part of women's groups to form a women's movement independent from the Left as merely one of a number of initiatives of so-called self-liberation groups (*Selbstbefreiungsgruppen*) in West Germany, which organized politically primarily around their own social experiences. Those groups' seemingly self-involved actions were seen by Marxist revolutionary activists as undermining the concentration on a shared class struggle: "in this respect, the situation of the women's movement is merely symptomatic of the entire situation of the former revolutionary left, who does not even realize their own permanent politics of retreat and because of that has lost all perspective." [72] Women's liberation, Tiedemann concludes, needs to happen in the context of revolutionary struggle, echoing Heike's position at the beginning of this chapter: "for me, women's liberation cannot be disconnected from the class struggle, it is part of the class struggle, or in other words: women's only true social, political and sexual liberation finds its expression in the active participation in the revolutionary struggle against a system in which women's oppression is only one component of the oppression of the exploited classes."[73]

The fact that Tiedemann did not return to this topic in later letters with Caroline conveys the political insignificance she attributed to the women's movement during that time. The political debates resulted in a fallout between Tiedemann and Caroline that was in no way connected to their discussion of the women's movement, but that rather pertained to their discord over the question of the consolidation of political prisoners that occupied the leftist radical scene at the time. Tiedemann began to distance herself from the radical differentiation between "political" and "social" prisoners popular with hardliners of the movement and disapproved of Caroline's reliance on a rhetoric of armed struggle in her argument.[74] Simultaneously with the change in her attitude towards feminist politics that coincided with the end of this pen friendship in 1983, Tiedemann apparently distanced herself from the belief that armed struggle is the only form of effective resistance. This change in political identity resulted in an alienation not only from her correspondent but also from other radical activists.

## Letters #2: The Women's Movement as "Laboring around at a Secondary Contradiction of Society"

The second set of letters is the correspondence between Tiedemann and her close pen friend Beate, a teacher of German as a foreign language to migrant children and the life partner of Tiedemann's attorney. The feminist attitude of this pen friend inspired Tiedemann to return to the topic of women's emancipation in her letters starting in 1982. After organizing for some time as an activist, Beate had retreated from the leftist political scene and was only again confronted with movement politics and issues like "prison and resistance" because of her relationship with Tiedemann's attorney.[75] Tiedemann's correspondence with Beate lasted five and a half years, between January 1982 and August 1987, during which Tiedemann was incarcerated in the maximum security prison in

Hindelbank.[76] In the so-called Hindelbank letters with Beate, one finds the most comprehensive and extensive discussion about the women's movement in Tiedemann's prison correspondence.[77]

The context of everyday life (in prison) forms an important background for this exchange of letters. As Grisard demonstrates, at this point in time Tiedemann sought to be placed in normal detention (*Normalvollzug*), which contrasted with her prior efforts towards the placement of political prisoners into shared detention, also referred to as the consolidation of political prisoners (*Zusammenlegung*). Her dealings with authorities also pointed to a change in tactics in negotiating prison conditions: in this period of her imprisonment, she appealed for improved prison conditions through temporary (*befristete*) hunger and work strikes as well as through letters of complaint, while before she had pursued her demands with open-ended hunger strikes and lawsuits.[78] These less confrontational strategies—moving from what Goffman classified as *disruptive* to *contained* underlife practices—can be understood to reflect a moderated political attitude in Tiedemann. Her "deradicalization"[79] took place at a time when the heated public debates around left-wing terrorism had largely abated and also seems to have been influenced by her "experiences as long-term prisoner,"[80] many of which took place in the isolation of maximum security. At the same time, one finds a heightened engagement with feminist ideas in her letters.[81]

From the beginning, the letters that Tiedemann and Beate exchanged are personal, and an abstract theorizing of political positions is absent; instead, in the course of time a friendship developed between the two women. The reality of imprisonment calls for alternative ways to develop intimacy and confidentiality than a direct interpersonal contact allows for. Tiedemann writes on November 7, 1982, "after just three letters, one *cannot* know each other. trusting and knowing each other are mutually dependent and involve a long, a very long process. and then there's censorship, which makes much impossible."[82] However, the two women successfully overcame the limitations set by Tiedemann's detention, and their correspondence is characterized by mutual appreciation and affection. The fact that feminism is important in this exchange of letters is explained by the significance the women's movement had for Beate.

In the early stages of her discussion with Beate, Tiedemann expresses a deep skepticism of the basic assumptions of the women's movement, such as that patriarchy primarily affects women negatively and that the individual man needs to be made accountable for the general oppression of women. For her, women's liberation does not mean "emancipation against men, but, in the end, always only *with* him."[83] Tiedemann reiterates her dislike of what she calls a "new form of racism"[84] expressed by radical feminists against men and rejects the notion of "man as enemy":[85] "of course patriarchal thinking is women's enemy, but it is not the man as such, the male gender (sex), who/that is this enemy. [...] not only do i think this position to be politically wrong, but also somehow inhuman."[86] Men, she argues, also suffer under patriarchy, from their "own socialization [and want to] liberate themselves from this socialization."[87] Patriarchal gender relations, states Tiedemann, equally harm men and women. She expresses a "deep dislike"[88] of separatist feminists—including the "radical lesbians" (*radikallesben*) who advocate for gender-separated social and political spaces. And she positions herself as an activist for whom the autonomous women's movement was a means for her personal emancipation, not a political movement as such: "the women's movement [was] a purpose for one's own emancipation, not politics as such [...], but a means to return, with all the powers one has developed through the women's movement, to and for a politics for all, whether man or woman."[89]

Looking back on her experiences as a twenty-year-old in a women's group in Berlin, Tiedemann concedes that women's groups within leftist political initiatives made it possible for women to attest to each other's solidarity, to get themselves on equal footing with men in the movement in terms of knowledge of political theories, and to gain strength and confidence. She views this form of solidarity between women as legitimate, but only with the ultimate "goal of carrying back whatever has been experienced and learned there"[90] into the broader leftist movement, where, according to her, "actual" political work was performed. To her, the only purpose of women's political groups was to form a "counterweight to the work of mixed political groups," never to be stand-alones.[91] Here Tiedemann quotes a friend who was incarcerated with her and with whom, she says, she shared "identical opinions" about gender relations: "we can only win together [...] i simply can't blame men if i, as a woman, carry around any complexes, because it is primarily up to me to change myself."[92] At this stage—in November 1982—sexism for Tiedemann is not a political but a personal problem, and politics for women mean nothing but a "laboring around at a secondary contradiction of society."[93] Feminism, she claims, addresses a minor or secondary contradiction—"*Nebenwiderspruch*"—of the class struggle, which addresses the primary contradiction of human relations produced by capitalism: class difference. The feminist postulate that "the personal is political" does not seem to resonate with her, as in her letters she reads feminist politics as exclusive and separatist. Against the background of her change of conviction regarding feminist politics that occurs later, it is significant that in this letter she states that "in my own political practice, the man-woman problem was not a problem, it never was an issue for us."[94] The "man-woman problem" was resolved through a shared political experience (the "political practice"). This echoes her earlier point that a woman's personal emancipation most effectively happens through her participation in armed struggle.

Tiedemann's analysis of gender relations here is clearly rooted in a left-radical discourse of the 1970s, with its particular notions of gender and power (and their relation to the class struggle). This analysis differs from that of the women's movement of the mid-1970s and 1980s, which clearly distances itself from beliefs of the Left and instead defines gender relations as social power structures that needed to be countered with legislative as well as cultural measures.[95] In a letter from 1983, her correspondent does criticize the tendency of many women's groups to politically retreat. [96] However, Beate views this tendency not as an inherent separatism but as a result of leftist groups' overall rejection of the women's movement, reflected in their refusal to integrate the sexual division of labor—reproductive labor versus paid/productive labor—into their Marxist critique of capitalism and imperialism. According to her, women and the domestic work they perform are not considered as an economic factor in a Marxist social analysis. The refusal of leftist men to view the oppression of women as material, argues Beate, points to the fact that men profit from this gender-specific division of labor. Tiedemann's friend, who in her writing understands men to be "unreliable allies" and women to be the actual "progressive force" with a shared standpoint,[97] quotes from the text "Feminismus und Sozialismus" ("Feminism and Socialism") by feminist author Anja Meulenbelt to substantiate her argument.[98] In her answer from August

23, 1983, Tiedemann admits that five years in prison might have locked her into an outdated perspective on the women's movement, and she voices an interest in engaging more closely with feminist ideas, which until this point were not a priority to her.[99] While she dismisses as "vulgar Marxism" (*vulgärmarxismus*)[100] Meulenbelt's argument that women as a social group share a consciousness that differs from men's, she does admit that the Left did not deal enough with the implications of domestic work and the sexual division of labor. Tiedemann clearly views these as the basis for the oppression of women that manifests most harshly for the full-time housewife and the female worker: "even if an emancipated partnership exists on this individual level, the woman still carries around the burden of centuries-long oppression of women, because her individual liberation has to assert itself against the domination of men in the entire society again and again."[101] This becomes discernable in the socialist countries, says Tiedemann, where an early state-mandated liberation of women in all social areas "gradually was backtracked on, resulting in barely anything remaining of 'women's liberation' other than women's jobs [in paid work]."[102] But she doubts the accuracy of Meulenbelt's conclusion that women, because of their social position as reproductive workers, should be regarded as the true revolutionary progressive force: to view "the female part of society as its own class with an avant-garde function," she states, unimpressed, "is for me, coming from the socialist corner, rather 'revolutionary.'"[103] Since Tiedemann categorizes the classic Marxist theory of consciousness as determined by material reality as outdated, it is not surprising that she is skeptical of Meulenbelt's "feminist social theory."[104]

That Tiedemann emphasizes in a letter from 1984 that she at this point possesses only a little knowledge of feminist theory[105] (in an activist milieu that generally mandated the rigorous theorizing of any political position) points to the low significance that feminism had in radical leftist circles. Tiedemann justifies her own ignorance by referring to the lack of any overlap between her radical political work (armed struggle and life underground) and feminist issues: "my political practice outside—as an activist and later underground—focused on completely different issues."[106] Her personal emancipation, she claims, was not influenced by the women's movement but "came, so to speak, from myself, were [my] own impulses and thought processes, that i developed because of my own experiences."[107] She rejects an automatic claim for solidarity between women that is based on a shared material (i.e., feminist) standpoint.[108] At this point she displays a remarkable theoretical naïveté in her assumption that any of one's "own impulses and thought processes" can be generated autonomously from within a person's experience, or can be separated from ideas brought to her attention externally or from shared social experiences.

However, despite her skepticism of feminism, in a letter from February 9, 1984, she emphasizes that she finds it easier to establish political as well as personal relationships with women than with men. In this very personal letter (which she describes as a "chat letter"),[109] she tries to explain the conflict between Marxist political theory (sexual differences are not a basis for political collaboration) and personal experience (emotional affinity with women):

> well, and we women are the better half of humanity anyway. i say this irrespective of any discussions about the women's liberation movement, any theories or anything else. it is my feeling, my experience, that i get along so much better with women, can personally develop, can trust, that there is depth, intensity, happiness, without question, in a way that i experience much more rarely with men—and i always have to fight to gain it, fight against them, the competition, the power struggle between men and women.[110]

At the time when Tiedemann composed this letter, women were central to her life, since in prison, a social space that prescribes absolute gender segregation, her survival depended on the presence of, and her friendships with, women. Her expressed attachment to the women around her does not necessarily diverge from her earlier position that gender liberation comes through women emancipating themselves in their personal lives, not through a particular political effort. However, in this segment of the text, which simultaneously is a very personal "declaration of love to all my girlfriends,"[111] Tiedemann displays an increased awareness of women possessing particular *social* traits and skills that they acquire in society. According to standpoint theory, these shared traits produce a solidarity felt in everyday life that potentially leads to a political one. This awareness prepares the ground for the clear shift in

Tiedemann's thinking towards an understanding of women's oppression as political and systemic, with women as the social group primarily affected by patriarchy.

### Letters #3: Feminism as "Struggle for Full Equality between Men and Women"

In the letters Tiedemann wrote to Amin—an Iranian leftist activist who was living in exile in West Germany—in the mid-1980s, the shift in her thinking regarding the significance of women's liberation in the context of leftist politics becomes visible. Here she classifies women's oppression as political, not personal, and views it as playing a central role in the general struggle against oppression. Tiedemann and Amin debated this topic in an exchange of letters from October 1985 through June 1986, following a multiyear correspondence between the two. Amin, who visited her multiple times in prison and who also knew Tiedemann's mother, discussed a variety of political themes in his correspondence (such as the overthrow of the shah, the repression of leftist activists by the Khomeini regime, and questions around Iranian nationalism).[112] However, he also wrote very personal letters to Tiedemann that reflect on his experiences with xenophobia and racism as an Iranian in exile in West Germany, his interpersonal relationships, and his feelings of loneliness, and that also refer to his composing of (political) poetry and to general philosophical questions. It is therefore not surprising that the two correspondents, with their "odd, 'platonic'"[113] relationship as a basis, would have a discussion about the status (and liberation) of women in the context of leftist politics. Their exchange about feminism takes place in the context of other political discussions, and unlike in other matters, on this they do not agree. The correspondence between Tiedemann and Amin ends—after a two-year break—with a farewell postcard from Amin.[114]

In the months in which the letters about feminism were composed (October 1985 through June 1986), Tiedemann was incarcerated in Hindelbank in Switzerland and was one year away from being extradited to West Germany. During this period of her incarceration—according to her own disclosures—she time and again lived through phases when she was physically and psychologically unwell.[115] Both she and

Amin thought their friendship to be stagnating at that time, and they attempted to become closer again by approaching new topics. Tiedemann mentions in a letter from October 14, 1985, that lately she had been engaging more with feminism and asks Amin if he were interested in this political topic, particularly considering the situation of women in Iran.[116] In the same letter, Tiedemann writes that because of her detention she has increasing difficulties productively engaging with political topics that are far removed from her living space and experiences that because of this "only become increasingly abstract to me."[117] She goes on to say that this "weighs heavy on me and frightens me."[118] It is important to point out that at this stage she perceived feminism clearly as something that politically spoke to her life directly, and that she viewed the situation of women in Iran as a topic for discussion that would connect Amin's realm of experiences as an Iranian to hers as a woman.

Tiedemann viewed this correspondence with Amin as a productive exchange of opinions; they even discussed the "cursed topic"[119] during one of his visits. On November 28, 1985, Amin responds in detail to Tiedemann's question about his understanding of feminism,[120] whereupon she answers on January 27, 1986, that she appreciates that he as a man is thinking about women's liberation. Unfortunately, she writes, it cannot be taken for granted "that men—even men disposed to revolutionary thought—deal with it."[121] For the longest time, she continues, women's liberation had been dismissed as "something that just women should need to deal with, because it is exclusively their problem"[122]—if it was mentioned in political discussions at all.

At this point, there are two major differences in her approach to women's oppression from that expressed in earlier letters. First, Tiedemann objects to the position expressed by Amin that women's oppression is secondary, a minor contradiction—which was exactly the position that Tiedemann herself formulated in 1982. Second, she now insists that this issue impacts her differently than it impacts him—that her standpoint is different—and that with the question of gender relations her personal liberation is at stake, since, she writes, "it is, so to say, existential to me, because it affects my existence."[123] In contrast, for him as a man this issue will always remain abstract, since his social experiences—unlike hers—do not overlap with those of other women. For the first time, Tiedemann unambiguously declares that patriarchy affects women differently than men, who, on the basis of their position within the system, also know advantages.

This change in paradigm forms the basis for her following discussion with Amin, in which Tiedemann asks, "what political significance does the struggle for women's liberation have, how do we integrate it into the general struggle against exploitation and oppression?"[124] She dissents from his tendency to view the women's movement as one of many "issues" that as symptoms of capitalism ignite resistance (noticeable by their prefix "anti-," "e.g. 'anti-noise, anti-militarism, anti-nuclear, anti-forest decline' etc."),[125] an outlook she had voiced earlier in her political development. To equate these countermovements with the women's movement now means to her to "very much trivialize [the problem of women's oppression], to misconceive its significance or even to perform a wrong analysis."[126] After all, Tiedemann writes, capitalism, compared to patriarchy, is a recent phenomenon in the history of oppression of some social groups by others, as she passionately lays out:

> since the beginning of humanity, all social systems have one thing in common: the dominance of patriarchy; it is the social, cultural and therefore also political basis for all different types of societies and can thus by no means be viewed as disconnected [from the primary contradiction], i.e. the attempt to view it separately disregards or ignores an important root of human oppression as such, and with that continues to produce systems that because of a false analysis are not capable of resolving this contradiction. this is is not an empty claim, but reality.[127]

One even detects a slight impatience in her tone, when she responds to her friend's observation that patriarchy is a complicated thing with the following statement: "i do not really comprehend this, because these 'complicated and delicate problems' are exactly the dominance of patriarchy, which i don't find complicated but rather crystal clear."[128]

Tiedemann makes the case with Amin that women's oppression rather forms a part of the primary contradiction since patriarchy and capitalism/imperialism form a unit of systemic oppression—that "births" our exploitative societies[129]—which would also explain why patriarchal structures continue to exist in postrevolutionary societies, precisely because sexism is *not* a secondary contradiction that disappears with the abolition of capitalism. Tiedemann prioritizes neither of the two systems (a tendency of some feminists that she criticizes); instead she declares that they constitute each other: "one cannot solve the one problem without the other."[130]

Tiedemann also emphasizes that it would be wrong to reject feminism as inherently bourgeois and that instead one should be aware that there are several orientations of feminist politics, that feminism is "not a homogenous movement."[131] Despite all differences, she writes, "all have the goal [in common] to take the struggle for women's rights and for their liberation into their own hands, here and now."[132] She deems it legitimate to reject those "strands" of feminism that refuse to recognize the extent to which capitalism and sexism rely on each other (e.g., parts of the bourgeois/liberal and the radical feminist movement). But for her this no longer means that women's liberation *as a political movement* should be rejected—a radical shift in her opinion, which she articulated in 1978 and reiterated as late as 1982. Tiedemann had always assumed that a woman's emancipation begins "at home" (with her personal relationships and her sexuality) and that this was the prerequisite for any *political* liberation of a woman. This does not change in her later letters. However, unlike before, in the mid-1980s she views men and women as affected very differently by patriarchy: men profit in everyday life from women's oppression. To then expect that "men and women fight 'shoulder to shoulder'" assumes "ideal conditions" between the genders that is unrealistic for today's society.[133] She understands "perforce [. . .] this liberation often will have to be directed against men, as long as the majority of men are not willing to accept women as equal."[134] It appears that while she is happy to politically work with men who are engaging critically with their privilege, she has no patience with those who refuse to do so.

Tiedemann's increasingly feminist attitude manifests in a letter from June 3, 1986, in which she defines feminism as follows: "an umbrella term for the struggle whose aim it is to achieve full equality between women and men and that also postulates women's complete self-fulfillment on an individual, social, cultural and political level."[135] She abolishes the traditional differentiation between "political" and "cultural" changes and declares both to be valid targets of activism.[136]

Amin openly doubts whether "the personal is political" ("das persönliche [private] ist politisch")—the core message of the women's liberation movement; that is, he doubts whether the changes a woman achieves in her private life are politically effective. In her response, Tiedemann adamantly rejects the right of the larger political Left—i.e., men—to determine or judge whether a woman's resistance to her oppression—even if it happens on a personal level—is effective or not. "i wonder if this is not again a form of typical male paternalism, when men—in this case you—disqualify women's struggle for their rights as worthless!"[137] She emphasizes that men, even if they politically support the fight against gendered discrimination, can never fully grasp the extent of the phenomenon and thus cannot adequately judge women's resistance to an oppression that remains abstract to them. Here Tiedemann clearly claims a feminist standpoint that ascribes to women an epistemological advantage: only they can assess sexism realistically and they therefore possess political and cultural authority in the fight against it. Men—since they experience advantages through gender discrimination—inevitably have a different, less knowledgeable perspective. Women cannot afford to wait until after the revolution for leftist men to finally take women's oppression as a political task seriously: "women themselves must fight for their liberation, it is mainly and primarily their own struggle. men cannot and should not be allowed to 'take over' this struggle or fight it for them, they can only support them as best they can."[138]

Tiedemann views women's liberation in the private sphere as necessary for successful political change, and particularly for the revolution. Men needed to acknowledge that sexism impacts every woman's everyday life and that the fight against personal experiences of discrimination constitutes a political act. This diverges from Tiedemann's former position that women become most effectively liberated through participation in armed struggle. Instead she now politicizes individual emancipation as such as a necessary part of the leftist movement, without which successful resistance is not possible. The most important shift here is the emphasis on personal resistance in everyday life *as political*. She insists

> that individual or social steps towards liberation that are (still) intrinsically part of the system can also constitute a step towards a general revolutionizing of social structures. does a revolutionary process not always consist of a multitude of such steps? because the revolution itself is a pro-

cess and today precisely not anymore the great spectacle of seizure of power by the revolutionary class.[139]

Accordingly, women's liberation must happen on both a personal and a political level, for only then is true social transformation—a revolution—possible: "for liberation is a process that cannot be pre-scribed through laws or decrees. it is a live process, a prolonged process. [. . .] only when they de facto stand 'shoulder to shoulder' with men does a joint struggle become possible."[140]

The importance that the women's movement and its theoretical as-sumptions had for Tiedemann significantly changed during the eight years between 1978 and 1986 in which the letters analyzed here were written. As an activist living underground and during the early years of her detention she viewed—congruent with the radical Left in general—the women's movement as negligible, if not obstructive, to the armed struggle. Early on in her prison correspondence, she dismisses women's liberation efforts as those of a counterrevolutionary "self-liberation group." While Tiedemann in a later phase of her incarceration still called the women's movement nothing more than a "laboring around at a sec-ondary contradiction of society," she nevertheless sought out discussion of the topic, in particular with regard to the question of whether patriar-chal structures impress the (political) consciousness of women and men differently. In the mid-1980s she inhabited a clearly feminist position. In 1986, finally, the former terrorist criticized a "revolutionary" attitude that does not view patriarchy as the basis of all oppression, and told her at that time active pen friend that she was planning on educating herself further on the topic.[141]

Tiedemann's development mirrors the larger social development of the Left in West Germany (the deradicalization of a militant scene and the turn towards self-fulfillment through internalization, the "long march through the institutions" ["lange Marsch durch die Insti-tutionen"]), on the one hand, and that of the women's movement on the other.[142] However, Tiedemann's feminist analysis never loses sight of the power relations created by economic differences: her continu-ous commitment to radical leftist politics, which view class conflict as the primary social conflict, departs from the political conviction of most groups in the autonomous women's movement, and so does her unwavering belief that—ultimately—this is a struggle that can only be won *with* men. She remains wary of—albeit ambivalent about—an assumed solidarity among women based on their gender alone; like the authors of the autobiographies, she seems to have experienced underground as a gender-"neutral" space, a space that allowed for women to be agents of their politically controversial activism. Disturbingly absent from her reflections on class and gender is a critical engagement with race and ethnicity, and one wonders how far her isolation from current issues "outside" (i.e., the increased dealings with questions of ethnicity and race in the women's movement and feminist scholarship) limited a comprehensive development of her analysis. The question remains how her criticism of a revolutionary ethos that excludes the struggle for gender equality (i.e., her growing belief that revolution can only take place when gender equality has been achieved or is a primary goal for revolution) coincides with her general distancing from terrorism as a means for revolutionary politics. Towards the end of the period of her imprisonment covered by the letters, Tiedemann disassociates herself from the dogma of the unconditional dedication of the revolutionary subject to armed struggle. But she never explains more closely how the political consciousness of a woman that not only reflects the class struggle but also patriarchal power relates to political violence.[143] Among other things, Tiedemann's letters make apparent the need for more research on how gender relations and feminist politics influenced militant women.

The autobiographies and letters by former female terrorists at hand—if read for moments of engagement with questions of gendered power—reveal that gender and sexuality were very much on the minds of women in armed groups. The autobiographical texts (re)construct a concern with gender politics that, if perhaps unreliably capturing the actual moment, nevertheless place leftist politics in relation with feminist ones; they re-member a body of shared politics that has been depicted as completely severed. The letters by Tiedemann participate in this remembering by letting the reader witness the theoretical struggles of that process, making visible their effects as feminist practices through their reinstituting of a feminist concern for gender equality into the core of revolutionary politics.

These readings contradict a general understanding prevailing in the literature that makes invisible armed women's feminist concerns, which politically connect leftist radicals with issues of the women's movement. Organizationally, there were clear separations; however, the overlap in the individual activists' personal histories (and retrospective desires) denies that these organizational separations included all conceptual similarities. Recognizing these overlaps locates feminist practices *outside* the organizational boundaries of the autonomous women's movement and into the (at times failed) attempts of women in armed underground groups to integrate gender politics into their lives, if not their politically violent actions.[144] Feminist practices are then not only rooted in the "truth" of women's efforts to integrate feminist issues into leftist politics, but find their origin in the political—and in the imagined, desired— histories of armed women whose actions at times were influenced by an acute awareness of gender and sexual oppression, and haunted by the gendered failure of their revolution.

# Conclusion

## "Can Political Violence Be Feminist?"

The topic of women terrorists elicits a variety of responses: from the feminist "commonsense" reaction of condemning their political violence as morally indefensible while conceding that not every woman is a "feminist" assumed always to have nonviolent politics; to the equal-opportunity response of "gender does not matter in discourse on terrorism"; to the more conservative "yes, something is clearly off about these women *as* women and see—women can be violent, too!" Feminists' vehement answer "No!" to the question "Can violence be feminist?" clearly indicates that the feminist position has most at stake here: female terrorists necessitate a clear *Abgrenzung* (separation) of their actions from the goals of the women's movement, in order for the latter not to be discredited within the discourse on liberal democratic politics. Ultimately, it is violence that marks political actions as unfeminist.

When in the winter of 2012 I was visiting the Infoladen Frankfurt am Main, a volunteer-run local activist library, community center, and archive, one of the volunteers, a white German woman in her fifities, asked me about the focus of my research. Her reaction to my answer was significant and thought-provoking: she was absolutely thrilled that someone was making an effort to better understand the gender politics of the RAF and of the group's impact on German society. She was tired of people demonizing the women and tired of feminists' silence on that aspect of political activism. She explained to me that as a working-class woman in the late 1970s and '80s, she had always felt slightly out of place in most women's groups that were organizing, and that she had felt more "at home" with the militant women who remained committed to class as a major political focus. For her, she told me, the RAF women's actions were more "real"—even though the violence was difficult to come to terms with. She would like to see feminist scholars examine the fissure between the middle-class autonomous women's movement's push towards peace politics, motherhood, and personal empowerment and the political concerns of working-class women activists. The volunteer's remarks resonated with what I found during my archival research and my studying of the "grey literature" of the 1970s and '80s (movement publications and political statements). I was struck by how the definition of feminist politics as nonviolent has made invisible large numbers of women whose feminist sensibilities were turned off by exclusionary and ultimately separatist attitudes of many women in the autonomous women's movement. The pain caused by conflicting feminist concerns, or rather, by the prioritizing of certain concerns over others, it seems, is still very much present: my encounter at the Infoladen speaks to the importance of resisting the creation of a one-dimensional cultural memory of feminist politics that declares alternative feminist positions to be inauthentic and unfeminist.

My analysis discloses that because terrorists symbolize a violent departure from the social contract and challenge the promise of democratic political measures, they are often demonized in public debates. However, the main tenor in the public debate on, and official response to, female terrorists seems to be that while terrorism/armed struggle as political strategy is condemned in general, the participation of women seems a fundamental contradiction in terms, as we see in the media coverage of female terrorists. Men believing in armed struggle are understood to be ideologically misguided but do not pose a mystery (they are seen as acting out some power fantasy that is in accord with masculine aspirations), while the very nature of terrorism precludes women's participation.[1] Some feminist theories on violence as patriarchal provide a powerful frame of analysis of how relationships to violence—institutional, personal, and political—are, in fact, gendered. Women appear to be positioned (structurally or naturally) as victims of violence, while men are predisposed to becoming perpetrators, and these theoretical presumptions are backed up by statistical findings of a prevalence of male criminal violence over female criminal violence, including occurrences of violence between intimate partners and sexual violence. Women, the argument goes, are consequently more predisposed towards peaceful politics, and have skills that make them more competent in negotiating the terms of those politics.

This prominence of the notion of violence as male/masculine within feminist theories is problematized by Hanna Hacker in her book *Gewalt ist: keine Frau* (Violence Is: Not Woman). She observes that violence against the (female) body is still almost exclusively claimed by authoritative discourses on "violence against women" (a violence that is conceptualized as concrete and direct). At the same time, poststructuralist feminist approaches (including those informed by Foucault's ideas of decentralized power and resistance) hold a monopoly on the textual construction of the body through cultural inscription, but have developed little on concrete bodily violence (one exception being Judith Butler's writing on normative violence on bodies in her gender theory). According to Hacker, feminist theories have so far failed to effectively theorize gender and violence—the assumed relationship (women as victims of male violence) determines our readings of women's actions. Instead, she asks if we should rather be looking closely to see if those actions do not challenge said assumed relationship.[2] Following Hacker, my analyses of discourses on terrorist women's actions suggest that defining gender (and sex) as category, not role or identity per se,[3] destabilizes the idea of the feminist "subject" and makes an examination of the practice of performing gender—and politics—possible. In this grey gendered area is where we find the RAF women and what Jean-Luc Nancy defines as their "violent truth." This "violent truth" establishes an effect that challenges the norms of the gender regime: it is in fact the violence of the women's actions that constitutes them as potential feminist practices.

## Experiencing Violence and Violent Resistance

Understanding the limitations of feminist theories' (and the women's movement's) claims that women's relationship to violence is necessarily one of oppression is central in making visible the ultimately *diverse* relationships women have to violence. As compelling as these feminist models of gender and violence might appear in their powerful rejection of violence, they are based on two flawed assumptions: by privileging a universal women's "experience," these models effectively leave armed women outside of any theorizing of gendered violence, and they discount as feminist politics any resistance other than nonviolence.

The idea that women's experiences are important to feminist politics is derived not just from the concept that "the personal is political" but also from a materialist understanding of structural social experiences as gendered. However, an assumed universal women's standpoint (based in women's shared experiences *as women*) can become problematic in its erasure of standpoints shaped by categories such as race and class, which generate different relationships to state and structural violence (what Žižek terms "objective violence") and which often produce a need for measures of counterviolence that a more privileged standpoint might not generate.[4] These limitations extend to (neo)imperialism and global relations and their at time violent manifestations. An assumed peaceful disposition releases Western women from examining calls for solidarity and their own privilege, which allows a pacifist strategy. Instead of constituting an ahistoric, universal truth, women's presumed nonviolence is actually a discursively produced assumption based on the privileging of specific voices and actions. As chapter 1 demonstrates, signs of this became visible in the early autonomous women's movement's privileging of reproductive rights and sexual/domestic violence and its overall focus on "the personal is political," which effectively eclipsed voices of nonwhite German women as well as international calls to solidarity. The most consequential gesture of the women's movement was the embrace of the binary model of female victims of male violence that defined women's standpoint as centering around their victimization through patriarchal violence. However, as discussed in chapter 2, maternal ethics' inability to account for the actions of RAF women who left their children to join the armed struggle makes apparent the unreliability that comes with theorizing violent women's actions within a framework of gendered violence as binary.

In much feminist criticism of male violence, the role of the state and its effects on women (especially poor women and women of color) remains undertheorized. The types of gendered experiences of violence that are prioritized will shape feminist discourse—the emphasis on reproductive rights and sexual violence as the major failures of the state to protect women's rights by the West German women's movement made invisible the gendered forms of structural "objective" violence women experienced, often based on their class and/or nationality (such as guest workers in Germany). The ways in which women in the RAF and Movement 2nd June posed a particularly gendered threat to the state becomes visible in chapters 3 and 4, which analyze how the state and media constructed the feminized body as violent threat to a masculine system of reason. This can be seen both in terms of actual gender, exemplified by the women wanted and prosecuted by the state and its law enforcement agencies, and in terms of a perceived structural position of the hunger-striking gendered body within prison as feminine. While prison does not speak to the experience of every woman, its gendered spaces and the construction of the body as a femininized entity in relation to a masculine state provides crucial insights into the way power operates along gendered lines. The foregrounding of the body in the political hunger strikes raises important questions regarding the state's gendering of the hunger-striking prisoner as well as about the construction of alternative identities to a liberal political subjectivity. Finally, chapter 5 makes visible how the issue of women's experiences of patriarchal violence is reflected on in the memoirs and letters of (former) terrorists and how a link to revolutionary (and thus implicitly violent) politics is forged by the authors. The analyses throughout these chapters account for violent women's effects on a gender regime threatened by their gender transgressions.

The second flawed assumption brought forward by the feminist model of patriarchal violence oppressing women is the necessary discounting of any violent resistance as nonfeminist. Inherent to the concept of violence as male is that the only viable feminist response to an existing condition (violence) is its opposite (nonviolence). Violent female resistance would then reinforce the violent status quo. The effect of this is that feminist resistance to violence has been naturalized as nonviolent; otherwise the woman resisting would participate in what is understood to be *patriarchal* behavior and perpetuate the cycle of violence. However, if we avoid the binary logic that violence can only be countered with nonviolence, counterviolence becomes a viable option in feminist politics. I trace this in the militant women's relationship to violence as well as in the relationship that feminist activists had to violence as it is expressed in movement publications and letters, such as with the analysis of feminist responses to media coverage in chapter 3, and in the autobiographies and letters by (former) female terrorists discussed in chapter 5. So despite its compelling elements, the feminist construction of the dialectic of violence as masculine and nonviolence as feminine comes up short when one accounts for the diversity of both women's realities and their means of resisting.

The various points of analysis presented in this book offer ways of understanding RAF women's actions and their discursive significance as feminist practices. This understanding is an alternative to the presentation of female terrorists as separate from feminist politics both ideologically and in terms of action: violence is instead understood as resistance to the experience of violence. The book makes this point in two ways. First, it demonstrates that many feminist activists had a more ambivalent relationship to political violence than usually is claimed by popular accounts of the autonomous women's movement. This is an intervention in the historicization of women in the RAF and Movement 2nd June as separate from feminist politics. Second, it questions whether feminist politics are exclusively defined as actions of a feminist *subject* or whether they should not rather be understood as feminist *practices*, which can be contradictory to other feminist practices and also morally questionable. This is an intervention into theorizing feminist politics.

## Political Violence as Feminist Practice

In my analysis of women and political violence, I aim at maintaining a balance between historical and cultural specificity (a specific gender ideology confronting RAF women in post–World War II Germany) and a broad critique of patriarchal "readings" of political women globally (RAF women as encountering ideological responses that converge with or diverge from women's experiences in other national settings). In fact, the concept of feminist practice as I have used it throughout the book is inspired by feminists of color's intervention into a Western feminist discourse of liberation and global sisterhood: the primacy of the subject—i.e., a conscious feminist identity—in defining feminist politics then reproduces hegemonic cultural and political "truths" that make women's experiences and politics outside of those "truths" invisible. Concepts that challenge the political "truth" of "women's experience" and that inform my analysis include Chandra Talpade Mohanty's politics of engagement versus politics of transcendence[5] (transcendence as erasing difference without resolving the power structures underlying it) and Karen Kaplan's call to theorize feminist transnational practices as critiques of location in order to produce "the grounds for a rejection of unitary feminism in favor of solidarity and coalitions that are not based on mystified notions of similarity or difference."[6] Feminist practices are based in the historical, cultural, and political context that the woman who acts finds herself in—not in some universal notion of a liberated feminist subject. Acknowledging women's varied experiences then does not prevent feminist politics but instead allows for examination, evaluation, and support of feminist practices *outside one's own experiences.*

Sara Mahmood's ethnographic study of Egyptian women's participation in the Islamic revival movement, *The Politics of Piety,* effectively questions the theoretical viability of the feminist subject as the marker for sustainable gender politics. Feminist subjectivity, she argues, has been conceptualized in terms of freedom and autonomy, "liberal presuppositions [that] have become naturalized in the scholarship on gender," on the one hand, and a feminist poststructuralist discourse that overwhelmingly "conceptualize[s] agency in terms of subversion or resignification of social norms,"[7] on the other. While I am not willing to abandon all "liberationist" notions as the basis for progressive politics (and thus contribute to the poststructuralist feminist scholarship that views the subversion of social norms as furthering social justice), I appreciate Mahmood's focus on practice[8] and not identity when evaluating women's aspirations to viable and sustained lives. My approach to reading actions by women in the RAF and Movement 2nd June as feminist practices that undermine the existing gender status quo thus is informed by these theorists' prioritizing of shared political beliefs and declared solidarity over shared experiences as well as by the questioning of the feminist subject as the center of feminist politics.

In the context of West German terrorism, I view feminist practices to be actions whose gender constellations trouble, challenge, and potentially redirect existing oppressive gender regimes. These practices need not be "consciously" feminist in their orientation;[9] they have discursive effects and shape power in ways that undermine essentialist notions of femininity and masculinity, and thus a heterosexist economy of desire. "Feminist" then is a marker less of progressive identity than of practices that affect gender relations in ways that challenge conservative and static traditions, and these practices might be controversial in their moral and ethical implications.[10] When one tries to measure the discursive impact of a woman's political action, the focus needs to be on the specificity of the context: the historical moment is important when one tries to assess the discursive relevance of political actions as gendered. What were the gender politics with which the RAF and Movement 2nd June women's actions interacted? And how did these gender politics influence the actions and tactics of terrorist groups?

When Andreas Baader's prison break was organized in 1970, the women planning the action were clearly thinking about gender: they anticipated a situation determined by dominant, conservative gender norms. They assumed that the action would be complicated by gender expectations that they as women would evoke, since any threat of violence posed by them would be dismissed by the male guards. They were acutely aware of the fact that women wielding weapons would not be taken seriously and that that might actually force the use of violence. The RAF women solved this dilemma by hiring a man to take part in the prison break, hoping that his presence would lend masculine authority to their action. In the end, the gendered dynamics that clearly were considered in the planning backfired. "The fact that shots were fired during Baader's escape was—well, how do I put it—ironic. That was not based on some ideological reason, but developed out of the makeup of the group," former RAF member Barbara[11] reflects.

> We knew there would be two armed guards in the room and after all, it was 1970, and unlike today, when every time you turn on the TV a female detective jumps out at you, if women had marched in with weapons back then, they would have said: "Come on, girl! Let it be" and then we would have *had* to shoot. So in order to be taken seriously, we asked another man to take part in the break, who promptly was the one who lost his nerve and used his gun when there was absolutely no reason to do so.[12]

The cultural assumption that violence is masculine, which the RAF women were afraid would generate a need to demonstrate their seriousness about taking Baader with them, in fact was reproduced by the one man in the group. Barbara reminds us that there had been no real challenge to the gendered concept of (political) violence prior to this point—while the movements of the 1960s might have destabilized gender norms, they did not politically and openly counter them. The response RAF women generated was grounded in an actual risk they posed not just to national security but to a normative gendered ideology that was only being openly criticized by an emerging autonomous women's movement starting in 1972. "In a situation like this," Barbara insists, "very different from today, women would not have been able to assert themselves. We felt we had to rely on the presence of a man to be taken seriously as a threat." There had been no feminist movement to openly question naturalized gender roles when it came to the use of violence, and both the RAF women's astute reading of the situation as it related to the success of their action and the hysterical response of the public and state to the existence of female terrorists attest to the powerful impact the gesture of women taking up arms had on gender discourse.[13] This awareness of how expectations around gender roles in the 1970s differed from those of today is echoed in Margit Schiller's reflections on the necessity to historicize women's political actions, such as with the women's decision to ask a man to partake in the freeing of Baader, which young women in 2001 could not understand: "For an eighteen-year-old it seems to be close to inconceivable [   ] that the women's movement in the 1970s was just in its beginnings and that men had no experiences with collective confidence and active resistance from women."[14] This shift in discourse on gender that the women's movement forced is also reflected in the request to deny a medical expert in the trial against RAF member Christine Kuby, which she presented in court in January 1979 and which was titled "Zu Frauen in der Guerilla" (On Women in the Guerilla). In this document, Kuby is able to refer to a by-now-established feminist critique of the sexist practices and theories of the medical (in particular the psychiatric) establishment in West Germany that reduce women to supposed biological traits. Her claim that the "starting point of the raf is the position and experience of strength, i.e. to be as a *woman* what anyone can be, rebellion, guerilla"[15] references a feminist discourse on equality that was not available in the same way to women in the RAF in 1970.

The claim that women's political violence creates a discursive moment is congruent with poststructuralism and its decentering of power and thus of (single) identities as the basis for politics. This further complicates the polarization of women's peacefulness and men's violence that is argued for in both mainstream gender ideology and much of feminist theory. Theories of intersectionality and assemblages (the latter of which, as Jasbir Puar states, conceptualize race, sexuality, and gender "as concatenations, unstable assemblages of revolving and devolving energies, rather than intersectional coordinates")[16] identify a variety of sources of violence experienced by women (the state, poverty, heterosexism, racism, colonialism, nationalism, other women) and draw on Foucault's idea of discursive power, which locates sites of resistance outside established political mechanisms.[17] Furthermore, the notion of gender performativity put forth by Judith Butler in *Gender Trouble* locates gendered behavior as originating not in bodies/individual identities but in regulatory norms, destabilizing both mainstream ideologies of passive women and radical feminist positions declaring women to be naturally peaceful: women in violent political groups perform their gender in ways that become unintelligible to existing norms—they become what Hacker conceptualizes as "nonwomen," female actors unidentifiable as having the identity (and designation) of woman.[18] As Hacker argues, much of feminist theorizing participates in the erasure of politically and otherwise violent women from public discourse on women's social roles. She instead calls for a feminist theorizing of gender that makes possible the historicization of actors outside the binary of woman-man firmly bookended by the concepts of femininity and masculinity.

Recent feminist scholarship (including Hacker's) has contributed to this retheorizing of violent women more generally and their representation in public debates, as well as of politically violent women in particular. As Bielby argues in *Violent Women in Print*, news coverage on violent women rarely makes a distinction between politically motivated and personal violence: in their representations of these women, "there is no such thing as a politically violent woman; regardless of why she might *think* she is being violent, it is actually all about her body, her sexuality, her oedipal history, and her uncontrollable emotions."[19] Beyond media coverage however, I would argue that it is the extreme threat that a *politically* violent woman constitutes that necessitates the total depolitization of her actions. What amplifies the threat she poses is the political motivation behind her violence—it forces an engagement with political claims that criminal violence does not. The fact that the *state* is the primary target of her violence catapults her deviation into the realm of national security, not simply criminal pathology. These feminist theoretical interventions into a rigid gender theory of naturalized femininity and masculinity (gender performativity, violence as "degendering," and discursive political power as intersecting with gender) make a reevaluation of actions by RAF and Movement 2nd June women possible. This reevaluation does not rely on an understanding of them as deviant and instead accounts in a more thorough manner for the power of gender as a structuring discursive force, which continues to couple normative bodies with violent/nonviolent behavior and declares diverging ones to be unnatural and damaged.

Since early on, feminist theories thus have complicated the violence-against-women paradigm that conceptualizes men/masculinity as the source of violence. Simultaneously they maintained a critical framework in which masculinity and femininity function as social norms that regulate gendered behavior. This acknowledgment that gendered norms define much of our understanding of violence (masculinity as historically associated with violence), on the one hand, and the offering of sophisticated views of deviations from this norm as part of a troubling of gender that exceeds the binary identities of man-woman (violent women are not unnatural; their assumed nonviolence is a discursive "truth," not a natural one), on the other, makes possible a critique of patriarchal violence *and* a revisiting of violence as a potentially feminist political means of engagement. Women in the RAF and other leftist politically violent groups are figures around which these discursive efforts converge.

A thorough examination of the tension between understanding violence as a feminist tool of resistance and understanding violence as patriarchal is an important aspect of building feminist political communities and collective resistance. An insistence on contextualizing women's experiences and political decisions resists a universal notion of "women's" activism—and thereby resists a universal definition of "feminist." In the process of building cultural memory, feminists, in their continued attempts to make sense of these contradictions, need to be cautious not to dismiss this tension by evoking a "peaceful" tradition of women's political work. This is especially dangerous in our contemporary global situation of a rising neoliberalism and the wars that have been raging in the name of (U.S.) "freedom" and imperialism. Declaring one form of activism as "feminist" and another as "unfeminist" on the basis of universal notions of gender can itself be an imperialist gesture and reduces the diverse and necessarily contradictory positions that make up feminist practices. Recognizing contentious political strategies within feminist histories—of which militancy is a part—is necessary in our ongoing debates on feminist practices in a transnational world.

Accepting the premise that feminist politics cannot presuppose a feminist subject has implications for feminist theories of violence. Above all, it removes the problematic privileging of a liberated feminist subject as the measure for feminist politics. The universalizing of "the" feminist subject makes invisible the power of location and the hegemonic understanding of what it means to be a liberated woman by naturalizing the experiences and beliefs of "the" feminist subject that form the basis for feminist politics. If instead it is the discursive impact on a gender regime (or lack thereof) that becomes the starting point for examining feminist practices, then any feminist politics is open to scrutiny in regard to its political sustainability, moral defensibility, and effect on women's lives. A declared feminist sensibility (that often is coupled with a privileged position within the global order) then does not suffice to claim feminist politics that can be assumed to be "good" politics and to withstand critical moral evaluations. Feminist practices demand the investigation of women's politics by not relying on the automatic equation of feminist politics with unambiguously sound politics. Instead of weakening the concept of feminist politics, the notion of feminist practices reinvests in discussion of accountability, transnational locations, and morality by demanding an engagement with uncomfortable contradictions and beliefs within women's experiences. This approach invites a reexamination of criteria that establish the category of feminist.

Two difficult aspects accompany the concept of feminist practices in the context of women in the RAF and Movement 2nd June. First, if it is the effect on gender discourse, not the subjectivity of the political actor, that is the defining moment of feminist politics, does this mean that the violence of right-wing women activists constitutes feminist practices? A close examination of whether those women's actions actually challenge an existing gender regime or whether their role in political violence does not ultimately reify dominant gender ideologies would be necessary in order to pursue this question, as well as a closer discussion of notions of political resistance (against a state/dominant groups), as opposed to reactionary political violence aimed at domination and exclusion (e.g., the historical constellation of German antifascist versus fascist activists). The evaluation of feminist practices as viable, or partly viable, would have to include their contribution to an overall more socially just society.[20]

The second potentially troubling aspect of the concept of feminist practices lies in the focus on an analysis of *discursive effects*, which shelves important questions of ethics and morality that politically violent actions raise, and threatens to make invisible the loss and grief experienced by victims of political violence. Here it is imperative to emphasize that a feminist practice does not automatically signal "good" politics exempt from scrutiny; unlike the claim to feminist subjectivity, feminist practices do not presume a moral high ground. Instead, they demand an examination of these feminist practices in terms of their sustainability and morality, enabling a critical debate on women's political practices that is aware of divergent and contradictory political values and strategies.

Finally, recasting the question of whether political violence can be feminist as one that examines these actions as historically rooted practices and as women's differing feminist politics changes our understanding not only of gender and violence but also of terrorism.[21] Violent political acts then become less objects of automatic condemnation but instead demand an examination of axes of power that structure people's lives and an engagement with the complicated assemblages of gender, sexuality, race, and nationalisms that form the discourse on terrorism.[22]

Maybe the most significant implication of women's political violence for feminist theories on violence is to allow dissonances within the theorizing of gendered political subjectivity and to foreground the necessity of reading women's political history as one of diverse—and diverging—feminist practices aimed at changing the status quo *towards* liberation, not as a progressive historical movement towards feminist subjectivity *through* liberation. The reflexive gesture of denying any link between women's social emancipation and violence would then be viewed as limiting an analysis of why women make political choices: acknowledging the ambivalence that certainly was part of an earlier feminist debate enriches our understanding of the subversive power of what Judith Butler termed "gender trouble," i.e., the *failed* performance of femininity. While murder and violence pose real moral questions, and might be indefensible to many, women's participation in these acts still poses a powerful threat to an existing gender order. In that sense, the question of whether women active in the RAF and Movement 2nd June engaged in feminist practices and what the wider implications of that might be for feminist politics—both in a productive and a counterproductive way—becomes a necessary one to ask.

# Notes

## Notes to Introduction

1. Deutsches Zentralinstitut für Soziale Fragen. The first epigraph for this chapter is a translation of "Müsse nun nicht . . . 'jeder Bürger' damit rechnen, daß ihm eines Tages 'der gewaltsame Tod in Gestalt eines jungen Mädchens gegenübertritt'?" ("Frauen im Untergrund," *Der Spiegel* 22). The second epigraph is Jean-Luc Nancy, "Image and Violence" 16; emphasis his.

2. See interview by Arno Luik with author Jutta Dithfurth in Luik's "'Sie War die Große Schwester der 68er'" (She Was the Big Sister of the 68ers) (60).

3. "Terroristenmädchen" (Schreiber, "Wir fühlten uns einfach stärker" 100).

4. "Der gewaltsame Tod in Gestalt eines jungen Mädchen" (quoted in *Der Spiegel*, "Frauen im Untergrund" 22).

5. There exist a variety of translations of the term "Bewegung 2. Juni," including "June 2 Movement," "Movement of June 2 (MJ2)," and "Movement 2 June." I believe the last term best expresses the German meaning and most closely reflects its spoken rhythm. I use the ordinal number "2nd" so the date will not be as visually jarring to the reader.

6. MacDonald xiv. According to journalist Eileen MacDonald in *Shoot the Women First*, this was "reputedly an instruction given to recruits to West Germany's anti-terrorist squad, and also the advice offered by Interpol to other European squads . . . [T]hough none [of the members of antiterrorist squads] would confirm that they ever had been given such an instruction, they considered it to be a damn good piece of advice" (xiv).

7. Important exceptions to this rejection of violence as masculine was the feminist armed group the Rote Zora (Red Zora), starting in the 1970s, and left militants, like Frauen gegen Imperialistischen Krieg (Women Against Imperialist War) in the 1980s. These feminists saw armed struggle as *grounded* in a feminist consciousness that viewed violence as the only effective way of resisting patriarchal domination. See chapter 1 for a discussion of these diverging feminist positions in the movement.

8. Saša Vukadinović, "Feminismus im Visier" (An Eye on Feminism) 54. Dominique Grisard uses the term "Emanzipationsthese" (emancipation thesis; *Gendering Terror* 38) to describe this phenomenon.

9. "Feminist" activism need not be synonymous with "women's" activism, since not all women activists organize for the liberation of women from patriarchal restrictions (see Waylen, "Rethinking Women's Political Participation and Protest: Chile 1970–1990" for a critical differentiation of the two). Here I am less interested in the analytical demarcation of feminist versus women; my focus is on how naturalized assumptions about women's innate political dispositions inform notions of what constitutes feminist politics.

10. §129 was introduced to the West German criminal code in August 1976. It states that it is criminal to found a terrorist organization, as well as to be a member of such an organization, or to support or advertise it. It enabled the legal system to punish thought before action (to "support," "advertise," or "be" a member does not necessitate action) and contributed to the general atmosphere of fear of state repression and social *Abgrenzung* (exclusion/demarcation) within the circles of left-leaning Germans.

11. See Karrin Hanshew's *Terror and Democracy in West Germany* for an in-depth analysis of the dealings of the German state and the German public with the phenomenon of left-wing terrorism.

12. Sozialistischer Deutscher Studentenbund. See Gerd Koenen, *Das rote Jahrzehnt* (The Red Decade) on the rapidly expanding leftist activism within K-groups (communist groups) and other political formations that far exceeded the immediate political presence of the SDS. Also see chapter 1.

13. See Sarah Colvin, *Ulrike Meinhof and West German Terrorism* (2009) and Clare Bielby's *Violent Women in Print* (2012) for a recently developing focus on gender in the scholarship on the RAF.

14. See chapter 1.

15. See chapter 4.

16. See chapters 2, 4, and 5.

17. I conducted qualitative interviews in 2005 and in 2006 with three former members of the RAF and Movement 2nd June, who throughout the book will be referred to as Heike, Karin, and Barbara. In each case, I conducted two formal interviews of 1–1.5 hours and at least one additional informal (unrecorded) conversation. The women I interviewed requested to remain anonymous; all references paraphrase (rather than directly quote) the content of the interviews. In general, this particular population is difficult to access: while some former members of West Germany's radical Left, especially armed groups like the RAF and Movement 2nd June, have either spoken or published about their experiences (including all three of the women I interviewed), many remain reluctant to go on record about any of their experiences and beliefs or distrust the state (and researchers) to a degree that makes it impossible for them to engage in any in-depth interview situation.

18. My study excludes the field of creative cultural texts inspired by the RAF, including movies, literary fiction, and texts in the performing arts. While this body of creative works does important discursive work, doing it justice goes beyond the scope of this book. Work being done in this area in English includes the European collection of essays on the RAF, *Baader Meinhof Returns*, edited by Gerrit-Jan Berendse and Ingo Cornils, as well as the influential chapter on films on the RAF in Nora Alter's study of German historical cinema, *Projecting History*. Also inspired by the release of the Oscar-nominated film *Baader-Meinhof* (2008), based on Stefan Aust's account of the group, several journals have taken up the RAF debate in special issues and individual articles.

19. See chapter 3.

20. See Jeremy Varon, *Bringing the War Home* 2, 7.

21. See Varon 314, n. 3.

22. In this I agree with Varon, who "describe[s] members of the RAF and other German groups variously as guerrillas or terrorists, depending on context." Using both terms,

he seeks "to reproduce some of the ambiguities that define the group's existence and that haunt efforts to reach definitive judgments on political violence" (Varon 314, n. 3).

23. Žižek, *Violence* 1. Subjective violence is what makes the news in the Western world, that which produces an incident and directly impacts victims: "[T]he obvious signals of violence are acts of crime and terror, civil unrest, international conflict" (1).

24. Žižek 1.

25. Žižek 2.

26. Butler, *Precarious Life* xiv.

27. Nancy, "Image and Violence" 16.

28. Nancy, "Image and Violence" 16.

29. Nancy, "Image and Violence" 17. Violence's force is "pure, dense, stupid, impenetrable intensity" (17) and "exercises itself without guarantor and without being accountable" (20).

Thank you to Eugenie Brinkema for bringing Nancy's reflection on violence to my attention.

30. Brinkema 366.

31. Nancy, "Image and Violence" 17.

32. "Truth" here signifies philosophical truth, a system of beliefs held and/or the state of "pure" being that is thought to preexist language and discourse. In the context of theories of discourse and power, "truths" are usually understood to be produced by claims of knowledge; they are "truth-effects" that declare something to be "true," "natural," "prediscursive."

33. Nancy, "Image and Violence" 17.

34. Brinkema 366.

35. Nancy, "Image and Violence" 18.

36. Nancy, "Image and Violence" 18; emphasis mine.

37. Nancy, "Image and Violence" 17.

38. According to Judith Butler, regulatory gender norms are part of the apparatus that bestows the category "human" on us—or that withholds it: referring to the Hegelian concept of "recognition" as that which makes us socially viable beings, she states, "The terms by which we are recognized as human are socially articulated and changeable. [. . .] As a result, the 'I' that I am finds itself at once constituted by norms and dependent on them" (*Undoing Gender* 3); performing a non-normative gender places the "I" outside the category human and the "I" becomes "threatened with unviability, with becoming undone altogether, when it no longer incorporates the norm in such a way that makes this 'I' fully recognizable" (3). This concept of norms as regulatory and necessary for subjects to be articulated and able to live echoes Hacker's observation in *Gewalt ist: keine Frau* (Violence Is: Not Woman) of the ways in which violence de-genders—or rather, un-genders—women, making them something less than human as "nonwomen."

39. Nancy, "The Image—the Distinct" 1; emphasis his.

40. Nancy, "The Image—the Distinct" 2. Part of this distinction is "the force—the energy, pressure, or intensity" that sets it apart from mere representation: the image "is the intimate and its passion, distinct from all representation" (Nancy, "The Image—the Distinct" 2 and 3). The image is—as violence and truth are—"of the

order of the monster" (Nancy, "Image and Violence" 22); it demonstrates separate from the thing, disputes its presence.

41. Brinkema 366.

42. "[T]he distinct is visible [. . .] because it does not belong to the domain of objects, their perception and their use, but to that of forces, their affections and transmissions. The image is the obvious of the invisible" (Nancy, "The Image—the Distinct" 12).

43. An image that is "indecent, shocking, necessary, heartrending" (Nancy, "Image and Violence" 15).

44. This gender transgression is also racialized and classed within the context of post–World War II Germany during both economic growth and crisis and its division of its society into citizens versus guest workers. The image of the female terrorist was very much that of the daughter of well-off Germans, educated and privileged, who had strayed from her path.

45. In this assessment of the feminist subject as limited for conceptualizing feminist politics, I am particularly inspired by "Third World" feminists' intervention into Western feminism's definition of both women's liberation and feminist subjectivity since the 1990s, such as in the early essays in *Feminist Genealogies, Colonial Legacies, Democratic Futures*, edited by Chandra Talpede Mohanty and M. Jacqui Alexander (1996); *Scattered Hegemonies,* edited by Inderpal Grewal and Caren Kaplan (1994), and *Third World Women and the Politics of Feminism,* edited by Chandra Talpede Mohanty with Lourdes Torres and Ann Russo (1991).

46. For example, the politics of European Imperial feminists or social reformers can actually be seen as "being violent" towards those women who did not conform to their feminist version of a woman. These women's racialized citizen status as colonial subjects, while often considered part of the "first" feminist movement, in fact marginalized and oppressed women of color and poor women. Instead of trying to reconcile their racism with a feminist subjectivity, their feminist practices can be evaluated according to their impact on a gender regime in which these women inhabited different racialized positions. Within this analytical approach, the viability of what is usually understood to be their feminist politics then can be seriously challenged.

47. Michel Foucault's theory of power states that power is *productive,* i.e., it is produced and circulates through discourse. Discourses are systems of knowledge whose claims produce, regulate, and discipline the subject. The body also is a product of discourse, a notion that denaturalizes gender and sexual relations. Important here is the concept that power relations and ideology never operate in/from one direction; instead, power and knowledge circulate through discursive technologies and can be resisted with reverse discourse (see Foucault, *The History of Sexuality*).

48. Judith Butler's theory on gender performativity puts forth the idea that instead of being an inherent, naturally constituted identity, gender is instead produced discursively, through political and social powers that privilege heterosexuality. She understands gender to be "an identity tenuously constituted in time, instituted in exterior space through a *stylized repetition of acts*" (*Gender Trouble* 140; emphasis hers). The idea of "gender as performative" conceptualizes it as a parody of an ideal gender identity, which is itself an illusion and therefore unattainable. This concept explicitly deconstructs the notion of a core gender identity based on a "natural" (i.e.,

prediscursive) sex and radically destabilizes normative gendered and sexual behavior. This "performativity" is not voluntary—*identifications* are real to the subject; its subversive potential lies in the *melancholic failure* of attaining the ideal, not in the playfulness of consciously "performing" a gender by choice. The regulatory mechanisms of discourse regarding gender are punitive and real: gender performativity takes place within a set of norms that both enable identity and deny it; these changing norms define what "does and does not count as recognizably human" (*Undoing Gender* 31).

49. "[D]ass Geschlecht sowohl auf der persönlichen Ebene wie auch auf der institutionellen und der symbolischen Ebene konstitutiv für das Phänonmen des Linksterrorismus ist" (Grisard, *Gendering Terror* 11–12).

50. Colvin, *Ulrike Meinhof* 190.

51. "[D]er Krieg findet gegen uns alltäglich statt" (Brockmann 110).

52. See chapter 9 in *Die Neue Frauenbewegung*, edited by Ilse Lenz: "Wenn Frauen nein sagen, dann meinen sie auch nein! Die Bewegung gegen Gewalt gegen Frauen" (When women say no, they mean no! The movement against violence against women), 281–324.

53. A recent example is Mary Hawkesworth's comprehensive study of women's politics globally, *Political Worlds of Women*.

54. The excellent collection *Women and Revolution in Africa, Asia, and the New World*, edited by Mary Ann Tétreault, highlights the conflicted relationship women historically have had with revolutionary movements, which, once social change is enforced, not only seem to forget women's contribution to the revolution but neglect to put "women's issues" on the newly nationalist agenda.

55. See Robert Moeller, *Protecting Motherhood*, for a discussion of how the new nation's stability was framed in terms of traditional family and gender roles. Dagmar Herzog in *Sex after Fascism* argues that sexuality and sexual norms were central in the conflict between the emerging youth countercultures of the 1960s and their parent generation, in which sexuality became a key component in (re)defining a democratic, antifascist subjectivity. In their extensive collection of primary documents and media reports, *Germany in Transit: Nation and Migration, 1955–2005*, editors Deniz Göktürk, David Gramling, and Anton Kaes thematize the cultural and social marginalization of *Gastarbeiter* from the mid-1950s into the 1970s, based on a racialized German national identity that only starting in the 1970s was problematized in public discourse.

56. Außerparlamentarische Opposition. After the German government formed a "Great Coalition" between the two major parties, students and other activists who viewed Parliament as devoid of any true opposition defined their political activism as extraparliamentary opposition. See chapter 1.

57. Important divergences from this trend are recent studies of the RAF that apply a gendered and/or feminist analysis, such as the work by Bielby and Colvin in the English-based context, and Grisard and Diewald-Kerkmann in the German-language-based one.

58. See Dagmar Herzog, *Sex after Fascism*.

59. See the RAF paper "Das Konzept Stadtguerilla" (The Concept of the Urban Guerilla) from April 1971, in which the group argues for the avant-garde position of

underground armed struggle in the revolution for social change (*Rote Armee Fraktion* 27–48).

60. See also Katharina Karcher's work for a discussion of how female terrorists consciously used and undermined expectations around gender presentation.

61. In *Gendering Terror*, Grisard examines the participation of citizens in the phenomenon of left-wing terrorism in Switzerland through their denouncing of suspected leftist radical activists (285–85). In "Deutschland, deine Denunzianten" (Germany, Your Informers), political scientist Gerhard Paul discusses the historical precedence for Germans denouncing their neighbors during the terrorism discourse of the 1970s (he states that between 1974 and 1981 the number of citizens reported to the police for political work grew six-fold) as having a long history in German culture, including both West and East Germany (*Die Zeit* 10 September 1993).

62. Their illegal existences differentiated the RAF and Movement 2nd June from other West German militant armed groups, such as the Revolutionäre Zellen (Revolutionary Cells) and their feminist contingent, Die Rote Zora (the Red Zora), whose members operated while maintaining "legal" lives. While the Revolutionary Cells and the later autonomous Red Zora formed important elements of militant and terrorist activism in West Germany, and appear to have remained more integrated with the leftist scene than the RAF, it is the particular political space of underground living and its effects on gendering terrorism as it was taking place in West Germany that is of analytical relevance to this project. Consequently, the RAF and Movement 2nd June are the focus of this study's examinations of gender and violence. What set the RAF and Movement 2nd June apart from other militant groups was that they operated from underground (i.e., they gave up their legal existence and all contact with persons who could link them to their old identity); they believed that only a true separation from the social order enables revolutionary action. It is this conceptual and experiential break with situational street militancy that sets the armed guerilla apart from the more fluent and conflicted debates on political violence.

63. See Clare Bielby's analysis of media coverage of RAF women's life underground as hypersexual and their pleasure as derived from violence (*Violent Women in Print* 106–7).

64. See Laura Sjoberg and Caron Gentry's *Mothers, Monsters, Whores*, Miranda Alison, *Women and Political Violence,* and V. G. Julie Rajan, *Women Suicide Bombers* for an international feminist political science and communication studies framing of the issue. Also see Ruth Glynn, *Women, Terrorism, and Trauma in Italian Culture.*

65. See in particular Grisard's *Gendering Terror*, in which she makes this argument for the Swiss context.

66. In the 1970s and into the 1990s, mass media consisted primarily of print and television. The discourse on terrorism and media since 9/11 needs to be considered in terms of the Internet, social media, and other new media; these are media venues that did not exist in the times of the RAF's conflict with the German state. Accordingly, print media then had a much more significant role in shaping and voicing public debates than is attributed to it today.

67. For example, for the past twenty-five years, mainstream and public discourse on the RAF has been dominated by one journalist's account of the group's operations: Stefan Aust's *The Baader-Meinhof Complex* not only still serves as a major source of

reference but has been made into an action thriller in 2008, *Der Baader-Meinhof Komplex,* which has gained international acclaim and which in highly problematic fashion cements the sensationalized and gendered/sexualized interpretation of the RAF initiated in Aust's work.

68. See note 10.
69. See Bielby, *Violent Women in Print,* for a comprehensive analysis of that discursive mechanism.
70. See the following works for a discussion of how "terrorist experts" derived their gendered theories on RAF women's violence from century-old flawed "science" on the pathology of female violence: Colvin, *Ulrike Meinhof* (especially chapter 6); Grisard, *Gendering Terror* (especially part 2, chapter 1); chapter 6 in Hanno Balz, *Von Terroristen, Sympathisanten, und dem starken Staat* (On Terrorists, Sympathizers, and the Strong State); and Clare Bielby, *Violent Women in Print* (especially chapter 3).
71. Colvin, *Ulrike Meinhof* 192.
72. *Der Baader-Meinhof-Report* 14, 17, 33.
73. "von der Natur kümmerlich bedacht" " (*Baader-Meinhof-Report* 43, 47). See also Colvin's discussion of the *Baader-Meinhof-Report* in *Ulrike Meinhof.*
74. Colvin, *Ulrike Meinhof* 189.
75. Gilcher-Holtey, "Transformation by Subversion?" 157.
76. Gilcher-Holtey 157.
77. In her thoughtful essay on policial strategies beyond the polarized positions of terrorism and retreat into the private sphere, Belinda Davis in "Jenseits von Terror und Rückzug" (Beyond Terror and Retreat) discusses the various positions within the Left regarding political violence. She credits especially the women's movement and nonviolent gender-mixed groups with developing sustainable and productive "kitchen table politics" ("Politik am Küchentisch" 182), informal congregations in local spaces, such as bars, small offices, apartments, etc., that contributed to a newly critical public sphere. However, she does not further investigate the theoretical underpinnings of a feminist theory of patriarchal violence and how it differs from the leftist construction of a potentially fascist, repressive state violence.
78. In the past ten years, this relationship has been the object of its own scholarly *Gewaltdebatte* whose main actors attempt to draw a direct line from the "1968" movement to the RAF in terms of idealizing and legitimizing terrorist violence.
79. Gilcher-Holtey argues that the New Left's relationship to violence is rooted more in their attempt to subvert and transform society by violating its rules and expectations, less in a concrete goal to "conquer political power" (160). Symbolic violence is strategically then more important than "actual" violence, which in the larger movement mostly "is ignited by the process of interaction" (160)—such as with police brutality.
80. Gilcher-Holey 158.
81. See Alexander Holmig, "Die aktionistischen Wurzeln der Studentenbewegung" (The Actionistic Roots of the Student Movement) and Mia Lee, "Umherschweifen und Spektakel: Die situationistische Tradition" (Wandering and Spectacle: The Situationist Tradition).
82. See Martin Klimke, *The Other Alliance* 109.

83. See Gilcher-Holtey 163.
84. See Della Porta 34 and 39.
85. See Varon 31; see Della Porta 35.
86. Gilcher-Holtey 163.
87. According to Davis, police brutality shaped discussions on violence from the beginning (as early as 1962) of the New Left's organizing (see "Jenseits von Terror und Rückzug" 162).
88. "Wie sich Gewalt gegen Sachen, also eine überwigend symbolische Geste, zur Gewalt gegen Personen verhielt" (Davis, "Jenseits Terror und Rückzug" 158).
89. Davis, "Jenseits von Terror und Rückzug" 160.
90. Gilcher-Holtey 165.
91. See Davis, "Jenseits von Terror und Rückzug" 159.
92. *"bleierne Zeit."* Originally used in German poet Friedrich Hölderlin's (1770–1843) "Der Gang aufs Land," this term is used both to signify the decade after 1945 (as the static and culturally and politically dead time of economic reconstruction in West Germany) and the time periods roughly between 1972 and 1977 when the conflict between state and groups like the RAF and Movement 2nd June developed and escalated.
93. Notstandsgesetze. See chapter 1.
94. As employees of West Germany's public higher education system, university professors are public servants. See Davis, "Jenseits von Terror und Rückzug" 165–66.
95. See Georgy Katsiaficas, *The Subversion of Politics* 64 and Colvin, *Ulrike Meinhof* 135. The decree was terminated in 1976.
96. *Sympathisanten* is the German term used by law enforcement and media to define an activist environment populated by individuals sympathetic to the RAF's politics. By the mid-1970s, the classification as "sympathizer" would designate an activist as a target of state surveillance and potential arrest (see also Colvin, *Ulrike Meinhof* 135).
97. The paralysis experienced by many radicals was met with the organization of the Tunix-Kongress (do-nothing Congress) in 1978 by the Sponti scene in Berlin. This gathering provided a forum for the "nondogmatic" Left to reorganize and reenergize after the German Autumn. Projects and events of the new social movements were introduced at the gathering, and it is generally understood to be the beginning of the Autonomen scene in Berlin (see Katsiaficas 6; von Dirke, *"All Power to the Imagination!"* 111–12; also see Hanno Balz and Jan-Henrik Friedrichs, eds., *"All we ever wanted"*).
98. "Kinder, Küche, Kirche."

## Notes to Chapter 1

1. "Die Frauen tragen auf ihren Schultern die Hälfte des Himmels und sie müssen sie erobern. Mao Tse Tung."
2. "Die militärische Linie der Bewegung 2. Juni ist nicht von der politischen Linie getrennt und ist ihr nicht untergeordnet. Wir betrachten beide Linien als untrennbar verbunden. Sie sind zwei Seiten derselben revolutionären Sache" ("Bewegung 2. Juni–Programm" 11).
3. "Practice" here needs to be understood as in contrast to theory, i.e., as in action versus talk. "Die Rote Armee Fraktion redet vom Primat der Praxis. Ob es richtig ist, den bewaffneten Widerstand jetzt zu organisieren, hängt davon ab, ob es möglich

ist; ob es möglich ist, ist nur praktisch zu ermitteln" ("Das Konzept Stadtguerilla," *Rote Armee Fraktion* 40).

4. Gilcher-Holtey 164.

5. See in particular Kraushaar, "Rudi Dutschke und der bewaffnete Kampf" (Rudi Dutschke and the Armed Struggle).

6. For example, see Belinda Davis, "Jenseits von Terror und Rückzug" (Beyond Terror and Retreat).

7. Until more recently, the RAF and other armed groups were viewed as an extreme section of the dissolving student movement, who were disappointed in what many viewed as failure to start a revolution. In "Rudi Dutschke und der bewaffnete Kampf," social historian Wolfgang Kraushaar makes the controversial case that violence—specifically that of underground armed struggle—was a logical consequence of the 1968 movement, not an aberrant development of a few extremists. Instead, I agree with Gilcher-Holtey, not so much in that the armed groups did not share the basic values of the New Left (those were, after all, not as homogeous as that statement assumes), but in that they radicalized the forms of actions of the 1968 movement while they "rejected its strategy of transformation" (164). I find both positions—that the armed struggle was a logical consequence of a latently violent 1968 movement, presented by scholars such as Kraushaar, and the opposite position, that the RAF and other groups were in the end separate from the New Left, as argued by Gilcher-Holtey—counterproductive and reductive. Neither position accounts for the complexities and heterogeneity of a complicated political and cultural landscape.

8. Außerparlamentarische Opposition.

9. Sozialisitisches Patientienkollektiv.

10. The Autonomen were leftist activists prominent in the squatter and alternative political scene in West Germany's urban centers. They became known as loosely connected groups of street militants and local activists, in particular in the 1980s. See Hanno Balz and Jan-Henrik Friedrichs, *"All we ever wanted."*

11. See Jeremi Suri, *"Ostpolitik* as Domestic Containment," for a discussion of the contradiction produced by the Cold War in the late 1960s that cast student radicals and dissidents as more of an internal threat to the FRG than the Eastern bloc as external adversary.

12. Notstandsgesetze. A point of public contention since the early 1960s, these laws were eventually passed in 1968 with the majority votes of the Great Coalition (also see Varon 31).

13. Sozialdemokratische Partei Deutschlands; Christlich Demokratische Union; Christlich-Soziale Union.

14. Originally, the SDS was the SPD's youth wing, until its expulsion in 1959, when the party took issue with the students' continued commitment to socialism.

15. See Varon 31–35, 39.

16. See Varon 31–32.

17. Gasserts and Steinweis 2.

18. Varon 33. See Detlef Siegfried, "Don't Look Back in Anger," for a discussion of criticisms of these continuities from the Nazi era within youth culture and media; and Michael Schmidtke, "The German New Left and National Socialism," for a discussion of the New Left's dealings with the recent past.

19. Gasserts and Steinweis 2.

20. The most prominent among these was Kurt Kiesinger, who as chancellor oversaw the government of the Great Coalition from 1966 to 1969. Kiesinger had been a member of the NSDAP from 1933 on, and from 1940 to 1945 had held an important position in Hitler's foreign ministry's department of radio propaganda. He became the student movement's symbol of the postwar republic's failure to successfully eradicate fascist influences in the reconstruction period. Kiesinger famously got his ears boxed by the German-born French citizen Beate Klarsfeld in November 1968 at the CDU's National Party Convention. Klarsfeld stated that she wanted to draw attention to the young generation's dissatisfaction with former Nazi officials running the country. She was sentenced to a year in prison but was able to evade the sentence because of her French citizenship; the disproportionately high sentence was responded to by protests by the SDS.

21. Varon 33.

22. The *Kinderladen* inititative created independent co-op childcare facilities throughout urban areas in Germany. *Kinderladen* literally means "children's shops" and refers to the fact that many of the *Kinderläden* rented empty store fronts. See also chapter 2.

23. For a comprehensive overview of the complicated relationship the Left has had with Germany's fascist past, see Gasserts and Steinweis, eds., *Coping with the Nazi Past*.

24. See Slobodian, *Foreign Front* 203 and 208.

25. As Slobodian demonstrates, Iran was a major point of organization from 1960 at least.

26. Slobodian 7.

27. I appreciate Slobodian's argument throughout *Foreign Front* that while the problematic abstraction introduced by an anti-imperialist view of world politics is helpful in understanding the increased distance from actual Third World subjects and the lack of practical collaboration after 1966, it is necessary to recognize the relationship of the Left to Third World issues as grounded in more than simply a projection of West German activists' fantasy of revolutionary struggle.

28. The unarmed student Benno Ohnesorg was shot by policeman Heinz Kurras. In 2009 it became known that Kurras was working for the East German government. The armed group Movement 2nd June named their group after the day Ohnesorg was shot to signify its meaning as what they viewed to be a political murder that called for political counterviolence. The RAF would develop the custom of naming actions (such as bombings, assassinations, etc.) after late members of the group, declaring these actions a continuation of the dead's political work.

29. As Martin Klimke observes in *The Other Alliance*, "[T]his interpretation [of blacks as comprising an internal colony that need to use violence to end their oppression] was strengthened by an anti-imperialism accelerated by the escalation of the war in Vietnam, which, for parts of the West German movement, linked the United States and its foreign policy semiotically to the crimes of National Socialism" (108).

30. Those included organizational ties to the radical SNCC (Student Nonviolent Coordinating Committee, later renamed the Student National Coordinating Committee), work with black GIs stationed in West Germany, as well as the Black Panther Solidarity Committee. Most activists were aware that the violence inherent in the experience of being black in the United States did not compare to their

experience of post–World War II bourgeois and static West Germany—in particular as white, ethnic Germans. However, leftist paranoia and sense of separation from mainstream society did at times evoke analogies between their social marginalization as leftists and members of an anti-establishment subculture (identified by their long hair and clothing) and being stigmatized as Jews and/or "Negroes." Detlef Siegfried, in "White Negroes," views the identification with especially black culture (such as music and aesthetics) by German activists as a "creative act of appropriation" (206) that did not claim original authenticity but constituted the construction of one's own style. Slobodian sees evidence of a more problematic dynamic of this identification with the "other" in the emergence of what he calls "corpse polemics" and points to the attempts of some members of the New Left to move beyond the sensationalist use of dead bodies as political instruments (135–69).

31. Klimke 113.
32. Varon 40. See also chapter 3. Dutschke survived the shooting heavily injured. He later died of complications from the injuries.
33. The publishing house became a target of the RAF's May Offensive, a series of bombings, in 1972.
34. "Vom Protest zum Widerstand."
35. Karin Bauer traces the origin of the slogan "from protest to resistance" to Carl Davidson, leader of the American Students for a Democratic Society (SDS), as he was quoted in a *New York Times* article in May 1967 (Bauer, "'From Protest to Resistance'" 171).
36. "Protest ist, wenn ich sage, das und das paßt mir nicht. Widerstand ist, wenn ich dafür sorge, daß das, was mir nicht paßt, nicht länger geschieht. Protest ist, wenn ich sage, ich mache nicht mehr mit. Widerstand ist, wenn ich dafür sorge, daß alle anderen auch nicht mehr mitmachen" (Meinhof, "Vom Protest zum Widerstand"; translation by Karin Bauer, "'From Protest to Resistance'" 171).
37. See Koenen, *Das rote Jahrzehnt* 18. The name was used in particular by rivaling leftist activists and the media; the letter "K" refers both to the small size of the individual party (*Kleinpartei*) and the self-identification of the parties as communist (*kommunistisch*).
38. The term "Spontis" is derived from the German term for spontaneous, "*spontan*," referring to the loosely organized, anarchist-leaning activism associated with the Spontis.
39. Both groups named themselves after the longest-operating urban guerilla group, the Tupamaros in Urugay.
40. The Red Zora was the only armed group in West Germany that identitified as feminist and that planned explicitly feminist actions. See Katharaina Karcher's work on the Red Zora and other militant feminists. For various essays on the formation and operation of nonfeminist groups, see Wolfgang Kraushaar, ed., *Die RAF und der linke Terrorismus*, vol. 1.
41. According to Kraushaar, *Agit 833* could boast of a circulation number ranging at any given moment from as low as four to seven thousand to as high as ten thousand (see Kraushaar, "*Tupamaros West-Berlin*" 517).
42. The defendants were Gudrun Ensslin, Andreas Baader, Thorwald Proll, and Horst Söhnlein. They received a three-year prison sentence for arson with intention to harm (see Sara Hakemi and Thomas Hecken, "Die Warenhausbrandstifter" 316–31).

43. "Die Rote Armee aufbauen."
44. "Die Konflikte auf die Spitze treiben heißt: Daß die nicht mehr können, was die wollen, sondern machen müssen, was wir wollen" ("Die Rote Armee aufbauen" 26).
45. See Tobias Wunschik, "Die *Bewegung 2. Juni*" (The Movement 2nd June) for a comprehensive attempt at creating a chronological history of the group, as well as Kraushaar's "Die *Tupamaros West-Berlin*" for an account of the predecessors and influences of the group, such as the Blues.
46. "Halb Subkultur, halb Polituntergrund" (Wunschik 547).
47. See Wunschik 548.
48. West Berlin was officially a part of the FRG; however, its geographical isolation as a West German enclave within the GDR, its special standing (*Sonderstatus*) in the FRG, and its distinct local (radical) culture set it apart from the rest of the FRG.
49. "Unser Ziel ist nicht die Schaffung einer 'Diktatur des Proletariats' sondern das Zerschlagen der Herrschaft des Kapitals, der Parteien, des Staates. Das Ziel ist die Errichtung einer Rätedemokratie" ("Bewegung 2. Juni—Programm" in *Der Blues* 10).
50. "Sie [die Bewegung 2. Juni] versteht sich als antiautoritär" (The Movement 2nd June identifies as anti-authoritarian, "Bewegung 2. Juni—Programm" 10). See also Kraushaar, *Tupamaros West-Berlin*.
51. For discussions of theoretical influences on armed groups in Germany, see Bernhard Gierds, "Che Guevara, Régis Debray, und die Focustheorie" (Che Guevara, Régis Debray, and the Focus Theory); Sabine Kebir, "Gewalt und Demokratie bei Fanon, Sartre, und der RAF" (Violence and Democracy in Fanon, Sartre, and the RAF); Klimke, *The Other Alliance* 108–42.
52. Aside from the Vietnam War, the rise of Black Power after the civil rights movement was the most influential political formation for West German radical leftists. The support of the Black Panthers in West Germany ranged from general protests against the trial of Angela Davis and the liberal usage of Black Panther iconography in particular (the black panther as printed in movement publications) and Black Power more generally (the raised fist as a generalized symbol of revolution) to concrete collaborations between black and German activists. Some of these collaborations included an outreach campaign driven by the West German Black Panther Solidarity Committee (instituted on November 23, 1969) to black American G.I.s stationed in Germany in order to politically radicalize them, which resulted in an increased visibility of black American military personnel in protests against the Vietnam War and for the release of black militants from U.S. prisons (see Maria Höhn, "The Black Panther Solidarity Committee and the Trial of the Ramstein 2").
53. See Slobodian for a comprehensive study of the influence of foreign activists who were living and organizing in West Germany, especially Iranian dissidents and African activists, on the New Left. Slobodian demonstrates "that socialist [West German] students drew conclusions from their interactions with Third World students—even when those conclusions often boomeranged attention back to German subjectivity" (13). He cautions against the popular tendency to "blame" international revolutionary theories emerging from the Third World's struggle against colonialism for the emergence of left-wing terrorism, which both constructs the Third World subject as violent and "barbaric" and simultaneously trivializes any solidarity with other peoples' struggles as "inauthentic." So it is important to emphasize that while West German activists found a theoretical framing for

domestic unease in their engagement with Third World groups, the issues and theoretical debates included German-specific historical points of reference, such as Germany's recent past of fascism, a long history of military aggression, and a history of militant leftist resistance.

54. In *The Wretched of the Earth* (1961), Frantz Fanon engages with anticolonial struggles and the role violence plays. He states that colonial violence can only be defeated by counterviolence, not by nonviolent negotiations. Counterviolence against colonial violence liberates the individual's psyche from the alienation produced by colonial oppression. Revolutionary violence here is understood as counterviolence and as a means to end colonial oppression as well as to disrupt the pathology created by racist violence in the psyches of both colonized and colonizer.

55. While some West German activists rejected the USSR's brutal repression of reforms (such as in the Prague Spring), others took a neutral position because they felt the conservative party in West Germany, the CDU, was using the repression as a weapon to bolster Cold War divisions. Overall, the Soviet Union's role in the Cold War remained underscrutinized by the New Left's critique of imperialism.

56. Hailed as "the midwife of new societies" by Che Guevara ("Guerilla Warfare" 75), violence in his experience becomes a necessary element of any revolutionary change. Calling for armed resistance of the people against the oppressive state in texts such as "The Essence of Guerrilla Struggle" (1960) and "Guerrilla Warfare" (1963), Guevara's call to arms was extended to a call for international solidarity in the struggle against U.S. imperialism, such as in his address to the Tricontinental conference shortly before his murder, "Create Two, Three, Many Vietnams" (1967).

57. "Das Konzept Stadtguerilla."

58. "Rote Armee Fraktion und Stadtguerilla sind diejenigen Fraktion und Praxis, die, indem sie einen klaren Trennungsstrich zwischen sich und dem Feind ziehen, am schärfsten bekämpft werden. Das setzt politische Identität voraus; das setzt voraus, daß einige Lernprozesse schon gelaufen sind" ("Das Konzept Stadtguerilla" 42).

59. See Varon for extensive discussions on the influences of Marcuse, and the Frankfurt School more generally, on the RAF and U.S. radicals.

60. As part of the ideological battle of the Cold War, and more specifically as an expression of the intra-German conflict along the ideological battle line of the hostile allies, the Communist Party of Germany (Kommunistische Partei Deutschlands, KPD) was outlawed in West Germany in 1951. The KPD was force-merged with the SPD in the USSR-occupied Eastern Zone of later East Germany and formed the Unified Socialist Party of Germany (Sozialistische Einheitspartei Deutschlands, SED), the later governing party in the GDR's one-party government system.

61. "Lange Marsch durch die Institutionen."

62. See Davis, "Jenseits von Terror und Rückzug."

63. Die Grünen.

64. Slobodian 204.

65. See Martin Kloke's work for an analysis of the German Left's complicated relationship to Israel, in particular his *Israel und die deutsche Linke* (Israel and the German Left).

66. To the dismay of many participants in the debate on 1968 and the RAF, in the current moment it appears that the aim of some scholars (including Kraushaar, who

also leads the historic position that the terrorism of the 1970s is a logical conclusion of the New Left's movement) is to descredit all of the New Left as inherentlty anti-Semitic, or, more specifically, to argue that German terrorism was rooted in anti-Semitism and hatred for Jews.

67. See Belinda Davis, "New Leftists and West Germany: Fascism, Violence, and the Public Sphere, 1967–1974," for a discussion of how the concept of "fascism" circulated and how its retrospective linking of present politics to the past influences activists; also see Michael Schmidtke, "The German New Left and National Socialism." See chapter 4 for a discussion of how images of concentration camp survivors were used to create analogies between hunger-striking RAF prisoners and Holocaust victims.

68. It is particularly difficult in a U.S. context to understand the uncompromising position in German discourse that pronounces it impossible to be critical of Israel's politics without being anti-Semitic, since there are numerous leftist U.S. Jewish writers and intellectuals who have been very outspoken in their criticism of Israel and who react quite sharply to the criticism of being anti-Semitic Jews. See, for example, Judith Butler's "No, It's Not Anti-Semitic."

69. See chapter 4.

70. "Politik in der ersten Person." McCormick translates the term as "politics of the self." It indicates a forgrounding of one's own experiences and identity in one's political agenda. The New Left's envisioning of a new social order included a necessary change in one's self/subjectivity that would facilitate a new society, hence the strong countercultural element of the 1968 movement. However, much of the New Left's utopian vision was founded in a socialist, internationalist understanding of power that differed from that of the women's or gay rights movements, or from much of the personalized fear of a nuclear holocaust within the peace movement. The differentiation, however, is primarily helpful in terms of analysis.

71. Von Dirke, *"All Power to the Imagination!"* 68.

72. See Hanno Balz and Jan-Henrik Friedrichs, *"All we ever wanted"* 17–18.

73. See von Dirke for a discussion of the Greens' synergy of environmentalism and parliamentary politics (183–208).

74. Aside from environmental concerns and the infringement on residents' quality of life because of airplane noise, many activists feared that the new runway would be utilized by NATO forces.

75. The NATO's Dual Track policy—simultaneous modernization and armament control—included stationing new U.S. nuclear weapons in Western Europe while offering negotiations on disarmament of certain other nuclear weapons to members of the Warsaw Pact.

76. "Euren Frieden wollen wir nicht!" (Hanno Balz and Jan-Henrik Friedrichs, *"All we ever wanted"* 13).

77. See Hanno Balz, "Der 'Sympathisanten'-Diskurs im Deutschen Herbst" (The "Sympathizers" Discourse during the German Autumn).

78. The term "autonomous women's movement" (*autonome Frauenbewegung*) was to signal independence from the New Left, as well as the state and the established women's movement, which had close ties to the political parties.

79. Aktionsrat zur Befreiung der Frau (literally: Action Council for the Liberation of Women).

80. "[W]e state that within its organization the SDS is a reflection of the larger social circumstances" ("[W]ir stellen fest, dass der SDS innerhalb seiner organization ein spiegelbild gesamtgesellschaftlicher verhältnisse ist" [Sander, in Lenz 58]).

81. Schulz 83.

82. "Konterrevolutionär . . . Agent des Klassenfeindes" ("SDS: Hü und Hott," *Der Spiegel* 39 [1968] 77–78 [quoted in Schulz 83]).

83. See Schulz 85. The term "1968 movement" is often used to refer to the New Left in the late 1960s and early 1970s.

84. *autonome Frauenbewegung.*

85. "wichtigstes Merkmal der neuen Frauenbewegung" (Gerhard, "Frauenbewegung" [Women's Movement] 203).

86. "der männerdominierten Linken und Männern überhaupt" (Gerhard 203).

87. "Das Private ist politisch.""

88. See Thomas Schultze and Almut Gross, *Die Autonomen* 174. For a historical discussion of the new women's movement in West Germany see Florence Hervé, ed., *Geschichte der deutschen Frauenbewegung*; Gerhard; Ilse Lenz, ed., *Die Neue Frauenbewegung in Deutschland Abschied vom kleinen Unterschied*; Kristina Schulz, *Der lange Atem der Provokation.*

89. See Gerhard 204 ff.

90. See chapter 2 for a discussion of the role motherhood played in the autonomous women's movement.

91. See Schultze and Gross 174; for a discussion on "autonomy and money"—the acceptance of state funding with a simultaneous preservation of self-determination of the projects—see Gerhard 209.

92. See flyer of the *Aktionsrat* at http://www.frauenmediaturm.de/themen-portraets/chronik-der-neuen-frauenbewegung/vorfruehling-1968–1970/flugblatt.

93. *Nebenwiderspruch.*

94. See Schulz 81–85.

95. Also see chapter 2 for a discussion of the *Kinderladen* movement.

96. See Herzog.

97. "befreit die sozialistischen eminenzen von ihren bürgerlichen schwänzen" (Lenz 63).

98. See Schulz 88–89.

99. Since its inception into the German criminal code in 1871, §218 criminalized abortion; in 1927 it was modified to include a medical exception. In 1970, it was illegal to have an abortion unless the life of the mother was in danger. Upon pressure from the women's movement, the social-liberal coalition in 1972 passed legislation that allowed abortions until the end of the first twelve weeks of pregnancy (*Fristenlösung*). The conservative parties challenged this in front of the Supreme Court, which in 1975 declared it to be an unconstitutional violation of the right of the unborn. The compromise reached in 1976 included the provision that abortions were allowed until a certain point under certain circumstances that were clearly indicated (*Indikationslösung*): medical indication (the health of the mother or a damaged embryo/fetus), criminal indication (rape), or social indication (social distress of the mother). After reunification in 1990 there was no shared abortion law between the newly unified German states: the former GDR had an unrestricted right to abortion until the end of the first twelve weeks of pregancy. Only in 1995 did lawmakers—against the protests of East and West German feminists, who favored

the law of the former GDR—formulate a shared law that, while declaring abortion illegal, refrains from prosecuting if the woman has received counseling at least three days before the abortion, which needs to take place within the first twelve weeks of the pregnancy. Abortions with a medical or criminal indication are always legal.

100. See Lenz 74–75.

101. "[Frauen] verdichteten und stabilisierten ihre Netzwerke. Mit dem ersten Bundesfrauenkongress in Frankfurt am Main 1972 begannen sie eine bundesweite Vernetzung und Strategiedebatte" (Lenz 69).

102. See Lenz 69.

103. "Ich habe abgetrieben," published in *Stern* 6 June 1971.

104. Reluctant because many socialist feminists believed the *Stern* initiative to be "reformist" and "bourgeois."

105. See Schulz 145–52.

106. "Mein Bauch gehört mir!" The literal translation is "my belly belongs to me," expressing self-ownership of the reproductive function.

107. See *FrauenMediaTurm* 1973 and 1974, available at http://www.frauenmediaturm.de/ themen-portraets/chronik-der-neuen-frauenbewegung/1973 and http://www. frauenmediaturm.de/themen-portraets/chronik-der-neuen-frauenbewegung/1974.

108. The feminist publication *Courage* (1976 to 1984) is associated with cultural feminism.

109. *Emma* (since 1977), Alice Schwarzer's feminist magazine, has always taken a strong constructionist approach to feminist analyses of power.

110. Schulz argues for the distinction between "cultural" and "social," which echoes the distinction between "cultural" and "radical": "If one advocated in the name of a cultural feminism for a society that recognizes/values the 'other,' social feminism aimed at the overcoming of the 'other.' If representatives of cultural feminism sought to abolish gender *hierarchies*, social feminists were committed to the overcoming of gender *differences*" ("Plädierte man dergestalt auf Seiten des kulturellen Feminismus für eine Gesellschaft, die das 'Andere' anerkannte, zielte der soziale Feminismus auf die Überwindung des 'Anderen.' Strebten Vertreterinnen des kulturellen Feminismus an, Geschlechter*hierarchien* aufzuheben, setzten sich soziale Feministinnen für die Überwindung von Geschlechter*differenzen* ein" [Schulz 204; emphasis hers]). While I appreciate Schulz's attempts to broaden the distinctions between different feminist currents to avoid comparing the proverbial apples with oranges ("essentialism" as a basis for women's identity versus "materialism" as an analysis of oppressive structures), her distinction does not include the differentiation within her category of "social" feminism between what some term "radical" feminism (radical in that it prioritizes patriarchy as a system of oppression that demands a radical social reconfiguration) and "socialist" feminism, which insists on capitalism as a major enabler of patriarchy.

111. Available at http://www.frauenmediaturm.de/themen-portraets/ chronik-der-neuen-frauenbewegung/1974.

112. *Alltagsgewalt*.

113. "[D]er Krieg findet gegen uns alltäglich statt" (Brockmann, "Frauen gegen den Krieg, Frauen für Frieden—gegen welchen Krieg, für welchen Frieden eigentlich?" [Women against War, Women for Peace—against Which War, for Which Peace Anyway?] 110).

114. Hagemann-White 49:

    [D]aß Mißbrauch Teil eines Kontinuums von Unterdrückung und Ausbeutung von Frauen ist, [. . .] Frauenhäuser als Teil des Kampfes gegen diese Unterdrückung, nicht etwa als Lösungsversuch eines umschriebenes soziales Problem. [. . .] Mißhandlung in der Ehe [. . .] als strukturellen Teil einer die gesamte Gesellschaft durchziehenden Gewalt gegen Fraue, einer Gewalt, die heute erst recht Prinzip dieser Gesellschaft, nicht Abweichung ist. .

115. It was also the first "autonomous women's project" that was publicly funded, beginning a debate on cooperation with the state on feminist projects.

116. See Lenz 282–83.

117. "Denn jeder Mann—Ehemann, Vater, und auch der Bruder ist für uns als potentieller Vergewaltiger anzusehen" (Beitrag der Gewaltgruppe München zum Kongress zum Thema Vergewaltigung 297).

118. Tanz in den Mai.

119. See Lenz 286. On the National Women's Conference of the Autonomous Women's Movement in Munich in March 1977, the activists decided to protest annually against sexual violence on Walpurgisnacht.

120. See Lenz 288.

121. See chapter 9 in *Die Neue Frauenbewegung*, edited by Ilse Lenz: "Wenn Frauen nein sagen, dann meinen sie auch nein! Die Bewegung gegen Gewalt gegen Frauen" (When women say no, they mean no! The movement against violence against women), 281–324.

122. "Die Männergewalt hat sich in meinem Körper eingenistet, hat meine Stimme gebrochen, meine Bewegungen gefesselt, meine Fantasie blind gemacht: Frauenkörper-Mikrophysik der patriarchalen Gewalt, gesichtslose Identität, gestaltlose Geschichte, unsichtbare Arbeit, genannt Liebe" (Brockmann 110).

123. See introduction and chapter 3.

124. See introduction and chapter 3.

125. Frauenfriedensbewegung.

126. "Die Friedensbewegung teilte mit der Frauenfriedensbewegung eine gemeinsame [. . .] friedenspolitische Zielsetzung" (Maltry 32).

127. "bewußte[n] Bezugnahme auf die weibliche Geschlechtszugehörigkeit bei der Begründung des individuellen Friedensengagements und/oder bei der Formulierung der friedenspolitischen Forderungen und Zielsetzungen" (Maltry 31).

128. "die bewußt geschlechtsbezogenen Friedensaktivitäten der Frauen in separaten politischen Handlungsstrukturen" (Maltry 32).

129. See Melzer, "'Frauen gegen Imperialismus und Patriarchat zerschlagen den Herrschaftsapparat'" ("Women against Imperialism and Patriarchy Smash the Power Structure") 173.

130. Even though this is a historically specific development of the Cold War era, there is some continuity in middle-class ("bourgeois") women's movements in emphasizing the gendered relations men and women have to violence as rooted in natural differences, while women in radical labor movements and/or anarchist groups, such as Rosa Luxemburg in Germany and Emma Goldman in the United States, rejected as a product of bourgeois ideology the idea of women's natural disposition as nonviolent.

131. This maternal figure of peace has traveled through various new social movements since the late 1970s, including the antinuclear movement, such as with the political group Mothers against Nuclear Power (Mütter gegen Atomkraft) that formed in 1986 and that is still active today. See http://www.muettergegenatomkraft.de.
132. "Ist die Gewalt in der Frauenbewegung angekommen?"
133. "Ist die Abgrenzungsdebatte in der Frauenbewegung angekommen?" This is a reference to the general climate of surveillance and fear during the second half of the 1970s, when state persecution of radical leftist activists intensified, often compelling people to *abgrenzen* (separate/demarcate) themselves from those targeted by the state. The need to visibly and openly denounce militant left activism produced painful schisms among political activists, including within feminist groups, as the conflicting positions of the authors of the two pieces demonstrate.
134. Frauen-Befreiungsfront.
135. "in eigener Sache" (Meinhof, "Die Frauen im SDS oder in eigener Sache" [Women in the SDS: Acting on Their Own Behalf]).
136. See *Früchte des Zorns*, 594–633, for interviews with and statements of the Red Zora from 1977 to 1988. See also Karcher, *Sisters in Arms?*.
137. Frauen gegen imperialistischen Krieg.
138. See Melzer, "'Frauen gegen Imperialismus und Patriarchat,'" for a detailed discussion of Women Against Imperialist Wars.
139. "Denn so, wie jeder Gewaltakt gegenüber einer Frau ein Klima von Bedrohung gegenüber allen Frauen schafft, so tragen unsere Aktionen, auch wenn sie sich nur gegen einzelne Verantwortliche richten, mit dazu bei, ein Klima zu entwickeln: Widerstand ist möglich!" ("Interview mit der Roten Zora" 605).
140. See chapter 3.
141. Another related discursive convergence takes place in connection to the peace movement, that, while being a clearly male-dominated campaign that rarely credited women for their organizational work, by the 1980s rhetorically appropriated the position taken by the Women's Peace Movement (Frauensfriedensbewegung) of embracing more "feminine" (i.e., nonviolent) values and presenting the state and countries engaged in the armed race as masculine and male-identified (see Davis, "'Women's Strength against Their Crazy Male Power'").

## Notes to Chapter 2

1. For information about interviews, see Introduction, note 17.
2. Parts of this chapter previously appeared in Patricia Melzer, "Maternal Ethics and Political Violence: The 'Betrayal' of Motherhood among the Women of the RAF and 2 June Movement."
3. See Eager 1.
4. "Lied von der Glocke"; "da werden Weiber zu Hyänen."
5. Hacker 10, 17–21.
6. Zwerman 135.
7. See Diewald-Kerkmann, "Bewaffnete Frauen im Untergrund: Zum Anteil von Frauen in der RAF und der *Bewegung 2. Juni*" 663, 666.
8. See Melzer, "'Death in the Shape of a Young Girl'" 36–37, 41–42.

9. Originally published in 1985 and translated as *The Baader-Meinhof Complex* in 1987, the book has been revised and reissued several times in German as well as in English.
10. See Koenen, *Vesper, Ensslin, Baader.*
11. See Aust.
12. See Seifert.
13. Herzog 141. Herzog counters the prevailing notion that the 1960s sexual revolution was a response to a lingering sexual repression during the Third Reich and instead argues that it in fact exposed a moral conservatism developed in a defensive gesture after the post–World War II years to relieve Germans of the guilt of fascism. Herzog evaluates the rising conservatism in the 1950s with its censoring of promiscuity in general and particularly that of women, and its virulent condemnation of (male) homosexuality that followed the relatively liberal sexual politics of the immediate postwar years: "One powerful initial impetus for sexual conservatism in postwar Germany lay in the fact that incitement to sexual activity and pleasure had been a major feature of National Socialism. Turning against nudity and licentiousness in the early 1950s, especially in the name of Christianity, could, quite legitimately and fairly, be represented and understood as a turn against Nazism" (103).
14. See also Heinemann, "Single Motherhood and Maternal Employment in Divided Germany," and Moeller, *Protecting Motherhood.*
15. See Heinemann, "The Hour of the Woman." From 1942 on, with the war failing catastrophically and a large number of German men absent at the front, women increasingly were fending for themselves and their families, contradicting the conservative ideal of a mother at home with her children, with a male breadwinner protecting the family. Instead, German women were coping with Allied bombings and flight from Eastern territories as they were trying to escape the approaching Soviet Army. These experiences, however, did not trigger a new discourse on gender ideologies during the founding of the FRG. Instead, the creation of collective memory that shaped the discourse around reconstruction and the founding of a democratic state utilized the gender-specific experiences of women to define a new German national identity. As Elizabeth Heineman argues in "The Hour of the Woman," collective memory appropriated women's war and postwar experiences in the process of redefining German postwar national identity. Experiences of bombing raids, evacuations, flight, and rape, which were predominantly female, were degendered and translated into experiences of "ordinary" Germans and represented the general victimization of Germany by the Soviet Army in particular and Allied bombing and the war in general. During the reconstruction years, 1945–48, which were characterized by a *Frauenüberschuss* (surplus of women), the *Trümmerfrau* (Woman of the Rubble) represented Germany's postwar effort at rebuilding (Heinemann 378). This symbol was contrasted with German women's fraternization and prostitution with occupying soldiers; the fraternizer symbolized the moral decay of Germany and distracted from the international discourse of Nazi Germany crimes against humanity as ultimate signifier of moral decay.
16. Moeller, "Reconstructing" 143–45.
17. Moeller, "Reconstructing" 150.
18. Moeller, "Reconstructing" 155.

19. The German debate was unlike those in other West European countries, such as Sweden, where the "citizen," not the "family," was the focus of social policy, based on the "assumption that all adults would work outside the home and that single women with children needed particular assistance so that their children's standard of living would not fall below that of families with two incomes" (Moeller, "Reconstructing" 158).

20. Moeller, "Reconstructing" 160.

21. Moeller, "Reconstructing" 164. The focus on "natural" gender differences in the post–World War II debate continued the idealization of woman as mother that dominated Nazi politics. As Leila Rupp elaborates in "Mother of the *Volk*," the official party line of the NSDAP prescribed that the "ideal Nazi women owed service to the state above all else" (Rupp 368) and that this could be best delivered in her role as mother in the domestic sphere; any social power allocated to her as a "major influence on society was exerted through the medium of the family" (369). Motherhood epitomizes women's designated role in German fascism. Her influence on the fate of the Fatherland only extended to her role as mother of the nation, by her producing racially pure offspring (particularly soldiers) who would enable the Reich to grow and flourish. Enlisted in a racialized "battle of births" (Bridenthal, Grossmann, and Kaplan, "Introduction" 19) over *Lebensraum* (living space), only skills related to her ability to reproduce were relevant for a woman: housekeeping and cooking, emotional and practical support for children, husband, and other household members, cultural cultivation of a nationalist identification, etc. This "maternal" duty was later extended to prescribed public activities in approved organizations that created an illusion of political participation; this also applies to men's public activities (see Stephenson 19). However, as some feminist scholars have pointed out, there is no one category "woman" for any given political system. Instead, class, religion, ethnicity, geographical habitat, etc., are all variables in how women will experience a society in general, and Nazi Germany in particular (See Koonz, *Mothers in the Fatherland* 663; Stephenson 11–16); "women" in the Third Reich were subjected to highly differentiated ideological classifications. The cult of motherhood was applied exclusively to "Aryan" women who were "fit" to reproduce. "The distinctions drawn between different racial and ethnic groups, between victors and vanquished, between 'responsible' and 'asocial,' between 'hereditarily healthy' and 'hereditarily diseased,' cut across conventional class barriers" (Stephenson 14). When looking at continuous gender ideologies, though, an analysis of the prevailing social *ideal*—that which is politically and socially sanctioned—can be helpful. Thus the homogeneous (if internally contradictory) construction of what makes a "German woman" that emerged under Nazi rule following the contradictory gender configurations of the Weimar Republic can be an indicator of ideological forces that shaped the 1950s.

22. Focusing on the "normal" family became a mechanism that allowed Germans to shift their predisposition from guilt and shame to moral righteousness: "The reconstitution of a private family sphere [as opposed to an institution for the national good] was vital to reaching the 'end of ideology' in the fifties [. . .] [T]he family could serve as a vehicle for anti-Nazi *and* anti-communist rhetoric" (Moeller, "Reconstructing" 162). Also see Bielby's discussion of violence, motherhood, and

German nationalism in *Violent Women in Print*, in particular chapter 1, "The Violent Woman, Motherhood, and the Nation."

23. Grundgesetz.

24. West Germany's Grundgesetz was adopted in 1949. It guaranteed that "men and women have the same rights," a clear break with "women's political exclusion under the Nazis and a recognition of women's experiences during the war and after 1945" (Moeller, "Reconstructing" 141). However, the Grundgesetz also mandates the special protection of marriage and family, reflecting a belief that women need to be protected and that the family is "the realm where women might best exercise their equality" (Moeller, "Reconstructing" 141). Thereby, family was exclusively defined as a married heterosexual couple. "Incomplete" or "half-families" (Moeller, "Reconstructing" 153) (those without fathers, that is, those headed by unwed, divorced, and widowed mothers) were excluded from benefits of family allowances that were established in 1954. "Men, not women, 'founded families,' and it was the male *Leistungslohn* that should be the basis for this construction" (Moeller, "Reconstructing" 144). By 1954, families with three or more children were eligible for payments—paid directly to fathers; single mothers rarely had three or more children and so did not receive assistance (see Moeller, "Reconstructing" 154).

25. *Kinderladen* literally means "children's shop." Also see note 22 in chapter 1.

26. See Schulz 71–72.

27. See Herzog 162.

28. See Herzog 163, 165; Naumann 56.

29. See Meike Sophia Baader's edited collection *"Seid realistisch, verlangt das Unmögliche!": Wie 1968 die Pädagogik bewegte* ("Be Realistic, Demand the Impossible!": How 1968 Influenced Pedagogy) on the ideas of anti-authoritarian childrearing and their effects on German educational theories.

30. See Herzog 231–32; Schulz 76–96.

31. See Ilse Lenz's *Die Neue Frauenbewegung in Deutschland* for a collection of foundational lesbian texts from the 1970s (223–66).

32. See Naumann 56–57.

33. See Hochgeschurz 161–63; Schulz 143–74.

34. Naumann 58–59. "Autonomy"—a key word used by the early women's movement that signified anti-institutional, antistate, and grass-root activism—characterized much of the activism of the time. The autonomous women's movement, more than any other political formation, took the concept the furthest: separatism became a part of necessary political action, such as from established women's organizations and political parties and, of course, from men. In comparison with other European countries, West German feminists relied on the term more heavily for identity-forming signification, and rigidly autonomous activism and analysis became characteristic for the West German more so than for her European counterparts. The insistence on separatist spaces and actions put feminists at odds with many of the Left's men, who dismissed those as unpolitical and as a retreat into the private sphere (see Gerhard 204).

35. See Davis, "'Women's Strength against Their Crazy Male Power'" 251, 255; Melzer, "'Death in the Shape of a Young Girl'" 39; Zwerman 34.

36. Frauensfriedensbewegung. See chapter 1.

37. "Wer Leben zur Welt bringt, hat zum Frieden ein besonderes Verhältnis" (Quistorp, back cover).
38. See Meyer and Whittier 277.
39. See Quistorp 9.
40. Feminist work on "ethics of care" followed the discursive intervention of Sara Ruddick's work on maternal thinking (1980) and Carol Gilligans's book *In a Different Voice* (1982). The latter locates difference in moral reasoning and the development of ethics within the structures of sexual difference. Even though it was criticized for its class and race assumptions, which generated a gendered theory based on the experience of primarily white, middle-class girls/women, Gilligan's work had an important impact on subsequent feminist theorizing on gender and ethics and, ultimately, political activism.
41. The argument that motherhood as an identity elevates women morally—and with that politically—is of course not new. In the late nineteenth and early twentieth centuries throughout the Western world, women argued for their political importance based on their role as mothers and their inherent peaceful positions, including in Germany (see for example Ann Taylor Allen, "Mothers of the New Generation"), a line of argument that has been echoed in feminist theories on the ethics of mothering since the 1980s. In Germany, the Bund für Mutterschutz (Association for the Protection of Mothers, founded in 1904) "hailed motherhood as the highest individual fulfillment and the mother-child bond as the most sacred of ties [and] placed major emphasis on the right to become a mother with the full respect and support of society" (Allen 424, 425). They were quite radical in their demands for social reform: unlike mainstream ideology (and state policies) that blamed mothers for a high infant death rate (which spurred the breastfeeding campaign) and that viewed unwed mothers as immoral (a position espoused by bourgeois feminists) the Bund für Mutterschutz foregrounded *any* mother's rights to social and political support and advocated "free love" that released motherhood from the restriction of the patriarchal nuclear family (see Allen 428).
42. Ruddick 244.
43. Other prominent examples of texts that defined the debate on maternal ethics early on are collected in the 1984 anthology *Mothering: Essays in Feminist Theory*, edited by Joyce Treblicot, which makes available essays from 1972 to 1984 that contemplate the role mothering plays in understanding gendered relations.
44. Ruddick 220.
45. Ruddick 242.
46. Held, "The Obligations of Mothers and Fathers."
47. Whitbeck 186; 189–91.
48. Held, "Feminism and Moral Theory."
49. See Wuschnik 556.
50. Außerparlamentarische Opposition (extraparliamentary opposition). See chapter 1.
51. See chapter 1 for a discussion of the debate on political violence in the German Left.
52. See Irmgard Möller in Tolmein 20; Koenen, *Vesper, Ensslin, Baader* 288
53. See Aust, *Baader-Meinhof: The Inside Story of the R.A.F.* 54, 55; Koenen, *Vesper, Ensslin, Baader* 244.
54. See Prinz 214–15.

55. See Zwerman's study of women in U.S. armed groups, who were mothers at the time of their political activities, which included aiding in planning and executing acts of political violence.

56. Edschmid 44:
Ohne Kinder konnte sie sich keine bessere Welt vorstellen. Später konnte sie nicht verstehen, daß Ulrike Meinhof und Gudrun Ensslin ihre Kinder aufgaben und in den Untergrund gingen. Wenn wir nicht in der Lage sind, sagte sie sich, mit unseren Kindern die Welt zu verändern, dann können wir es auch nicht ohne sie. [. . .] An den Kindern wurde die Utopie konkret.

57. See Elaine Brown and Assatua Shakur for reflections on motherhood in the Black Power Movement.

58. Driven by decreasing birthrates and economic depression, the Nazis actively encouraged German women to be mothers (e.g., through honoring multiple mothers with the Honor Cross and giving loans to families with a male breadwinner and a mother at home). This of course was limited to "Aryan" households: "Women were [. . .] made responsible for the preservation of the purity of the 'Aryan' race" (Rupp 371); those deemed racially and/or hereditarily "worthless" (Stephenson 12) were discouraged (through antimarriage laws) or actively prevented from reproducing (through sterilization and murder). Those who were excluded from the nationalist project of the Thousand Year Reich were denied any benefits that the rigid gender ideology might have brought German women. While devoid of racist differentiations, political debate and legislation in the 1950s enacted pro-natal policies that reflected key elements of those of the 1930s and '40s: conservatives "insisted that *family* policy should not be confused with National Socialist or communist *population* policy"; however, as Moeller points out, they "protested far too much" ("Reconstructing" 159) to make their arguments less problematic.

59. Ulrike Meinhof followed Ensslin's, Baader's, and their two accomplices' trial in Frankfurt and interviewed Ensslin for the leftist news magazine *konkret*, which she ran with her husband. It is said that it is in her conversation with Ensslin that Meinhof was confronted with the question of "doing, not talking" that would make her a founder of the RAF (see Aust, *Baader-Meinhof: The Inside Story* 39).

60. Bernward Vesper, son of the "Blut-und-Boden-Dichter" (German nationalist poet) Will Vesper, was editor until he committed suicide in 1971. His only piece of creative writing, his autobiographical novel fragment *Die Reise* (The Journey), was posthumously published in 1977, and is often viewed as the bequest of an entire generation.

61. "Felix . . . Ich weiss nur, dass ich ihn vom ersten Augenblick an bedingungslos geliebt habe, und dass er, eh' er geboren war, schon einen Prozess intensiviert hat, Dich und mich entblösst hat [. . .] und Handlungen und Haltungen losgelöst hat, die uns beide . . . über uns selbst die Augen geöffnet hat [sic]" (Harmsen, Seyer, and Ullmaier 129).

62. For an analysis of Meinhof's career as journalist and of her political activism, see Karin Bauer, "In Search of Ulrike Meinhof."

63. See Jörg Herrmann, "'Unsere Söhne und Töchter': Protestantismus und RAF-Terrorismus in den 1970er Jahren," for a discussion of how Protestantism and its ethics influenced members of the early RAF.

64. See Koenen, *Vesper, Ensslin, Baader* 155, 206.

65. See Ditfurth 272.

66. In 2003, Koenen's *Vesper, Ensslin, Baader* was the first work to discuss the (at that time unpublished) letters between Ensslin and Vesper, setting the tone for their interpretation. In 2009 they were published as *Notstandgesetze von Deiner Hand*, edited by Caroline Hamsen, Ulrike Seyer, and Johannes Ullmaier. In 2011, the film *Wer wenn nicht wir,* based on Koenen's book and directed by documentary filmmaker Andreas Veiel, was released.

67. See Koenen, *Vesper, Ensslin, Baader* 207.

68. "Die Fotos [von Felix] sind wunderschön, jedes Wort dazu bleibt mir im Hals stecken. [. . .] Aber laß es um Gotteswillen, mir Sätze vorzuhalten . . . und nie (ich *schrei* das Wort) wollte ich die Trennung von Felix" (Harmsen, Seyer, and Ullmaier 182–83; emphasis Ensslin's).

69. "[W]enn ich rauskomme . . . 'will' ich Felix ganz schrecklich, aber ich will ihn Dir doch dabei und damit nicht wegnehmen, ein- und für allemal, das *ist* Ernst" (Harmsen, Seyer, and Ullmaier 184; emphasis Ensslin's).

70. "[B]in langsam sicher, daß wir immer einen Weg finden werden, der keinen von Felix trennt; und irgendwann wird er begreifen, daß er eben zwei Zärtlichkeiten und zwei Welten hat" (Harmsen, Seyer, and Ullmaier 106).

71. "Du hast nicht eine Minute Dir konkret meine Situation vorgestellt [. . .], wenn ich rauskomme. *Was* werde ich tun, *wie* werde ich leben, *wo* werde ich leben, *wie* werde ich Geld verdienen etc. . . . gut, das alles muß *ich* erst sehen, ehe ich—was ich sehr will—mich Felix werde nähern können, klar?" (Harmsen, Seyer, and Ullmaier 246; emphasis Ensslin's).

72. *Ehelichkeitserklärung.*

73. See Koenen, *Vesper, Ensslin, Baader* 199–200, 206.

74. See Koenen, *Vesper, Ensslin, Baader* 152.

75. Harmsen, Seyer, and Ullmaier 204.

76. *Der kaukasische Kreidekreis.*

77. See Harmsen, Seyer, and Ullmaier 237, 240. First performed in German in 1954, Berthold Brecht's piece tells the story of a poor servant lovingly raising the child of a rich woman who abandoned him during a civil war only to claim him as hers afterwards. Their dispute is settled by a judge who announces that whoever succeeds in pulling the child out of a circle drawn in chalk will gain custody. The foster mother, out of fear of hurting the child, releases her hold, and because of her maternal love the judge declares her the rightful mother. Brecht's critique of bourgeois notions of parental rights devoid of care (language of the blood) borrows from Chinese culture, which features the chalk circle as a determining test of motherhood, as well as the Old Testament, in which King Solomon executes a similar test.

78. Harmsen, Seyer, and Ullmaier 246.

79. See Harmsen, Seyer, and Ullmaier 247.

80. See Koenen, *Vesper, Ensslin, Baader* 246.

81. From May 11 to 24, 1972, the RAF executed several bombings throughout Germany, targeting U.S. military facilities, German law enforcement agencies, a federal judge, and the publishing house Axel Springer. Known as the "RAF May Offensive," the series of attacks was followed by a national manhunt that resulted in the arrest of most RAF leaders by the beginning of July of the same year.

82. The trial of RAF leaders Gudrun Ensslin, Ulrike Meinhof, Andreas Baader, and Jan-Carl Raspe would take place from May 1975 to April 1977 in a building constructed just for their trial. During that time they were incarcerated in the maximum-security prison Stammheim, near Stuttgart.

83. "Außerdem vielleicht 2 [Fotos] von Felix. Felix is kein RAF-Mitglied, Felix ist mein Sohn; weißt Du was von ihm?" (Ensslin and Ensslin 37).

84. "Aber paß' auf, daß Du nicht in die Fürsorger-Scheiße fällst [...]; was Du nicht *für Dich* tust, laß' sein, wenn Du das richtig verstehst—auf eine caritative Tante kann [Felix] nämlich nur scheißen" (Ensslin and Ensslin 84; emphasis hers).

85. "habe ihre affektive Bindung an das eigene Kind hinter die 'politisch-revolutionäre Zielsetzung' zurückgestellt" (Diewald-Kerkmann 669).

86. Koenen, *Vesper, Ensslin, Baader* 219.

87. "Im Sommer 1969 zu sagen 'Nicht ohne mein Kind,' wäre eine erste Chance für Gudrun gewesen, 'Ich' zu sagen" (Koenen, *Vesper, Ensslin, Baader* 219).

88. "die Banalität des Alltags" (Koenen, *Vesper, Ensslin, Baader* 219–20).

89. *das info* is a communication system the RAF established during the period 1973–1977 among members incarcerated in various prisons, primarily to organize their hunger strikes. *das info* consisted of letters that were illegally delivered by RAF defense attorneys. Selected and edited versions of the letters were published as *das info* by Pieter Bakker Schut in 1987. See also Colvin, *Ulrike Meinhof* 161–65.

90. See Schut 292.

91. "es gibt [...] niemand in der alten gesellschaft, der entfremdung [...] unmittelbarer erfährt als die frauen" (Schut 294).

92. "wirklich als gruppe zu denken und zu handeln [...] da liegt das stück, das tanten typen voraus [haben]" (Schut 293). "*Tante*," literally "aunt," is a slang term used for women in the RAF correspondence, with men often being referred to as "*Typ*," "guy."

93. See Schut 294.

94. "damit ist aber auch die dialektik ihrer situation klar—wenn sie nach den besonderen brutalitäten ihrer domestitizierung [...] überhaput *sich* wollen, *sich* denken—müssen sie radikal *und* subversiv denken: ein inhalt und eine form, die sie für illegalität prädestiniert" (Schut 294; emphasis hers).

95. See Aust, *Baader-Meinhof: The Inside Story* 203–5; 214–15; 252–55.

96. See chapter 1.

97. Colvin 200.

98. *Mütterarbeit*.

99. *erpreßt*.

100. "So werden die Frauen mit ihren Kindern erpreßt, und das dürfte das Menschliche an ihnen sein, daß sie sich mit ihren Kindern erpressen lassen, daß sie die Forderung, primär für ihre Kinder dazusein, selbstverständlich akzeptieren" (Meinhof, "Falsches Bewußtsein" 128).

101. "Die Frauen sitzen in einer Klemme, in der Klemme zwischen Erwerbsfähigkeit und Familie, genauer: Kindern—vorhandenen, zu erwartenden, gehabten" (Meinhof, "Falsches Bewußtsein" 128).

102. "Ideologisierung ihrer Mutterrolle" (Meinhof, "Falsches Bewußtsein" 129).

103. See Meinhof, "Falsches Bewußtsein" 131. ·

104. "Der Protest is fällig. Er findet nicht statt" (Meinhof, "Falsches Bewußtsein" 131).

105. See Ditfurth 212.

106. "Ulrikes Problem in jener Zeit ist überhaupt nicht der Mann oder ein anderer Mann oder überhaupt Mann gewesen, sondern Politik gewesen. [. . .] Ihr 'Engagement' [. . .] also die Betroffenheit und die Aktivität, waren so stark, dass der Mann dazu überhaupt nicht existierte" (Ditfurth 215).

107. See Ditfurth 217.

108. See Ditfurth 234, 257.

109. See Ditfurth 260.

110. Aust's translation in *Baader-Meinhof: The Inside Story*:
Von den Bedürfnissen der Kinder her gesehen ist die Familie [. . .] der stabile Ort mit stabilen menschlichen Beziehungen notwendig und unerläßlich. [. . .] Das ist natürlich viel einfacher, wenn man ein Mann ist und wenn man also eine Frau hat, die sich um die Kinder kümmert. [. . .] Und wenn man Frau ist und also keine Frau hat, die das für einen übernimmt, muß man das alles selber machen—es ist unheimlich schwer. (54)

111. "Also ist das Problem aller politisch arbeitenden Frauen—mein eigenes inclusive—dieses, daß sie auf der einen Seite gesellschaftlich notwendige Arbeit machen. [. . .] Aber auf der anderen Seite mit ihren Kindern genauso hilflos dasitzen wie alle anderen Frauen auch" (Aust, *Der Baader Meinhof Komplex* 152; my translation).

112. "Wenn man es so will, ist das die zentrale Unterdrückung der Frau, daß man ihr Privatleben als Privatleben in Gegensatz stellt zu irgendeinem politischen Leben. Wobei man umgekehrt sagen kann, da, wo politische Arbeit nicht was zu tun hat mit dem Privatleben, da stimmt sie nicht, da ist sie perspektivisch nicht durchzuhalten" (Aust, *Der Baader Meinhof Komplex* 152; my translation).

113. See Ditfurth 270. In this strategy, Röhl was supported by the mass media. As Clare Bielby points out in "Attacking the Body Politic: The *Terroristin* in 1970s German Media," after Baader was sprung from prison, the weekly magazine *Der Stern* ran an article that depicted former wife and mother Meinhof as a woman who was initially tender and loving but who then failed as a single mother with alternative notions of childrearing in an out-of-control social and political environment in Berlin (see 32).

114. See Ditfurth 260.

115. See Ditfurth 271–72.

116. See Ditfurth 271.

117. See Ditfurth 291.

118. See Ditfurth 284.

119. See Ditfurth 290.

120. See Aust, *Baader-Meinhof: The Inside Story of the R.A.F.* 75–77.

121. See Ditfurth 292. In 2010, Anja Röhl (half-sister to Regine and Bettina Röhl) came forward with accusations against Klaus Röhl that he sexually abused her (and the twins) when they were young girls. In response, Ulrike Meinhof's daughter, Bettina Röhl, published several statements and interviews claiming that the breaking of the story was a strategic move to whitewash Meinhof's decision to send her children away instead of having them raised by their father. Röhl does not deny that her father sexually abused her ("lightly") but insists that this occurred after 1970 (when Meinhof was gone already) (Röhl, "Meine Eltern").

122. "He Mäuse! [. . .] [B]eißt die Zähne zusammen. Und denkt nicht, daß Ihr traurig sein müsst, daß Ihr eine Mami habt, die im Gefängnis ist. Es ist überhaupt besser,

wütend zu werden als traurig zu sein. Au warte—ich werd' mich freuen, wenn Ihr kommt" (Aust, *Der Baader Meinhof Komplex* 375; my translation).

123. See Aust, *Baader-Meinhof: The Inside Story of the R.A.F.* 187–88.

124. "Ich mach' mir jetzt ziemlich viele Gedanken über Euch. . . . Und besucht mich! Und schreibt—los! Oder malt mir was, ja? Ich finde, ich brauche mal wieder ein neues Bild. Die ich hab', kenn' ich jetzt auswendig" (Röhl, "Unsere Mutter" 106).

125. "Ihr zwei. Eure Mami" (Aust, *Der Baader Meinhof Komplex* 381, my translation; see also Aust, *Baader-Meinhof: The Inside Story* 188).

126. See Meinhof, "Die Frauen im SDS."

127. "Du willst die Fotzen an ihrer Emanzipation hindern" (Koenen, *Vesper, Ensslin, Baader* 285). The term "*Fotze*" or "*Votze*"/"cunt" to signify women, like "*Schwanz*"/"dick" to signify men, was liberally used in leftist political circles during the 1970s to signify a break with traditional outlooks. However, the terms, especially "*Votze*," generally maintained their insulting connotation, including in the RAF's, especially Baader's, application of the word to women, and Meinhof and Ensslin preferred "*Tante*" (aunt) as the more neutral term for women (See Colvin, *Ulrike Meinhof* 208–9). See Colvin for a discussion of how Meinhof's (and other RAF members') use of "cunt" "conflates the ideas 'woman,' 'capitalist,' and 'traitor'" (188, 209).

128. See Koenen, *Vesper, Ensslin, Baader* 93.

129. See Bressan and Jander 421–22; Koenen, *Vesper, Ensslin, Baader* 338–39.

130. See Bressan and Jander 412.

131. See the article in *Der Spiegel* from 1981 by Marion Schreiber, "Wir fühlten uns einfach stärker" (We Simply Felt Stronger), a report on women in the underground. The images reproduced in the article are part of a repertoire of iconic images of female terrorists that had been circulated in media coverage since the early 1970s. Ensslin's participation in an avant-garde film that featured some nudity in the early 1960s provided sexualized images on the discourse on her terrorism. See Bielby, *Violent Women in Print*.

132. See Ensslin and Ensslin, eds., 162–65.

133. Colvin, "Chiffre und Symbol für Wut und Widerstand?" 102.

134. See Röhl, "Unsere Mutter"; Seifert. Bettina Röhl, Meinhof's daughter, seems very much invested in the idea that her mother was "turned" by external influences as well as by her communist convictions from a sane, maternal figure into a crazy, unnatural woman; Seifert, in his mostly nostalgic reminiscing about Meinhof's political activism before she "went bad," also constructs an idealized authentic and real Meinhof that is contrasted with the later, inexplicably changed terrorist. Bielby points out that explaining terrorists in term of this binary of "before" and "after" brought about by external events or people was a strategy the mass media reserved for female terrorists (male terrorists seem to have undergone linear developments as political activists). She discusses how the tabloid *Bild* resurrected Meinhof's maternal and tragic image after her suicide on "Mother's Day," when she, so Bielby argues, did not pose a threat anymore (see Bielby, "Attacking the Body Politic" 12).

135. This contrast is visible in reports such as in the new magazine *Stern*, "Der Mordbefehl" (Command to Murder), from 1972 after Meinhof was arrested. In this

article, images of Meinhof's arrest are contrasted with photos of her and her family from years before the RAF was founded.

136. See Herrmann, "Ulrike Meinhof und Gudrun Ensslin" 112.

## Notes to Chapter 3

1. Brigitte Mohnhaupt, Christian Klar, and Susanne Albrecht.
2. Deutscher Herbst.
3. "Die Grausamkeit wird in diesem Fall nicht über die offene Brutalität, sondern in stereotypischer Weise über die Hinterhältigkeit der weiblichen Täter(innen) mit dem Blumenstrauß reconstruiert" (Steinseifer 362).
4. "Der Abschied von der Küche bedeutet den direken Weg in den Knast" ("Terrorismus, der Exzeß der Emanzipation" 3).
5. "mörderischen Mädchen" (from the magazine *Quick*, as quoted in Steinseifer 362–63).
6. See Hanno Balz, "Gesellschaftsformierungen: Die öffentliche Debatte über die RAF in den 1970er Jahren" (Social Formations: Public Debate on the RAF in the 1970s).
7. Bielby, "Attacking the Body Politics" 2.
8. *Terroristenmädchen* and *Wilde Furien* (Schreiber, "Wir fühlten uns einfach stärker," *Der Spiegel*).
9. "Straffälligkeit und Nicht-Straffälligkeit einer Frau werden mit *biologischen Eigenschaften* von Frauen erklärt und müssen immer etwas mit *Sexualität* zu tun haben" (Klein 10; emphasis hers). See also Sarah Colvin, *Ulrike Meinhof and West German Terrorism* (especially chapter 6) and Clare Bielby's *Violent Women in Print* on the history of biological gender theories—in particular on the physical roots of women's criminal and violent behavior—in German criminology.
10. Hacker 17. The German terms are "*Nicht-Frau*" and "*Nicht-Weiblichkeit*." "*Weiblichkeit*" can mean either femininity or femaleness.
11. See Hacker 9.
12. For excellent analyses of West German media representations of female terrorists in the 1970s, see Bielby's *Violent Women in Print*, which places the representation of RAF women in the broader context of media depictions of violent women in general, and Balz's chapter in his study on media and public discourse on the RAF, *Von Terroristen, Sympathisanten, und dem Starken Staat*: "Das Feindbild der 'bewaffneten Mädchen'" (The Enemy Concept "Armed Girls").
13. Portions of this chapter previously appeared in Patricia Melzer, "'Death in the Shape of a Young Girl': Feminist Responses to Media Representations of Women Terrorists during the 'German Autumn' of 1977."
14. For a discussion of feminist theories of political violence in the 1970s, see chapter 1.
15. In "'Women's Strength against Their Crazy Male Power,'" Belinda Davis addresses gendered (rhetorical) concepts that circulated in the peace movement, which at the same time did not translate into egalitarian treatment of women (leaders) in the movement by their male counterparts. See Micaela Di Leonardo's review essay "Morals, Mothers, and Militarism: Antimilitarism and Feminist Theory" for a critical discussion of the development of the theoretical linkage of feminism and peace politics.
16. See Davis, "'Women's Strength against Their Crazy Male Power'" 245; Echols 243–86.
17. Meyer and Whittier 277.

18. See Davis, "'Women's Strength against Their Crazy Male Power'" 251.

19. Meyer and Whittier 287.

20. Davis, "'Women's Strength against Their Crazy Male Power'" 251, 255.

21. This position is developed in the following works in various ways: Helen Caldicott's *Missile Envy: the Arms Race and Nuclear War*; Cynthia Enloe's *Does Khaki Become You?*; and the edited volumes by Pam McAllister, *Reweaving the Web of Life: Feminism and Non-Violence*, Eva Quistorp, *Frauen für den Frieden* (Women for Peace), and Diana Russel, *Exposing Nuclear Phallacies*.

22. Zwerman 34.

23. For example see Zwerman's "Mothering on the Lam: Politics, Gender Fantasies, and Maternal Thinking in Women Associated with Armed, Clandestine Organizations in the United States," a study examining maternal ethics—and their potential for peaceful politics—among women in armed groups. While initially critical of an unexamined, assumed connection of feminism and pacifism, Zwerman in the end contributes to the construction of armed women (and mothers) as delusional in their assessment of gender equality in armed groups, including by giving not-always-convincing interpretations of quotations from her interviews with former activists. In contrast, Georgina Waylen's study of Chilean women's activism provides a more careful presentation of why women chose to organize in certain ways and not others; the material and representations in discourse cannot be separated when examining women's activism. Utilizing traditional gender roles in stating political concerns and demands then might be read more as a political strategy than a moral feminist subject position, an evaluation the author leaves to the reader.

24. Cynthia Enloe's work is absolutely central here. From her early study *Does Khaki Become You?* (1984) to *Maneuvers* (2000), she has provided the framework for a feminist analysis of the effects of militarization on women's (and men's) everyday lives. Women's participation in military culture as wives, mothers, and soldiers is understood to be structured by patriarchal priorities, on the one hand, while also affecting those structures, on the other. The severe oppression experienced by women in Argentina and Chile at the hands of the military juntas is documented in Ximena Bunster-Bunalto's "Surviving beyond Fear: Women and Torture in Latin America." Bunster-Bunalto makes visible the sexual and gendered violence the state employs against women it deems threatening, a violence that also is the object of women's activism and research against "femicide," the "mass murder of women during peace time" (Hawkesworth 130).

25. See Hackett and Haslanger.

26. One of the earliest texts that in the U.S. context of the second wave women's movement formulated a biological base for women's politics was former Weather Underground member Jane Alpert's "Mother Right: A New Feminist Theory." In this 1974 piece, she denounces armed struggle as inherently patriarchal and declares women to be superior to men because of their—potential and actual—biological ability to produce life. A comparable text appeared in Germany in 1976, by Gunild Feigenwinter, titled *Manifest der Mütter* (Mothers' Manifesto).

27. Examples include Jean Elshtain's *Women and War*, Margarete Mitscherlich's *Die Friedfertige Frau* (The Peacable Sex), and Sara Ruddick's *Maternal Thinking*. A prominent voice of cultural feminism is Robin Morgan, who in *Demon Lover* defines political violence as inherently male.

28. Examples of this position include 1970s publications from women active in the U.S. militant group Weather Underground ("A Weatherwoman: Inside the Weathermachine" 322–26; "Honky Tonk Women" 313–20), as well as the West German activist publication of the 1980s, *Frauen die Kämpfen sind Frauen die Leben* (Michel, Women Who Fight Are Women Who Live). A more recent activist publication that criticizes the exclusive political strategy of pacifism as only supporting the violence of the state, including nonviolent feminist politics, is Peter Gelderloos's *How Non-Violence Protects the State*.

29. See for example Danielle Djamila Amrane-Minn's "Women and Politics in Algeria from the War of Independence to Our Day," Márgara Millán's "Zapatista Indigenous Women," and Mary Ann Tétreault's *Women and Revolution in Africa, Asia, and the New World*.

30. The incident of 9/11 has generated an increased focus on political violence within feminist scholarship and activism, especially regarding religious fundamentalism, militarism, and women living under Muslim laws (see, for example, the special issue of *Signs* 32 [2007]). It signifies a changing political context for the debate on gender and political violence, as evinced in Rajan's study of the discourse on female suicide bombers, *Women Suicide Bombers: Narratives of Violence*.

31. This discussion is evinced in print primarily in movement publications, and in book publications airing activist women's voices, such as the West German essay collection edited by Ruth-Esther Geiger and Anna Johannesson, *Nicht Friedlich und Nicht Still* (Not Peaceful and Not Quiet). One of the few early attempts at looking systematically at women's participation in left-wing terrorism by feminist scholars includes the collection of essays edited by Susanne von Paczensky in 1978, *Frauen und Terror* (Women and Terror).

32. Neither Herrad Schenk's early historical account of German feminism, *Die feministische Herausforderung* (The Feminist Challenge, 1983), nor the later *Der lange Atem der Provokation* (The Long Breath of Provocation) by Kristina Schulz (2002) even mention women's activism in armed groups. In contrast, the activism-focused publication edited by Kristine Soden, *Der große Unterschied: Die neue Frauenbewegung und die Siebziger Jahre* (The Major Difference: The New Women's Movement and the 1970s, 1988), includes a chapter on women in the RAF in its chronicle of women's activism, social concerns, and feminist politics in the 1970s. The chapter is highly critical of armed struggle, but its presence in a volume on women's politics in the 1970s indicates a degree of discussion lacking in most later feminist publications.

33. An obvious example of this is the voluminous collection of primary documents of the West German Autonomous Women's Movement edited by Ilse Lenz and published in 2010, *Die Neue Frauenbewegung in Deutschland* (The New Women's Movement in Germany). The only reference to women's violent political activism in the over-one-thousand-page-long volume concerns the Rote Zora, an armed group that defined itself as feminist. The editor dismisses this claim to feminist politics as appropriation and as inauthentic, stating that the entire women's movement rejected any idea of violence as a part of sustainable politics (see Lenz 269).

34. Bielby, "Attacking the Body Politic" 3.

35. The term "autonomous" women's movement originated in activists' rejection of the state taking any role in feminist politics, on the one hand, and in an effort at demarcation from the New Left more generally, on the other. See chapter 1.

36. See Balz, "Gesellschaftsformierungen" 180; Balz, *Von Terroristen, Sympathisanten, und dem starken Staat* 46.

37. In the 1970s and '80s, print media, together with television, made up the most important media outlets in terms of influencing public debates and state policies. Also see note 67 in the introduction.

38. "Austragungsorte ideologischer Auseinandersetzungen" (Balz, *Von Terroristen* 30).

39. "Im Rahmen einer modernen 'Mediendemokratie' ist die Trennung von politischem und medialem Apparat kaum noch aufrechtzuerhalten. Vielmehr sind die Medien, und vor allem die Nachrichtenmedien, die entscheidene Instanz des politischen Diskurses" (Balz, *Von Terrroristen* 33).

40. See Elter 1064.

41. See Elter for a detailed discussion of terrorism's strategic use of media as means of communication.

42. Marighella 30. Marighella's *Mini-Manual* discusses mass media in the context of a state-controlled media system within a dictatorship that the urban guerilla needs to manipulate and subvert. In contrast, the RAF was confronted with a mass media that, though basically free of state censorship, nevertheless pursued political agendas and influenced state policy. The RAF believed the media was "brainwashing" Germans as effectively as any state-run mass communication system would (such as during the Nazi regime).

43. See Balz, *Von Terroristen* 67.

44. "Ihr Konzept beinhaltet sowohl eine symbolische Politik als auch eine explizite Form der Öffentlichkeitsarbeit, wie beispielsweise das Verschicken von Kommuniqués an internationale Presseagenturen" (Balz, *Von Terroristen* 70).

45. "als massen-medialen Vermittler ihrer Botschaften" (Elter 1071). In his essay, "Die RAF und die Medien" (The RAF and the Media), Elter argues that mass media not only reported on terrorism but was actively used by the RAF, extending the original concept of the "propaganda of the deed" to a strategic thinking about the *Vermittlung* (conveyance, dissemination) of a violent act through media, i.e., about media's "potential propaganda effect" ("deren potentieller propagandistische Wirkung," Elter 1069). Not unlike any organization, the RAF seemed to have developed "PR"-communication-related strategies of how best to "handle" various media outlets and information. The significance of the media in West Germany's dealings with the RAF was reiterated in the RAF exhibit in Berlin of 2005, which included a complete exhibit floor chronologically displaying selected news coverage of the RAF. See Steinseifer for a discussion of the exhibit's treatment of media coverage (Steinseifer 351–52).

46. See Elter 1070–72.

47. Balz points out that this dilemma of a "revolt with and against the media" is typical of the 1968 movements more broadly but becomes visible in particular with the RAF (see 70–76).

48. See Elter 1072; Steinseifer 370–71.

49. "Am Ende ist der hegemoniale Diskurs [. . .] in Teilen grundsätzlich auch ein Verstärker für die RAF, deren deutlichstes Souveränitätsmerkmal die Fähigkeit ist,

durch ihre Initiative die Stimmen in den Diskursen als auch die politischen Institutionen zur Reaktion zu zwingen" (Balz, *Von Terroristen* 76).

50. See Balz, *Von Terroristen* 75.

51. See Kraushaar, "Kleinkrieg gegen einen Grossverleger" 1083.

52. In "Die Achtundsechziger-Bewegung zwischen etablierter und alternativer Öffentlichkeit" (The Sixty-Eighter Movement between Established and Alternative Public Spheres), Dominik Lachenmeier lays out the countermovement's investment in creating public spheres and the activists' symbiotic relationship with mass media. See also the edited volume by Martin Klimke and Joachim Scharloth, *1968 Handbuch zur Kultur und Mediengeschichte der Studentenbewegung* (1968 Handbook on Cultural and Media History of the Student Movement).

53. For an extensive discussion of the anti-Springer campaign and the RAF's bombing of the Springer building, see Wolfgang Kraushaar, "Kleinkrieg gegen einen Grossverleger" (Guerilla Warfare against a Publishing Giant). Also see chapter 1.

54. "Allerdings muss die hier veröffentlichte nicht unbedingt mit der öffentlichen Meinung übereinstimmen" (Balz, "Der 'Sympathisanten'-Diskurs im Deutschen Herbst" 321; emphasis mine).

55. See Balz, "'Sympathisanten'-Diskurs" 321.

56. See introduction and chapter 1.

57. "Kampf um die Köpfe" (Balz, "Gesellschaftsformierungen" 180).

58. "So lässt sich sagen, dass die bundesrepublikanische Gesellschaft zwischen 1970 und 1977 in der Auseinandersetzung nicht *mit* der RAF, sondern *über* sie ein Bild von sich selbst entwarf" (Balz, "Gesellschaftsformierungen" 180; emphasis his).

59. "Ist die Linksterrorismus-Debatte als dezidierte politische Intervention gegen den Feminismus zu verstehen" (Vukadinović, "Feminismus im Visier" [An Eye on Feminism] 58).

60. See Bielby, *Violent Women in Print*.

61. "Ermächtigung eines Subjektstatus mit Waffe" (Balz, *Von Terroristen* 200).

62. See Hauser 54–55, 112, 209; Bielby, "Revolutionary Men and the Feminine Grotesque."

63. Paczensky 9:
    [A]lle Personen, die sich öffentlich sichtbar mit dem Terrorismus befaßten—der Krisenstab, die Fahndungsorgane, die Rettungsmannschaft bis hin zu den ernsten Experten, die [. . .] über Hintergründe und Folgen des Geschehens diskutierten— allesamt waren Männer. [. . .] Doch die Betroffenen—die Geiseln in der "Landshut" und ihre Kidnapper, die RAF-Gefangenen, die freigepreßt werden sollten, bis zu der Figur, die gemeinhin "der Mann auf der Straße" genannt wird—die Betroffenen waren überwiegend Frauen. [. . .] nach den Gewalttaten des Jahres 1977, wurde deutlich, wie ungewöhnlich die Geschlechterverteilung bei den Terroristen ist.

64. "[V]on den Fahndungsplakaten blicken die glatten Mädchengesichter, doch ihre Verfolger und ihre Erforscher und selbst ihre Verteidiger sind Männer" (Paczensky 9).

65. "Irgendwas Irrationales in dieser ganzen Sache [. . . daß da so viele Mädchen dabei sind . . .] Vielleicht ist das ein Exzeß der Befreiung der Frau, was hier deutlich wird" ("Löwe los" [Loose/Escaped Lion]). Vukadinović argues that this would be the most influential line of reasoning in the discourse on left-wing terrorism in the years to come ("Feminismus im Visier").

66. "Einerseits wurde das Leben von Frauen im Untergrund als Emanzipationserfahrung präsentiert, andererseits wurde die Gleichung aufgestellt,

dass feministisches Aufbegehren gegen patriarchale Strukturen der eigentliche politische Hintergrund für den Terrorismus sei und Terroristinnen eine pervertierte, exzessive Emanzipation verkörperten" (Bandhauer-Schöffmann, "'Emanzipation mit Bomben und Pistolen'?" ["Emancipation with Bombs and Guns"?] 5).

67. Bielby, "Remembering the Red Army Faction" 142.

68. For an elaboration of this point, see Bielby, "Attacking the Body Politic" and "Remembering the Red Army Faction" and Balz, *Von Terroristen*, 198–231.

69. "Vielmehr kommentiert die Story, während sie Tatsachen erzählt" (Balz, *Von Terroristen* 43).

70. *Medienlandschaft.*

71. "Between 1970 and 1980 *Der Spiegel*'s circulation increased from 911,405 to 984,783" ("Zwischen 1970 und 1980 steigt die Auflage des *Spiegel* von 911.405 to 984.783") (Balz, *Von Terroristen* 44).

72. "Schon 1970 erreichte er fast ein Viertel der Gesamtbevölkerung ab 14 Jahren" (Balz, *Von Terroristen* 44).

73. See Balz, *Von Terroristen* 44–45.

74. See Balz, *Von Terroristen* 45.

75. *Meinungsführer* (Balz, "Der 'Sympathisanten'-Diskurs" 320).

76. See chapter 2.

77. Schreiber, "Wir fühlten uns einfach stärker," *Der Spiegel* 90, 106.

78. Bielby provides an analysis of Meinhof's representation, especially in *Bild*, as contrast figure to the ideal German mother ("Remembering the Red Army Faction" 141–42).

79. Schreiber, "Wir fühlten uns einfach stärker," *Der Spiegel* 98, 90.

80. Bielby, "Remembering the Red Army Faction" 142.

81. Balz, *Von Terroristen* 207.

82. *Der Spiegel* reprinted the image of a struggling Meinhof paraded by police after her arrest in 1972 in its article from 1981 by Schreiber, "Wir fühlten uns einfach stärker," an image that had been prevalent in media coverage since 1972. Steinseifer points to the distorted images of women underground, as if terrorism has a physically transformative effect on femininity (363). See Bielby, *Violent Women in Print*, for a feminist reading of the shifting representations of terrorist women in the media.

83. *Der Spiegel* 12 July 1976.

84. "Ausbruch der Frauen" 20.

85. This photo was taken during the OPEC Conference siege in Vienna in 1975. See chapter 5 for a discussion of Tiedemann's prison letters.

86. "Ausbruch in Berlin: 'Das ist eine Riesensache'" 21.

87. See chapter 1 for a closer analysis of the actual number of women documented to have been members of the RAF/Movement 2nd June and public perception of terrorism *as* female.

88. Grisard in *Gendering Terror* extensively discusses the discursive production of "left-wing terrorism" as an object of knowledge (see especially part 2, chapter 1).

89. See chapter 1 for a discussion of the autonomous women's movement's organizational structure.

90. "markieren den triumphalen Einzug der antifeministischen RAF-Debatten in die westdeutsche Printmedienlandschaft" (Vukadinović, "Feminismus im Visier" 57).

91. This particular cover indicates a moment when media directly influences political decisions. Steinseifer points out that Albrecht's portrait photo printed on the *Der Spiegel* cover later was used as a wanted image by the police (Steinseifer 363 n. 33). One would assume that the high recognition factor generated by the cover image influenced the decision to use this photo on wanted posters.

92. "Die anonymen Autoren des Artikels wirkten als Schaltstelle zwischen den zitierten Wissenschaftlern und dem Lesepublikum" (Vukadinović, "Feminismus im Visier" 58).

93. "Frauen im Untergrund" 22–23.

94. See Balz, *Von Terroristen* 210–12.

95. Balz also points to the fact that women calling out women on their actions and declaring them to be "abnormal" resonates much more powerfully than men defining violent women as deviant.

96. *Mädchen.*

97. "makaber"; "die sich mit selbstzerstörerischer Lust in die Niederungen von Mord und Totschlag hinabbegeben haben" ("Frauen im Untergrund" 22).

98. "Klar war Männern wie Frauen, daß hier Mädchen tief aus ihrer angestammten Rolle gefallen waren. Ihre Tat fügt sich nicht ins herkömmliche Bild von jenem Geschlecht, das im Englischen 'the fair sex' genannt wird, das schöne, das anstän-dige, das helle" ("Frauen im Untergrund" 22–23).

99. In 1975, the Movement 2nd June kidnapped Berlin politician Peter Lorenz. The West German government exchanged him for five political prisoners. Two months later, the RAF seized the West German embassy in Stockholm, Sweden, with the aim of freeing twenty-six political prisoners, including RAF leaders Ulrike Meinhof, Gudrun Ensslin, Andreas Baader, and Jan-Carl Raspe. The West German govern-ment this time did not compromise; the incident ended in the deaths of two diplomats and two terrorists, and the arrest of the remaining four terrorists. After the kidnapping of Jürgen Ponto failed, the RAF abducted Hans Martin Schleyer in September 1977, demanding the release of several political prisoners. The govern-ment refused an exchange, and Schleyer was killed by his kidnappers the day after Ensslin, Baader, and Raspe were found dead in their cells on October 18, 1977, ending the "German Autumn." Also see chapter 1.

100. "Frauen im Untergrund" 23. Steinseifer mentions the media's visual emphasis on the degenerative effect of living underground on *female* terrorists' faces in particular (Steinseifer 363).

101. "Schneller konnten sie den westdeutschen Wohlstandsbürgern kaum plausibel machen, wer nun am Drücker ist" ("Frauen im Untergrund" 22).

102. "äußerste Grenze menschlicher Perversion" ("Frauen im Untergrund" 22).

103. "Müsse nun nicht [. . .] 'jeder Bürger' damit rechnen, daß ihm eines Tages 'der gewaltsame Tod in Gestalt eines jungen Mädchen gegenübertritt'?" ("Frauen im Untergrund" 22).

104. "Frauen im Untergrund" 23.

105. "Frauen im Untergrund" 29.

106. Bielby, "Attacking the Body Politic" 2.

107. Bielby, "Attacking the Body Politic" 2. The symbolic meaning of the stroller that was hiding weapons that RAF members used to slow down the motorcade of Hanns-Martin Schleyer in September 1977 is discussed in Bielby's "Remembering the Red

Army Faction." The driver's distraction by a stroller being pushed by a woman across the street is usually viewed as the key aspect that enabled the industrialists' kidnapping. The stroller is a centerpiece in the section on West Germany's terrorist past in the German History Museum's permanent exhibition (Bielby 137).

108. "Frauen im Untergrund" 23.

109. *Mädchen-Militianz.* "Frauen im Untergrund" 25.

110. See Balz, *Von Terroristen* 203–8.

111. "die 'dunkle Seite der Bewegung für volle Gleichberechtigung'" ("Frauen im Untergrund" 23).

112. "'weibliche Supermänner'" ("Frauen im Untergrund" 25).

113. "Die Knarre im Kosmetikkoffer" ("Frauen im Untergrund" 25).

114. "'gelassen, ruhig, beherrscht, ungemein cool'"; "irren Nerven" ("Frauen im Untergrund" 25).

115. See Vukadinović, "Feminismus im Visier" 58.

116. See Balz, *Von Terroristen* 212–14.

117. Mauz in "Frauen im Untergrund" 32–33.

118. "Frauen im Untergrund" 22.

119. *Weibergewalt* ("Frauen im Untergrund" 23).

120. "Das mag wohl sein" ("Frauen im Untergrund" 23).

121. "Die höhere Tochter eines Tages als Politkillerin—das ist der real gewordene Alptraum. Aus seinen Nischen in der Industriegesellschaft kann ein derart getarntes Mordsystem unvermutet, kaum parierbar, zuschlagen" ("Frauen im Untergrund" 38).

122. See Leserbriefe, *Der Spiegel* 7.

123. "Die gegen Frauen gerichteten Schikanen bei der Terroristenfahndung in der BRD nahmen breiten Raum in den Frauenzeitschriften ein" (Bandhauer-Schöffmann, "Emanzipation" 74). Bandhauer-Schöffmann's article "'Emanzipation mit Bomben und Pistolen'?" ("Emancipation with Bombs and Guns"?) offers a comprehensive analysis of the cross-regional feminist publications' dealings with the *Feminismusverdacht* and their debating of political violence.

124. "Black" here is not a reference to skin color or racial identity, but instead connotes a link to West German anarchists and Autonomen, whose radical leftist politics were not as much rooted in Marxism as in anarchist thought.

125. The magazine was published from 1976 to 1987; its circulation in 1976 was approximately three thousand (see http://de.wikipedia.org/wiki/Die_Schwarze_Botin).

126. It was published from 1976 to 1984 and at times is claimed to have had a circulation of thirty thousand (see http://de.wikipedia.org/wiki/Courage_%28Zeitschrift%29).

127. *Emma* was founded by Alice Schwarzer in 1977 and its first circulation reached two hundred thousand issues. It was modeled after the U.S. *Ms.* in layout, distribution, targeted audience, and content. *Emma* still is published today and is Germany's most prominent feminist magazine; in 2010 it had a circulation of over forty thousand (see http://de.wikipedia.org/wiki/Emma_%28Zeitschrift%29).

128. Published in 1972, it was the first German-language feminist periodical, issuing its last volume in 2011 (see www. http://auf-einefrauenzeitschrift.at).

129. See Bandhauer-Schöffman, "Emanzipation" 77.

130. See Bandhauer-Schöffmann, "Emanzipation" 81.

131. See Bandhauer-Schöffmann, "Emanzipation" 83.

132. See Bandhauer-Schöffmann, "Emanzipation" 75.
133. See Bandhauer-Schöffmann, "Emanzipation" 79.
134. See Bandhauer-Schöffmann, "Emanzipation" 82.
135. A brief critique of *Der Spiegel* coverage also can be found in *WIR: Frauenzeitung* 7 (1977), a small women's center publication, which again criticizes the equation of terrorism with female liberation: "Exzeß der Emanzipation."
136. "aus Gewalt gegen Frauen wird, dass auch Frauen Gewalt anwenden" ("Frauen und Gewalt oder Gewalt und Frauen" 32).
137. The necessity to prepare women to engage in counterviolence is evident in the self-defense groups that tried to develop women's abilities to physically resist violent attacks, especially sexual assault.
138. "[A]ls seien diese Frauen, die da auch nicht vor Gewaltanwendung zurückschrecken, um für sich und andere ein menschenwürdigeres Leben zu erkämpfen, nicht mehr ganz normal, als politischer Faktor nicht Ernst zu nehmen" ("Frauen und Gewalt oder Gewalt und Frauen" 33).
139. "'Auswuchs der Emanzipationsbestrebungen'" ("Frauen und Gewalt oder Gewalt und Frauen" 33).
140. "Sie wollen immer noch nicht wahrhaben, dass sie es mit einem politischen Gegner zu tun haben, dessen Ziel ein menschenwürdigeres Leben ist und der sein [sic] eigenes Leben dafür einsetzt" ("Frauen und Gewalt oder Gewalt und Frauen" 34).
141. "tatsächlichen Gründe" ("Terrorismus, der Exzeß der Emanzipation" 3).
142. "Terrorismus, der Exzeß der Emanzipation" 3.
143. "Frauen, die jahrelang engesperrt sind, neigen nun mal zu lesbischen Kontakten. Eine Umarmung, ein Streicheln und vielleicht ein mütterlicher Kuß wirkt bei manchen Frauen schon wie eine Explosion des Liebesrausches" ("Fahndung nach Frauen" [Manhunt for Women] 9).
144. "Es ist durchaus möglich, daß die Ausbrecherinnen von Lesbierinnen versteckt werden" ("Fahndung der Frauen" 9).
145. "Gudrun Ensslin—Die Eiskalte Verführerin," *Bild am Sonntag* 14.
146. "Terrorismus, der Exzeß der Emanzipation" 3.
147. "Heim- und Herdideologie" ("Terrorismus, der Exzeß der Emanzipation" 3).
148. The original text states "*weibliche Natur*," which can be translated as either "female" or "feminine" nature. "Diese Frauen negieren demonstrativ alles, was weibliche Natur ausmacht" ("Terrorismus, der Exzeß der Emanzipation" 3).
149. "Der Abschied von der Küche bedeutet den direkten Weg in den Knast" ("Terrorismus, der Exzeß der Emanzipation" 3). One way in which terrorists rejected traditional female roles was by leaving families with children. The two most prominent examples of women who "abandoned" their children are Ulrike Meinhof, whose ex-husband seized custody of the seven-year-old twin daughters she had sent to Italy, seemingly on their way to a Palestinian orphanage camp, and Gudrun Ensslin, who left an infant son with his father when committing political arson in 1968 in Frankfurt, and when going underground in 1970. See chapter 2.
150. "Frauen, die sich wehren sind verrückt" ("Terrorismus, der Exzeß der Emanzipation" 4).
151. "wird von ihren politischen Motiven gänzlich abgelenkt" ("Terrorismus, der Exzeß der Emanzipation" 4).

152. "Strategie und Taktik für die Entwicklung linker Politik für schädlich erachten" ("Frauenbewegung seit 'Deutschland im Herbst,'" *Frauen gegen den Strom II* 7).
153. "Selbsterfahrung und Selbstuntersuchung" ("Frauenbewegung seit 'Deutschland im Herbst,'" *Frauen gegen den Strom II* 7).
154. Bandhauer-Schöffmann, "Emanzipation" 80.
155. "Aufruf an alle Frauen zur Erfindung des Glücks." In tantric iconography, the yoni symbolizes the vulva.
156. "Die Mütter, die Töchter, die Frauen dieses Landes verlangen, aus der Nation, die nur Unglück hervorbringt, entlassen zu werden" ("Aufruf an alle Frauen zur Erfindung des Glücks" 16).
157. "Wir die Frauen aller Altersklassen, leben schon immer im Exil. Aus unseren tausend Exilen verkünden wir: Das Glück befindet sich jenseits der Maschinenvernunft und der seichten Gefühle" ("Aufruf an alle Frauen zur Erfindung des Glücks" 16). "Machine-reason": a reference to Max Horkheimer's critique of instrumental reason, which he saw dominating late-capitalist societies, in his *Kritik der instrumentellen Vernunft* (1967).
158. "Deshalb erklären wir die Marktplätze und die Politik zum Müllhaufen der Geschichte, auf dem wir abladen werden, womit wir gepeinigt wurden" ("Aufruf an alle Frauen zur Erfindung des Glücks" 16).
159. "Seid leichtmütig, werdet Ausbrecherinnen aus der Gewaltnation, Ausbrecherinnen aus der Schreckensherrschaft. Tanzt, tanzt aus der Reihe!" ("Aufruf an alle Frauen zur Erfindung des Glücks" 16).
160. "Frauenbewegung seit 'Deutschland im Herbst'" 8 (emphasis hers):
    Unser "Glück" ist eben nicht unabhängig vom gesellschaftlichen Kräfteverhältnis, zu dessen Veränderung wir aktiv beitragen wollen und müssen. Und *wie* sollen wir "aus der Reihe tanzen," wenn wir tagtäglich in unseren elementarsten Grundrechten beschnitten werden und die Repression gegen uns immer weiter verschärft wird? Wohl nur, wenn wir uns Scheuklappen anlegen! Dieser "Aufruf" ist wohl eher dazu angetan, uns dorthin zurückzuholen wo uns die Herrschenden eh haben wollen!
161. I came across this undated pamphlet in the APO-Archiv, where it is filed in the section "Women's Movement" *(Frauenbewegung)*.
162. This ridiculous-sounding observation is derived from the police's directions to citizens on what to look out for in neighbors' behavior that might indicate terrorist activities. A toilet that is flushed abnormally often could point toward a group of terrorists inhabiting an illegally rented apartment.
163. "Ihr Weg zum Terrorimus ist vorgezeichnet, denn [. . .] Sie ist 'zuweilen aggressiv' (Bild); [. . .] sie stammt aus guter Familie (Stern); [. . .] sie hat ein 'selbstbewußtes Auftreten' (Bild); [. . .] Studentinnen rutschen leichter in sowas hinein (Spiegel)."
164. Paczensky 11–12:
    Wenn der Kampf gegen Terrorismus unversehens zum Kampf gegen Emanzipation ausartet, wenn die weiblichen Verdächtigen nicht nur wegen ihrer Straftaten, sondern darüber hinaus als unbotmäßige Frauen verfolgt und gebrandmarkt werden, dann richtet sich diese Verfolgung auch gegen mich und mein Bemühen um Veränderung. [. . .] Wenn die Ablehnung von Gewalt, das Entsetzen vor einer Gruppe, die sich selbst und unserer Gesellschaft zerstören will, zugleich in eine Ablehnung tatkräftiger Frauen, in den Verzicht auf Protest

und notwendige Wut umgemünzt wird, dann lähmt mich dieser Konflikt zwischen zwei Solidaritäten.

165. An example of some of this work being done is Bielby's essay "Revolutionary Men and the Feminine Grotesque," in which she argues that "[t]hrough being represented as grotesquely feminine, the male revolutionary becomes a power-less object of derision, designed to provoke laughter on the part of the reader and the West German 'imagined community,' which is able to constitute itself as masculine through this process" (226).

166. "Es genügt nicht, den Zusammenhang zwischen Terror und Emanzipation einfach zurückzuweisen, um unserer eigenen Loyalitätskonflikte willen müssen wir ihn genau und gewissenhaft untersuchen" (Paczensky 12).

## Notes to Chapter 4

1. The original German version of the epigraph for this chapter is "Gegen ihr terroristisches Programm gibts allerdings nur eins—zu kämpfen und auch aus der äußersten Defensive der Isolation raus sie anzugreifen, mit dem, was sie uns auch hier nicht nehmen können ohne uns zu töten: unser kollektives Bewußtsein und unseren Willen zu siegen. Es ist eine Machtfrage."

2. For information about the interviews see Introduction, note 17.

3. The case of Volker Leschhorn, chief physician in Berlin prisons, who committed suicide on January 11, 1982, was extremely controversial. He committed suicide after having disagreements with superiors and a disciplinary investigation conducted against him that resulted in his demotion after he medically treated RAF prisoners against the directions of government officials. See Passmore, "The Ethics and Politics" 481–82; "Wahrhaft christlich" (Truly Christian), *Der Spiegel*; "In tödlicher Gewissensnot" (In a Deadly Struggle of Conscience), *Die Zeit*. Also see the final report on the independent investigation of the death of Dr. V. Leschhorn in the publication Arbeitsgruppe Haftbedingungen/ Strafvollzug, *Haftbedingungen in der BRD* (Prison Conditions in the FRG) 87–112.

4. See Passmore, "The Ethics and Politics" 481.

5. See introduction and chapter 3.

6. For example, see Gerd Koenen, "Camera Silens: Das Phantasma der Vernichtungshaft."

7. For example, see the work of Leith Passmore ("The Art of Hunger" and "The Ethics and Politics"), Dominique Grisard's *Gendering Terror*, and Hanno Balz's *Von Terroristen, Sympathisanten, und dem Starken Staat*.

8. "[J]ahrelang voneinander isoliert und von jedem gemeinsamen politischen Prozess und der Aussenwelt abgeschlossen, sind wir entschlossen, mit unserem einzig wirksamen Mittel—dem kollektiven unbefristeten Hungerstreik—die Trennung zu durchbrechen und uns die Bedingungen für kollektive Lern- und Arbeitsprozesse zu erkämpfen, um als Menschen zu überleben" ("Hungerstreik-Erklärung vom 6.2.1981" 286).

9. While federal regulations recommended force-feeding, the application of the practice varied by state (*Bundesland*), of which a number did not force-feed. The fact that the ultimate decision lay with the medical director of the prison in question complicated the debate on force-feeding considerably.

10. Holger Meins died on November 9, 1974, and Sigurd Debus on April 16, 1981, as a result of prolonged hunger strikes. A third death associated with the RAF hunger strikes was that of Dr. Leschhorn, who committed suicide after professional defamation for refusing to force-feed prisoners under his care during the hunger strike of 1981.

11. See introduction and chapter 3.

12. There were local exceptions to this general pattern, such as the Swiss media spectacle created around German-Jewish Petra Krause, a German incarcerated in Swiss prisons for terrorist charges who was on hunger strike. Through the extensive media coverage—and extremely gendered images—her case generated, she succeeded in her demand to be extradited to Italy without standing trial in Switzerland (see Dominique Grisard's analysis of the Petra Krause case in *Gendering Terror* 71–82).

13. This tendency extends beyond RAF scholarship on hunger strikes: Allen Feldman's book-length study of the body in the conflict in Northern Ireland, including IRA hunger strikes, *Formations of Violence*, completely neglects to provide any analysis of gender in these configurations of the body and violence. More recently, in Patrick Anderson's study of hunger and (political) performance, *So Much Wasted*, a gendered (if not necessarily feminist) analysis is central. The author focuses primarily on how the performance of hunger transforms and challenges assumptions about masculinity (both in male patients of clinical anorexia and male performance artists) and in his chapter on a political hunger strike in Turkey demonstrates how the participation of women is interpreted (by Westerners) as much through sexuality and race/ethnicity as it is through gender. Ultimately, Anderson's analysis provides important additions to the discourse on the politics of starving in terms of masculinity and performance more than in terms of female political subjectivity.

14. One of the few examples in which political hunger strikes are examined in Western feminist literature is in the context of the suffragist movements, such as the historical occurrence of force-feeding of UK, Irish and U.S. suffragettes who were on hunger strike while incarcerated. A feminist analysis of the gendered nature of the conflict between female activists and the state usually is restricted to force-feeding, which is analyzed as a dichotomous "feminist/female body as violated by a patriarchal/male state/medical establishment" that mirrors the original political conflict. See Caroline Howlette, "Writing on the Body?" Force-feeding was also widely used as a treatment for neurasthenia and hysteric conditions in the early twentieth century. Aside from the case of the suffragists, the political hunger strike has rarely been the object of feminist analyses.

15. Aretxega's important work on women in the IRA includes the ethnographic study *Shattering Silence* and her essays in *States of Terror*.

16. While discourse on terrorism today is very much influenced by religion as a declared major catalyst/force for attacks/countermeasures, the left-wing terrorism that dominated global conflicts in the 1960s and '70s was mainly framed in terms of Marxist/anticolonial groups versus capitalist, imperialist states. Criticisms of the groups' political violence in Western European discourse positioned them as irrational and in violation of the liberal social contract. For example, the mainstream media routinely referred to RAF and other militant groups as "anarchists,"

placing them into the Marxist-anarchist tradition of Russian anarchists who used political violence. Anarchism, especially the communist anarchism that dominated much of Russian activism in the preceding century, as a political theory was thus constructed as synonymous with terrorism, with liberal society and state as target.

17. Ellmann 4.

18. Vandereycken and Van Deth, *From Fasting Saints to Anorexic Girls*, and Joan Jacobs Brumberg, *Fasting Girls,* in their historical and sociological studies of anorexia nervosa describe this genealogy of self-starvation as one primarily of women: medieval saints, hunger artists, and anorexia nervosa in a rising bourgeois society. All of these studies focus on white European or American women. Works by scholars like Doris Witt (*Black Hunger*) point to the limits of this genealogy, whose focus on *self-starvation* misses the connection to other eating disorders that are historically rooted in racist exploitation. Patrick Anderson's chapter on male anorexia in *So Much Wasted* points to an increased theoretical engagement with masculinity and hunger.

19. Ellmann 1. According to Kenny, Silove, and Steel, the World Medical Association (WMA) has "defined a hunger striker as a 'mentally competent person who has indicated that he [or she] has decided to refuse to take food and/or fluids for a significant interval'" (237). See Williams, "Hunger-Strikes: A Prisoner's Right or a 'Wicked Folly'?" for a categorization of five types of hunger strikers (287).

20. Ellmann 7.

21. Ellmann 5.

22. The characterization of suffragettes as "hysterical" was in accord with existing medical notions that linked mental illnesses and/or non-normatively gendered behavior (criminal, political, creative, etc.) to "nervous" physiological conditions. Representative of the medical tradition that pathologized women's non-normative behavior was physician Silas Weir Mitchell (1829–1914), whose "rest cure" was extremely influential. He prescribed it primarily to treat women diagnosed with neurasthenia and hysteria, and by extension to women he felt were hypochondriacs or lazy. His very popular treatment included absolute bed rest, lack of any intellectual stimuli, very limited social contacts, and a strict diet. This prescribed diet often would include force-feeding through the nose or rectum (Mitchell 32), at times with terrible consequences for the patient (Poirier 30). His theories today are generally understood to be informed by sexist notions of women's "nature" and a personal dislike he felt for them (see Poirier 23). Thank you to K. Surkan for bringing this issue to my attention.

23. See Peter Gelderloos's book, *How Nonviolence Protects the State* for a comprehensive discussion of how nonviolent activism is viewed (and used) by the state.

24. As I discuss extensively in previous chapters, the gendering of political activism is complicated and riddled with contradictions—as is all patriarchal ideology: thus masculinity is usually associated with violence and femininity with nonviolence, but if women employ violence, it is viewed as deranged femininity, which is much more virulent than any masculinity. So it is in the perceived *irrationality* of their violence that male terrorists are feminized, while their violent actions *as violent actions per se* do not challenge their masculinity.

25. For this study, the *group* hunger strike is relevant, even though there have been many instances of individual prisoners on hunger strike protesting their conditions of detention.

26. Ellmann 19.
27. Ellmann refers to Kafka's story "A Hunger Artist" (1922), in which a man dies of hunger only when he is removed from public display in a cage, i.e., from the public gaze, to make the case that "[s]elf-starvation is above all a performance" (17) that necessitates an audience that is implicated in the spectacle it witnesses.
28. Ellmann 17.
29. The WMA has established guidelines for doctors involved in the care of prisoners on hunger strike: "The Declaration of Tokyo (1975) and the Declaration of Malta (1991) both prohibit the use of non-consensual force-feeding of hunger strikers who are mentally competent" (Kenny, Silove, and Steel, "Legal and Ethical Implications of Medically Enforced Feeding" 237, 239). For aspects of the debate on force-feeding also see Peel, "Hunger Strikes"; the *Der Spiegel* cover story, "RAF-Hungerstreik: Zwangsernährung, Rettung oder Folter?" (RAF Hunger Strike: Force-Feeding, Rescue, or Torture?); Williams, "Hunger-Strikes: A Prisoner's Right or a 'Wicked Folly'?"
30. Ellmann 21; emphasis hers.
31. Balz, *Von Terroristen* 139.
32. See introduction, chapters 1 and 3.
33. Kristeva 4.
34. Kristeva 4; emphasis mine.
35. Kristeva 4.
36. From July 27 to August 3, 1994, RAF prisoners organized a hunger strike whose end date was predetermined (*befristet*) (see *Rote Armee Fraktion* 498). *Befristet* hunger strikes like this one have a more strictly symbolic function than *unbefristet* ones, since the threat to the prisoner's health and/or life is limited.
37. See Martin Jander's discussion of the report by German psychiatrist Wilfried Rasch on the psychological and physical damages done to prisoners under solitary confinement and his recommendations about the minimum number of prisoners within a group required to maintain basic health in "Isolation: Zu den Haftbedingungen der RAF-Gefangenen" (Solitary: On the Prison Conditions of RAF Prisoners 983–84).
38. Movement archives hold numerous flyers, brochures, and other movement publications, as well as petitions and initiatives of prisoners' families, that claim the refusal of necessary medical treatment of political prisoners. Jander, in his research on prison conditions of RAF prisoners, mentions that on several occasions prisoners were denied examination and treatment by doctors of their choice (980). This can be understood as a clearly political move on the side of the state, as RAF prisoners routinely rejected examinations by prison medical staff because they suspected them to be biased towards the state's goals.
39. As Jander points out, there exists very little scholarship on the actual prison conditions of RAF prisoners. He attributes this problematic lack of historical research to a reluctance of scholars to be absorbed into either position in this highly polarized debate (974).
40. From the hunger strike statement about the seventh strike, April 20, 1979: "In Ireland, Spain, Italy, Austria, Switzerland, France, Israel prisoners fight against prison conditions, through which their political identity is to be broken and they

physically destroyed—prison conditions, whose implementations in most cases was enforced by the FRG [Federal Republic of Germany]" ("In Irland, Spanien, Italien, Österreich, der Schweiz, Frankreich, Israel kämpfen Gefangene gegen Haftbedingungen, deren Einführung in den meisten Fällen von der BRD durchgesetzt worden sind") (*Rote Armee Fraktion* 282).

41. See Passmore, "The Art of Hunger" 35.

42. See Passmore, "The Art of Hunger" 42.

43. See Aust, *Der Baader Meinhof Komplex* 431–33.

44. "Lauter Polizisten auf dem Kudamm? *Spiegel* Interview mit Berlins Justizsenator Gerhard Moritz Meyer (FDP) über Hungerstreik und Krawalle" (Lots of Police on the Kudamm? *Spiegel* Interview with Berlin's Minister of Justice Gerhard Moritz Meyer (FDP) on Hunger Strikes and Riots 114–15):

    Wir müssen davon ausgehen, daß wir es in Berlin wie in vielen anderen Großstädten mit mehreren hundert ständig zu Gewalttaten bereiten Menschen zu tun haben, die insbesondere den Anlaß des Hungerstreiks der RAF-Häftlinge benutzen, um Krawalle zu begehen. Und wir wissen ja auch, daß es nach dem Hungerstreik-Tod von Holger Meins 1974 nicht nur krawallartige Ausschreitungen, sondern auch Anschläge auf Personen und Sachen gegeben hat.

45. Passmore refers to these two realms of communication networks as "*info*" (synonymous with the secret letters sent between prisoners), an internal information exchange and a way to keep the collective in check ("Art of Hunger" 37) and "*out-fo*," which communicated RAF ideas from prisons to the outside support network and that "became more than a line of communication between comrades; it evolved into a network of publication and event management" ("Art of Hunger" 40).

46. An exception was the sixth hunger strike, for which no declaration exists.

47. "Unser Hungerstreik ist dabei nichts als unsere einzige Möglichkeit zu solidarischem Widerstand in der Isolation. Ohne die Macht, die Gewalt der Straße, ohne die Mobilisierung der antifaschistischen Bürger, die für Menschenrechte und gegen Folter eintreten, auf deren Loyalität die Schweine noch angewiesen sind—hebt unser Hungerstreik unsere Ohnmacht nicht auf" ("Hungerstreik-Erklärung vom 8. Mai 1973" 189).

48. The most prominent example is Birgit Hogefeld, who was incarcerated from 1993 to 2011. In *Die Geschichte der RAF verstehen*, she explains how her involvement in prison rights activism during the hunger strikes radicalized her and made her seek RAF membership (see Hogefeld, "Zur Geschichte der RAF" (On the History of the RAF).

49. Ellmann discusses Sinn Fein's narrative creation of a tradition of hunger striking against an oppressor, which effectively erased the actual political precedent of a hunger strike by suffragette Hannah Sheehy Skeffington in 1912. In the context of the suffragettes' radical resistance, Sinn Fein initially had declared hunger striking to be a "womanish" thing (see Ellmann 12). Also see Sweeney, "Irish Hunger Strikes and the Cult of Self-Sacrifice" and "Self-Immolation in Ireland."

50. Ellmann 54.

51. 183 centimeters, 39 kilograms (see Aust, *Der Baader Meinhof Komplex* 415).

52. Denazification and reeducation efforts by Allied forces after World War II included the display of emaciated and abused Nazi prisoners, forcing Germans to confront

(often for the first time) the realities of the Nazi regime's terrorism against Jews and other persecuted groups. See Barbie Zelizer's *Remembering to Forget* and Habbo Knoch, *Die Tat als Bild* (The Deed as Image). See Alice Weinreb's "'For the Hungry Have No Past nor Do They Belong to a Political Party'" for an analysis of how within a few years and within the context of an international human rights discourse in the postwar time, the discourse on hunger shifted from charging Germany's aggression and terror regime with causing (world) hunger to treating the German population as victims of starvation originating in causes outside of their control: "Defeated Germany was rapidly reconceptualized: the most powerful and threatening enemy nation was transformed into the primary hotspot of postwar hunger. Hunger became, in the eyes of both Germans and the Western Allies, the defining attribute of the German experience of post–World War II occupation" (52).

53. See Habbo Knoch's "The Return of the Images" for a discussion of the role images of Nazi crime played in shaping public discourse on the Holocaust in the decade of 1955–65.

54. The largest German concentration and death camp, Auschwitz-Birkenau, where approximately 1.1 million Jews were murdered between 1941 and 1945, functions universally as a placeholder for the genocide committed against Jews during the time of National Socialism in Germany. It was regularly used by German radical leftist rhetoric in the 1960s and '70s to evoke fear of what activists claimed was a resurging fascist West German state (also see Petra Terhoeven, "Opferbilder–Täterbilder").

55. Kristeva 4.

56. In contrast, a picture of Meins's corpse on his death bed that was circulated, instead of triggering abjection, evokes very different imagery related to Christian religion and martyrdom.

57. Even though both images show the men's genitals, the context in fact "un-mans" them: Meins's death and brutal arrangement on the autopsy table places him outside of the symbolic, beyond the law of the father, while the barbed wire that indicates the concentration camp as context for the survivor's body stands for a dehumanized symbolic order of violence that denies subjectivity to the human body.

58. See Passmore, "The Red Army Faction's 'Revolution under the Skin'" (6).

59. "weil der ausgemergelte Mensch so viel Ähnlichkeiten mit KZ-Häftlingen, mit den Toten von Auschwitz hat" (Hogefeldt, "Zur Geschichte der RAF" 40).

60. Passmore, "The Ethics and Politics" 483.

61. See Passmore's "The Art of Hunger" for a comprehensive analysis of the role *das info* played not only in maintaining an internal network of RAF prisoners on hunger strike in the early 1970s but also in rhetorically defining the political and ideological meaning of the strikes in terms of "virtue, sacrifice and martyrdom" (58). Klaus Theweleit, in "Bemerkungen zum RAF-Gespenst" (Comments on the Specter of the RAF), views the extreme group mentality of the RAF as constructing *one collective body* in *das info* that forces each member into identification with the group, an *Über-Leib* (super-body) that factually erases the physical existence of the individual (54). Interestingly, despite Theweleit's commitment to a gendered analysis of power and violence in German history in much of his other work, here this super-body is not gendered.

62. See for example Passmore's "The Art of Hunger" and Colvin, *Ulrike Meinhof*.

63. See Balz, *Von Terroristen, Sympathisanten, und dem starken Staat*; Colin, de Graaf, Pekelder, Umlauf, eds., *Der "Deutsche" Herbst und die RAF in Politik, Medien, und Kunst* (The "German" Autumn and the RAF in Politics, Media, and Art); Elter, "Die RAF und die Medien" (The RAF and the Media); Weinhauer, Requate, Haupt, eds., *Terrorismus in der Bundesrepublik* (Terrorism in the Federal Republik).

64. "Dies könnte mit dem [. . .] Anblick eines femininen Körpers zu tun haben. Holger Meins' Körperbild ließ die MedienkonsumentInnen im Ungewissen über den Status des Terroristen—war dies der Körper eines Staatsfeinds, der Körper eines Opfers von Staatsgewalt oder beides?" (Grisard, *Gendering Terror* 154).

65. See their statement about the tenth hunger strike: "Hungerstreik-Erklärung vom 1.2.1989" 389–91.

66. According to Passmore in "The Art of Hunger," the early RAF hunger strikes (until 1977) were affecting public awareness to a much greater degree than the later ones; he points to the relative obscurity with which the death of Sigurd Debus took place in 1981, which contrasts sharply with the public outcry that met Holger Meins's death in 1974.

67. See Balz, *Von Terroristen, Sympathisanten, und dem starken Staat* 139–50.

68. See Balz, *Von Terroristen, Sympathisanten, und dem starken Staat* 142–43.

69. See Balz, *Von Terroristen, Sympathisanten, und dem starken Staat* 140, and Passmore, "Art of Hunger" 32, 34.

70. The newsmagazine's cover story—"RAF-Hungerstreik: Zwangsernährung, Rettung, oder Folter?"—included the title story by Christian Habbe, "Hungerstreik—'Grünes Licht' für den Tod?" (Hunger Strike—A "Go-Ahead" for Death?) and "'Würden Sie nicht sagen, das ist Mord?'" (Would You Not Call That Murder?), an interview with medical experts by Axel Jeschke and Hans-Wolfgang Sternsdorff, as well as a report on the effects of force-feeding on the prisoner by RAF member Karl-Heinz Dellwo, "Der Kopf fängt an zu dröhnen" (The Head Begins to Roar).

71. See Dellwo 34–37.

72. See Karl-Heinz Krumm, "Hungerstreik—und niemand weiß einen Ausweg" (Hunger Strike—and No One Knows the Solution).

73. Außerparlamentarische Opposition (Extra-Parliamentary Opposition). See introduction and chapter 1.

74. Schiller, "Margit Schiller zum Hungerstreik: Gefangene seit 10 Jahren isoliert" (Margit Schiller on the Hunger Strike: Prisoners in the Past 10 Years Isolated).

75. "Inhaftierte Terroristen im Hungerstreik fordern die Zusammenlegung aller Häftlinge. Die *Zeit* diskutiert," *Die Zeit*, 7 April 1989.

76. See Grisard, *Gendering Terror* (38–45), and Colvin, *Ulrike Meinhof* (190–93), for a discussion of gender theories in criminology.

77. For a comprehensive analysis of media and other public discourse on the RAF in the 1970s, see Balz's *Von Terroristen, Sympathisanten, und dem starken Staat*.

78. "Das Ziel ist, den Rechtsstaat und seine Ordnung funktionsunfähig zu machen und gleichzeitig der Lächerlichkeit preiszugeben. Im Bewußtsein, daß die hochgestellten Sympathisanten ihre Partei ergreifen, unternehmen die Terroristen den Versuch, sich als politische Kraft in den Haftanstalten zu etablieren" (Matthias Weber, "Den armen Baader lassen sie verhungern" [They Let Poor Baader Starve]).

79. "Die neuerlichen Gewaltaktionen scheinen daher nur der Auftakt einer Terrorwelle zu sein, welche sich nach dem Tod eines Häftlings in eine hochgefährliche Eskalation steigern könnte" (Hans Wüllenweber, "Löst Hungerstreik Terror aus?" [Does Hunger Strike Cause Terror?]).

80. "Mehrheit gibt Justiz keine Schuld an Meins-Tod" (Majority Does Not Fault Justice System for Meins's Death): Nur zwölf Prozent der Bundesbürger sehen es als ein Versagen der Behörden an, daß der Untersuchungshäftling Holger Meins an den Folgen eines Hungerstreiks gestorben ist. 78 Prozent sind dagegen der Ansicht, man könne den Behörden keinen Vorwurf daraus machen, wenn ein Hungerstreik tödlich ausgehe. [. . .] Fünf Prozent zeigten sich unentschieden, welcher Ansicht sie sich anschließen sollten, weitere fünf Prozent äußerten sich nicht zu diesem Thema."Mehrheit gibt Justiz keine Schuld an Meins-Tod" ["Majority does not fault justice system for Meins' death").

81. Kristeva 4.

82. "Klaus-Bericht," a report about the evaluation of evidence confiscated on July 16 and 18, 1973, in the cells of eight RAF prisoners. The report was submitted by investigator Alfred Klaus in April 1974.

83. Klaus-Bericht: Danach verbirgt sich hinter den Folterprotesten nicht so sehr die Notwendigkeit, Leben und Gesundheit der angeblich gefolterten zu schützen, sondern vor allem die Absicht, die Guerillaorganisation ungestört aufzubauen. [. . .] Und die Menschenrechtsfunktion von Amnesty International soll, wie sich aus dem zweiten Absatz ergibt, eine politische Dimension in Richtung bewaffneter Kampf erhalten. In der Einzelhaft und anderen Sicherheitsmaßnahmen "Aussageerpressungsmethoden" zu sehen, entbehrt jeder realen Grundlage und dürfte auf die überreizte Phantasie und das Mißtrauen der RAF-Gefangenen zurückzuführen sein.

84. Dokumentation "Baader-Meinhof-Bande," published according to the records of the Federal Bureau of Criminal Investigation in Wiesbaden and the State Bureau of Criminal Investigation (Landeskriminalamt) Rhineland-Palatinate of the Ministry of the Interior Rhineland-Palatinate on November 22, 1974: Die anläßlich der Strafprozesse gegen anarchistische Gewalttäter seit längerer Zeit laufende Kampagne gegen die Justiz wurde aktiviert und "durch den Hungerstreik auf den Weg gebracht." Tatsächlich wird mit der Aufhebung der Isolation jedoch die politische Beeinflussung der Mitgefangenen und deren Aufputschung mit dem Ziel angestrebt, Gefängnisrevolten herbeizuführen—nicht zuletzt aber auch eine Befreiung zu erleichtern. (33)

85. "Lauter Polizisten auf dem Kudamm" 114–15: Gehen Sie davon aus, daß hinter der aus Ihrer Sicht unerfüllbaren Kernforderung der RAF auf Großgruppenbildung die alte Strategie steckt: Hungerstreik, Passivität drinen, schafft neue Anhänger, Aktivität draußen? [. . .] Es ist eine wirklich schlimme Entwicklung, daß durch solche Hungerstreiks eine emotional bestimmte Solidarisierung entsteht. Ich muß allerdings nach wie vor auch davon ausgehen, daß es sich um eine lang geplante und gezielte Aktion handelt, gerichtet auf den Aufbau einer neuen Befehlszentrale der RAF.

86. One such case was that of Lutz Taufer and Karl-Heinz Dellwo, two RAF prisoners, when the Higher Regional Court (Oberlandesgericht) Düsseldorf ruled to have

their hands tied after force-feeding to prevent self-induced vomiting in 1977 (Beschluss des Oberlandesgericht Düsseldorf).

87. See Passmore, "The Ethics and Politics of Force-Feeding," for a detailed discussion of the law regarding force-feeding and its implications.

88. Neumaier, "Für das Leben verloren?" (Lost to Life?):

Die Bundesärztekammer bekennt sich unverändert zu der Aufgabe des Arztes, das menschliche Leben mit allen ihm zur Verfügung stehenden Möglichkeiten zu erhalten und zu retten. Diese Verpflichtung des Arztes muß jedoch dort ihre Grenze finden, wo ein eindeutiger, auf freier Willensbildung beruhender Beschluß des einzelnen Menschen vorliegt, die ärztliche Behandlung abzulehnen und sich ihr sogar aktiv zu widersetzen. Kein Arzt darf zu einer derartigen Zwangsbehandlung verpflichtet werden.

89. Bundespräsident Gustav Heinemann: Was wenn ein Mensch seinen "selbstgewollten Tod als Kampfmittel, als Ausdruck seiner Freiheit und Selbstbestimmung, auch in der Haft einsetzen will?" (Neumaier, "Für das Leben verloren?"). The conservative national daily newspaper *Die Welt* counters Heinemann's deliberations with the argument that for the state to maintain its constitutional judicial system, "the plaintiff is barred from morally blackmailing the state with his [sic] death," expressing a commonly held opinion ("daß der Angeklagte den Staat nicht mit seinem Tod moralisch erpressen darf" [Ohnesorge, *Die Welt*]).

90. "Offener Brief an den [sic] Anstaltsärzten [sic] in der Bundesrepublik."

91. In 1981, ten members of the Provisional Irish Republican Army (PIRA) (an Irish nationalist, armed organization that was fighting for Northern Ireland's independence from Great Britain and for unity with the Republic of Ireland) died during hunger strikes carried out to protest the state denying them the status of political prisoner (see Aretxaga, "Striking with Hunger: Cultural Meaning of Political Violence in Northern Ireland"). Force-feeding was not allowed in Great Britan, and British authorities refused to negotiate with the prisoners.

92. "Recht an der Grenze: Mediziner und Juristen streiten: Muß Zwangsernährung sein?" (The Limits of the Law: Medical and Law Experts Argue; Is Force-Feeding a Must?):

Wie lange die Justiz mit hungernden Gefangenen um Leben und Tod pokert, ist in das Ermessen der Länder gestellt. Das Gesetz erhält nur Vages: Es erlaubt den Aufsehern, ihre Häftlinge fast, wenn auch nicht ganz verhungern zu lassen. Die Grenze, an der das Recht der Anstaltärzte, die Hungernden von Hohenasperg [Gefängniskrankenhaus] mit Gewalt zu ernähren, zur Pflicht wird, zieht Paragraph 101 des Strafvollzugsgesetzes—dort, wo der Häftling in "absoluter Lebensgefahr" ist oder wo nicht mehr "von einer freien Willensbestimmung des Gefangegen ausgegangen werden kann."

93. "hatte die Justiz Mühe, genügend Ärzte zu finden, die zur Zwangsernährung der Hungernden bereit waren"("Recht an der Grenze" 71).

94. "'Verletzung der Würde des Häftlings'" ("Recht an der Grenze" 71). It is significant that the dignity of prison staff subjected to violent resistance by prisoners against being force-fed became an aspect within the discourse and was raised as one reason *not* to force-feed, such as in a letter by the prison director of the Stammheim prison to the Oberlandesgericht Stuttgart (Leitender Regierungsdirektor Nusser, Betr.:

Untersuchungsgefangene Baader, Ensslin, und Raspe; *hier*: Hungerstreik [Director Nusser, Re.: remand prisoners Baader, Ensslin, Raspe; *here*: hunger strike]).

95. "Recht an der Grenze: Mediziner und Juristen streiten; Muß Zwangsernährung sein?"

96. "Zwangsernährung soll nur noch geboten sein, wenn der Hungernde nicht mehr Herr seiner Sinne ist" ("Recht an der Grenze: Mediziner und Juristen streiten: Muß Zwangsernährung sein?")

97. De-escalation through concessions and negotiations through the modification of prison conditions took place in Austria, where the state dealt with the few political hunger strikes strategically in a nonconfrontational way. The result was an effective depoliticization of the strikes and waning public sympathy with the prisoners (see Bandhauer-Schöffmann, "Hungerstreiks in Österreichischen Gefängnissen" [Hunger Strikes in Austrian Prisons]).

98. A notable exception is the work of Dominique Grisard, whose sophisticated use of Foucault in her analysis of public discourse on terrorism in Switzerland foregrounds the role notions of gender play in the construction of the terrorist subject.

99. *biopolitische Intervention* (Grisard, *Gendering Terror* 155).

100. "[Der Hungerstreik] könnte [. . .] durchaus als 'weiblicher' Gewaltakt am eigenen Körper interpretiert werden: als Manipulation anderer mittels dem eigenen Körper zugefügter Gewalt" (Grisard, *Gendering Terror* 155).

101. Communism, whose Marxist theory underlies much of the RAF's ideological thinking, was absent in public West German debate as an actual political alternative to fascism. As the political system of the "other" Germany, the German Democratic Republic, it symbolized the second evil to fascism and any propagation of communism was viewed as extreme and fringey (the KPD was banned in West Germany). The severe anticommunism of the West German government preceding Chancellor Willy Brandt's Ostpolitik in the early 1970s was understood by leftist activists as a replication of the anticommunism of the Weimar Republic that paved the way for a takeover by the fascists, who were communist activists' prime enemies.

102. "androzentrischer Kern" (Appelt, "Staatsbürgerin und Gesellschaftsvertrag" [The Female Citizen and the Social Contract] 540).

103. Until the eighteenth century, the dominant scientific model for gender/sex viewed physical differences between male and female bodies as a question of degree, not as absolute differences—the "basic" natural body was considered male, and the female body was an inverted version of it, not an inherently different one. Biological difference was not ontological, but social. E.g., sex changes were possible through the behavioral appropriation of mannerisms and professions of the opposite sex. Consequently, a strict code regarding clothes and social behavior to regulate social gender was necessary. This was succeeded by the biological determinism of the two-sex model, which declared male and female bodies to be *fundamentally* different and thus needing to be assigned social roles and responsibilities that were *natural* to them. A naturalization of gender roles thus occurred (see Laqueur, *Making Sex*, and Maihofer 28–33).

104. "Den Frauen wurden nun aufgrund ihres Geschlechts gerade *die* Fähigkeiten und Eigenschaften abgesprochen, die eben zur Grundlage allgemeiner Menschen- und Bürgerrechte erklärt worden waren" (Maihofer 32; emphasis hers).

105. Daß "die bestehende bürgerlich-patriarchale Geschlechterordnung und die mit ihr verbundene geschlechtsspezifische Arbeitsteilung in der biologischen Natur der Geschlechter, insbesondere der Frau, begründet sind" (Maihofer 33).

106. Appelt emphasizes that masculinity and property were not only prerequisites for citizen status, but the latter actually *constituted* bourgeois masculinity, which was defined as independent of any other's will: "Entscheidend für das Selbstverständnis des aufgeklärten Bürgertums war, daß nicht nur Männlichkeit und wirtschaftliche Unabhängigkeit Voraussetzungen für den Staatsbürgerschaftsstatus darstellten, sondern dieser umgekehrt bürgerliche Männlichkeit, die als Unabhängigkeit vom Willen anderer formuliert wurde, konstituierte" ("Staatsbürgerin" 555).

107. The citizen status of colonized people was much more complicated than presented here and depended on the colonizing state's regulations. The point here is that they were denied full citizenship based on their race/colonial status, thus further limiting the universal claim of liberal citizenship.

108. See Appelt, "Staatsbürgerin" 546.

109. See Appelt, "Staatsbürgerin" 547.

110. See Plumwood, *Feminism and the Mastery of Nature*, for the development of dualistic thinking in Western philosophy that inherently produces (and legitimizes) relationships of domination. See also Appelt, "Vernunft versus Gefühle?" (Reason versus Emotions?).

111. In "Racism and Sexism in Nazi Germany: Motherhood, Compulsory Sterilization, and the State," Gisela Bock briefly recounts the pre-1933 eugenics movement in Germany, whose ideology of racial hygiene resonated in National Socialism's ideals of racial purity and the role of women within that ideology (273–75). See Stefan Kühl's important study of the influence of U.S. genetic thinking and policies in the name of "science" on Nazi Germany's race ideology and legislation, *The Nazi Connection*.

112. The place that women took in empire building during colonialism might not have been "political" but was nevertheless central, as laid out in Lora Wildenthal's *German Women for Empire* and Anette Dietrich's *Weiße Weiblichkeiten* (White Femininities).

113. See chapter 1 for a discussion of leftist activists' rather problematic equation of the West German state—but especially the United States and Israel—with elements of German fascism, and the absence of real discussions of National Socialism. While the Left's unqualified and broad usage of the term "fascist" needs to be viewed in the context of a postwar general population reluctant to examine remnants of Nazi Germany in its cultural, social, and political formations, the troubling evidence of actual anti-Semitism in the New Left—including the RAF—needs to be part of an analysis of radical politics in West Germany.

114. This anxiety not only plagued conservatives, but also, as Bridenthal, Grossmann, and Kaplan discuss in "Introduction: Women in Weimar and Nazi Germany," both the bourgeois and the socialist women's movement, "although they were bitter political enemies shared a commitment to women's traditional roles in the family and to ideals of female duty, service, and self-sacrifice. Their feminism [included] a peculiarly German deference to the whole community, whether perceived as the class or the nation" (2).

115. Bridenthal, Grossmann, and Kaplan 13.

116. Bridenthal, Grossmann, and Kaplan 11:

The "new women"—who voted, used contraception, obtained illegal abortions, and earned wages—were more than a bohemian minority or an artistic convention. They existed in office and factory, bedroom and kitchen, just as surely as—and more significantly than—in café and cabaret. Their confrontation with the rationalized workplace, their heightened visibility in public spaces, and their changing sexual and procreative options preoccupied population experts and sex reformers. Also see Claudia Koonz's *Mothers in the Fatherland* (93–123).

117. See Stephenson 143.

118. The volume edited by Bridenthal, Grossmann, and Kaplan, *When Biology Became Destiny: Women in Weimar and Nazi Germany* (1984), is an early attempt by feminist scholars to examine the role that gender as biologically determined played in the roots and rise of German fascism and gives some insight into how the body positions the fascist subject in relation to politics.

119. While local Nazi officials' take on women's role differed according to regional issues and was strategically interpreted, official Nazi doctrine, especially after the party's takeover of power in 1933, viewed men's and women's worlds as distinctly separate, if codependent. The man's "larger" world of the state, economics, and fascist struggle (i.e., militarism) was complemented by the woman's "small" world of family and community (see Stephenson's quote of Hitler on this issue in *Women in Nazi Germany*, 142).

120. Koonz, "The Competition for Women's *Lebensraum*" 213.

121. See Stephenson 16.

122. See Stephenson 19.

123. See Bock for a discussion of forced sterilization and antinatal legislation against Jews, the mentally ill, and the disabled, as well as those classified as "asocial" in Nazi Germany.

124. Stephenson quotes Hitler, who states that "men's and women's spheres of activity [are of a] natural order" (142) that has been displaced by democratic liberalism and women's emancipation projects. He emphasizes that fascist society rests on this natural order of the sexes: "[T]here can be no conflict in the relations between the two sexes as long each fulfills the function assigned to it by nature" (Stephenson 142).

125. Stephenson points out the contradication that exists in designating the domestic sphere as "a woman's domain" while maintaining the legality of the Civil Code, which effectively places all authority with the man of the house (Stephenson 19).

126. Bridenthal, Grossmann, and Kaplan 24.

127. As Koonz points out, this ideology "conceived an intensely communal vision of motherhood that aimed at incorporating women into civic activities, welfare work, patriotic and folk organizations, and housewives' associations" (*Mothers in the Fatherland* 122).

128. See chapter 2.

129. "Es wird deutlisch, daß Macht und Geschlecht sich dem modernen Subjekt nicht etwa lediglich additiv hinzufügen, sondern diesem immanent sind" (Maihofer 110).

130. See Maihofer 116.

131. See also Wilde, "Der Geschlechtervertrag als Bestandteil moderner Staatlichkeit" (The Sexual Contract as Part of Modern Statehood).

132. See Ludwig 95.

133. See Ludwig 97.
134. Ludwig 100.
135. See Bordo, "The Body and the Reproduction of Femininity" 22–23.
136. Though the female saints are outside a liberal discourse, they point to a historical continuity of women using their bodies to enter the public/political realm. See Caroline Walker Bynum's extensive study on starving female saints in medieval times and the significance of gendered relations to food, *Holy Feast and Holy Fast*.
137. Feminist literature since the late 1980s, when the "epidemic" proportions of the spread of anorexia became known, focuses primarily on the population most affected by it, i.e., women. Current publications by scholars such as Patrick Anderson point to the invisibility of male anorexics in both feminist literature and clinical diagnostics and to the neccessity to revisit the gendered implications of the pathology (see Anderson's chapter, "The Archive of Anorexia" in *So Much Wasted* 30–56).
138. See for example "'A Way Outa No Way': Eating Problems among African-American, Latina, and White Women" by Becky Wangsgaard Thompson. Doris Witt's *Black Hunger* is a study of the relationship between food and African American since the 1960s. Witt examines the role of debates on soul food as both perpetuating and challenging racial stereotypes. She addresses the ways race (and class and sexuality) shapes the gendered relationship to food—the nourishment of the body—both in black masculinities and black femininities.
139. A well-known publication that makes the argument that anorexia needs to be understood as a gesture of resistance against patriarchal norms (not simply as individual pathology) is Susie Orbach's *Hunger Strike*, originally published in 1993.
140. Bordo, "The Body and the Reproduction of Femininity" 20.
141. Bordo, "The Body and the Reproduction of Femininity" 20.
142. Research on anorexia in particular does show that the anorexic at times perceives her refusal to eat as a political act, and it definitely takes place in opposition to external control. Discovery of the condition then often draws it into a public sphere of school doctors and therapists, as the family is scrutinized. However, the sense of empowerment and the starving itself take place in secrecy, and force-feeding usually takes place in hospitals and nutrition clinics, technically keeping the condition within the private sphere. So-called ana (pro-anorexia) sites on the Internet have created a public forum that situates the disorder in a more public realm. In what way this politicizes the practice is still to be debated. Anorexia at times is seen as more of an act of political resistance, a view that portrays anorexic women less as victims than as employing desperate measures of resistance.
143. Bordo differentiates between "discursive" demonstrations and the simply "embodied" protest of the anorexic patient. It remains unclear whether this distinction can be made, especially in light of Ludwig's persuasive linking of Gramsci's hegemonic *integral state* (internalized by subject), Foucault's power of governing, and Butler's performativity—especially the latter two, which clearly present the body *as* embodied discourse.
144. See the autobiographical publications by Margit Schiller, *Remembering the Armed Struggle* (first published in German in 1999 as *Es war ein harter Kampf um meine*

*Erinnerung*) and Gabriele Rollnik and Daniel Dubbe, *Keine Angst vor niemand* (Not Afraid of Anybody).

145. "Der Kampf hört auch im Gefängnis nicht auf, die Ziele verändern sich nicht, nur die Mittel und das Terrain, auf dem die Auseinandersetzung Guerilla/Staat, der Krieg weiter ausgetragen werden, und so reagiert der Staat auch in dieser Situation: gefangen und unbewaffnet—auf einen kollektiven Hungerstreik wie auf einen bewaffneten Angriff" ("Hungerstreik-Erklärung vom 6.2.1981" 286).

146. This forging of a collective identity through hunger strikes is not restricted to the RAF but also applies to other organized group hunger strikes, such as the IRA's in Northern Ireland. However, in the 1970s, participation in the RAF hunger strike was absolutely defining in terms of group membership.

147. This, of course, is based on classic Marxist politics of proletarian solidarity.

148. "[Solidarität] ist der praktische Ausdruck des Bewußtseins jedes Einzelnen, daß individuelle und kollektive Befreiung kein Widerspruch ist, wie die klägliche Apologie individueller Bedürfnisbefriedigung meint, sondern ein dialektisches Verhältnis—wie Befreiung hier vom Befreiungskampf der Völker der Dritten Welt nicht zu trennen ist" ("Hungerstreik-Erklärung vom 6.2.1981" 287).

149. "Wo Herrschaft durch Trennung, Differenzierung, Vernichtung einzelner, um alle zu treffen und den ganzen Prozeß zu lähmen funktioniert, ist Solidarität eine Waffe. Es ist die erste starke subjektive politische Erfahrung für jeden, der hier zu kämpfen anfängt, der Kern revolutionärer moral: Solidarität als Waffe—konkret, materiell, Aktion aus der eigenen Entscheidung für diesen Krieg" ("Hungerstreik-Erklärung vom Dezember 1984" 322–23).

150. Ellmann 7.

151. See chapter 5 for a discussion of Erving Goffman's concept of prison as an "absolute institution."

152. Within the—limited—comparison with anorexia nervosa and political hunger strikes, this constitutes an important difference: the anorexic's reliance on secrecy contains the act of hungering within the personal space—even if we understand it as an act of resistance against, not just as a symptom of, patriarchal power.

153. Ellmann 33.

154. Quoted in Ellmann 33.

155. See Caroline Howlette's analysis of written accounts by suffragettes of force-feeding and their role in "the construction of a shared suffragette subjectivity" ("Writing on the Body?" 3). According to Howlette, the strategic usage of terms like "outrage" to describe the violence experienced by the body, which is the equivalent to today's use of "rape," not only signified a gendered and sexualized conflict but was also used to "combat representation's resistance to pain" (3).

156. Some RAF scholars might disagree with me on this point and argue that the group calculated on the death of one or more prisoners to make the strikes more effective—thus making death a strategic goal within the practice, and the way the death of Holger Meins in 1974 was used to mobilize for the RAF prisoners is well documented. I still maintain that the power of the hunger strike, unlike other acts of political self-destruction, only is effective in its *threat* of death, while others necessitate death within the strategy. This is complicated by the group identity of

the RAF hunger strikes (and those of other organized groups), where the individual's identity (and body) is subordinated—or rather incorporated—into a collective one: one starves for all.

157. "Wenn unser Schreiben kein Gehör findet, werden auch unsere Körper die Quälereien beweisen, die Ihr täglich an uns begeht" ("Baader/Meinhof: Macht kaputt").

158. "Tatsächlich ermöglichte ihnen die Widerstandspraxis des Hungerstreiks, die repressive Seite des freiheitlich-demokratischen Staats und sein vermeinlich humanitäres Interssse am 'Erhalt des Lebens' blosszustellen. So besehen ist der Hungerstreik gleichzeitig als Akt der Gewalt gegen das Selbst und gegen den Staat zu lesen" ("Transversale Widerstandspraktiken?" 206; emphasis mine). At a different point she states, "The violence against the self is violence against the state" ("Die Gewalt gegen das Selbst ist Gewalt gegen den Staat" [*Gendering Terror* 157]).

## Notes to Chapter 5

1. "Was macht uns Frauen den Männern gleicher als eine Waffe?" (anonymous woman in Social Center, Berlin, 1973).

2. For information about the interviews see Introduction, note 17.

3. See Lenz 281–89.

4. See chapter 3 for news coverage of this prison break.

5. Such as Gisela Diewald-Kerkmann, *Frauen, Terrorismus, und Justiz* (Women, Terrorism, and the Justice System); Vojin Saša Vukadinović, "Der unbegründete Feminismusverdacht" (The Unfounded Accusation of Feminism); Sylvia Schraut, "Terrorismus und Geschlecht" (Terrorism and Gender).

6. Within the German-speaking countries, the Red Zora (Rote Zora), the feminist wing of the Revolutionary Cells (Revolutionäre Zellen) from which they eventually seceded, was the only armed group with an explicitly feminist orientation: it limited its political violence to objects and property and committed attacks against institutions the group viewed as antiwomen or antifeminist (see the collection of texts by the Rote Zora in *Die Früchte des Zorns* [Grapes of Wrath], 593–633). They did not operate underground and instead as feminist activists maintained strong ties to the radical leftist scene (see chapter 1).

7. Vukadinović, "Der unbegründete Feminismusverdacht" 92.

8. See Patricia Melzer, "'Death in the Shape of a Young Girl': Feminist Responses to Media Representations of Women Terrorists during the 'German Autumn' of 1977." Also see chapter 1 and chapter 3 for discussions of feminist debates about this topic as they were taking place in movement publications.

9. Alice Schwarzer is (West) Germany's most prominent feminist activist and the founder and editor of *Emma*, Germany's most widely circulated feminist magazine. A journalist in mainstream media outlets, Schwarzer was not active in the New Left before politically engaging with women's issues. Many of the movement's controversies and debates manifested in or through Schwarzer positioning herself center stage as the women's movement representative in the media and in public. She declared the women's movement to have emerged only through the abortion-rights campaigns of 1971—dismissing the continuous earlier feminist work of leftist women such as in the Aktionsrat zur Befreiung der Frau, founded by women in the

SDS in 1968, and the group that emerged from that work, Brot und Rosen (Bread and Roses) (see also Schulz 188–90).

10. Smith and Watson, eds., 3.

11. The following are life narratives that have contributed to a personalizing of revolutionary politics in the German debate on terrorism: Ralf Reinders and Ronald Fritzsch, *Die Bewegung 2 Juni* (The Movement 2nd June, 1995); Dieter Kunzelmann, *Leisten Sie keinen Widerstand!* (Don't Resist! 1998); Till Meyer, *Staatsfeind: Erinnerungen* (Enemy of the State: Memories, 1998); Irmgard Möller and Oliver Tolmein, *RAF—Das war für uns Befreiung* (RAF—That Meant Liberation to Us, 1997); Ralf Pohle, *Mein Name ist Mensch: Das Interview* (My Name Is Human Being: The Interview, 2002); Thorwald Proll, *Mein 68: Aufzeichnungen, Briefe, Interviews* (My 68: Notes, Letters, Interviews, 1998); Thorwald Proll and Daniel Dubbe, *Wir kamen vom anderen Stern* (We Were from Another Planet, 2003); Gabriele Rollnik and Daniel Dubbe, *Keine Angst vor Niemand* (Not Afraid of Anybody, 2004); Margrit Schiller, *Es war ein harter Kampf um meine Erinnerung* (Remembering the Armed Struggle: Life in Baader-Meinhof, 1999); Inge Viett, *Nie war ich furchtloser: Autobiographie* (Never Was I More Fearless: Autobiography, 1996) and *Einsprüche! Briefe aus dem Gefängnis* (Objections! Letters from Prison, 1996); and Stefan Wisnieswski, *Wir waren so unheimlich konsequent* (We Were So Extremely Consistent, 1997). Earlier memoirs include Marianne Herzog, *Nicht den Hunger verlieren* (Hold on to the Hunger, 1980), and the controversial writings by former RAF member Jürgen-Peter Boock, such as *Abgang* (Exit, 1988) and *Schwarzes Loch: Im Hochsicherheitstrakt* (Black Hole: In Maximum Security, 1988). Some of Gudrun Ensslin's letters from prison were posthumously published by her brother and sister: Christiane and Gottfried Ensslin, eds., *Gudrun Ensslin: "Zieht den Trennungsstrich, jede Minute"* ("Draw the Demarcation Line, Every Minute," 2005), and Caroline Harmsen, Ulrike Seyer, and Johannes Ullmaier, eds., *Gudrun Ensslin/Bernward Vesper, "Notstandsgesetze von Deiner Hand": Briefe 1968/1969* ("Emergency Laws Written by Your Hand": Letters 1968–1969, 2009).

12. Publications that foreground the victims of the RAF/Movement 2nd June and their families include Anne Siemens, *Für die RAF war er das System, für mich der Vater* (To the RAF He Was the System, to Me He Was My Father, 2007) and Julia Albrecht and Corinna Ponto, *Patentöchter: Im Schatten der RAF—ein Dialog* (Goddaughters: In the Shadow of the RAF—a Dialogue, 2011).

13. See chapter 2. For a general analysis of specifically *women's* autobiographies as a literary genre and as historical source see Sidonie Smith and Julia Watson, eds., *Women, Autobiography, Theory: A Reader.*

14. E.g., Jamie Trnka in "Frauen, die unzeitgemäß schreiben" (Women Whose Writing Is Outmoded) reads RAF women's memoirs as a variation of the (feminist) testimonies genre, in particular Margrit Schiller's book. Sarah Colvin in "Chiffre und Symbol für Wut und Widerstand?" (Cipher and Symbol for Rage and Resistance?) views the prison letters by Gudrun Ensslin to her siblings less as an opportunity to idealize her as resistance fighter (which at times seems to be the aim of the editors) and more as a chance for "the acknowledgment of the historical conditions of being human, and because of that, Gudrun Ensslin's humanness" ("die Anerkennung des historisch bedingten Mensch-Seins und damit der Menschlichkeit von Gudrun Ensslin") (102).

15. She was born Gabriele Tiedemann and married Norbert Kröcher in 1971. She separated from him shortly afterward and later divorced him while in prison (see Diewald-Kerkmann, *Frauen, Terrorismus, und Justiz* 75). Almost all sources refer to her last name as "Kröcher-Tiedemann," partly because that is the name with which she was initially charged in court. However, she herself signed with "Tiedemann," and since this was her legal and preferred name when she died, I will use it throughout this analysis.

16. Very few secondary sources on Gabriele Tiedemann exist. The primary source for this analysis is Tiedemann's bequest, which is archived in the International Institute for Social History in Amsterdam. The most detailed study on Gabriele Tiedemann to date can be found in Dominique Grisard, *Gendering Terror*. For biographical dates, see also Diewald-Kerkmann, *Frauen, Terrorismus, und Justiz* (74–76). The main sources in Diewald-Kerkmann are "criminal, investigation, and trial files" ("Kriminal-, Ermittlungs- und Prozessakten") while Grisard, in addition to Swiss police and court files, also consults the letters in the bequest of Tiedemann as well as media coverage.

17. This critical approach to the category "experience" in feminist historiography was introduced by Joan Scott in "The Evidence of Experience" in 1991.

18. Purvis 127 n. 5.

19. Smith and Watson 5.

20. Smith and Watson 13.

21. Smith and Watson 10.

22. Smith and Watson 13.

23. Smith and Watson 196.

24. Smith and Watson 196.

25. Smith and Watson 196.

26. The number of times these women were able to escape from prison seems astonishing. Security measures and architectural layouts of prisons in the 1970s predated the hugely intensified imprisonment of convicts today, where maximum security measures have become almost routine. Women were also not expected to attempt to escape their punishment; the actions of RAF women and other terrorists resulted in many a local "security update" of women's prisons in Germany and in Switzerland.

27. For more information on the SPK, see chapter 1.

28. "Die Doppelbelastung der Frau in Familie und Beruf" (Rollnik and Dubbe 9).

29. "Die Frauen verdienten auch grundsätzlich weniger für die gleiche Arbeit" (Rollnik and Dubbe 12).

30. Schiller, *Remembering* 23.

31. Schiller, *Remembering* 12.

32. Schiller, *Remembering* 18.

33. "Schiller setzt Konzeptionen von Sexualität und Geschlechtlichkeit ein *und* wiedersetzt sich einer Sexualisierung ihres Körpers und ihrer politischen Aktivität, indem sie die Aufmerksamkeit auf den sexuellen Charakter staatlicher Gewalt richtet" (Trnka 222, emphasis hers).

34. Viett 66:

Nirgendwo ist das ökonomische Abhängigkeitsverhältnis der Frauen so ungetarnt, das Warenverhältnis in der Geschlechterbeziehung so nackt, die Liebe und Lust so illusionär wie in den Vergnügungsghettos der Städte. Eingerichtet, betrieben und kontrolliert von und für Männer. Die Frauen schaffen, produzieren für sie. [. . .] "Das älteste Gewerbe der Welt," zwinkert das Patriarchat und meint damit seine Welt, in der die jahrhundertealte Unterdrückung und Ausbeutung der Frau als anthropologische Gegebenheit gerechtfertigt wird.

35. "Sie ist den vorgezeichneten Weg gegangen, der auch für mich bestimmt war" (Viett 38).

36. Viett 88.

37. Schiller, *Remembering* 35.

38. Schiller, *Remembering* 35.

39. Schiller, *Remembering* 89.

40. "Ihre Solidarität ist selbstverständlich und furchtlos" (Viett 111).

41. Viett 188.

42. "ist die vehemente Entfaltung der Eigenständigkeit von uns Frauen, die umfassende Entwicklung von Fähigkeiten, wie sie die Männer nicht von Frauen gewöhnt waren. [. . .] [D]as konnte schon diesen oder jenen Genossen einschüchtern, wenn er neu in die Gruppe kam und sich einer Übermacht entscheidungsfreudiger Frauen gegenübersah. Da wurde ihm nirgendwo ein Rollenvorsprung zuerkannt" (Viett 188).

43. Rollnik and Dubbe 92–93:
Von da an haben wir uns gegenseitig mehr Luft zum Atmen gelassen. Sie war sowieso schon knapp. [. . .] Du bist selbst unter einer solchen Bedrohung und Anspannung von außen, daß du immer guckst: Verhalten wir uns alle immer richtig? [. . .] Man beobachtet sich selbst so sehr, daß es sehr schnell zerfleischend werden kann. Aber als wir es gemerkt hatten, konnten wir uns anders verhalten. [. . .] Wir haben uns nicht fertig gemacht, sondern wir sind heute noch befreundet..

44. Schiller, *Remembering* 46.

45. Schiller, *Remembering* 46.

46. "Nein, Hausfrau nie. So war's, bei allen Fehlern, doch schon besser" (Rollnik and Dubbe 119).

47. See Viett 51.

48. Viett 110:
Frauen brechen selten aus, sie sind das Dulden, Warten und Hoffen gewöhnt. Manchmal versuchen sie den Rahmen ihrer Rolle zu dehnen, schaffen vielleicht, ihn zu sprengen, wenn ihre Kraft reicht. Das Lebensgefängnis brechen sie auf, manchmal, und entkommen ihm mühevoll. Dieses eherne Gefängnis aber, aus Stahl, Schlüsseln und Beton, diese Konzentration von Menschenmacht über Menschsein oder—nichtsein, diese rohe kahle Ecke, in die die Herrschenden alle kehren, die ihrem System der Lebensordnung nicht gewachsen sind, diese absolute Gewalt überwältigt die Frauen mit einer hoffnungslosen Endgültigkeit, die keinem weiterführenden Gedanken an Überwindung lebendig werden läßt.

49. For example, Schiller joined an anti-imperialist women's group before going into exile to Cuba in 1985. In the afterword to the German paperback edition of her memoir, she explicitly discusses how she is struck by contemporary young women's inability to comprehend the radicalism of RAF women's gesture of arming themselves, saying that roles are different today than they were in the 1970s in Germany (see Schiller, *Es war ein harter Kampf* 214).

50. The collections of West German movement archives attest to this; the "grey literature" archived there includes countless flyers, calls to solidarity actions, protest announcements, and position papers regarding political prisoners, in particular those of the RAF. Chapters of the organization Rote Hilfe (Red Aid) were formed in the early 1970s with the aim of assisting leftist prisoners legally and through social contacts and still are active today.

51. Goffman xiii.

52. Goffman 7.

53. See Goffman 7–8.

54. One example of a disruptive practice is the hunger strike of the prisoner. See chapter 4 for a discussion of RAF hunger strikes.

55. Goffman 199–200.

56. Warren 12.

57. Mary Corcoran, quoted in Warren 12.

58. See Weigel, *"Und selbst im Kerker frei . . . !" Schreiben im Gefängnis* ("Free Even in the Dungeon . . . !" Writing in Prison) 18.

59. "was allerdings zu meinem frust beigetragen hat ist die beschissene regelung, die ich neuerdings einhalten muss, dass ich nur 2 seiten schreiben kann" (letter from GT to Henner on September 9, 1979).

60. "Unterlebensstrategie" (Weigel 7).

61. See Weigel 18.

62. See Wunschik 551.

63. See Diewald-Kerkmann on Tiedemann's supposed connections to "Carlos" and the OPEC Conference attack (*Frauen, Terrorismus und Justiz* 76–77). Also see Grisard, *Gendering Terror* 24.

64. Tiedemann's involvement in the kidnapping was established primarily with evidence such as pistol magazines, portions of the ransom money, and the bags it was transported in, which were found in Tiedemann's possession. This circumstantial evidence pointed to a connection between Tiedemann and Christian Möller and the Austrians Thomas Gratt and Othmar Keplinge. Gratt and Keplinger received several years of prison sentences because of their participation in the Palmers kidnapping. Tiedemann was never charged with participation in the kidnapping (see the following documents archived in the Tiedemann bequest, Archiv GT: letter from Schweizerischen Bundesanwaltschaft [Swiss Federal Prosecutor], 12 May 1978; Rapport Officiel des Synthese dans l'affaire: Kroecher et Moeller des Ministre Public de la Confederation Suisse 1 March 1978 [8 and 31]; Vollmacht [power of attorney] by Walter Palmers to his attorney to act in his interest with all Swiss officials in regaining the ransom money).

65. Tiedemann's bequest includes not only letters to Tiedemann but also carbon copies of the letters she wrote on the typewriter. The letter exchange with Caroline took place between July 8, 1978, and February 15, 1983, and contains fifty letters and/or postcards. In the time period from June 1, 1982, to August 20, 1987, Tiedemann exchanged altogether fifty-nine letters/cards with Beate. Of her pen friendship with Amin that took place between April 4, 1981, and May, 7 1988, forty-four letters/cards remain. Of these, carbon copies of Tiedemann's responses to Amin's correspondence only exist from September 18, 1983, on. Also see Melzer, "'Wir Frauen sind eh

die bessere Hälfte der Menschheit': Revolutionäre Politik und Feminismus in den Gefängnisbriefen einer Ex-Terroristin."

66. Even though the archive of Tiedemann's bequest is publicly accessible (after submission of a written request for access to the administration of the archive), I am using pseudonyms for the names of the authors throughout this analysis.

67. See also Grisard, "Selbststilisierungen einer inhaftierten Terroristin," especially for a detailed discussion of the rhetorical strategies Tiedemann employed in her self-presentation in letters and official documents.

68. "ich muss sagen, dass ich die politik vieler frauengruppen für ziemlich beschissen halte" (letter from GT, Bern, to C, September 2, 1978). Like many activists in the 1960s and '70s, Tiedemann used only lower-case letters in her writing. This departure from conventional spelling was a visible offense against what were viewed as bourgeois norms and carried political meaning. All original quotations are spelled as in the original documents and lower-case spelling is maintained in my translations.

69. "der zwischen kapital und arbeit/metropole und dritter welt."

70. "die traditionelle frauenemanzipation ändert an dem hauptwiderspruch nichts, im gegenteil, sie stabilisiert ihn. [. . .] wenn die zielvorstellung darin besteht, dass die herrschenden Verhältnisse nur dadurch stabilisiert werden sollen, so ist so ne politik genauso zu bekämpfen, [sic] wie jede andere sozialdemokratische politik" (letter from GT, Bern, to C, September 2, 1978). The role of the SPD (German Social Democratic Party) in post–World War II politics in West Germany was an object of great derision by leftist activists, especially after their denouncement of communists from their party and in particular their involvement with the conservative Christian Democratic Party to form a Great Coalition in the 1960s. The term "social democratic politics" was used by activists to denote politics as reformist (in contrast to radical) and ultimately as close to the system.

71. "Emanzipation bedeutete Befreiung durch Änderung der gesellschaftlichen Verhältnisse. [. . .] Der Gleichberechtigungsanspruch stellt die gesellschaftlichen Voraussetzungen der Ungleichheit zwischen den Menschen nicht mehr in Frage [. . .] er verlangt nur [. . .] Gleichheit in der Ungleichheit" (Meinhof, "Falsches Bewußtsein" 118) (see also chapter 2).

72. "insofern ist die situation der frauenbewegung auch nur symptomatisch für die gesamtsituation der ehemals revolutionären linken, die ihre eigene permanente rückzugspolitik schon gar nicht mehr realisiert und die darüber jegliche perspektive verloren hat" (letter from GT, Bern, to C, September 2, 1978).

73. "für mich kann die frauenemanzipation nicht losgelöst sein vom klassenkampf, sie ist bestandteil des klassenkampfes oder anders: die einzig wahre gesellschaftliche, politische und sexuelle emanzipation der frau findet ihren ausdruck in der aktiven teilnahme am revolutionären kampf gegen ein system, in dem die unterdrückung der frau nur bestandteil ist von der unterdrückung der ausgebeuteten klassen" (letter from GT, Bern, to C, September 2, 1978).

74. Letter from GT, Hindelbank, to C, June 8, 1981, and letter from GT, Hindelbank, to C, September 21, 1981. The status of "political," so it was argued, warrants a different treatment by the state: political prisoners should be placed in small groups together, a demand that was initially formulated to protest the complete isolation of prisoners

incarcerated for their politically motivated crimes (the state isolated them from other prisoners so as to minimize a potential recruitment effect). The opposing position was to advocate for an integration of political prisoners into the general prison population, which offered more humane conditions to the prisoner, but also indicated a loss of the symbolic status as political prisoner.

75. Letter from BS, Bellikon, to GT, June 1, 1982.

76. At this point in time, Tiedemann was corresponding with "circa a good dozen" people ("ein rundes dutzend circa") (letter from GT, Hindelbank, to BS, February 9, 1984).

77. Tiedemann writes, "it was only through my contact with you that i started to even engage more closely with [the women's movement and feminist theories] and then also had a good exchange of experiences with your namesake [B.A., who was detained with Tiedemann]" ("ich fing dann erst durch dich an, mich [mit der Frauenbewegung und feministischen Theorien] überhaupt näher zu beschäftigen, und hatte dann auch einen guten erfahrungsaustausch mit deiner namensvetterin [der mitinhaftierten B.A.]" (letter from GT, Hindelbank, to BS, January 16, 1984).

78. See Grisard's discussion of this development in "Selbststilisierungen" (131–33).

79. "Entradikalisierung" (Grisard, "Selbststilisierungen" 134).

80. "Erfahrungen als Langzeitgefangene" (Grisard, "Selbststilisierungen" 131).

81. It is still unclear to what extent Tiedemann's revision of her leftist positions and her assessment of feminist politics influenced each other.

82. "nach drei briefen *kann* man sich nicht kennen. sich-kennen und sich-vertrauen bedingt sich gegenseitig und ist ein langer, sehr langer prozess. und dann ist da immer noch die zensur, die vieles verunmöglicht" (letter from GT, Hindelbank, to BS, July 11, 1982; emphasis in the original).

83. "nicht gegen den Mann zu emanzipieren, sondern immer nur mit ihm, letztendlich" (letter from GT, Hindelbank, to BS, July 11, 1982; emphasis mine).

84. "neue art rassismus" (letter from GT, Hindelbank, to BS, July 11, 1982).

85. "mann als feind" (letter from GT, Hindelbank, to BS, July 11, 1982).

86. "natürlich ist patriarchalisches denken ein feind der frau, aber es ist doch nicht der mann an sich, das männliche geschlecht, der/das dieser feind ist [. . .] ich finde diese haltung nicht nur politisch falsch[,] sondern irgendwo auch unmenschlich" (letter from GT, Hindelbank, to BS, July 11, 1982).

87. "eigenen erziehung [und wollen] sich von dieser erziehung befreien" (letter from GT, Hindelbank, to BS, July 11, 1982).

88. "tiefe abneigung" (letter from GT, Hindelbank, to BS, July 11, 1982).

89. "die frauenbewegung [war] zweck [. . .] für die eigene emanzipation, keine politik an sich [. . .] , sondern ein mittel, um mit allen eigenen kräften, die man durch die frauenbewegung entwickelt hat, wieder zurückzugehen in und für eine politik für alle, egal ob mann oder frau" (letter from GT, Hindelbank, to BS, July 11, 1982).

90. "mit dem anspruch, dort erfahrenes und gelerntes wieder zurückzutragen" (letter from GT, Hindelbank, to BS, July 11, 1982).

91. "gegengewicht zu [der] arbeit in gemischten politischen gruppen" (letter from GT, Hindelbank, to BS, July 11, 1982).

92. "identische Ansichten"; "gewinnen können wir nur zusammen [. . .] ich kann einfach nicht den männern die schuld daran geben, wenn ich als frau irgendwelche komplexe mit mir rumschleppe, weil es in erster linie an mir liegt, mich zu verändern" (letter from GT, Hindelbank, to BS, July 11, 1982).

93. "rumlaborieren an einem nebenwiderspruch der gesellschaft" (letter from GT, Hindelbank, to BS, July 11, 1982).
94. "in [ihrer] eigenen politischen praxis [. . .] das problem mann-frau kein problem [war], es war niemals ein thema für uns" (letter from GT, Hindelbank, to BS, July 11, 1982).
95. See Kristina Schulz, *Der lange Atem der Provokation* (The Long Breath [Stamina] of Provocation) for an overview of the feminist politics of the 1970s and 1980s (226–45). Also see chapter 1.
96. Letter from BS, Zürich, to GT, June 20, 1983.
97. "unzuverlässige verbündete"; "fortschrittliche kraft" (letter from BS, Zürich, to GT, June 20, 1983). In the past twenty years, the opinion that the Marxist premise that the proletariat's class status, i.e., its material situation (relation to production), defines it as the revolutionary agent of change needs to be expanded to include the sexual division of labor has been developed into a sophisticated theory of a feminist standpoint (feminist standpoint theory). Feminist standpoint theory presumes that a feminist consciousness develops in interrelation with other social factors such as race and class, always in connection with material conditions, including those of reproduction. For this reason, because of their shared social (i.e., material) experiences, a shared foundation for knowledge is laid that can be excavated and developed through shared political work. See Linda Alcoff and Elizabeth Potter, *Feminist Epistemologies,* and Sandra Harding, ed., *The Feminist Standpoint Theory Reader,* for an introduction to feminist standpoint theory and the debates this theoretical approach generated.
98. The lengthy quotation Beate gives in her letter (June 20, 1983) is from Anja Meulenbelt's collection of essays, *Feminismus: Aufsätze zur Frauenbefreiung* (Feminism: Essays on Women's Liberation).
99. Letter from GT, Hindelbank, to BS, August 23, 1983. In the same letter she comments that she feels since her detention that she has been "living under a rock" when it comes to certain topics since access to information in books and political papers is limited; prison effectuates "an isolation from discussions that are taking place outside" ("hinterm mond zu leben"; "die abschottung von diskussionen, die draussen laufen").
100. Letter from GT, Hindelbank, to BS, August 23, 1983. In the following letter to BS, Tiedemann declares that the classic Marxist theory of the proletariat as the avant-garde in a revolution is outdated; history has proven, so Tiedemann argues, that Marx's understanding of the role of the proletariat was bound to the historical context of the days of the origins of Marxism. The Russian Revolution and also the worldwide political movements of the 1960s did not originate in the proletariat but emerged out of different sections of the population. In fact, the proletariat, she claims, has by now a self-understanding (self-image) of itself as the petty bourgeoisie and is most of the time hostile towards political change (letter from GT, Hindelbank, to BS, January 16, 1984).
101. "doch selbst wenn auf dieser individuellen ebene eine emanzipierte partnerschaft vorhanden ist, trägt die frau immer noch die bürde der jahrhundertelangen unterdrückung d[e]r frau mit sich herum, weil ihre individuelle befreiung sich immer wieder von neuem gegen die herrschaft des mannes in der ganzen gesellschaft behaupten muss" (letter from GT, Hindelbank, to BS, August 23, 1983).

102. "nach und nach wieder kehrtwendungen eingeschlagen wurden und von 'frauenbefreiung' dann kaum noch mehr übrig blieb als die berufstätigkeit der frau" (letter
from GT, Hindelbank, to BS, August 23, 1983).

103. "den weiblichen Teil der gesellschaft als eigene klasse [anzusehen], der eine
avantgarde-funktion zukommt, dies ist für mich, als aus der sozialistischen ecke
kommend, doch recht 'revolutionär'" (letter from GT, Hindelbank, to BS, January 16,
1984).

104. Letter from GT, Hindelbank, to BS, January 16, 1984.

105. Letter from GT, Hindelbank, to BS, January 16, 1984.

106. "meine politische praxis draussen—in der legalität und in der illegalität später—
hatte ganz andere schwerpunkte" (letter from GT, Hindelbank, to BS, January 16,
1984).

107. "kam sozusagen aus mir selbst heraus, waren eigene anstösse und denkprozesse, die
ich aufgrund eigener erfahrungen entwickelte" (letter from GT, Hindelbank, to BS,
January 16, 1984).

108. It is interesting that Tiedemann—from a letter dated October 5, 1983, on—
increasingly uses the unofficial indefinite pronoun "frau" (female) rather than
the official "man" (male) to mean "one," such as "which *frau* has never seen
before" ("den *frau* noch nie gesehen hat") (letter from GT, Hindelbank, to BS,
October 5, 1983). This signals a latent assumption that men and women experience language—and thus the social world—differently; otherwise a
differentiation would not be necessary. Here a perception of women as a specific
social group with shared characteristics becomes already discernable in
Tiedemann's writing.

109. "Klön-Brief" (letter from GT, Hindelbank, to BS, February 9, 1984).

110. Letter from GT, Hindelbank, to BS, February 9, 1984:
na, und wir frauen sind eh die bessere hälfte der menschheit, dies ganz unbeschadet
jetzt aller fb[frauenbewegungs]-diskussionen, aller theorien und was sonst noch. es
ist mein gefühl, meine erfahrung, dass ich mit frauen oft so viel mehr kann,
entwickeln kann, vertrauen haben kann, tiefe, intensität, glück da ist, so selbstverständlich, wie ich es mit männern nur sehr viel seltener erlebe—und dies immer
erst erkämpfen muss, gegen sie, gegen die konkurrenz, den machtkampf zwischen
man und frau.ary 9,1984).

111. "liebeserklärung für alle meine freundinnen" (letter from GT, Hindelbank, to BS,
February 9, 1984).

112. See Quinn Slobodian, *Foreign Front*, for a recent study of the influences of Third
World politics and activists on the student movement prior to 1968 (in particular
chapter 4 on Iranian dissidents in West Germany). The context Slobodian establishes provides an important background to Tiedemann's relationship with Amin.

113. "merkwürdig, platonische" (letter from GT, Hindelbank, to AM, September 23,
1984). With this expression, Tiedemann comments on the fact that the two only
knew each other from their letters and Amin's visits to prison. She does not view
this type of friendship as necessarily less important or less intensive than others:
"sure, the written communication in the end is always 'platonic,' but it can take place
on a level where the *entire* person brings themselves across" ("sicher, die schriftliche
kommunikation ist letzlich immer, 'platonisch,' doch sie kann auch auf einer ebene
stattfinden, wo sich der *ganze* mensch vermittelt").

114. It is not apparent from the correspondence why either the long break or the ending of the pen friendship occurred.

115 Letter from GT, Hindelbank, to AM, October 14, 1985, and letter from GT, Hindelbank, to AM, June 3, 1986.

116. Letter from GT, Hindelbank, to AM, October 14, 1985.

117. "die nur noch zunehmend abstrakt für mich werden" (letter from GT, Hindelbank, to AM, October 14, 1985).

118. "etwas was mich selbst sehr belastet und auch erschreckt" (letter from GT, Hindelbank, to AM, October 14, 1985).

119. "verhexten thema" (letter from AM, Dortmund, to GT, March 17, 1986), and her answer in her letter from June 3, 1986.

120. Letter from AM to GT, November 28, 1985.

121. "dass sich männer—auch revolutionär gesinnte männer—damit auseinandersetzen" (letter from GT, Hindelbank, to AM, January 27, 1986).

122. "etwas womit sich dann halt nur die frauen beschäftigen sollen, weil dies ausschliesslich ihr problem sei" (letter from GT, Hindelbank, to AM, January 27, 1986).

123. "es für mich sozusagen existenziell ist, weil es meine existenz betrifft" (letter from GT, Hindelbank, to AM, January 27, 1986).

124. "welchen politischen stellenwert nimmt der kampf für die befreiung der frau ein, wie ordnen wir ihn ein in den kampf gegen ausbeutung und unterdrückung allgemein?" (letter from GT, Hindelbank, to AM, January 27, 1986).

125. "z.b., dem 'anti-lärm, anti-militarismus, anti-atom, anti-waldsterben' etc." (letter from GT, Hindelbank, to AM, January 27, 1986).

126. "sehr zu verharmlosen, seinen stellenwert zu verkennen oder gar, eine falsche analyse machen" (letter from GT, Hindelbank, to AM, January 27, 1986).

127. Letter from GT, Hindelbank, to AM, January 27, 1986:
allen gesellschaftlichen systemen seit beginn der menschheit ist eins gemeinsam: die herrschaft des patriarchats; sie ist die soziale, kulturelle und damit auch politische basis aller verschiedener formen von gesellschaften und kann damit keineswegs [von dem Hauptwiderspruch] losgelöst betrachtet werden, bzw. wird der versuch, es davon losgelöst zu betrachten eine der wichtigen wurzeln von unterdrückung des menschen überhaupt missachten oder ignorieren und damit immer nur weiter systeme produzieren, die aus einer falschen analyse heraus diesen widerspruch gar nicht zu lösen imstande sind. dies ist keine leere behauptung sondern realität.

128. "dies finde ich wenig einsichtig, denn diese 'komplizierten und feinen probleme' sind genau die herrschaft des patriarchats, was ich nicht kompliziert sondern sehr klar finde" (letter from GT, Hindelbank, to AM, January 27, 1986). See also the letter of June 3, 1986.

129. Here Tiedemann opts to use the rather strange metaphor of reproduction to illustrate her argument that the emergence of the nuclear family is coupled with the emergence of private property (she refers to Friedrich Engels's "Origin of the Family, Private Property, and the State"): "put this way, one can view the patriarchal system as the egg cell of the family—and thus also of the state—and private property (later of means of production) as the sperm and that which was born was the class society, that has manifested over the centuries in different ways until today" ("wenn man so will, kann man das patriarchale system als die

eizelle der familie—und damit auch des staates—betrachten und das privateigen-
tum [später an produktionsmitteln] als den samen und das, was geboren wurde,
war die klassengesellschaft, die sich über jahrhunderte in jeweils verschiedenen
formen bis heute manifestiert") (letter from GT, Hindelbank, to AM, June 3,
1986).

130. "man kann das eine problem nicht ohne das andere lösen" (letter from GT,
Hindelbank, to AM, January 27, 1986). While Tiedemann insists that capitalism and
patriarchy constitute each other without either being merely a symptom of the other
system, she emphasizes neither imperialism nor racism as discreet elements of
oppression. This refusal to recognize other categories of oppression alongside
capitalism can either be understood to be in the tradition of (international) leftist
revolutionary and liberation movements, which insisted that imperialism exists
through capitalism, or it can be seen as a continuous refusal by (white) leftist
activists in the industrialized nations to reflect on their privileges within imperialism, which are structured around racist criteria.

131. "keine homogene strömung ist" (letter from GT, Hindelbank, to AM, January 27,
1986).

132. "allen gemeinsam ist aber das ziel, den kampf um die rechte der frauen und um ihre
befreiung in die eigenen hände zu nehmen, und dies hier und jetzt" (letter from GT,
Hindelbank, to AM, January 27, 1986).

133. "mann und frau, 'schulter an schulter' kämpfen"; "idealzustand" (letter from GT,
Hindelbank, to AM, January 27, 1986).

134. "[sich] eben notgedrungen [. . .] diese befreiung oft gegen den mann richten [wird],
so lange die mehrheit der männer nicht willens ist, die frau als gleichberechtigt zu
akzeptieren" (letter from GT, Hindelbank, to AM, January 27, 1986).

135. "ein überbegriff des kampfes, der sich sowohl die volle gleichberechtigung zwischen
frau und mann zum ziel gesetzt hat, wie auch die volle entfaltung der frau auf
individueller, sozialer, kultureller, politischer ebene postuliert" (letter from GT,
Hindelbank, to AM, June 3, 1986).

136. This follows a letter in which Amin calls "women's liberation" politically and socially
important but dismisses "feminism" as ideological (Tiedemann refers to this letter
from Amin as "your letter from December 22" ["deines briefes vom 22.12."]. The
actual letter is not in the files of her bequest) (letter from GT, Hindelbank, to AM,
June 3, 1986). At this point, Tiedemann does not make that distinction anymore.

137. "ich frage mich, ob es nicht schon wieder eine typisch männliche bevormundung ist,
wenn mann—also in diesem fall du—einen kampf von frauen, die sie um ihre rechte
führen, als wertlos abqualifiziert!" (letter from GT, Hindelbank, to AM, June 3, 1986).

138. "die frauen selbst müssen um ihre befreiung kämpfen, es ist hauptsächlich und in
erster linie ihr eigener kampf. die männer können und dürfen diesen kampf nicht
'übernehmen' oder für sie führen, sie können sie nur nach besten kräften darin
unterstützen" (letter from GT, Hindelbank, to AM, June 3, 1986).

139. Letter from GT, Hindelbank, to AM, June 3, 1986:
dass individuelle oder gesellschaftliche schritte zur befreiung, die (noch) system-
immanent sind, auch einen schritt zu einer generellen umwälzung der
gesellschaftstrikturen [sic] darstellen können. ist denn ein revolutionärer prozess
niicht [sic] auch immer zusammengesetzt aus einer vielzahl solcher schritte? denn

die revolution selbst ist ja ein prozess und eben heeue [heute] nicht mehr das grosse spektakel der machtübernahme der revolutionären klasse.

140. "denn befreiung ist ein prozess, der nicht durch gesetze oder dekrete verordnet werden kann. er ist ein lebendiger prozess, ein langwieriger prozess" (letter from GT, Hindelbank, to AM, June 3, 1986). "erst dann, wenn die frauen die männer zwingen, umzudenken, erst dann wenn sie de facto 'schulter an schulter' mit den männern stehen, ist auch ein gemeinsamer kampf möglich" (letter from GT, Hindelbank, to AM, January 27, 1986).

141. Letter from GT to AM, January 27, 1986. She writes, "but to be honest it has been a long while that i have theoretically engaged with patriarchy and it is thus not completely present with me anymore. (something i by the way would like to remedy and once again read some texts about it)" ("aber es ist ehrlich gesagt ziemlich lange her, dass ich mich theoretisch mit dem patriarchat beschäftigt habe und mir daher nicht mehr völlig präsent. [dem will ich jetzt übrigens abhilfe schaffen und einmal wieder texte dazu lesen]").

142. Many thanks to Kathrin Melzer, whose input into this chapter was central to its completion.

143. The conviction that due to their gender-specific oppression, women in particular are destined for radical resistance was by all means present underground. See Gudrun Ensslin's letter in *das info*: "for this reason, though, the dialectic of their [the women's] situation also becomes clear—if, after the particular brutalities of their domestication [. . .] they even want *themselves*, to think *themselves*—they need to think radically *and* subversively: a content and a form that predestines them to illegality" ("damit ist aber auch die dialektik ihrer [der Frauen] situation klar—wenn sie nach den besonderen brutalitäten ihrer domestizierung- [. . .] überhaupt *sich* wollen, *sich* denken—müssen sie radikal *und* subversiv denken: ein inhalt und eine form, die sie für illegalität prädestiniert" (her emphasis, Bakker Schut 294; see also chapter 2).

144. This overlap was very visible in the Red Zora after the mid-1970s and actually was openly discussed and analyzed by militant feminists in the Autonomen, the leftist-radical political scene, in West Germany, after 1980. See Patricia Melzer, "'Frauen gegen Imperialismus und Patriarchat zerschlagen den Herschaftsapparat'" ("'Women against Imperialism and Patriarchy Smash the Power Structure'").

## Notes to Conclusion

1. While *Death in the Shape of a Young Girl* and other work by feminist scholars such as Colvin and Bielby make this point in relation to the specific historical moment of the RAF, current feminist scholarship on perceptions of women's (political) violence today show a remarkable consistency in the gendering of political activists globally (see Glynn; Sjoberg and Gentry; Rajan).

2. See Hacker 282.

3. This follows Butler's concept of gender as performative, in contrast to the notion that gender is an intrisic, prediscursive identity.

4. One example is the way activists' narratives relate their first encounter with violence and their process of arriving at the point of viewing violence as a necessary tool of resistance. Memoirs by Black Panther activists, such as Elaine Brown and Assata

Shakur, evoke the presence of a violent state and racist environment that create confrontations that the activists can only mitigate with counterviolence. Memoirs by white activists, on the other hand, including those by RAF women, encounter state violence primarily through *seeking* the confrontation with the state. The state's violent response then radicalizes them. The relationship to violence as either an immediate or a latent presence is often shaped by race, ethnicity, and/or nationality (racism), as well as by class (poverty, foster care, etc.).

5. Mohanty, *Feminism without Borders* 122.

6. Kaplan 148

7. Mahmood 14–15.

8. In the context of Mahmood's study, this is defined more in relation to religious rituals.

9. As I discuss in chapter 1, there were several militant groups that declared their feminist politics, such as the Red Zora. While militant feminism in German leftist politics constitutes an important element, the concept of feminist practices as I develop it here is particularly interesting in the context of militant women who did not identify as feminists.

10. See also the introduction.

11. For information about the interviews see Introduction, note 17.

12. Georg Linke, an employee of the Institute for Social Research, where Baader and Meinhof met that day, was seriously wounded.

13. See Karcher's "'Die Perücke ist ein Element das Alle Katzen Grau Macht': Femininity as Camouflage in the Liberation of the Prisoner Andreas Baader in 1970" for a discussion of how femininity was strategically employed by the women organizing the break, which "both reinforced and challenged predominant gender norms" (99).

14. "Für eine 18jährige sei es demnach heute kaum mehr vorstellbar [. . .] daß die Frauenbewegung in den 70ern gerade in den Anfängen steckte und Männer noch keine Erfahrungen mit kollektiven Selbstbewußtsein und aktiver Gegenwehr von Frauen hatten" (Schiller, *Es war ein harter Kampf um meine Erinnerung* 214).

15. "der ausganspunkt der raf ist die position und die erfahrung der stärke, d.h. als *frau* zu sein, was jeder sein kann, rebellion, guerilla" (Kuby 5; emphasis hers).

16. Puar 195.

17. If we understand violence at times to be relational, i.e., to have some causal origin, then violence extends beyond any isolated incident and instead needs to be evaluated within a distinct historical context. Frantz Fanon's argument that the violence of colonialism necessitates violent decolonization (see *The Wretched of the Earth*, especially the chapter "Concerning Violence") speaks of how violence produces counterviolence that is distinct to the colonial process and its racism. Achille Mbembe's analysis of how Foucault's biopower manifests in what Mbembe terms late modern colonial "necropower" also links narratives of nation and race to violence. Necropower combines "the disciplinary, the biopolitical, and the necropolitical" (Mbembe 27) and justifies the complete subjugation of one with the right to sovereignty of the other (Mbembe describes apartheid South Africa and the occupation of Palestine as manifestations of necropolitics). This absolute domination produces terror and death as forms of resistance, a "preference for death over continued servitude" (Mbembe 39)—acts of what Žižek describes a subjective violence that appear outrageous in the naturalized context of objective violence.

18. This resonates with Nancy's notion of violence "denaturalizing" the system it assaults (see Introduction).
19. Bielby, *Violent Women in Print* 1.
20. That reevaluation would for example also include actions of white, colonial, middle-class feminists and their effect on both an impoverished and exploited female population in their industrialized home countries and the female population of the colonies, or those of the second-wave women's movements in the West and their effect (or lack thereof) on poor women and women of color and their communities.
21. I am grateful to Carol Dougherty and Eugenie Brinkema for this thought.
22. See Puer, *Terrorist Assemblages*.

# References

## Primary Sources

Articles from Newspapers and Other Serials

"Aufruf an alle Frauen zur Erfindung des Glücks." *Emma* 12 (1977): 16.

"Ausbruch der Frauen: Die Terroristen machen mobil." *Der Spiegel* 12 July 1976: cover page.

"Ausbruch in Berlin: 'Das ist eine Riesensache.'" *Der Spiegel* 12 July 1976: 17–27.

"Baader/Meinhof: Macht kaputt."*Der Spiegel* 22 January 1973: 54–55.

Dellwo, Karl-Heinz. "Der Kopf fängt an zu dröhnen." *Der Spiegel* 13 April 1981: 34–37.

"Der Mordbefehl." *Stern* 25 June 1972: 14–20.

"Fahndung nach Frauen." *Courage* 1 (1976): 9–10.

"Frauen im Untergrund: 'Etwas Irrationales.'" *Der Spiegel* 8 August 1977: 22–33.

"Gudrun Ensslin—Die Eiskalte Verführerin." *BILD am Sonntag* 11 June 1972: 14.

Habbe, Christian. "Hungerstreik—'Grünes Licht' für den Tod?" *Der Spiegel* 13 April 1981: 24–27.

"Ich habe abgetrieben." *Stern* 6 June 1971.

"In tödlicher Gewissensnot." *Die Zeit* 5 February 1982: 14.

"Inhaftierte Terroristen im Hungerstreik fordern die Zusammenlegung aller Häftlinge. *Die Zeit* diskutiert." *Die Zeit* 7 April 1989: 3.

Jeschke, Axel, and Hans-Wolfgang Sternsdorff. "'Würden Sie nicht sagen, das ist Mord?'" *Der Spiegel* 13 April 1981: 27–32.

Krumm, Karl-Heinz. "Hungerstreik—und niemand weiß einen Ausweg." *Frankfurter Rundschau* 7 April 1981.

"Lauter Polizisten auf dem Kudamm?" *Der Spiegel* 20 April 1981: 114–15.

Leserbriefe. *die tageszeitung* 5 May 1981 and 6 May 1981.

Leserbriefe. *Der Spiegel* 22 August 1977: 7.

"Löwe los." *Der Spiegel* 22 February 1971: 26–30.

Luik, Arno. "'Sie War die Große Schwester der 68er.'" *Stern* 74 (2007): 54–60.

"Mehrheit gibt Justiz keine Schuld an Meins-Tod." *Frankfurter Rundschau* 4 January 1975: 4. HIS Ba, A/017, 006 (RAF-Sammlung).

Meinhof, Ulrike. "Die Frauen im SDS oder In eigener Sache." *Konkret* 12 (1968).

———. "Vom Protest zum Widerstand." *Konkret* 5 (1968).

Neumaier, Eduard. "Für das Leben verloren?" *Die Zeit* 13 December 1974.

Ohnesorge, Henk. *Die Welt* 10 December 1974: 4. HIS, Ba A/017, 003 RAF-Sammlung.

Paul, Gerhard. "Deutschland, deine Denunzianten." *Die Zeit* 10 September 1993.

Plogstedt, Sybille. "Ist die Gewalt in der Frauenbewegung angekommen?" *Courage* 6:9 (1981): 30–35.

"RAF—Hungerstreik: Zwangsernährung, Rettung oder Folter?" *Der Spiegel* 13 April 1981: 24–37.

"Recht an der Grenze: Mediziner und Juristen streiten: Muß Zwangsernährung sein?" *Der Spiegel* 14 January 1985: 71.

Röhl, Bettina. "Meine Eltern." *Der Spiegel* 31 Mai 2010, available at http://www.spiegel.de/spiegel/print/d-70701741.html (accessed 18 April 2014).

———. "Unsere Mutter—'Staatsfeind Nr. 1.'" *Der Spiegel* 17 July 1995: 88–109.

Schiller, Margit. "Margit Schiller zum Hungerstreik: Gefangene seit 10 Jahren isoliert." *die tageszeitung* 1 February 1981. HIS, Ordner: Pol. Gef. IV/HS (RAF-Sammlung).

Schreiber, Marion. "Wir fühlten uns einfach stärker." *Der Spiegel* 11 May 1981: 82–108.

"Die Terroristinnen: Frauen und Gewalt." *Der Spiegel* 8 August 1977: cover page.

"Wahrhaft christlich." *Der Spiegel* 1 February 1982: 82–83.

Weber, Matthias. "Den armen Baader lassen sie verhungern." *Deutsche Wochen-Zeitung* 13 December 1974. HIS Ba, A/017, 003 (RAF-Sammlung)

Wüllenweber, Hans. "Löst Hungerstreik Terror aus?" *Kieler Nachrichten* 13 April 1981. HIS, Ordner: Pol. Gef. IV, HS.

## Autobiographies, Published Interviews, Memoirs

Albrecht, Julia, and Corinna Ponto. *Patentöchter: Im Schatten der RAF—ein Dialog.* Cologne: Kiepenheuer & Witsch, 2011.

Boock, Jürgen-Peter. *Abgang.* Göttingen: Lamuv, 1988.

———. *Schwarzes Loch: Im Hochsicherheitstrakt.* Hamburg: Rowohlt, 1988.

Brown, Elaine. *A Taste of Power: A Black Woman's Story.* New York: Doubleday, 1992.

Herzog, Marianne. *Nicht den Hunger verlieren.* Berlin: Rotbuch Verlag, 1980.

Kunzelmann, Dieter. *Leisten Sie keinen Widerstand! Bilder aus meinem Leben.* Berlin: Transit, 1998.

Meyer, Till. *Staatsfeind: Erinnerungen.* Munich: Goldmann, 1998.

Pohle, Ralf. *Mein Name ist Mensch: Das Interview.* Berlin: Kramer, 2002.

Proll, Thorwald. *Mein 68: Aufzeichnungen, Briefe, Interviews.* Book on Demand: Verlag von Hoher See, 1998.

Proll, Thorwald, and Daniel Dubbe. *Wir kamen vom anderen Stern: Über 1968, Andreas Baader und ein Kaufhaus.* Hamburg: Nautilus, 2003.

Reinders, Ralf, and Ronald Fritzsch. *Die Bewegung 2. Juni: Gespräche über Haschrebellen, Lorenzentführung, Knast.* Berlin: ID-Verlag, 1995.

Rollnik, Gabriele, and Daniel Dubbe. *Keine Angst vor niemand. Über die Siebziger, die Bewegung 2. Juni und die RAF.* Hamburg: Nautilus, 2003.

Schiller, Margrit. *Es war ein harter Kampf um meine Erinnerung. Ein Lebensbericht aus der RAF.* Hamburg: Piper, 1999.

———. *Remembering the Armed Struggle: Life in Baader-Meinhof.* London: Zidane, 2009.

Shakur, Assata. *Assata: An Autobiography.* Chicago: ZedBooks, 1987.

Siemens, Anne. *Für die RAF war er das System, für mich der Vater: Die andere Geschichte des deutschen Terrorismus.* Munich: Piper, 2007.

Tolmein, Oliver. *RAF–Das war für uns Befreiung. Ein Gespräch mit Irmgard Möller über bewaffneten Kampf, Knast und die Linke.* Hamburg: Konkret, 2002.

Viett, Inge. *Nie war ich furchtloser. Autobiographie.* Reinbek bei Hamburg: Rowohlt Taschenbug Verlag,1999.

Wisnieswski, Stefan. *Wir waren so unheimlich konsequent: Ein Gespräch zur Geschichte der RAF.* Berlin: ID-Verlag, 1997.

Government Documents (published and unpublished)

Beschluss des Oberlandesgericht Düsseldorf. Vorsitzender des 4. Strafsenats Müller, Vorsitzender Richter am Oberlandesgericht, 20 September 1977. HIS, RA 02/012,009 (RAF-Sammlung).

*Der Baader-Meinhof-Report: Dokumente Analysen Zusammenhänge.* Mainz: Hase und Koehler, 1972. Cilip-Archiv.

Dokumentation "Baader-Meinhof-Bande" herausgegeben nach Unterlagen des Bunder-kriminalamtes Wiesbaden und des Landeskriminalamtes Rheinland-Pfalz vom Ministerium des Inneren Rheinland-Pfalz am 22.11.1974. HIS, S Be 670–679.

Klaus-Bericht (Bericht über die Auswertung des am 16.7. bzw. 18.7.1973 in den Zellen von 8 RAF-Gefangenen gefundenen Beweismaterials. 18 April 1974: 92–93. HIS, SO 09/004,002 (RAF-Sammlung).

Leitender Regierungsdirektor Nusser, "Betr.: Untersuchungsgefangene Baader, Ensslin und Raspe; *hier*: Hungerstreik." Brief an das Oberlandesgericht Stuttgart. 30 March 1977. HIS, Ba, A/019,001 (RAF-Sammlung).

Interviews Conducted by Author

Barbara, Oberursel and Frankfurt, Germany, 10 August 2005, 8 January 2006.

Heike, Hamburg, Germany, 9 January 2005, 20 July 2005.

Karin, Berlin, 10 November 2005, 3 January 2006.

Letters (Unpublished and Published)

Ensslin, Christiane, and Gottfried Ensslin, eds. *Gudrun Ensslin: "Zieht den Trennungsstrich, jede Minute." Briefe an ihre Schwester Christiane und ihren Bruder Gottfried aus dem Gefängnis 1972–1973.* Hamburg: Konkret Literatur Verlag, 2005.

Gabriele Tiedemann Nachlass (Bequest), Archiv GT (Gaby Tiedemann Papers), International Institute of Social History, Amsterdam, The Netherlands:

1/1: Information zur Person GT [Gabriele Tiedemann].

4/3: Letter from BS, Bellikon, to GT, June 1, 1982, 3 pages.

4/3: Letter from GT, Hindelbank, to BS, July 11, 1982, 2 pages.

4/3: Letter from BS, Zürich, to GT, June 20, 1983, 4 pages.

4/3: Letter from GT, Hindelbank, to BS, August 23, 1983, 2 pages.

4/3: Letter from GT, Hindelbank, to BS, October 5, 1983, 2 pages.

4/3: Letter from GT, Hindelbank, to BS, January 16, 1984, 2 pages.

4/3: Letter from GT, Hindelbank, to BS, February 9, 1984, 2 pages.

5/1: Letter from GT, Hindelbank, to AM, September 23, 1984, 2 pages.

5/1: Letter from GT, Hindelbank, to AM, October 14, 1985, 2 pages.

5/1: Letter from AM to GT, November 28, 1985, 3 pages.

5/1: Letter from GT, Hindelbank, to AM, June 3, 1986, 4 pages.

5/1: Letter from AM, Dortmund, to GT, March 17, 1986, 3 pages.

5/1: Letter from GT, Hindelbank, to AM, January 27, 1986, 4 pages.

11/2: Vollmacht unterzeichnet von Walter Palmers: Offizielles Formular des bernischen Anwaltverbandes, Bern, January 23, 1978, 1 page.

11/2: Rapport Officiel des Synthese dans l'affaire: Kroecher et Moeller des Ministre Public de la Confédération Suisse, Bern, March 1, 1978, 35 pages.

11/2: Letter from Schweizerischen Bundesanwaltschaft, Bern, to den Präsidenten der Anklagekammer des Berner Obergerichtes, May 12, 1978, 2 pages.

13/2: Letter from GT, Bern, to C, September 2, 1978, 4 pages.

13/2: Letter from GT, Hindelbank, to C, June 8, 1981, 2 pages.

13/2: Letter from GT, Hindelbank, to C, September 21, 1981, 2 pages.

13/2: Letter from GT, Lausanne, to Henner, September 9, 1979, 2 pages.

Harmsen, Caroline, Ulrike Seyer, and Johannes Ullmaier, eds. *Gudrun Ensslin/Bernward Vesper, "Notstandsgesetze von Deiner Hand": Briefe 1968/1969*. Frankfurt: Suhrkamp Verlag, 2009.

Schut, Pieter Bakker, ed. *das info: Briefe von Gefangenen aus der RAF aus der Diskussion 1973–1977*. Hamburg: Malik, 1987.

Viett, Inge. *Einsprüche! Briefe aus dem Gefängnis*. Hamburg: Nautilus, 1996.

## Manuscript Sources (Archives)

"Anarchiv," International Institute of Social History, Amsterdam, The Netherlands.

Archiv "APO und soziale Bewegungen" (Extraparliamentary Opposition and Social Movements), Freie Universität Berlin, Fachbereich Politik- und Sozialwissenschaften, Otto-Suhr Institut für Politikwissenschaft, Germany (APO-Archiv).

Archiv "Protest, Widerstand, und Utopie in der BRD" (Protest, Resistance, and Utopia in the FRG), Hamburger Institut für Sozialforschung, Hamburg, Germany (HIS).

Cilip-Archiv (Archiv des Instituts für Bürgerrechte und öffentliche Sicherheit, e.V. (Institute for Civil Rights and Public Safety), Freie Universität, Berlin.

Das Archiv und Dokumentatationszentrum, *FrauenMedia Turm*, www.frauenmediaturm.de.

Denkträume, Hamburger Frauenbibliothek, Hambug, Germany.

"Gaby Tiedemann Papers," International Institute of Social History, Amsterdam, The Netherlands (Archiv GT).

Infoladen und Archiv, Community Archive and Library, Frankfurt a.M., Germany.

Papiertiger, Community Archive and Library, Berlin.

## Movement Publications ("Grey Literature")

Aktionsrat der Frau, flyer. Available at http://www.frauenmediaturm.de/themen-portraets/chronik-der-neuen-frauenbewegung/vorfruehling-1968–1970/flugblatt.

Alpert, Jane. 1974. "Mother Right: A New Feminist Theory." Available at http://scriptorium.lib.duke.edu/wlm/mother (accessed 5 April 2014).

Arbeitsgruppe Haftbedingungen/Strafvollzug (Abschlußbericht des unabhängigen Untersuchungsausschusses zum Tode von Dr. med. V. Leschhorn). *Haftbedingungen in der BRD: Theoretische und praktische Beträge zum Strafvollzug und zur Gefangenenhilfe* Eds. Kommitee für Grundrechte und Demokratie. Sensbachtal: Selbstverlag, 1982. 87–112. Available at http://archiv.dusnet.de/sb/a/txtarc/haft1982o1bro_txto1.html.

*AUF*. Available at http://auf-einefrauenzeitschrift.at.

"Bewegung 2. Juni–Programm." *Der Blues: Gesammelte Texte der Bewegung 2. Juni*. Dortmund: Antiquariat "Schwarzer Stern," 2001. 10–11.

"Das Konzept Stadtguerrilla." *Rote Armee Fraktion: Texte und Materialien zur Geschichte der RAF*. Berlin: ID-Verlag, 1997. 27–48.

*Der Blues: Gesammelte Texte der Bewegung 2. Juni*. Vols. I und II. Dortmund: Antiquariat "Schwarzer Stern," 2001.

*Die Früchte des Zorns: Texte und Materialien zur Geschichte der Revolutionären Zellen und der Roten Zora.* Vols. I and II. Berlin: Edition ID-Archiv, 1993.

"Die Rote Armee aufbauen." *Rote Armee Fraktion: Texte und Materialien zur Geschichte der RAF.* Berlin: ID-Verlag, 1997. 24–26.

"Exzeß der Emanzipation." *WIR: Frauenzeitung Hannover* 7 (1977): 9. APO-Archiv, Ordner: Frauenbewegung.

"Frauen und Gewalt oder Gewalt und Frauen." *Dokumentation zur Situation in der BRD und zum Verhältnis BRD-Schweiz.* 1977: 31–34. Cilip-Archiv.

"Frauenbewegung seit 'Deutschland im Herbst.'" *Frauen gegen den Strom II* (1978): 7–10. APO-Archiv, Ordner: Frauenbewegung.

"Hungerstreik-Erklärung vom 8.5.1973. 2. *Hungerstreik, 8.5–29.6.1973.*" *Rote Armee Fraktion: Texte und Materialien zur Geschichte der RAF.* Berlin: ID-Verlag, 1997. 187–90.

"Hungerstreik-Erklärung vom 20.4.1979. 7. *Hungerstreik, 20.4.–20.6.1979.*" *Rote Armee Fraktion: Texte und Materialien zur Geschichte der RAF.* Berlin: ID-Verlag, 1997. 281–82.

"Hungerstreik-Erklärung vom 6.2.1981. 8. *Hungerstreik, 6.2.–16.4.1981.*" *Rote Armee Fraktion: Texte und Materialien zur Geschichte der RAF.* Berlin: ID-Verlag, 1997. 285–88.

"Hungerstreik-Erklärung vom Dezember 1984. 9. *Hungerstreik, 4.12.84–3.2.85.*" *Rote Armee Fraktion: Texte und Materialien zur Geschichte der RAF.* Berlin: ID-Verlag, 1997. 322–27.

"Hungerstreik-Erklärung vom 1.2.1989. 10. *Hungerstreik vom 1.2.–14.5.89.*" *Rote Armee Fraktion: Texte und Materialien zur Geschichte der RAF.* Berlin: ID-Verlag, 1997. 389–91.

"Ihr Weg zum Terrorismus ist vorgezeichnet, denn . . ." Pamphlet, APO-Archiv, Ordner: Frauenbewegung.

"Interview mit der Roten Zora. *Juni 1984.*" *Die Früchte des Zorns: Texte und Materialien zur Geschichte der Revolutionären Zellen und der Roten Zora.* Vol. II. Berlin: Edition ID-Archiv, 1993. 598–605.

Kuby, Christine. "Zu Frauen in der Guerilla." Antrag zur Ablehnung von Arnold, vom Gericht bestellter Sachverständiger im Prozeß gegen Christine Kuby. 22 January 1979. Denkträume, Hamburger Frauenbibliothek.

"Offener Brief an den [sic] Anstaltsärzten [sic] sin der Bundesrepublik." 80 holländische Ärzte. Amsterdam, den 18. Februar 1981. HIS, Politische Gefangene IV, HS (RAF-Sammlung).

Michel, Alexandra. *Frauen die Kämpfen sind Frauen die Leben.* Zürich: Selbstverlag, 1988.

*Rote Armee Fraktion: Texte und Materialien zur Geschichte der RAF.* Berlin: ID-Verlag, 1997.

"Terrorismus, der Exzeß der Emanzipation." *Frauen gegen den Strom II* (1978): 3–4. APO-Archiv, Ordner: Frauenbewegung.

## Secondary Sources

"A Weatherwoman: Inside the Weather Machine." *Weatherman.* Ed. Harold Jacobs. San Francisco: Ramparts Press, 1970. 321–26.

Alcoff, Linda, and Elizabeth Potter. *Feminist Epistemologies: Thinking Gender.* New York: Routledge, 1991.

Alexander, M. Jacqui, and Chandra Talpede Mohanty, eds. *Feminist Genealogies, Colonial Legacies, Democratic Futures.* New York: Routledge, 1996.

Alison, Miranda. *Women and Political Violence: Female Combatants in Ethno-National Conflict*. New York: Routledge, 2009.

Allen, Ann Taylor. "Mothers of a New Generation: Adele Schreiber, Helene Stöcker, and the Evolution of a German Idea of Motherhood, 1900–1914." *Signs: Journal of Women in Culture and Society* 10:3 (1985): 418–38.

Alter, Nora. *Projecting History: German Nonfiction Cinema, 1967–2000*. Ann Arbor: University of Michigan Press, 2002.

Amrane-Minn, Danielle Djamila. "Women and Politics in Algeria from the War of Independence to Our Day." *Research in African Literatures* 30:3 (1999): 62–77.

Anderson, Patrick. *So Much Wasted: Hunger, Performance, and the Morbidity of Resistance*. Durham, NC: Duke University Press, 2010.

Appelt, Erna. "Staatsbürgerin und Gesellschaftsvertrag." *Das Argument: Zeitschrift für Philosophie und Sozialwissenschaften* 37:210 (1995): 539–54.

———. "Vernunft versus Gefühle? Rationalität als Grundlage exklusiver Staatsbürgerschaftskonzepte." *Kritik der Gefühle: Feministische Positionen*. Ed. Agnes Neumayr. Vienna: Milena Verlag, 2007. 128–45.

Aretxaga, Begoña. *Shattering Silence: Women, Nationalism, and Political Subjectivity in Northern Ireland*. Princeton, NJ: Princeton University Press, 1997.

———. *States of Terror: Begoña Aretxaga Essays*. Ed. Joseba Zulaika. Reno: University of Nevada Press, 2005.

———. "Striking with Hunger: Cultural Meaning of Political Violence in Northern Ireland." *States of Terror: Begoña Aretxaga Essays*. Ed. Joseba Zulaika. Reno: University of Nevada Press, 2005. 31–56.

Aust, Stefan. *Baader-Meinhof: The Inside Story of the RAF*. Oxford: Oxford University Press, 2008.

———. *Der Baader Meinhof Komplex*. 1985. Hamburg: Hoffman und Campe, 2008.

Baader, Meike Sophia, ed. *"Seid realistisch, verlangt das Unmögliche!": Wie 1968 die Pädagogik bewegte*. Landsberg: Beltz, 2008.

Balz, Hanno. "Der 'Sympathisanten'-Diskurs im Deutschen Herbst." *Terrorismus in der Bundesrepublik: Medien, Staat, und Subkulturen in den 1970er Jahren*. Eds. Klaus Weinhauer, Jörg Requate, and Heinz-Gerhard Haupt. Frankfurt: Campus Verlag, 2006. 320–50.

———. "Gesellschaftsformierungen: Die öffentliche Debatte über die RAF in den 1970er Jahren." *Der "Deutsche Herbst" und die RAF in Politik, Medien, und Kunst: Nationale und Internationale Perspektiven*. Eds. Nicole Colin, Beatrice de Graaf, Jacco Pekelder, Joachim Umlauf. Bielefeld: transcript Verlag, 2008. 170–84.

———. *Von Terroristen, Sympathisanten, und dem starken Staat: Die öffentliche Debatte über die RAF in den 70er Jahren*. Frankfurt: Campus Verlag, 2008.

Balz, Hanno, and Jan-Henrik Friedrichs, eds. *"All we ever wanted . . .": Eine Kulturgeschichte europäischer Protestbewegungen der 1980er Jahre*. Berlin: Karl-Dietz Verlag, 2012.

Bandhauer-Schöffmann, Irene. "'Emanzipation mit Bomben und Pistolen'? Feministinnen und Terroristinnen in den deutschsprachigen Sicherheitsdiskursen der 1970er Jahre." *L'Homme: Europäische Zeitschrift für Feministische Geschichtswissenschaft* 20:2 (2010): 65–84.

———. "Hungerstreiks in Österreichischen Gefängnissen während der 1970er-Jahre: Behördenreaktionen, Medien, und die gesellschaftliche Konstruktion vergeschlechtlichter Körper." *Der Linksterrorismus der 1970er-Jahre und die Ordnung der Geschlechter*. Eds. Irene Bandhauer-Schöffmann and Dirk van Laak. Trier: Wissenschaftlicher Verlag Trier, 2013. 207–29.

Bauer, Karin. "'From Protest to Resistance': Ulrike Meinhof and the Transatlantic Movement of Ideas." *Changing the World, Changing Oneself: Political Protest and Collective Identities in West Germany and the U.S. in the 1960s and 1970s*. Eds. Belinda Davis, Wilfried Mausbach, Martin Klimke, and Carla MacDougall. New York: Berghahn Books, 2012. 171–88.

———. "In Search of Ulrike Meinhof." *"Everybody Talks about the Weather . . . We Don't": The Writings of Ulrike Meinhof*. Ed. Karin Bauer. New York: Seven Stories, 2008. 12–99.

Beitrag der Gewaltgruppe München zum Kongress zum Thema Vergewaltigung. *Die Neue Frauenbewegung in Deutschland*. 2nd ed. Ed. Ilse Lenz. Wiesbaden: VS Verlag, 2010. 297–99.

Berendse, Gerrit-Jan, and Ingo Cornils, eds. *Baader-Meinhof Returns: History and Cultural Memory of German Left-Wing Terrorism*. Amsterdam: German Monitor 70, 2008.

Bielby, Clare. "Attacking the Body Politic: The *Terroristin* in 1970s German Media." *Reconstruction: Studies in Contemporary Culture* 7:1 (2007). Available at http://reconstruction.eserver.org/071/bielby.shtml.

———. "Remembering the Red Army Faction." *Memory Studies* 3:2 (2010): 137–50.

———. "Revolutionary Men and the Feminine Grotesque in the German Media of the 1960s and 1970s." *Masculinities in German Culture: Edinburgh German Yearbook 2*. Ed. Sarah Colvin and Peter Daviews. Rochester, NY: Camden House, 2008. 213–28.

———. *Violent Women in Print: Representations in the West German Print Media of the 1960s and 1970s*. Rochester, NY: Camden House, 2012.

Bock, Gisela. "Racism and Sexism in Nazi Germany: Motherhood, Compulsory Sterilization, and the State." *When Biology Became Destiny: Women in Weimar and Nazi Germany*. Eds. Renate Bridenthal, Atina Grossmann, and Marion Kaplan. New York: Monthly Review Press, 1984. 271–96.

Bordo, Susan. "The Body and the Reproduction of Femininity: A Feminist Appropriation of Foucault." *Gender/Body/Knowledge: Feminist Reconstructions of Being and Knowing*. Eds. Alison Jaggar and Susan Bordo. New Brunswick, NJ: Rutgers University Press, 1989. 13–33.

———. *Unbearable Weight: Feminism, Western Culture, and the Body*. Berkeley: University of California Press, 1994.

Braunmühl, Carlchristian von, Birgit Hogefeld, and Jan Hubertus. *Versuche, die Geschichte der RAF zu verstehen: Das Beispiel Birgit Hogefeld*. 3rd ed. Gießen: Psychosozial Verlag, 2001.

Bressan, Susanne, und Martin Jander. "Gudrun Ensslin." *Die RAF und der Linke Terrorismus*. Volume I. Ed. Wolfgang Kraushaar. Hamburg: Hamburger Edition, 2006. 398–429.

Bridenthal, Renate, Atina Grossmann, and Marion Kaplan. "Introduction: Women in Weimar and Nazi Germany." *When Biology Became Destiny: Women in Weimar and Nazi Germany*. Eds. Renate Bridenthal, Atina Grossmann, and Marion Kaplan. New York: Monthly Review Press, 1984. 1–29.

———. *When Biology Became Destiny: Women in Weimar and Nazi Germany*. New York: Monthly Review Press, 1984.

Brinkema, Eugenie. "How to Do Things with Violences." *A Companion to Michael Haneke.* Ed. Roy Grundmann. Oxford, England: Wiley-Blackwell, 2010. 354–70.

Brockmann, Anna Dorothea. "Frauen gegen Krieg, Frauen für den Frieden–gegen welchen Krieg, für welchen Frieden eigentlich?" *Nicht Friedlich und Nicht Still: Streitschriften von Frauen zu Krieg und Gewalt.* Eds. Ruth-Esther Geiger and Anna Johannesson. Munich: Frauenbuchverlag, 1982. 105–16.

Brownmiller, Susan. *Against Our Will: Men, Women, and Rape.* New York: Ballantine Books, 1993.

Bunster-Bunalto, Ximena. "Surviving beyond Fear: Women and Torture in Latin America." *Women and Change in Latin America.* Eds. June Nash, Helen Safa, et al. Westport, CT: Greenwood, 1986. 297–325.

Butler, Judith. *Gender Trouble: Feminism and the Subversion of Identity.* New York: Routledge, 1990.

———. "No, It's Not Anti-Semitic." *London Review of Books* 24:16 (August 2003). Accessed online http://www.lrb.co.uk/v25/n16/judith-butler/no-its-not-anti-semitic.

———. *Precarious Life: The Powers of Mourning and Violence.* New York: Verso, 2004.

———. *Undoing Gender.* New York: Routledge, 2004.

Bynum, Caroline Walker. *Holy Feast and Holy Fast: The Religious Significance of Food to Medieval Women.* Berkeley: University of California Press, 1987.

Caldicott, Helen. *Missile Envy: The Arms Race and Nuclear War.* New York: Morrow, 1984.

Colin, Nicole, Beatrice de Graaf, Jacco Pekelder, Joachim Umlauf, eds. *Der "Deutsche" Herbst und die RAF in Politik, Medien, und Kunst: Nationale und Internationale Perspektiven.* Bielefeld: transcript Verlag, 2008.

Colvin, Sarah. "Chiffre und Symbol für Wut und Widerstand? *Gudrun ENSSLIN–Briefe aus der Haft,* herausgegeben von Christiane und Gottfried Ensslin." *NachBilder der RAF.* Eds. Inge Stephan and Alexandra Tacke. Cologne: Böhlau, 2008. 88–105.

———. *Ulrike Meinhof and West German Terrorism: Language, Violence, and Identity.* Rochester, NY: Camden House, 2009.

"Courage (Zeitschrift)." *Wikipedia: The Free Encyclopedia–Deutschland.* Wikimedia Foundation, Inc. 17 April 2014.

Davis, Belinda. "Jenseits von Terror und Rückzug: Die Suche nach politischem Spielraum und Strategien im Westdeutschland der siebziger Jahre." Translated by Alexander Vazansky and Klaus Weinhauer. *Terrorismus in der Bundesrepublik: Medien, Staat, und Subkulturen in den 1970er Jahren.* Eds. Klaus Weinhauer, Jörg Requate, and Heinz-Gerhard Haupt. Frankfurt/Main: Campus Verlag, 2006. 154–86.

———. "New Leftists and West Germany: Fascism, Violence, and the Public Sphere, 1967–1974." *Coping with the Nazi Past: West German Debates on Nazism and Generational Conflict, 1955–75.* Eds. Philipp Gasserts and Alan Steinweis. New York: Berghahn Books, 2006. 210–37.

———. "Women's Strength against Their Crazy Male Power': Gendered Language in the West German Peace Movement of the 1980s." *Frieden-Gewalt-Geschlecht: Friedens- und Konfliktforschung als Geschlechterforschung.* Eds. Jennifer A. Davy, Karen Hagemann, and Ute Kätzel. Essen: Klartext, 2005. 244–65.

De Cataldo Neuburger, Luisella, and Tiziana Valentine. 1992. *Women and Terrorism.* Translated by L. M. Hughes. New York: St. Martin's, 1996.

Della Porta, Donatella. "Politische Gewalt und Terrorismus: Eine vergleichende und soziologische Perspektive." *Terrorismus in der Bundesrepublik: Medien, Staat, und*

*Subkulturen in den 1970er Jahren.* Eds. Klaus Weinhauer, Jörg Requate, and Heinz-Gerhard Haupt. Frankfurt/Main: Campus Verlag, 2006. 33–58.

Di Leonardo, Micaela. "Morals, Mothers, and Militarism: Antimilitarism and Feminist Theory." *Feminist Studies* 11:3 (1985): 599–617.

"Die Schwarze Botin." *Wikipedia: The Free Encyclopedia–Deutschland.* Wikimedia Foundation, Inc. 31 October 2012.

Dietrich, Anette. *Weiße Weiblichkeiten: Konstruktionen von "Rasse" und Geschlecht im deutschen Kolonialismus.* Bielefeld: transcript Verlag, 2007.

Diewald-Kerkmann, Gisela. "Bewaffnete Frauen im Untergrund: Zum Anteil von Frauen in der RAF und der *Bewegung 2. Juni.*" *Die RAF und der Linke Terrorismus.* Volume I. Ed. Wolfgang Kraushaar. Hamburg: Hamburger Edition, 2006. 657–75.

———. *Frauen, Terrorismus, und Justiz: Prozesse gegen weibliche Mitglieder der RAF und Bewegung 2. Juni.* Düsseldorf: Droste, 2009.

Ditfurth, Jutta. *Ulrike Meinhof: Die Biografie.* Berlin: Ullstein, 2007.

Eager, Paige Whaley. *From Freedom Fighters to Terrorists: Women and Political Violence.* Aldershot/Burlington: Ashgate, 2008.

Echols, Alice. *Daring to Be Bad: Radical Feminism in America, 1967–75.* Minneapolis: University of Minnesota Press, 1989.

Edel, Uli. *Der Baader Meinhof Komplex.* 2008. Film.

Edschmid, Ulrike. *Frau mit Waffe: Zwei Geschichten aus terroristischen Zeiten.* Berlin: Rowohlt, 1996.

Ellmann, Maud. *The Hunger Artists: Starving, Writing, and Imprisonment.* Cambridge, MA: Harvard University Press, 1993.

Elshtain, Jean. *Women and War.* New York: Basic Books, 1987.

Elter, Andreas. "Die RAF und die Medien: Ein Fallbeispiel für terroristische Kommunikation." *Die RAF und der Linke Terrorismus.* Ed. Wolfgang Kraushaar. Volume II. Hamburg: Hamburger Edition, 2006. 1060–74.

"Emma (Zeitschrift)." *Wikipedia: The Free Encyclopedia–Deutschland.* Wikimedia Foundation, Inc. 17 April 2014.

Enloe, Cynthia. *Does Khaki Become You? The Militarization of Women's Lives.* Boston: South End Press, 1984.

———. *Maneuvers: The International Politics of Militarizing Women's Lives.* Berkeley: University of California Press, 2000.

Fanon, Frantz. *The Wretched of the Earth.* New York: Grove, 2005.

Feigenwinter, Gunhild. *Manifest der Mütter.* Basel: Edition Hexenpresse, 1976.

Feldman, Allen. *Formations of Violence: The Narrative of the Body and Political Terror in Northern Ireland.* Chicago: University of Chicago Press, 1991.

Foucault, Michel. *Discipline and Punish: The Birth of the Prison.* 2nd ed. New York: Vintage, 1995.

———. *The Government of Self and Others: Lectures at the College de France, 1982–83.* Basingstoke, England: Palgrave, 2010.

———. *The History of Sexuality: An Introduction.* Volume I. Translated by Robert Hurley. New York: Vintage Random House, 1978.

Gasserts, Philipp, and Alan Steinweis, eds. *Coping with the Nazi Past: West German Debates on Nazism and Generational Conflict, 1955–75.* New York: Berghahn Books, 2006.

Geiger, Ruth-Esther, and Anna Johannesson, eds. *Nicht Friedlich und Nicht Still: Streitschriften von Frauen zu Krieg und Gewalt.* Munich: Frauenbuchverlag, 1982.

Gelderloos, Peter. *How Non-Violence Protects the State.* Boston: South End Press, 2007.

Gerhard, Ute. "Frauenbewegung." *Die Sozialen Bewegungen in Deutschland seit 1945.* Eds. Roland Roth und Dieter Rucht. Frankfurt: Campus Verlag, 2008.

Gierds, Bernhard. "Che Guevara, Régis Debray, und die Focustheorie." *Die RAF und der Linke Terrorismus.* Volume I. Ed. Wolfgang Kraushaar. Hamburg: Hamburger Edition, 2006. 182–204.

Gilcher-Holtey, Ingrid. "Transformation by Subversion? The New Left and the Question of Violence." *Changing the World, Changing Oneself: Political Protest and Collective Identities in West Germany and the U.S. in the 1960s and 1970s.* Eds. Belinda Davis, Wilfried Mausbach, Martin Klimke, and Carla MacDougall. New York: Berghahn Books, 2010. 155–69.

Gilligan, Carol. *In a Different Voice: Psychological Theory and Women's Development.* Cambridge, MA: Harvard University Press, 1982.

Glynn, Ruth. *Women, Terrorism, and Trauma in Italian Culture.* Basingstoke, England: Palgrave Macmillan, 2013.

Goffman, Erving. *Asylums: Essays on the Social Institution of Mental Patients and Other Inmates.* Chicago: Aldine, 1961.

Göktürk, Deniz, David Gramling, and Anton Kaes, eds. *Germany in Transit: Nation and Migration, 1955–2005.* Berkeley: University of California Press, 2007.

Grewal, Inderpal, and Caren Kaplan, eds. *Scattered Hegemonies: Postmodernity and Transnational Feminist Practices.* Minneapolis: University of Minnesota Press, 1994.

Grisard, Dominique. *Gendering Terror: Eine Geschlechtergeschichte des Linksterrorismus in der Schweiz.* Frankfurt: Campus Verlag, 2010.

———. "Selbststilisierungen einer inhaftierten Terroristin: Arbeit am Terrorismusdiskurs der Schweiz der 1970er-Jahre." *Täterinnen und/oder Opfer?Frauen in Gewaltstrukturen.* Eds. Christine Künzel and GabyTemme. Berlin: LIT Verlag, 2007. 124–40.

———. "Transversale Widerstandspraktiken? Geschlechterrepräsentation von 'Selbst-mordattentäterinnen' und hungerstreikenden 'Terroristinnen' in den Massenmedien." *Gender in Tran-sit: Transkulturelle und transnationale Perspektiven/Transcultural and Transnational Perspectives.* Eds. Martina Ineichen, Anna Liesch, Anja Rathmann-Lutz, and Simon Wenger. Zürich: Chronos, 2009. 201–12.

Guevara, Che. "Create Two, Three, Many Vietnams." 1967. *Che Guevara Reader: Writing on Politics and Revolution.* Ed. David Deutschmann. 2nd ed. Melbourne: Ocean Press, 2003. 350–362.

———. "The Essence of Guerilla Struggle." 1960. *Che Guevara Reader: Writing on Politics and Revolution.* Ed. David Deutschmann. 2nd ed. Melbourne: Ocean Press, 2003. 64–69.

———. "Guerilla Warfare: A Method." 1963. *Che Guevara Reader: Writing on Politics and Revolution.* Ed. David Deutschmann. 2nd ed. Melbourne: Ocean Press, 2003. 70–84.

Hacker, Hanna. *Gewalt ist: keine Frau: Die Akteurin oder eine Geschichte der Trans-gressionen.* Königstein: Helmer, 1998.

Hackett, Elizabeth, and Sally Haslanger, eds. *Theorizing Feminisms: A Reader.* Oxford: Oxford University Press, 2005.

Hagemann-White, Carol. "Die Frauenhausbewegung." *Der große Unterschied: Die Neue Frauenbewegung und die Siebziger Jahre.* Ed. Kristine von Soden. Berlin: Elefanten Press Verlag, 1988. 48–52.

Hakemi, Sara, and Thomas Hecken. "Die Warenhausbrandstifter." *Die RAF und der Linke Terrorismus.* Volume I. Ed. Wolfgang Kraushaar. Hamburg: Hamburger Edition, 2006. 316–31.

Hanshew, Karrin. *Terror and Democracy in West Germany.* New York: Cambridge University Press, 2012.

Harding, Sandra, ed. *The Feminist Standpoint Theory Reader: Intellectual and Political Controversies.* New York: Routledge, 2003.

Hauser, Dorothea. *Baader und Herold–Beschreibung eines Kampfes.* Berlin: Alexander Fest Verlag, 1997.

Hawkesworth, Mary. *Political Worlds of Women: Activism, Advocacy, and Governance in the Twenty-first Century.* Boulder, CO: Westview, 2012.

Heinemann, Elizabeth D. "The Hour of the Woman: Memories of Germans' 'Crisis Years' and West German National Identity." *American Historical Review* 101:2 (April 1996): 354–95.

———. "Single Motherhood and Maternal Employment in Divided Germany: Ideology, Policy, and Social Pressures in the 1950s." *Journal of Women's History* 12:3 (Autumn 2000): 146–72.

Held, Virginia. "Feminism and Moral Theory." *Women and Moral Theory.* Eds. Eva Feder Kittay and Diana Tietjens Meyers. Savage, MD: Rowman and Littlefield, 1987. 111–28.

———. "The Obligations of Mothers and Fathers." *Mothering: Essays in Feminist Theory.* Ed. Joyce Trebilcot. Totowa, NJ: Rowman & Allanheld, 1984. 7–20.

Herrmann, Jörg. "Ulrike Meinhof und Gudrun Ensslin." *Zur Vostellung des Terrors: Die RAF.* Volume II. Ed. Klaus Biesenbach. Göttingen: Steidl, 2005. 112–14.

———. "'Unsere Söhne und Töchter': Protestantismus und RAF-Terrorismus in den 1970er Jahren." *Die RAF und der Linke Terrorismus.* Volume I. Ed. Wolfgang Kraushaar. Hamburg: Hamburger Edition, 2006. 644–56.

Hervé, Florence, ed. *Geschichte der deutschen Frauenbewegung.* 5th ed. Cologne: Papy-Rossa, 1995.

Herzog, Dagmar. *Sex after Fascism: Memory and Morality in Twentieth-Century Germany.* Princeton, NJ: Princeton University Press, 2005.

Hochgeschurz, Marianne. "Zwischen Autonomie und Integration: Die neue (west) deutsche Frauenbewegung." *Geschichte der deutschen Frauenbewegung.* Ed. Florence Hervé. 5th ed. Cologne: PapyRossa, 1995. 155–84.

Hogefeld, Birgit. "Zur Geschichte der RAF." *Versuche, die Geschichte der RAF zu verstehen: Das Beispiel Birgit Hogefeld.* Carlchristian von Braunmühl, Birgit Hogefeld, and Jan Hubertus. 3rd ed. Gießen: Psychosozial Verlag, 2001.

Höhn, Maria. "The Black Panther Solidarity Committee and the Trial of the Ramstein 2." *Changing the World, Changing Oneself: Political Protest and Collective Identities in West Germany and the U.S. in the 1960s and 1970s.* Eds. Belinda Davis, Wilfried Mausbach, Martin Klimke, and Carla MacDougall. New York: Berghahn Books, 2010. 215–39.

Holmig, Alexander. "Die aktionistischen Wurzeln der Studentenbewegung: Subversive Aktion, Kommune I, und die Neudefinition des Politischen." *Handbuch 1968: Zur Kultur- und Mediengeschichte der Studentenbewegung.* Eds. Martin Klimke and Joachim Scharloth. Stuttgart: Metzler, 2007. 107–18.

Honegger, Claudia. *Die Ordnung der Geschlechter: Die Wissenschaften vom Menschen und das Weib, 1750–1850.* Frankfurt: Suhrkamp, 1991.

"Honky Tonk Women." *Weatherman*. Ed. Harold Jacobs. San Francisco: Ramparts Press, 1970. 313–20.

Howlette, Caroline. "Writing on the Body? Representation and Resistance in British Suffragette Accounts of Forcible Feeding." *Genders* 23 (June 1996): 3–20.

Jacobs Brumberg, Joan. *Fasting Girls: The History of Anorexia Nervosa*. New York: Vintage, 2000.

Jander, Martin. "Isolation: Zu den Haftbedingungen der RAF-Gefangenen." *Die RAF und der Linke Terrorismus*. Volume II. Ed. Wolfgang Kraushaar. Hamburg: Hamburger Edition, 2006. 973–93.

Kaplan, Caren. "The Politics of Location as Transnational Feminist Critical Practice." *Scattered Hegemonies: Postmodernity and Ttransnational Feminist Practices*. Eds. Inderpal Grewal and Caren Kaplan. Minneapolis: University of Minnesota Press, 1994. 137–52.

Karcher, Katharina. "'Die Perücke ist ein Element das Alle Katzen Grau Macht': Femininity as Camouflage in the Liberation of the Prisoner Andreas Baader in 1970." *Der Linksterrorismus der 1970er-Jahre und die Ordnung der Geschlechter*. Eds. Irene Bandhauer-Schöffmann and Dirk van Laak. Trier: Wissenschaftlicher Verlag Trier, 2013. 99–119.

———. *Sisters in Arms? Female Participation in Leftist Political Violence in the Federal Republic of Germany since 1970*. Diss. University of Warwick, 2013.

Katsiaficas, Georgy. *The Subversion of Politics: European Autonomous Social Movements and the Decolonization of Everyday Life*. 2nd ed. Edinburgh, Scotland: AK Press, 2006.

Kebir, Sabine. "Gewalt und Demokratie bei Fanon, Sartre, und der RAF." *Die RAF und der Linke Terrorismus*. Volume I. Ed. Wolfgang Kraushaar. Hamburg: Hamburger Edition, 2006. 262–79.

Kenny, Mary A., Derrick M. Silove, and Zachary Steel. "Legal and Ethical Implications of Medically Enforced Feeding of Detained Asylum Seekers on Hunger Strike." *MJA* 180 (March 2004): 237–40.

Klein, Uta. "Kriminalität, Geschlecht, und Medienöffentlichkeit." *Hexenjagd: Weibliche Kriminalität in den Medien*. Eds. Petra Henschel and Uta Klein. Frankfurt: Suhrkamp Verlag, 1998. 9–20.

Klimke, Martin. *The Other Alliance: Student Protest in West Germany and the United States in the Global Sixties*. Princeton, NJ: Princeton University Press, 2010.

Klimke, Martin, and Joachim Scharloth, eds. *1968 Handbuch zur Kultur und Mediengeschichte der Studentenbewegung*. Stuttgart: Metzler, 2007.

Kloke, Martin. *Israel und die deutsche Linke: Zur Geschichte eines schwierigen Verhältnisses*. 2nd ed. Hanau: Haag & Herchen, 1994.

Knoch, Habbo. *Die Tat als Bild: Fotografien des Holocaust in der deutschen Erinnerungskultur*. Hamburg: Hamburger Edition, 2001.

———. "The Return of the Images: Photographs of Nazi Crimes and the West German Public in the 'Long 1960s.'" *Coping with the Nazi Past: West German Debates on Nazism and Generational Conflict, 1955–1975*. Eds. Philipp Gassert and Alam Steinweis. New York: Berghahn Books, 2006. 31–49.

Koenen, Gerd. "Camera Silens: Das Phatasma der 'Vernichtungshaft.'" *Die RAF und der Linke Terrorismus*. Volume II. Ed. Wolfgang Kraushaar. Hamburg: Hamburger Edition, 2006. 994–1010.

———. *Das rote Jahrzehnt: Unsere kleine deutsche Kulturrevolution, 1976–77*. 2nd ed. Frankfurt: Fischer, 2004.

———. *Vesper, Ensslin, Baader: Urszenen des deutschen Terrorismus*. Cologne: Kiepenheuer & Witsch, 2003.

Koonz, Claudia. "The Competition for a Women's *Lebensraum*, 1928–1934." *When Biology Became Destiny: Women in Weimar and Nazi Germany*. Eds. Renate Bridenthal, Atina Grossmann, and Marion Kaplan. New York: Monthly Review Press, 1984. 199–236.

———. *Mothers in the Fatherland: Women, the Family, and Nazi Politics*. New York: St. Martin's, 1987.

Kraushaar, Wolfgang. *Die RAF und der Linke Terrorismus*. Volumes I and II. Hamburg: Hamburger Edition, 2006.

———. "Die *Tupamaros West-Berlin*." *Die RAF und der Linke Terrorismus*. Volume I. Ed. Wolfgang Kraushaar. Hamburg: Hamburger Edition, 2006. 512–30.

———. "Kleinkrieg gegen einen Grossverleger: Von der Anti-Springer-Kampagne der APO zu den Brand- und Bombenanschlägern der RAF." *Die RAF und der Linke Terrorismus*. Volume II. Ed. Wolfgang Kraushaar. Hamburg: Hamburger Edition, 2006. 1075–1116.

———. "Rudi Dutschke und der bewaffnete Kampf." *Rudi Dutschke, Andreas Baader, und die RAF*. Hamburg: Hamburger Edition, 2005. 13–50.

Kristeva, Julia. *Powers of Horror: An Essay on Abjection*. New York: Columbia University Press, 1982.

Kühl, Stefan. *The Nazi Connection: Eugenics, American Racism, and German National Socialism*. Oxford: Oxford University Press, 2002.

Lachenmeier, Dominik. "Die Achtundsechziger-Bewegung zwischen etablierter und alternativer Öffentlichkeit." *1968: Handbuch zur Kultur- und Mediengeschichte der Studentenbewegung*. Eds. Martin Klimke and Joachim Scharloth. Stuttgart: Metzler, 2007. 61–72

Laqueur, Thomas. *Making Sex: Body and Gender from the Greeks to Freud*. Cambridge, MA: Harvard University Press, 1992.

Lee, Mia. "Umherschweifen und Spektakel: Die situationistische Tradition." *Handbuch 1968: Zur Kultur- und Mediengeschichte der Studentenbewegung*. Eds. Martin Klimke and Joachim Scharloth. Stuttgart: Metzler, 2007. 101–6.

Lenz, Ilse, ed. *Die Neue Frauenbewegung in Deutschland*. 2nd ed. Wiesbaden: VS Verlag, 2010. 281–324.

Ludwig, Gundula. "Performing Gender, Performing the State: Vorschläge zur Theoretisierung des Verhältnisses von modernem Staat und vergeschlechtlicher Subjektkonstitution." *Staat und Geschlecht: Grundlagen und aktuelle Herausforderungen feministischer Staatstheorie*. Eds. Gundula Ludwig, Birgit Sauer and Stefanie Wöhl. Baaden-Baaden: Nomos, 2009. 89–103.

MacDonald, Eileen. *Shoot the Women First*. New York: Random House, 1991.

Mahmood, Sara. *The Politics of Piety: The Islamic Revival and the Feminist Subject*. Princeton, NJ: Princeton University Press, 2005.

Maihofer, Andrea. *Geschlecht als Existenzweise: Macht, Moral, Recht, und Geschlechterdifferenz*. Frankfurt: Ulrike Helmer Verlag, 1995.

Maltry, Karola. *Die neue Frauenfriedensbewegung: Entstehung, Entwicklung, Bedeutung*. Frankfurt: Campus Verlag, 1993.

Marighella, Carols. *Mini-Manual of the Urban Guerilla*. Praxis-access no. I. Berkeley: Long Time Comin' Press, 1969.

Mbembe, Achille. "Necropolitics." Translated by Libby Meintjes. *Public Culture* 15:1 (2005): 11–40.

McAllister, Pam, ed. *Reweaving the Web of Life: Feminism and Nonviolence*. Philadelphia: New Society Publishers, 1982.

McCormick, Richard. *Politics of the Self: Feminism and the Postmodern in West German Literature and Film*. Princeton, NJ: Princeton University Press, 1991.

Meinhof, Ulrike. "Die Frauen im SDS oder In eigener Sache." *Die Würde des Menschen ist antastabar: Aufsätze und Polemiken*. 1968. Berlin: Wagenbach, 2004. 149–52.

———. "Falsches Bewußsein." *Die Würde des Menschen ist antastabar: Aufsätze und Polemiken*. 1968. Berlin: Wagenbach, 2004. 117–33.

Melzer, Patricia. "'Death in the Shape of a Young Girl': Feminist Responses to Media Representations of Women Terrorists during the 'German Autumn' of 1977." *International Feminist Journal of Politics* 11:1 (March 2009): 35–61.

———. "'Frauen gegen Imperialismus und Patriarchat zerschlagen den Herrschaftsapparat': autonome Frauen, linksradikaler feministischer Protest und Gewalt in Westdeutschland." *"All we ever wanted . . .": Eine Kulturgeschichte europäischer Protestbewegungen der 1980er Jahre*. Eds. Hanno Balz and Jan-Henrik Friedrichs. Berlin: Karl-Dietz Verlag, 2012. 157–77.

———. "Maternal Ethics and Political Violence: The 'Betrayal' of Motherhood among the Women of the RAF and 2 June Movement." *Seminar: A Journal of Germanic Studies* 47:1 (February 2011): 81–102.

———. "'Wir Frauen sind eh die bessere Hälfte der Menschheit': Revolutionäre Politik und Feminismus in den Gefängnisbriefen einer Ex-Terroristin." *Der Linksterrorismus der 1970er-Jahre und die Ordnung der Geschlechter*. Eds. Irene Bandhauer-Schöffmann and Dirk van Laak. Trier: Wissenschaftlicher Verlag Trier, 2013. 183–205.

Meulenbelt, Anja. *Feminismus: Aufsätze zur Frauenbefreiung*. Frauenoffensive: Munich, 1982.

Meyer, David, and Nancy Whittier. "Social Movement Spillover." *Social Problems* 41:2 (1994): 277–98.

Millán, Márgara. "Zapatista Indigenous Women." *Zapatista! Reinventing Revolution in Mexico*. Eds. John Holloway and Eloina Pelaez. London: Pluto Press, 1998. 64–80.

Mitchell, Silas Weir. *Lectures on Diseases of the Nervous System, Especially in Women*. 2nd ed. Philadelphia: Lea Brothers, 1885.

Mitscherlich, Margarete. *Die friedfertige Frau*. Frankfurt/Main: Fischer, 1987.

Moeller, Robert. *Protecting Motherhood: Women and the Family in the Politics of Postwar West Germany*. Berkeley: University of California Press, 1993.

———. "Reconstructing the Family in Reconstruction Germany: Women and Social Policy in the Federal Republic, 1949–1955." *Feminist Studies* 15:1 (Spring 1989): 137–69.

Mohanty, Chandra Talpade. *Feminism without Borders: Decolonizing Theory, Practicing Solidarity*. Durham, NC: Duke University Press, 2003.

Mohanty, Chandra Talpade, Lourdes Torres, and Ann Russo, eds. *Third World Women and the Politics of Feminism*. Bloomington: University of Indiana Press, 1991.

Morgan, Robin. *The Demon Lover: On the Sexuality of Terrorism*. New York: Norton, 1989.

*Mütter gegen Atomkraft*. http://www.muettergegenatomkraft.de

Nancy, Jean-Luc. "Image and Violence." *The Ground of the Image*. Translated by Jeff Fort. Bronx, NY: Fordham University Press, 2005. 15–26.

———. "The Image–the Distinct." *The Ground of the Image*. Translated by Jeff Fort. Bronx, NY: Fordham University Press, 2005. 1–14.

Naumann, Ingela. "Child Care and Feminism in West Germany and Sweden in the 1960s and 1970s." *Journal of European Social Policy* 15 (2005): 47–63.

Orbach, Susie. *Hunger Strike: Starving amidst Plenty*. 2nd ed. New York: Other Press, 2001.

Pasczensky, Susanne von, ed. *Frauen und Terror: Versuche, die Beteiligung von Frauen an Gewalttaten zu erklären*. Reinbek: Rowohlt, 1978.

Passmore, Leith. "The Art of Hunger: Self-Starvation in the Red Army Faction." *German History* 27:1 (2009): 32–59.

———. "The Ethics and Politics of Force-Feeding Terror Suspects in West German Prisons." *Social History of Medicine* 25:2 (2011): 481–99.

———. "The Red Army Faction's 'Revolution-under-the-Skin': Fitting the Worldwide Struggle into a West German Prison Cell." *Terror und Form/Terror and Form. Limbus: Australisches Jahrbuch für germanistische Literatur- und Kulturwissenschaft*. Eds. Franz-Josef Deiters, Axel Fliethmann, Birgit Lang, Alison Lewis, and Christine Weller. Berlin: Rombach Verlag, 2011.

Pateman, Carole. *The Sexual Contract*. Stanford, CA: Stanford University Press, 1988.

Peel, Michael. "Hunger Strikes: Understanding the Underlying Physiology Will Help Doctors Provide Proper Advice." *BMJ* 315 (October 1997): 829–30.

Plumwood, Valeire. *Feminism and the Mastery of Nature*. New York: Routledge, 1994.

Poirier, Suzanne. "The Weir Mitchell Rest Cure: Doctors and Patients." *Women's Studies* 10 (1983): 15–40.

Prinz, Alois. *Lieber wütend als traurig: Die Lebensgeschichte der Ulrike Meinhof*. Weiheim: Beltz Verlag, 2003.

Puar, Jasbir. *Terrorist Assemblages: Homonationalism in Queer Times*. Durham, NC: Duke University Press, 2007.

Purvis, June. "The Prison Experiences of the Suffragettes in Edwardian Britain." *Women's History Review* 4:1 (1995): 103–33.

Quistorp, Eva, ed. *Frauen für den Frieden: Analysen, Dokumente, und Aktionen aus der Friedensbewegung*. Frankfurt/Main: päd. extra buchverlag, 1982.

Rajan, V. G. Julie. *Women Suicide Bombers: Narratives of Violence*. New York: Routledge, 2011.

Ruddick, Sara. *Maternal Thinking: Towards a Politics of Peace*. New York: Ballantine, 1989.

Rupp, Leila. "Mother of the *Volk*: The Image of Women in Nazi Ideology." *Signs: Journal of Women in Culture and Society* 3:2 (1977): 362–79.

Russel, Diana, ed. *Exposing Nuclear Phallacies*. New York: Pergamon Press, 1989.

Schenk, Herrad. *Die feministische Herausforderung: 150 Jahre Frauenbewegung in Deutschland*. Munich: Verlag C.H. Beck, 1983.

Schmidtke, Michael. "The German New Left and National Socialism." *Coping with the Nazi Past: West German Debates on Nazism and Generational Conflict, 1955–75*. Eds. Philipp Gasserts and Alan Steinweis. New York: Berghahn Books, 2006. 176–93.

Schraut, Sylvia. "Terrorismus und Geschlecht." *Täterinnen und/oder Opfer? Frauen in Gewaltstrukturen*. Eds. Christine Künzel and GabyTemme. Berlin: LIT Verlag, 2007. 105–23.

Schultze, Thomas, und Almut Gross. *Die Autonomen: Ursprünge, Entwicklung, und Profil der Autonomen Bewegung*. Hamburg: Konkret Verlag, 1997.

Schulz, Kristina. *Der lange Atem der Provokation: Die Frauenbewegung in der Bundesrepublik und in Frankreich, 1968–1976*. Frankfurt/Main: Campus Verlag, 2002.

Scott, Joan. "The Evidence of Experience." *Critical Inquiry* 17 (Summer 1991): 773–97.

Seifert, Jürgen. "Ulrike Meinhof." *Die RAF und der Linke Terrorismus*. Ed. Wolfgang Kraushaar. Volume I. Hamburg: Hamburger Edition, 2006. 350–71.

Siegfried, Detlef. "Don't Look Back in Anger: Youth, Pop Culture, and the Nazi Past." *Coping with the Nazi Past: West German Debates on Nazism and Generational Conflict, 1955–75*. Eds. Philipp Gasserts and Alan Steinweis. New York: Berghahn Books, 2006. 144–60.

——. "White Negroes: The Fascination of the Authentic in the West German Counterculture of the 1960s." *Changing the World, Changing Oneself: Political Protest and Collective Identities in West Germany and the U.S. in the 1960s and 1970s*. Eds. Belinda Davis, Wilfried Mausbach, Martin Klimke, and Carla MacDougall. New York: Berghahn Books, 2010. 191–213.

Sjoberg, Laura, and Caron Gentry. *Mothers, Monsters, Whores: Women's Violence in Global Politics*. London: ZED Books, 2007.

Slobodian, Quinn. *Foreign Front: Third World Politics in Sixties West Germany*. Durham, NC: Duke University Press, 2012.

Smith, Sidonie, and Julia Watson. *Reading Autobiography: A Guide for Interpreting Life Narratives*. Minneapolis: University of Minnesota Press, 2001.

Smith, Sidonie, and Julia Watson, eds. *Women, Autobiography, Theory: A Reader*. Madison: University of Wisconsin Press, 1998.

Soden, Kristine von, ed. *Der große Unterschied: Die neue Frauenbewegung und die Siebziger Jahre*. Berlin: Elefanten Press, 1988.

Steinseifer, Martin. "Terrorismus als Medienereignis im Herbst 1977: Strategien, Dynamiken, Darstellungen, Deutungen." *Terrorismus in der Bundesrepublik: Medien, Staat, und Subkulturen in den 1970er Jahren*. Eds. Klaus Weinhauer, Jörg Requate, and Heinz-Gerhard Haupt. Frankfurt/Main: Campus Verlag, 2006. 351–81.

Stephenson, Jill. *Women in Nazi Germany*. Harlow, England: Longman Pearson Education, 2001.

Suri, Jeremi. "*Ostpolitik* as Domestic Containment: The Cultural Contradictions of the Cold War and the West German State Response." *Changing the World, Changing Oneself: Political Protest and Collective Identities in West Germany and the U.S. in the 1960s and 1970s*. Eds. Belinda Davis, Wilfried Mausbach, Martin Klimke, and Carla MacDougall. New York: Berghahn Books, 2010. 133–52.

Sweeney, George. "Irish Hunger Strikes and the Cult of Self-Sacrifice." *Journal of Contemporary History* 28 (1993): 421–37.

——. "Self-Immolation in Ireland: Hungerstrikes and Political Confrontation." *Anthropology Today* 9:5 (1993): 10–14.

Terhoeven, Petra. "Opferbilder–Täterbilder: Die Fotografie als Medium linksterroristischer Selbstermächtigung in Deutschland und Italien während der 70er Jahre." *Geschichte in Wissenschaft und Unterricht* 58: 7/8 (2007): 380–99.

Tétreault, Mary Ann, ed. *Women and Revolution in Africa, Asia, and the New World*. Columbia: University of South Carolina Press, 1994.

Theweleit, Klaus. "Bemerkungen zum RAF-Gespenst: 'Abstrakter Radikalismus' und Kunst." *Ghosts: Drei leicht inkorrekte Vorträge.* Frankfurt: Stroemfeld/Roter Stern, 1998.13–99.

Thompson, Becky Wangsgaard. "'A Way Outa No Way': Eating Problems among African-American, Latina, and White Women." *Gender and Society* 6:4 (1992): 546–61.

Tolmein, Oliver. "*RAF–Das war für uns Befreiung*": *Ein Gespräch mit Irmgard Möller über bewaffneten Kampf, Knast, und die Linke.* Hamburg: Konkret, 2002.

Trebilcot, Joyce, ed. *Mothering: Essays in Feminist Theory.* Totowa, NJ: Rowman & Allanheld, 1984.

Trnka, Jamie H. "Frauen, die unzeitgemäß schreiben: Bekenntnisse, Geschichte(en), und die Politik der Terrorismusliteratur." *NachBilder der RAF.* Eds. Inge Stephan and Alexandra Tacke. Cologne: Böhlau, 2008. 216–31.

Vandereycken, Walter, and Ron Van Deth. *From Fasting Saints to Anorexic Girls: The History of Self-Starvation.* New York: New York University Press, 1994.

Varon, Jeremy. *Bringing the War Home: The Weather Underground, the Red Army Faction, and Revolutionary Violence in the Sixties and Seventies.* Berkeley: University of California Press, 2004.

Veiel, Andreas, dir. *Wer wenn nicht wir,* 2011. Film.

Vesper, Bernward. *Die Reise: Romanessay.* Fragment. Ed. Jörg Schröder. Frankfurt: März-Verlag, 1977.

Von Dirke, Sabine. "*All Power to the Imagination!*": *The West German Counterculture from the Student Movement to the Greens.* Lincoln: University of Nebraska Press, 1997.

Vukadinović, Vojin Saša. "Der unbegründete Feminismusverdacht: Die RAF und die Frage der Frauenemanzipation." *Terroristinnen—Bagdad '77; Die Frauen der RAF.* Eds. Katrin Hentschel and Traute Hensch. Berlin: der freitag, 2009. 85–106.

———. "Feminismus im Visier: Zur Verknüpfung von Linksterrorismus und Feminismus in der BRD." *Ariadne: Forum für Frauen und Geschlechtergeschichte* 57 (2010): 54–59.

Warren, Kay. "Writing Gendered Memories of Repression in Northern Ireland: Begoña Aretxaga at the Doors of the Prison." *Anthropological Theory* 7 (1): 9–35.

Waylen, Georgina. "Rethinking Women's Political Participation and Protest: Chile 1970–1990." *Political Studies* 40:2 (1992): 299–314.

Weigel, Sigrid. "*Und selbst im Kerker frei . . . !*" *Schreiben im Gefängnis.* Marburg: Verlag Guttandin & Hoppe, 1982.

Weinhauer, Klaus, Jörg Requate, Heinz-Gerhard Haupt, eds. *Terrorismus in der Bundesrepublik: Medien, Staat, und Subkulturen in den 1970er Jahren.* Frankfurt: Campus Verlag, 2006.

Weinreb, Alice. "'For the Hungry Have No Past nor Do They Belong to a Political Party': Debates over German Hunger after World War II." *Central European History* 45 (2012): 50–78.

Whitbeck, Caroline. "The Maternal Instinct (1972)." *Mothering: Essays in Feminist Theory.* Ed. Joyce Trebilcot. Totowa, NJ: Rowman & Allanheld, 1984. 185–98.

Wilde, Gabriele. "Der Geschlechtervertrag als Bestandteil moderner Staatlichkeit: Carole Patemans Kritik an neuzeitlichen Vertragstheorien und ihre Aktualität." *Staat und Geschlecht: Grundlagen und aktuelle Herausforderungen feministischer Staatstheorie.* Eds. Gundula Ludwig, Birgit Sauer and Stefanie Wöhl. Baaden-Baaden: Nomos, 2009. 31–45.

Wildenthal, Lora. *German Women for Empire, 1884–1945*. Durham, NC: Duke University Press, 2001.

Williams, John. "Hunger-Strikes: A Prisoner's Right or a 'Wicked Folly'?" *Howard Journal* 40:3 (August 2001): 285–96.

Witt, Doris. *Black Hunger: Soul Food and America*. Minneapolis: University of Minnesota Press, 2004.

Wunschik, Tobias. "*Die Bewegung 2. Juni.*" *Die RAF und der Linke Terrorismus*. Volume I. Ed. Wolfgang Kraushaar. Hamburg: Hamburger Edition, 2006. 531–61.

Zelizer, Barbie. *Remembering to Forget: Holocaust Memory through the Camera's Eye*. Chicago: University of Chicago Press, 1998.

Žižek, Slavoj. *Violence: Six Sideways Reflections*. Picador: New York, 2008.

Zwerman, Gilda. "Mothering on the Lam: Politics, Gender Fantasies, and Maternal Thinking in Women Associated with Armed, Clandestine Organizations in the United States." *Feminist Review* 47 (1994): 33–56.

# Index

## About the Author

Patricia Melzer is Assistant Professor of German and Women's Studies at Temple University. She is the author of *Alien Constructions: Science Fiction and Feminist Thought.*